How Israel Made AIPAC

Books by Grant F. Smith

THE ISRAEL LOBBY ENTERS STATE GOVERNMENT
Rise of the Virginia Israel Advisory Board

BIG ISRAEL
How Israel's Lobby Moves America

SPY TRADE
How Israel's Lobby Undermines America's Economy

DIVERT!
NUMEC, Zalman Shapiro and the Diversion of U.S. Weapons Grade Uranium Into the Israeli Nuclear Weapons Program

NEOCON MIDDLE EAST POLICY
The "Clean Break" Plan Damage Assessment

DEADLY DOGMA
How Neoconservatives Broke the Law to Deceive America

VISA DENIED
How Anti-Arab Visa Policies Destroy U.S. Exports, Jobs and Higher Education

FOREIGN AGENTS
The American Israel Public Affairs Committee from the 1963 Fulbright Hearings to the 2005 Espionage Scandal

How Israel Made AIPAC

The Most Harmful Foreign
Influence Operation in America

Published by the Institute for Research: Middle Eastern Policy, Inc.
Calvert Station
PO Box 32041
Washington, DC 20007

First published in 2022 by the Institute for Research: Middle Eastern Policy

7 9 10 8 6
Copyright Institute for Research: Middle Eastern Policy, Inc.
All Rights Reserved

Paperback ISBN 978-0-9827757-2-1

Library of Congress Cataloging-in-Publication Data

Smith, Grant F.
  How Israel Made AIPAC : The Most Harmful Foreign Influence Operation In America / by Grant F. Smith.
     p. cm.
  Includes bibliographical references and index.

1. Zionists--United States--Political activity. 2. Jews--United States--Politics and government--20th century. 3. American Israel Public Affairs Committee. 4. United States. Dept. of Justice. 5. United States--Foreign relations--Israel. 6. Israel--Foreign relations--United States. 7. United States--Foreign relations--1945-1989. 8. United States--Foreign relations—1989

   Without limiting the rights under copyright reserved above, no part of this publication may be reproduced, stored in or introduced into a retrieval system, or transmitted, in any form or by any means (electronic, mechanical, photocopying, recording or otherwise), without the prior written permission of both the copyright owner and the above publisher of this book.

The scanning, uploading, and distribution of this book via the Internet or via any other means without the written permission of the publisher is illegal and punishable by law. Please purchase only authorized electronic editions and do not participate in or encourage electronic piracy of copyrighted materials. Your support of the author's rights is appreciated.

Praise for Grant F. Smith books about the Israel lobby

"Grant Smith renders great service. The secret documents reviewed in this volume will help any reader understand how a small but determined group of zealots for Israel have placed the United States in grave danger. It is a wakeup call that must be answered, if our noble experiment in representative government, which has long proclaimed justice for all people in all lands everywhere, is to survive. I choose those words carefully. This is no time to sit on our hands. Unwarranted fear of Israel has plunged us into an abyss that gets deeper all the time. All that is needed is a civilized discussion, one that this volume must surely bring forth." **Paul Findley, Member of Congress 1961-83, author of three books on the U.S.-Israeli relationship, including the Washington Post bestseller "They Dare to Speak Out: People and Institutions Confront Israel's Lobby"**

"This is vital reading for anyone interested in what really guides American attitudes towards Israel. Grant F. Smith reveals how the almost universal misunderstanding of the Israel-Palestine question in the United States, and the blind support for Israel in Government, the media and public opinion are not sentimental accident, but the result of assiduous plotting and planning by Israel, its agents, and friends to subvert the American system and freedom of speech over more than half a century." **Tim Llewellyn, former BBC Middle East Correspondent**

"The Israel lobby is one of the most influential interest groups in American history. Yet there is insufficient public knowledge about its origins and operations. Grant Smith's new book is a major step forward in correcting that problem. He provides a fascinating and disturbing account of how I.L. Kenen laid the groundwork for AIPAC, the most powerful organization in the lobby." **John J. Mearsheimer, the R. Wendell Harrison Distinguished Service Professor of Political Science at the University of Chicago and the author with Stephen M. Walt of "The Israel Lobby and U.S. Foreign Policy" (2007)**

"... Grant Smith has penetrated once again into the murky waters that underlie the observable control of U.S. Middle East policy by Israel and its aggressive American support base that have undermined the efforts of successive U.S. administrations, be they Democrat or Republican, to resolve the Israel-Palestine conflict... using recently declassified documents, Smith exposes the charade that the 'pro-Israel lobby' is simply a well-organized, overly zealous group functioning within the spirit of traditional American political advocacy. What we see is something far more sinister...[this] should be required reading for anyone concerned with preserving what is left of the U.S. political process." **Jeffrey Blankfort is the former editor of the Middle East Labor Bulletin and former host the international affairs program "Takes on the World" on KZYX Pacifica Radio in Mendocino, California.**

"This is an excellent book that brings together declassified material showing how the Israel lobby managed to sow corruption at the highest levels of the U.S. government and even break U.S. law. Like other excellent books by the author (e.g., Deadly Dogma and Foreign Agents), America's Defense Line breaks new ground in research into the destructive role of narrow special interests in U.S. domestic and foreign affairs. This latest contribution is a tour de force and is a must read for anyone interested to understand why we are embroiled in the quagmire of the Middle East and how we might get out of it (thus saving our economy and our global reputation)." **Dr. Mazin Qumsiyeh, Professor at Bethlehem University and author of "Sharing the Land of Canaan: Human Rights and the Israeli-Palestinian Struggle"**

"It has been a long honeymoon, but it may at last be coming to an end. The neoconservatives and the Iraq war have had the positive effect of exposing the ways that an ultra-Zionist agenda hurts the American interest (a subject of another Grant F. Smith book). And so today a new debate over Zionism has begun in America: how pro-Israel should the United States be? And how pro-Israel should the American Jewish community be? Given the success and power of Jews in this country, a factor that I.L. Kenen [the founder of AIPAC] and his adversaries would never have anticipated, this is not just an ethnic conversation; it is one that all Americans can join. I hope that the light Smith shines on a period in which Jews were far more ambivalent about Zionism will help to restart that debate." **Philip Weiss, co-founder of Mondoweiss**

Special thanks to James, who finally solved the mystery of Irene Bowman.

Table of Contents

About the Author i
Foreword: Why this Matters iii
Introduction 1
Chapter 1: AIPAC'S Founder 5
    Straight Journalist 7
    Journalism to Politics 7
    Lobbying for War 8
    Herzl's Plan 11
Chapter 2: Lobbying for a Country 16
    Truman and the Israel Lobby 17
    Jewish Agency Wins UN Representation 27
    Truman Recognizes Israel 31
    Feinberg Factor 34
    Israel Lobby Legacy 39
Chapter 3: Foreign Agents Act 43
    U.S. State Department Enforces FARA 45
    Department of Justice Takes Over FARA 47
    Viereck Goes to Prison 50
    1946 Lobbying Reform 51
    FARA Enforcement Malaise 53
Chapter 4: Arms Smuggling 56
    Irgun and the U.S. Treasury Department 58
    Haganah Arms Smuggling in the United States 63
    CIA Detects False-Flagging in Europe 66
Chapter 5: Israel Office of Information 69
    Deficient Declarations 71
    Marching orders from Mossad 73
    Kenen Makes a Clean Break 76
    Israel's American Lobbyist 80
Chapter 6: American Zionist Council 83
    American Israel Public Affairs Committee Born 87
    American Council for Judaism Dissents 95
Chapter 7: Near East Report 99
    Israel's Plank 103
    Lavon Affair Crisis 104
    Compliments of I. L. Kenen 107
Chapter 8: Senate Investigation 111

Kenen's Flight to Iran 112
Jewish Relief Fundraising Coup 113
AZC Funding from the Jewish Agency 116
Chapter 9: Fighting Justice 130
John F. Kennedy and the Israel Lobby 133
DOJ Forces AZC to Register as a Foreign Agent 135
FARA Ascendant 149
Dominican Republic 151
Nonproliferation and Dimona 152
Chapter 10: Secret Deal 157
Heavies Pull Out of AZC Registration Battle 159
Caveat 162
Katzenbach's Capitulation 165
Subvention Recipient Caveat 167
Bona Fide Dispute 169
AZC's Secret FARA Registration 172
AZC Resurgent 174
Chapter 11: Above the Law 177
Jewish Agency Metamorphosis 183
AIPAC in the 21st Century 189
Secrecy and Dissent 194
America's Defense Line 196
Afterword: Now What? 201
Israel spent $61 million making an American lobby 203
Appendices 209
Isaiah L. Kenen Chronology 210
Organizations 212
   World Zionist Organization 212
   World Zionist Organization–American Section 212
   Provisional Executive Committee for General Zionist Affairs 213
   Jewish Agency for Israel 213
   American Section–Jewish Agency for Israel 213
   United Jewish Appeal 214
   American Zionist Emergency Council 214
   American Zionist Council 214
   Conference of Presidents 215
   American Jewish Congress 215
   American Israel Public Affairs Committee 215
   American Jewish Conference 215
Foreign Agents Registration Act—6/8/1938-4/28/1942 216

Foreign Agents Registration Act—4/29/1942–10/03/1961 219
Israel Office of Information FARA Declaration—10/06/1948 231
Isaiah Kenen Personal FARA Declaration—09/01/1948 240
Israel Office of Information Deficiency Notice—06/17/1949 244
Israel Office of Information FARA Declaration—06/30/1950 245
Israel Office of Information Personnel—01/01/1951 253
FARA Section Memo on Kenen Visit—01/17/1951 254
Isaiah Kenen Letter to the FARA Section—02/13/1951 255
Isaiah Kenen Letter to the FARA Section—03/14/1952 256
: The Government of Israel and the Jewish Agency 257
AZC Internal Memo on Public Relations 1962-63 260
Alert to AG of Compelled AZC FARA 10/31/1962 262
FARA Registration Order to AZC 11/21/1962 264
DOJ Meeting with AZC Legal Counsel 5/2/1963 266
DOJ 72-Hour Warning to AZC 10/11/1963.. 269
Yeagley Memo to Katzenbach 10/7/1964... 270
AZC Disclosure 4/1/1962 to 6/30/1962 sent 3/2/1965............................. 271
Analysis of Cartoons from the Near East Report................................. 277
Other Incidents and Non-Enforcement 287
The Logan Act... 291
Delayed Disclosures 1933-2008... 292
Charter Memo of the Senate Foreign Relations Committee Investigation of Nondiplomatic Activities of Representatives of Foreign Governments, March 17, 1961 295
Index 299
Sources.. 305

Table of Figures

FIGURE 1 Official Logo of the Committee For A Jewish Army. 19
FIGURE 2 Truman Recognizes Israel 32
FIGURE 3 CIA: The Objectives and Activities of the Irgun Z'vai Leumi......... 57
FIGURE 4 Early Ner Cartoon with Arab Stereotypes 101
FIGURE 5 I. L. Kenen Presentation Card.. 107
FIGURE 6 Jewish Agency Payments to AZC.. 204
FIGURE 7 Jewish Agency Payments to AIPAC Founder Isaiah Kenen.......... 205
FIGURE 8 Jewish Agency Chief Gottlieb Hammer Senate Testimony........... 206
FIGURE 9 NER Cartoon: Armed, Mistrustful Arabs 278
FIGURE 10 NER Cartoon: Syria's Hafez Assad as Puppeteer........................ 280
FIGURE 11 NER Cartoon: Shiite Islam Killing Off Values 281
FIGURE 12 NER Cartoon: Syria as the Puppet Of Lebanon.......................... 282
FIGURE 13 NER Cartoon: Israel Jumped at the UN....................................... 283
FIGURE 14 NER Cartoon: Arabist State Department Official....................... 284
FIGURE 15 NER Cartoon: All The News That Isn't Fit................................. 285
FIGURE 16 NER Cartoon: The Arab Psyche 286

About the Author

Grant F. Smith lives in Washington, DC where he researches and writes about U.S. Middle East policy formulation. Smith is director of the nonprofit Institute for Research: Middle Eastern Policy (IRmep).

In his thirty-two-year professional career as a researcher, Smith has investigated financial services and global telecommunications industries, worked in twenty-two countries assessing the impact of regulatory and trade regime changes and managed multi-country research teams. Smith has a BA in International Relations from the University of Minnesota and MIM (Master of International Management) from the University of St. Thomas in St. Paul. Smith's first research experience examining lobbying took place in the late 1980s as a member of a Minnesota Citizen's League committee investigating public entities that used a significant percentage of their taxpayer-funded allocations to lobby elected officials for ever-larger appropriations.[a]

In 2014, Smith sued the Department of Defense in federal court and won release of a detailed report, contracted in 1987, about the advanced state of Israel's nuclear weapons program. *The Nation* wrote about it in the article "It's Official: The Pentagon Finally Admitted That Israel Has Nuclear Weapons, Too." In 2015, Smith sued the Central Intelligence Agency and won release of 131 pages of formerly classified information revealing its overseas agents obtained compelling evidence that Israel stole U.S. government-owned weapons-grade uranium in the 1960s to build its first atom bombs. The CIA's refusal to share this information thwarted two FBI investigations into the diversion. It is the subject of continuing Freedom of Information Act litigation as estimated toxic site cleanup costs approach half a billion dollars.

Smith's essays about the lobby are frequently published at the Antiwar.com news website and the *Washington Report on Middle East Affairs* magazine. This book is Smith's tenth about the Israel lobby. IRmep is co-

---

[a] "Because That's Where the Money Is: Why the Public Sector Lobbies" Citizens League Report, June 28, 1990

sponsor of the annual IsraelLobbyCon conference about Israel, the Israel lobby, Palestine, elections, and free speech held at the National Press Club. It has become a gathering point for a broad range of intellectuals, activists, reporters and educators determined to expose and defeat institutionalized corruption driving deadly and wasteful U.S. Middle East policy formulation.

Foreword: Why this Matters

Hi, I'm Grant F. Smith, author of the books "Big Israel," "The Israel Lobby Enters State Government" and "Foreign Agents" which are all about the Israel lobby in America. I'm director of IRmep which co-organizes a conference series about the Israel lobby at the National Press Club and other programs. This book is the transcript and fully sourced basis for a very special podcast that was broadcast in 2022 and which is still available on most major podcast platforms.

The American Israel Public Affairs Committee, or AIPAC has recently established its own political action committees. AIPAC is using tens of millions of dollars of PAC money to knock off candidates it believes won't be sufficiently deferential to the government of Israel.

There is a lot of analysis about this in social and even legacy media. Most of it has one thing in common: no historical basis about how, when or why AIPAC came into existence. What exactly is AIPAC and where does it come from? That's what we answer in the podcast and this book.

We answer some very basic questions, like, who founded AIPAC, and when? What did AIPAC's founder do before creating a lobby for Israel in the U.S.? What happened when he ran into trouble with the Senate and Department of Justice? And lastly, how much did Israel pay to set up AIPAC?

The answers to those questions through the eyes of its founder, Isaiah L. Kenen, and declassified U.S. government files are shocking, and increasingly relevant as AIPAC's power over politics in America expands into new areas.

AIPAC is the creation of Israel's government and was set up with foreign funding. Because AIPAC's founder and the organization never stopped collaborating with Israel's government, AIPAC was ordered to register as an Israeli foreign agent by the U.S. Department of Justice in 1962. But that Department of Justice order and files on the affair which were supposed to be publicly accessible were improperly kept secret...until we obtained them in the year 2008.

The podcast series and book was created and copyrighted by the Institute for Research: Middle Eastern Policy, Inc. If you would like to learn more about IRmep or support IRmep research, visit www.IRmep.org or send an email to info@irmep.com.

Introduction

On January 17, 1951, Isaiah L. Kenen walked into Nathan B. Lenvin's office at the Department of Justice Foreign Agent Registration section and launched an audacious deception. Kenen had worked as the director of the Israeli Embassy's new Information Office in New York City since 1948. The fledgling Israeli government wanted Kenen to break free of tight U.S. Department of Justice oversight and registration requirements placed on all agents of foreign principals. A public relations expert, Kenen knew after years of public and private efforts to establish a new state in Palestine that reframing Israel's interests as America's own would be impossible with an onerous "foreign agents" declaration on his every press release, newsletter, film clip, or radio tape circulated in the U.S.. His increasingly brash forays to Capitol Hill to lobby for arms and aid were less effective as an openly declared agent for Israel than they would be as a domestic lobbyist. Kenen and his cohorts circumvented Lenvin in the FARA section and the rest of the Department of Justice long enough to unify the current lead organization, the American Israel Public Affairs Committee (AIPAC), the largest and most secretive foreign lobby ever financed and assembled on U.S. soil. Along the way, Kenen and precursor Israel lobby umbrella group leadership also dodged investigations and enforcement actions from the Senate Foreign Relations Committee, the U.S. Department of State, and the FBI.

Because of the lobby's early and ongoing evasion of the Foreign Agents Registration Act public disclosure requirements, not much was known about the most intense behind-the-scenes public relations activities. For more than a half-century, relevant Department of Justice internal files and relevant registration statements were classified. However, in March of 2008, on the 20-year anniversary of Kenen's death, over 1,000 pages of documents related to his foreign agent activities on behalf of Israel were released in response to Freedom of Information Act filings. In June of 2008, highly sensitive internal Department of Justice documents revealing a secret battle to force AIPAC's precursor organization to register as a foreign agent were also abruptly released under FOIA.

Comparing Kenen's public statements, his lobbying newsletter, the *Near East Report*, and autobiographical accounts against Department of Justice Foreign Agents Registration Act filings, internal meeting minutes, deliberations whether to indict umbrella organization leaders, and other private correspondence reveals how Kenen and his key collaborators evaded FARA oversight. Deficient declarations, misleading statements, money laundering and misrepresentations had landed other lobbyists in jail or deportation proceedings. But purposeful omissions, shell corporations, and offshore operations created a dense smokescreen covering Israel's massive and secret public relations, lobbying, arms smuggling, and influence-peddling network, which is only now being revealed in declassified documents and biographical "end of career" accounts.

The following account tracks Isaiah Kenen from his birth in Canada through his career at the Jewish Agency for Palestine, the Israel Office of Information, the American Zionist Council, and the *Near East Report* to the foundation of AIPAC. Examining the circumstances in which AIPAC was created sheds light on a period of time when Israeli prerogatives were quietly institutionalized in Congress, the White House, Department of Defense, State Department, and other key government agencies, very often to the detriment of American citizens. We also reveals how little Americans typically know at any given point in time about the true catalysts determining U.S. Middle East policy—when such knowledge could actually affect deliberations and outcome.

AIPAC is understandably circumspect about its early history and founder. For many years AIPAC's website mentioned very little about that history, and there was no mention at all of Isaiah L. Kenen in the "What is AIPAC" section, which read:

> For more than half a century, the American Israel Public Affairs Committee has worked to make Israel more secure by ensuring that American support remains strong. From a small pro-Israel public affairs boutique in the 1950s, AIPAC has grown into a 100,000-member national grassroots movement described by *The New York Times* as "the most important organization affecting America's relationship with Israel."[1]

A more thorough search of the AIPAC website reveals that Kenen is referenced only a few dozen times, all within the *Near East Report* newsletter he established, owned, and ran as a separate unit beginning in 1957. This may be because a closer examination of precisely how Kenen and other leaders built AIPAC reveals too many troubling anomalies and legal exposures. Isaiah Kenen is not the single most important historical figure in the movement. However, his willingness to flout the law, engage in highly negative smear campaigns to cover up damaging facts, and then write frankly about much of it in two books is informative and sometimes even entertaining.

This is not a comprehensive review of AIPAC's lobbying activities or later encounters with U.S. law enforcement. We make extensive use of passages excerpted from declassified government documents, historical narratives from obscure scholarly journals, and Isaiah Kenen's two autobiographical works. Select original documents appear in the appendices and sufficient citations are provided to access the complete works referenced. In this sense, the structure attempts to leverage the strengths of a modern style of writing, the online web log or "blog," which frequently reproduces lengthy passages for criticism while linking to entire source documents. Readers may judge for themselves the opinions of experts and ideologues in their own words, from source documents that will probably never be found on the Internet, at key moments in history, contextualized within the larger narrative.

The following snapshots probe the creation, morphing, and maneuvering of global corporate entities and their subsidiaries operating in the United States juxtaposed against one of the very few laws designed to protect the American people from foreign influence on policymakers: the Foreign Agents Registration Act (FARA). The book uses Isaiah Kenen's activities and recently declassified archival documents as anchors to add further weight to the argument that the creation of Israel has been characterized by three developments of great political importance to Americans: timely intervention in U.S. foreign affairs by elite members of an opaque but coordinated global lobby, subversion of laws and enforcement mechanisms specifically designed to protect the American people from foreign influences, and the deployment of secrecy, sophisticated propaganda, espionage, money, and covert action to protect Israel lobby power and prerogative from the checks and balances long held to be critical to our democracy. Final chapters are sourced almost entirely from Department of Justice documents declassified in June of 2008 and reveal a shocking "caveat" that has been accepted at the highest levels of the U.S. government since the mid-1960s. It explains the curious and ongoing absence of warranted law enforcement in the United States in the face of years of serious, documented criminal violations by Israel lobby organizations.

The man behind Israel's lobby. The House vote authorizing billions in U.S. aid to Israel is a personal triumph for hardly known but potent Isaiah Kenen. Mr. Kenen, 68, does not appear in Who's Who. His Washington life is anonymousness personified. But his mind is a mixture of intelligence, skill and experience with Congress on behalf of Israel.[2] —**Great Bend Tribune, 1973**

Chapter 1: AIPAC'S Founder

Isaiah Kenen's frenetic energy in early life suggested that he might one day work to unite fractious Zionist groups into a massive foreign interest lobby in the United States. Kenen was born on March 7, 1905 in Canada. His parents were married in Portland, Maine but moved 226 miles northeast across the border to St. Stephen, where his intrepid father acquired an insurance agency. At the beginning of a pithy end-of-career memoir referenced often in the following pages, Kenen explained that Zionism was at the very core of his Orthodox family's early life:

> We were all Zionist activists. When we moved to Toronto, on April 1, 1911, my father established the first B'nai Zion club. My sisters Anna and Esther attended the first Hadassah convention in Rochester, New York, where they met Henrietta Szold, the founder of Hadassah. They decided to organize a Hadassah chapter in Toronto and they invited her to our Toronto home.
>
> On November 2—I was then 12—Arthur James Balfour issued the declaration that "his Majesty's government view with favor the establishment of a national home for the Jewish people and will use their best endeavors to facilitate the achievement of this objective." In my class at the Huron Street School, I raised my hand and asked my teacher whether I could make a short speech to the class. "This is a great day in the history of the Jewish people," I said. "The Jews are going to have their own state in Palestine at last. And the Bolshevik revolution promises an end to anti-Semitism in Russia."[3]

Kenen's father, originally from Kiev, frequently traveled abroad for business. Kenen's account of his father's World War I dealings from neutral territory in Sweden suggests his powerful influence over Isaiah's own ethics about business, personal conduct, and even nationality:

> I saw little of my father, who was often in Europe. In 1916, his brother Lippe, who had made a fortune in oil in Baku in 1890, suggested that they meet in Poland where Lippe commissioned my father to find a Canadian steel firm to build tank cars to transport oil to the embattled Russian army. That deal was intercepted by the Bolshevik revolution, but my father remained in Sweden to share in that country's wartime prosperity. He exploited Sweden's neutral middle ground. Germany and Russia, at war on the battlefield, were in a commercial war to buy all available merchandise, and my father prospered.[4]

Kenen also learned from his father the benefits of affiliation with religious relief and charitable organizations for lobbying and professional pursuits. Both deployed such affiliations as forms of international "letters of marque"[b] and moral force multipliers for lobbying and public relations influence. When a wartime business deal with Tsarist Russia went against Kenen's father in 1918 due to the Communist victory, he did not hesitate to aggressively press his case for compensation with a charitable credential:

> My father decided to go to Moscow, relying on his infallible powers of persuasion, his British passport and an authorization to represent the Jewish Relief Commission.[5]

Although Kenen's father was financially ruined and kept dreaming of "recovery of a million dollars from the Soviets," he was soon on the road again in Great Britain and Europe trying to rebuild his lost wartime fortune. Kenen's memories of his father's amateur human smuggling reveal consciousness of his father's somewhat ambivalent attitudes about law and international borders.

> My father opened up a store, the C.P. (Canadian Pacific) Tailoring Company, and he hired Jewish peddlers to sell his merchandise. He had

---

[b] The original function of a letter of marque (sometimes called a letter of reprisal) was to right a perceived wrong. If, for example, a foreign merchant had his goods stolen in Germany and could not gain cross-border compensation for loss through legal or diplomatic processes, he could be granted a letter of marque by his home government that allowed him to "capture" a German merchant as compensation for loss.

a little buggy, a two-seater with a fringe on top, and from time to time, when there were too many of them, he would smuggle one of the peddlers across the bridge to Calais, Maine.[6]

After Balfour's declaration, Kenen noticed many uncles and cousins planning to make their way to Palestine, and believed he would someday join them. Before that day arrived, he had to choose between tempting career paths as an actor, journalist, lawyer, and philosopher. Later in life, he successfully blended all four into intense activism.

Straight Journalist

Kenen worked as an usher and theatre property manager, and also took to the stage briefly as an actor in Toronto.[7] He planned to study at a New York seminary, but then considered becoming a Reform rabbi. Finally, he changed his mind yet again and majored in philosophy at the University of Toronto, becoming managing editor at the college daily. Upon graduation, he landed a job at the *Toronto Star* in May of 1925. He made clear distinctions between "straight reporting" and what is now referred to as "advocacy journalism." Kenen notes he was "never content just to be a reporter" and began to "champion many causes during the Depression."

A year later, Kenen took a job at the *Cleveland News*, where he soon began covering City Hall and Ohio politics at the Ohio State House. FBI files noted Kenen became a member of the Communist Party in 1937 while working as a newspaperman at the *Plain Dealer* in Cleveland.[8] . Kenen never mentioned such ties in his two autobiographies.

Kenen's persistence in getting a story won him praise but also rebukes and a night in jail. After a baker who overcame and disarmed an assailant refused Kenen's demand for a photo to accompany his news article, Kenen surreptitiously obtained it from the baker's church. At the age of 26, he was jailed for destruction of private property when, banging his press credentials against the glass, he broke a window trying to gain admission to a political event staged in an arena.

Journalism to Politics

During the Depression, Kenen wrote opinion pieces opposing new sales taxes meant to address plummeting revenue. He studied law at night and was admitted to the Ohio Bar Association. In 1933, he launched his first foray into Washington lobbying when his publisher sent him to convince the administration of President Franklin Delano Roosevelt (1882-1945) to pay off depositors who had lost money in Cleveland area bank failures. Like his father, Kenen now carried his own "letter of marque" for guaranteed access to politicians and power: his role as a "journalist providing news coverage." His press membership proved invaluable in his efforts to gain access and lobby media-hungry politicians:

> Within a few days of my arrival, I had established a lobby of Congressmen and journalists who thought as I did. All this was new to me, but for the next six weeks I interviewed many Senators and Representatives, rallying support for legislation authorizing the Administration to reimburse the depositors.[9]

After six weeks blending news coverage and lobbying, Kenen and his hastily assembled effort failed. But Kenen admired how players on both sides lobbied and "broadcast their views through the press."[10] He would achieve mastery over public relations, timely leaks, and effective media influence tactics over the next three decades. It should be noted that during his failed foray in Washington, Kenen was not yet even an American citizen. He was naturalized in the U.S. Northern District of Ohio Court on June 8, 1934.[11] But few rules governed federal lobbying until reforms were legislated a decade later.

Following reporter salary cuts reducing his pay from $65 a week to $50, Kenen was asked by a coworker to sign a petition for better conditions. Kenen scoffed at the idea that mere petitions would have any effect; instead, he went on to establish Local No. 1 of the American Newspaper Guild in Cleveland to negotiate higher-paying labor contracts. His successes drew the attention of other leaders: Kenen remembered that a "telephone call in 1940 changed his life" when a longtime friend sought to tap his organizing skills for the Zionist cause. Ezra Shapiro urged him to become president of the Cleveland Zionist District, and Kenen responded with gusto.

Lobbying for War

Now in his mid-thirties, Kenen conducted a fledgling public relations campaign designed to motivate the U.S. to enter WWII. Foreshadowing AIPAC's later tactics, it was focused on highly negative opposition research he compiled into a book targeting prominent Americans who opposed U.S. involvement. It was in the end, he noted, a wasted effort:

We were hopeful that Roosevelt would intervene, but he was under heavy pressure from many non-Jews who insisted that Americans must keep out of overseas problems and take care of themselves. Why must Americans intervene in European wars? How many isolationists were there? And who were they?

I thought that I should do some research. I was then covering the Cleveland City Hall, but I had a long lunch hour and I could always slip away to a nearby public library to look up the backgrounds and views of American leaders, especially those who couldn't care less about Jews. I spent many hours listing them, for I planned to write a monograph to be entitled "Isolate the Isolationists." I kept this up for several days until I had secured a long list.

Late one day I started for home and I picked up copies of my two favorite magazines: *The Nation* and *The New Republic*. My son Peter was at the curb waiting for the long ride to our home in South Euclid. I quickly thumbed through the pages of the two publications. Much to my dismay, both carried big feature stories about the isolationists. "Look Peter," I said, "that's terrible. I have been scooped after many days of hard work."

"What do you mean?" my nine-year-old cried. "They have many writers and readers and they will carry the names of many more people." No newspaper man likes to be scooped. Sadly, I threw away the pages of what was to have been my very first book.[12]

By 1943, Kenen had left the newspaper industry to work as the director of information for an organization called the American Emergency Committee for Zionist Affairs (AECZA) in New York. The AECZA was formed in 1939 to spread Zionist ideology to the largely indifferent non-Zionist majority of American Jews.[13] No longer personally subject to the military draft, Kenen was soon engaged in intense internecine combat within the AECZA for a harder ideological line. Kenen portrayed prominent antiwar Americans as isolationist, anti-Semitic, or when he thought justified, both.

They always held me back and thus to desist from significant action to overcome anti-Semitic isolationists. I had one major supporter, Louis Lipsky of Rochester, who was himself a veteran journalist and who always urged me to defy the moribund Committee and to write history-making press releases.[14]

The umbrella group's core issue framing challenge was not new: present Zionism to America as a "unified movement of the Jewish People."

This required combating more than apathy. Member Jewish opposition groups and their leaders rocked and subverted attempts to present a unified American Emergency Committee for Zionist Affairs message. Apathy had also undercut the AEZCA's precursor organization. During World War I, famed jurist Louis D. Brandeis (1856-1941) chaired a group called the Provisional Executive Committee for Zionist Affairs. This group was founded on August 30, 1914, when a group of 150 Zionist leaders met in New York City and elected Brandeis president. Movement membership blossomed from 12,000 in 1914 to 176,000 by 1919. But then momentum waned, according to author David Howard Goldberg:

> Internal disputes within the Zionist movement and/or the active opposition or passive ambivalence of non-Zionist American Jews scuttled the earlier efforts.[15]

Soon, however, troubling news of Nazi repression and atrocities would energize a broad reorganization effort to unify Jewish groups under temporary emergency Zionist umbrella organizations. The AEZCA became more effective in silencing and marginalizing dissident voices whose opposition seemed ever more theoretical and out of step with horrific facts coming in from the European theatre. They also targeted more militant front groups with competing messages.

Kenen's work late in World War II in New York City was atypical and more conflicted than most domestic nonprofit initiatives aiding the war effort as well as the work of traditional Jewish relief organizations. In combating 1939 British restrictions on Jewish immigration to Palestine and land acquisition efforts, Kenen and other leaders were also clearly antagonizing a United States ally. Great Britain authored restrictions on immigration to Palestine, outlined in the infamous "White Paper":

> We Zionists agreed that our major objective was to defeat Hitler and that we must not be diverted from it, but we accepted the epigrammatic dictum of Israel's David Ben-Gurion, who said, "We shall fight the White Paper as if there were no war, and we shall fight the war as if there were no White Paper."[16]

As the end of war became imminent, Kenen busily prepared for the inevitable peace conferences in Germany and Austria, documenting justifications for reparations and acquiring other evidence that might be useful in making a case for Israel.[17] He worked closely with Henry Monsky, a B'nai B'rith leader from Omaha. A core member of the task force was Louis Lipsky[c] (1876-1963), the super-activist former president of the Zionist Organization of America and founder of dominant Zionist fundraising organizations.

The Nuremberg prosecutions of Nazi leadership were held between November 14, 1945 and October 1, 1946. Kenen attended various international conferences on behalf of the American Jewish Conference between October 12, 1945 and December 7, 1945. He again departed the United States between June 20, 1946 and September 7, 1946, visiting the UK, France, Egypt, Palestine, and Germany representing the American Jewish Conference.[18]

Lingering dissent and disunity did not keep Kenen and other organizers from a major bid to achieve influence over the U.S. president discussed in Chapter 2. Soon after the creation of the State of Israel, the AEZCA was subsumed by yet another organization, the American Zionist Council. Ultimately, after the U.S. Department of Justice attempted to force it to openly register as a foreign agent, the American Zionist Council morphed into the American Israel Public Affairs Committee as the Israel lobby's push for unconditional U.S. political support and military and economic aid expanded geometrically.[19]

Herzl's Plan

In many ways, Isaiah Kenen's path through life can be seen as a focused and practical implementation of the vision laid out by the founder of modern political Zionism, Theodor Herzl (1860–1904). In hindsight, key aspects of Kenen's pursuits and actions seem modeled after Herzl himself, who, as Kenen noted, also began life as a journalist:

> A great number of Jews in Eastern Europe responded to the dramatic summons of Theodor Herzl, the visionary journalist who founded the modern-day Zionist movement, revolted by the infamous Dreyfus trial and the bigotry it exposed.[20]

Dreyfus, a French Jewish army captain, was accused and falsely convicted of spying for Germany. Herzl, who was of Austro-Hungarian heritage, covered the Dreyfus affair for a newspaper. The trial energized mass rallies in Paris where many chanted "Death to the Jews!" In June 1895

---

[c] In 1912, Lipsky became chairman of the Executive Committee of the Federation of American Zionists. He was an active participant lobbying for American support for the Balfour Declaration, and from 1922-1930 was chairman of the Zionist Organization of America. From 1954, he served as chairman of the American Zionist Committee for Public Affairs.

Herzl noted in his diary, "In Paris, as I have said, I achieved a freer attitude toward anti-Semitism...Above all, I recognized the emptiness and futility of trying to 'combat' anti-Semitism." Herzl's seminal work, *The Jewish State*, was translated into English and published in April 1896, making Herzl the leading spokesman for Zionism. The American Zionist Emergency Council itself published and distributed the book in 1946.

Theodor Herzl financed the First Zionist Congress in Basel, Switzerland and was elected chairperson. The Congress formulated a platform called the "Basel program" as well as the charter of the World Zionist Organization, which stated:

> Zionism seeks for the Jewish people a publicly recognized legally secured homeland in Palestine.[21]

Isaiah Kenen's father was the transmission belt between Herzl and Kenen, as he noted in his book *All My Causes*:

> Our family was always dedicated to Zionism. My father attended early meetings of the World Zionist Congress. He knew Herzl and other Zionist leaders. Herzl died in 1904. My father broke down and wept. I was born one year later and people used to say that I got the message.[22]

In 1898, Herzl began a series of programs to build diplomatic support for a Jewish state in Palestine. Herzl was granted audiences with the German emperor on several occasions, as well as the Ottoman emperor in Jerusalem, who rebuffed his territorial designs on Palestine.

Herzl's *The Jewish State* laid a very clear roadmap for Kenen's initiatives, including chartering and fortifying corporate umbrella entities that diverted general Jewish relief organization influence and funding into the Zionist cause. Herzl's great plan called for two primary corporations, one for public relations and the other for colonization:

> The plan, simple in design, but complicated in execution, will be carried out by two agencies: The Society of Jews and the Jewish Company.
>
> The Society of Jews will do the preparatory work in the domains of science and politics, which the Jewish Company will afterwards apply practically.
>
> The Jewish Company will be the liquidating agent of the business interests of departing Jews, and will organize commerce and trade in the new country.[23]

The first corporate entity, "the Society of Jews," would generate an ideological doctrine and nationalist drive for sovereignty and statehood through the sovereign branding concept of "the Jewish People." This drive called for an elite vanguard, able to transcend the masses and "internal schisms."

> A State is created by a nation's struggle for existence. In any such struggle it is impossible to obtain proper authority in circumstantial fashion beforehand. In fact, any previous attempt to obtain a regular decision from the majority would probably ruin the undertaking from the outset. For internal schisms would make the people defenseless against external dangers. We cannot all be of one mind; the gestor will therefore simply take the leadership into his hands and march in the van.
>
> The action of the gestor of the State is sufficiently warranted if the common cause is in danger, and the dominus is prevented, either by want of will or by some other reason, from helping itself.
>
> But the gestor becomes similar to the dominus by his intervention, and is bound by the agreement quasi ex contractu.[d] This is the legal relationship existing before, or, more correctly, created simultaneously with the State.
>
> The gestor thus becomes answerable for every form of negligence, even for the failure of business undertakings, and the neglect of such affairs as are intimately connected with them, etc. I shall not further enlarge on the negotiorum gestio[e], but rather leave it to the State, else it would take us too far from the main subject. One remark only: 'Business management, if it is approved by the owner, is just as effectual as if it had originally been carried on by his authority.'
>
> And how does all this affect our case?
>
> The Jewish people are at present prevented by the Diaspora from conducting their political affairs themselves. Besides, they are in a condition of more or less severe distress in many parts of the world. They need, above all things a gestor. This gestor cannot, of course, be a single

---

[d] Obligations that are not derived from the consent of the parties, but from either the voluntary act of one of the parties or imposition by law. In the US, these are referred to as "implied contracts" or "contracts implied by law."

[e] A situation in which the "gestor" takes action on behalf of a principal to the benefit of that principal, but without the consent of that principal. Later the action is ratified by the principal (from Roman and Dutch law).

individual. Such a one would either make himself ridiculous, or—seeing that he would appear to be working for his own interests—contemptible.

The gestor of the Jews must therefore be a body corporate. And that is the Society of Jews.[24]

Herzl charged the Society with surveying significant populations of Jews wanting to form a state, as well as gathering and compiling inside and outside views from "declarations of statesmen, parliaments, Jewish communities, societies, whether expressed in speeches or writings, in meetings, newspapers or books."[25] It was a clarion call for sustained and coordinated international lobbying to which many responded.

Herzl's second corporate entity, "the Jewish Company," would be in charge of the task of land acquisition and colonization, "the Jewish State."

> The Jewish Company is partly modeled on the lines of a great land-acquisition company. It might be called a Jewish Chartered Company, though it cannot exercise sovereign power, and has other than purely colonial tasks.[26]

The Jewish Agency, a corporation with a U.S. subsidiary headquartered in New York that employed Isaiah Kenen, David Ben-Gurion, and many others, would later list Herzl's concept of the colonization entity as one of the forebears of its own existence.[27] Herzl even provided a prescient glimpse of what awaited Kenen during his ill-fated attempt at immigration to Israel in 1951:

> The poorest will go first to cultivate the soil. In accordance with a preconceived plan, they will construct roads, bridges, railways and telegraph installations; regulate rivers; and build their own dwellings; their labor will create trade, trade will create markets and markets will attract new settlers, for every man will go voluntarily, at his own expense and his own risk...The emigrants standing lowest in the economic scale will be slowly followed by those of a higher grade. Those who at this moment are living in despair will go first. They will be led by the mediocre intellects which we produce so superabundantly and which are persecuted everywhere...

> This pamphlet will open a general discussion on the Jewish Question, but that does not mean that there will be any voting on it. Such a result would ruin the cause from the outset, and dissidents must remember that allegiance or opposition is entirely voluntary. He who will not come with us should remain behind.

Let all who are willing to join us, fall in behind our banner and fight for our cause with voice and pen and deed. [28]

Kenen honed his capabilities to fight for Herzl's cause "in voice, pen, and deed" in the movement's leadership, rather than enduring the early intense physical deprivations of state-building. But Kenen was never content to let dissidents and opposition go uncontested; as he both departed for Israel and "remained behind," he began his fight to overcome legal and national challenges to Israel's expanding prerogatives.

If we yield to the pressure of highly organized Zionist groups just now and make statements calculated to give support to their policies of the moment, we shall merely be encouraging them to make fresh demands and to apply pressure in the future whenever they conceive it to be in their interest...
—*Memo to President Harry S Truman, 9/12/1946, from acting Secretary of State William L. Clayton, declassified and released 7/15/1975*

...the Middle East could well fall into anarchy and become a breeding ground for world war.—***The Joint Chiefs of Staff, State-War-Navy Coordinating Committee, 6/21/1946; memo to Harry S Truman, declassified and released 1/16/1976***

Chapter 2: Lobbying for a Country

The formation of the State of Israel can clearly be seen in Herzl's plan as a "business startup." From this angle, the existing state is like the culmination of a business plan for a corporation. Different divisions and unit heads gathered the resources and legal basis to go public, executing Herzl's vision. However, unlike the corporate and entrepreneurial triumphs commonly splashed across the covers of popular business magazines, details about Israel lobbying programs in the United States are still emerging into the historical record, decades after they were launched and completed. A few illicit clandestine operations formerly confined to the fading memories of operatives and dusty intelligence files are also filling in critical gaps in the historical record. The transformative notion of creative destruction was also plainly at work in the evolution of corporate lobbying bodies.

In 1917, Zionist leader and chemist Chaim Weizmann (1874-1952) convinced the British government to declare support for establishing a Jewish national home in Palestine. This statement, the Balfour Declaration, was ratified by the League of Nations after WWI, and in 1922 Britain was appointed to rule Palestine.

Some Jews from across the globe immigrated to Palestine, especially from Germany after Nazi persecution began. This surge ignited Arab fear that Palestine would become an exclusively Jewish national homeland. By

1936, guerrilla fighting between Zionist settlers and Palestinians erupted across Palestine. In an attempt to quell the violence, the British issued an edict (the White Paper) that restricted Jewish immigration into Palestine in 1939. The British would ultimately become targets of terror bombings by Jewish colonizers and militant groups. Nazi atrocities provided a major catalyst for revitalizing Zionist organizations and more intense lobbying initiatives in the United States Congress. These efforts were overtly and covertly focused on circumventing British Displaced Person (DP) policies as well as securing arms. In Washington Herzl's most important concept in play was "negotiorum gestio": securing American recognition for a new state on the basis of applied special interest lobbying over broader competing foreign policy interests championed by the State Department and other U.S. government agencies. It would be the first of many instances of creating Israeli "facts on the ground" and then appealing for a U.S. president's approval.

Implementing Herzl's vision meant subverting all previous U.S. obligations and understandings with the Arabs. President Franklin D. Roosevelt assured Arab leaders that the United States would not intervene on any side without consulting all parties. But he was also the former governor of New York and extremely sensitive to the demands of Zionist activists. The original Balfour Declaration stated, "Nothing shall be done which may prejudice the civil and religious rights of existing non-Jewish communities in Palestine." Roosevelt's vice president, Harry S Truman (1884-1972), generally followed this evenhanded approach until Roosevelt died shortly after reelection in 1945. Roosevelt's longstanding appointees connected to the movement remained in place and growing entreaties from Zionist lobbyists were channeled through Truman's closest friends. The historical record reveals how Truman's policy on the Palestine question became heavily influenced by his need for campaign contributions for the looming 1948 presidential elections. This cycle repeats in the John F. Kennedy, Lyndon B. Johnson, and Robert F. Kennedy bids discussed later.

Truman and the Israel Lobby

When Harry S Truman became president on April 12, 1945, the Department of State and Department of War[f] did not support Zionist efforts to create a state in Palestine on geopolitical grounds and because it

---

[f] Renamed the Department of Defense in 1947.

did not benefit broader U.S. national interests, in their view. But the agencies' frantic, often confusing, and non-actionable warnings gave way to an intense ongoing lobbying campaign.

Truman served with Edward Jacobson (1891-1955) in WWI. Their military experiences and postwar retail business partnership made Jacobson an important channel for advisors concerned with realizing the Zionist dream of a state in Palestine. When Truman and Jacobson's store went bankrupt in 1921 and Truman began a career in politics, the future president learned the importance of tapping wealthy individuals and interest groups for campaign contributions. Truman worked hard to pay off his debts and launch a political career. In 1934, just as he was entering the Senate, a banker who acquired his failed retail business loan forgave a portion of it, discounted the rest to $1000, and contributed an equal amount to Truman's campaign. The money-for-influence message was clear. Truman also became a longtime beneficiary of "boss" Thomas Joseph Pendergast's (1873-1945) political machine, which thrived on winning and dividing public works contracts in Missouri. In 1940, Truman balanced competing economic special interest politics in his bid for Senate reelection with an appeal to the Freemasons: his fortunes were greatly boosted when he became Grand Master of their Missouri Grand Lodge. His campaign asserted that it proved he was trustworthy and of high principle,[29] but he did also win an unflattering nickname: "the Senator from Pendergast."

As a U.S. senator, Truman was under constant pressure from Pendergast's lobby to cater to the needs of the boss's Redimix concrete contracts. He also began receiving urgent pleas from Zionist interest groups, among the most unusual from Peter H. Bergson (aka Hillel Kook, born in Lithuania, 1915-2001) for the formation of a "Jewish Army" in the Middle East. Bergson's "Committee for a Jewish Army" circulated a plan to Congress calling for an army of 100,000 Jews in Palestine to fight Nazis and "fifth columnists" of Syria, Iraq, and Egypt. In reality, Bergson was leading a front organization for Menachem Wolfevitch Begin's (1913-1992) organization. Irgun Z'vai Leumi also lobbied Nazi Germany for a Jewish Army, as well as a formal alliance, between 1940 and 1941 when Hitler appeared to have the upper hand in Europe.

COMMITTEE FOR A JEWISH ARMY
OF STATELESS AND PALESTINIAN JEWS

Figure 1 Official logo of the committee during 1942 Washington lobbying.

Other members of Irgun included Avraham Stern (1907-1942) and Yitzhak Shamir (1915-2012), who later became Prime Minister of Israel. Irgun presented Nazi leaders with a January 11, 1941 proposal for a Jewish Army, also referred to as the National Military Organization (NMO). The alliance plan was fully titled "Fundamental Features of the Proposal of the National Military Organization in Palestine (Irgun Z'vai Leumi) Concerning the Solution of the Jewish Question in Europe and the Participation of the NMO in the War on the Side of Germany." Details of this stunning alliance would not emerge until years after the plan was drafted:

> The Solving in this manner of the Jewish problem and thus the bringing about with it of the liberation of the Jewish people once and for all, is the objective of the political activity and the years long struggle of the Jewish freedom movement, the National Military Organization (Irgun Z'vai Leumi) in Palestine.
>
> The NMO, which is well-acquainted with the goodwill of the German Reich government and its authorities towards Zionist activity inside Germany and towards Zionist emigration plans, is of the opinion that:
>
> 1. Common interests could exist between the establishment of a new order in Europe in conformity with the German concept, and the true national aspirations of the Jewish people as they are embodied by the NMO.
>
> 2. Cooperation between the new Germany and a renewed folkish-national Hebraium would be possible and,
>
> 3. The establishment of the historic Jewish state on a national and totalitarian basis, bound by a treaty with the German Reich, would be in the interest of a maintained and strengthened future German position of power in the Near East...

> Proceeding from these considerations, the NMO in Palestine, under the condition the above-mentioned national aspirations of the Israeli freedom movement are recognized on the side of the German Reich, offers to actively take part in the war on Germany's side.[30]

An ocean away, during the very month the U.S. entered the war, Truman was being lobbied by New York Congressman Andrew Somers (1895-1949) for the formation of the very same army.[31] Somers had also lobbied President Roosevelt and the secretary of state for the creation of a Jewish Army for Palestine composed of American Jews. Truman objected to any such segmentation of the full U.S. fighting force. He carefully relayed this to Andrew Somers two days after receiving his impassioned appeal and plan. But Truman did not object outright to a fighting force composed of Jews already in Palestine, and along with 32 other senators, lent his name to Somers's committee.[32]

> Appreciate very much your good letter of the Twenty Sixth, regarding the proposed Jewish Army.
>
> I have had a great deal of correspondence about this suggestion but so far as the United States is concerned I think the best thing for the Jews to do is to go right into our Army as they did in the last war and make the same sort of good soldiers as they did before.
>
> It is an honorable undertaking to organize an Army for Palestine but I think American citizens ought to serve in the American army.[33]

Bergson would form a succession of other front groups that competed with and diluted Isaiah Kenen's public relations on behalf of the Jewish Agency. Kenen was particularly worried about Bergson's PR strategy positioning Zionist efforts for a state as representative of universal Jewish aspirations. This not only encroached on the prerogatives of the American Jewish Conference but also diluted carefully constructed slogans. Bergson's effort was well executed and effective. Kenen noted that his Irgun competition was well armed for PR:

> These committees had a flair for publicity. They purchased advertising space, had literary talent, held public conferences, and submitted legislation to Congress. They confused many people because they diluted and watered-down programs, resorting to palatable and ambiguous euphemisms in order to win broad support. They rarely spoke of a Jewish state and they differentiated between the "Hebrews" of

Palestine and the Jews of the United States, a strange distinction which few Jews could understand and which sounded very much like the separatism of the American Council for Judaism.[34]

The militant committees found allies in Congress. While Kenen continued to be vexed by the American Council for Judaism (ACJ), the Irgun group concentrated on forming a "Team B" of allies in the U.S. Treasury while building up feeder paramilitary training camps in the U.S. and Europe. Bergson's later calls for U.S. visas and immediate evacuations of Jews from Europe found a widespread congressional following for their simplicity. But when Bergson threatened Kenen's Zionist groups' unified message, they lobbied the IRS to investigate and the U.S. State Department to deport Bergson, who ultimately left the U.S. of his own accord.[35]

Truman was angered and would have nothing to do with Bergson after one Jewish Army newspaper ad that also deeply bothered Kenen. Truman upbraided Bergson for the unauthorized use of Congress members' names in their advertising, and formally asked that his name be removed from the Committee for a Jewish Army on May 7, 1943.

> Senator Lucas yesterday called my attention to an advertisement in the New York Times to which was signed the names of some dozen or so Senators and to which the name of Senator Edwin C. Johnson was signed as Chairman.
>
> Senator Johnson informs me that this advertisement was never submitted to him for approval, and I have the same information from a number of other senators.
>
> I am withdrawing my name from your Committee, and you are not authorized under any circumstances to make use of it for any purpose in the future.
>
> This does not mean my sympathies are not with the down-trodden Jews of Europe, but when you take it on yourself without consultation to attack members of the Senate and House of Representatives who are working in your interest I cannot approve of that procedure.[36]

He copied his Senate letter to several colleagues and to the United Jewish Appeal, confirming his acquiescence to their lobbying pressure. But after he became president, Truman was bombarded with even more Zionist lobbying on Palestine that he privately found extremely irritating:

The facts were that not only were there pressure movements around the United Nations unlike anything that had been seen there before, but that the White House, too, was subjected to a constant barrage. I do not think I ever had as much pressure and propaganda aimed at the White House as I had in this instance. The persistence of a few of the extreme Zionist leaders—actuated by a political motive and engaging in political threats—disturbed and annoyed me.[37]

When Truman became president, Secretary of State Edward Stettinius (1900-1949) sternly warned him that he would become the target of concentrated pressure over Palestine and reminded him of his broader responsibilities:

It is very likely that efforts will be made by some of the Zionist leaders to obtain from you at an early date some of the commitments in favor of the Zionist program which is pressing for unlimited Jewish immigration into Palestine and the establishment there of a Jewish state.

As you are aware, the Government and people of the United States have every sympathy for the persecuted Jews of Europe and are doing all in their power to relieve their suffering. The question of Palestine is, however, a highly complex one and involves questions which go far beyond the plight of the Jews of Europe.[38]

Undersecretary of State Joseph C. Grew (1880-1965), who oversaw the establishment of the U.S. Foreign Service, echoed Stettinius's concerns and worryingly sent Truman a report of presidential commitments made to Saudi ruler Ibn Saud (1876-1953) before Roosevelt died:

I thought that you would like to know that although President Roosevelt at times gave expression to views sympathetic to certain Zionist aims, he also gave certain assurances to the Arabs which they regard as definite commitments on our part. On a number of occasions within the past few years, he authorized the Department to assure the heads of the different Near Eastern governments on his behalf that 'in the view of this Government there should be no decision altering the basic situation in Palestine without full consultation with both Arabs and Jews'. In his meeting with King Ibn Saud early this year, moreover, Mr. Roosevelt promised the King that as regards Palestine he would make no move hostile to the Arab people and would not assist the Jews as against the Arabs.[39]

On May 28, 1945, Grew sent Truman another memo urging him not to cave in to congressional pressure instigated by the American Christian

Palestine Committee.⁴⁰ Lessing J. Rosenwald⁸ (1891-1979), representing the dissident American Council for Judaism (ACJ), met with Truman at the White House on December 4, 1945, urging the president to avoid perpetual bloodshed over Palestine:

> We have saber rattling, boycott, recriminations, rioting, bloodshed and threats of still more bloodshed.
>
> The situation is not eased by the issuance of belligerent notes by sovereign states of the Near East, or by demonstrations and nationalist propaganda on the part of Zionists in and out of Palestine. It is high time to call an end to this dangerous course.⁴¹

Rosenwald laid out the ACJ's seven-point proposal calling for a UN declaration that Palestine not be an exclusively Muslim, Christian, or Jewish state, but rather enjoy freedom of expression and nondiscriminatory immigration. Rosenwald wanted the European Jewish DP issue to be disconnected from the Palestine question and treated separately under a research-oriented procedure for determining where and how DPs wanted to relocate in the postwar turmoil. He objected to simply propagandizing and sending them to Palestine. He also called for economic development of the Palestinian territory through internationally administered financial assistance.

However, Kenen and other movement leaders were incensed that an alternative "minority" group like the ACJ had such high-level administration access and press coverage. Kenen attributed the latter to what he saw as the inherent structural flaw of the American press:

> The American Council for Judaism included some ninety ultra-Reform rabbis and laymen who were able to gain newspaper space because the press invariably features and exaggerates minority dissent.⁴²

Lessing Rosenwald's and other appeals made an impact. A joint Anglo-American committee to study the Palestine question was formed and dispatched to the region. Truman signed Executive Order 9682 on January 19, 1946, providing resources and a charter to "examine political, economic and social conditions in Palestine as they bear upon the problem of Jewish immigration and settlement therein and the well-being of people now

---

⁸ Rosenwald was chairman of Sears, Roebuck and Company from 1928-1939. A major art philanthropist and book collector, Rosenwald donated 22,000 works of art worth $35 million (inflation adjusted) to the National Gallery of Art in Washington, DC in 1979.

living therein." The Anglo-American Committee was also to study the relocation desires of Jewish DPs in Europe and Palestine, as well as the views of Arab representatives in the region.

Before the committee reached any recommendations, Congressman Emanuel Celler (1888-1981) of New York began working to undermine the integrity of the UK team members from behind the scenes. He implored Truman to immediately permit the entry of 100,000 Jewish DPs into Palestine before the study was finished:

> It is clearly evident from the rift that has arisen between the American and British members of the Anglo-American Committee of Inquiry on Palestine that the British are determined to control completely this inquiry....I believe it is time to give serious consideration as to whether we shall continue in this inquiry...I respectfully submit that unless an interim report is published, recommending that 100,000 Jews be permitted entrance into Palestine immediately and unless the Committee is permitted to continue its inquiry in an unbiased, objective manner, unhampered by the British Foreign Office, that the American members of this Committee be withdrawn forthwith.[43]

Truman immediately responded that the committee still had four months to compile its report and it would be "premature to make comments on this report until it is in the hands of Prime Minister Attlee and myself." Celler was likely miffed at Truman's dismissive final words:

> I highly appreciate your interest, of course, but a premature comment on a report that is not made will not help the situation one little bit.[44]

Had Celler been closer to the committee preparing the report, he might have rested easier. But such privileged information was only being compiled and channeled to key Truman donors by David K. Niles (1890-1952). Niles acted as Truman's administrative assistant and political consultant to the president and had also served in the Roosevelt administration. A high-level gatekeeper between key Zionist lobbyists and the president, he sent Truman's appointment secretary Matthew J. Connolly (1908-1976) a confidential memo about the Anglo-American Committee report on May 1, 1946:

> The president may be interested in a conversation I had with Justice Frankfurter about midnight last night on the Palestine report.

Justice Frankfurter, as you probably know, is perhaps the most prominent supporter of Palestine in public life today among the Jews, and has been for many years. The great Zionist leader in this country and in the world, for many years, was Justice Louis D. Brandeis. Frankfurter and Brandeis had been intimate friends for many, many years. Frankfurter said to me, after reading the report, "I have only one regret." My heart sank a little bit and then Frankfurter continued, "My regret is that Justice Brandeis did not live to see this report. He would have called it a miracle." Then Frankfurter launched into a tirade against Silver and the other Zionist leaders who, he says, prefer a Jewish State on paper rather than doing something real for human beings.

I asked Justice Frankfurter if he had any objection to my quoting him on this and he said he did not and he would be glad to have me do so. You may be certain that I will use this to the limit with our friends in New York the next couple of days. [45]

This memo is one of the documented indicators, along with Truman's notice to the United Jewish Appeal about terminating his relationship with Bergson, of the importance of Israel lobby campaign contributors to the inner workings of the Truman administration. The issue of Israel would be omnipresent as they mapped out a plan for the 1948 election campaign, kept lines of communication open, and continued to channel closely held information to donors.

On June 20, under the leadership of Senator Robert F. Wagner of New York, nine more members of Congress sent Truman a letter demanding the admission of 100,000 Jewish DPs to Palestine and excoriating the British.[46] A day later, Truman's Joint Chiefs of Staff under A.J. McFarland presented the U.S. armed forces view of the Palestine question. McFarland urged that no U.S. forces be dispatched to carry out Anglo-American Committee recommendations. McFarland emphasized that any "pacification" effort involving the U.S. armed forces could result in conflict and the "Middle East could well fall into anarchy and become a breeding ground for world war." The Joint Chiefs also felt that implementation of the report by force would "prejudice British and U.S. interests in much of the Middle East and that British and U.S. influence would consequently be curtailed except as it might be maintained by military force."[47]

Militant Zionist groups now operating across Palestine, such as Stern and Irgun, were stepping up attacks and terror bombing campaigns against the British, including the July 22, 1946 bombing of the King David Hotel. UK Prime Minister Clement Richard Attlee (1883-1967) wrote

Truman on July 25, 1946, outraged over the terror attack but determined not to let terrorism affect the diplomatic process underway:

> The conversations between American and British officials on Palestine and related problems are now almost concluded and agreement has been reached on all matters of substance. I am sure you will agree that the inhuman crimes committed in Jerusalem on 22 July call for the strongest action against terrorism but having regard to the sufferings of innocent Jewish victims of Nazism this should not deter us from introducing a policy designed to bring peace to Palestine with the least possible delay.[48]

On October 4, Truman appealed for 100,000 Jews to be allowed to immigrate to Palestine, as well as endorsing a Jewish Agency plan for partition. In what would soon become a mainstay of American presidential electioneering (competition to see who was more "pro-Israel"), New York governor and presidential candidate Thomas Dewey upped the ante, calling for mass Jewish immigration to Palestine several days later. The British, sensing at once that U.S. electoral politics had become the driving factor in the Palestine question, hinted that Truman and Dewey's proposals were now motivated by domestic considerations.[49] Like the American people, they would not find out how true this was until long after it mattered.

By February 1947, Arab-Zionist communications in the region were frozen. The British proposed administering Palestine as a UN trusteeship pending total independence in five years. Within ten days, Isaiah Kenen and the Jewish Agency requested that the U.S. government align itself with the Zionist case and become "their voice," but received no satisfactory answer. Secretary of State George C. Marshall (1880-1959) in particular was firm that a resolution would only come from a "free and full conference between the representatives of the British government and the Jewish-Arab leaders...in a conciliatory spirit."[50] This evenhanded approach made circumventing the State Department an even more urgent matter for the Jewish Agency. Soon, the British turned the Palestine matter over entirely to the United Nations.

The UN General Assembly established the "Special Committee on Palestine" (UNSCOP) on April 2, 1947. The Jewish Agency immediately began recruiting staff for intensified lobbying operations in New York and Washington offices to win a favorable UN outcome. Isaiah Kenen formally became the Jewish Agency's Director of Information, and he was immediately granted a leave of absence from the American Emergency Committee for Zionist Affairs.[51]

Kenen was soon traveling with the 11-nation UNSCOP mission through Palestine and Europe as the Jewish Agency's liaison to the U.S. press.

> That evening I cabled New York that partition was assured—paradoxically because of UNSCOP's reaction to the testimony of partition's opponents.
>
> The Arab Higher Committee, led by the ex-Mufti, boycotted UNSCOP because its terms of reference had ignored their demands for independence and self-determination; but Arabs did meet UNSCOP diplomats at private parties where they could present their views without challenge.
>
> UNSCOP visited a school in Beersheba, where Arab students turned their heads away according to instructions. Left with little to do in empty classrooms, diplomats Enrique Fabregat of Uruguay and Jorge Garcia Granados of Guatemala and I played tic-tac-toe on the blackboard.
>
> UN diplomats had been snubbed in Jaffa and in every Arab town. They were swiftly evicted from the Golden Spindle, an Arab textile factory in Ramleh, after I had called Ralph Bunche's attention to children who were operating the machines. Jewish newspapermen were denied admission to an Arab cigarette factory in Haifa, and Arab City Councilmen boycotted the UNSCOP City Hall visit.[52]

Kenen quickly became confident of the mission's positive future outcome for the Jewish Agency, since Arabs were not even participating in the formal UN process. When they did attempt to make their case at the UN, Kenen would be ready.

Jewish Agency Wins UN Representation

On May 1, 1947, the Jewish Agency achieved a major lobbying victory by orchestrating a wave of public protests to the Truman administration designed to make itself a nonvoting representative in the United Nations. As the official spokesman, Kenen made a tactical decision to issue no statement about whether the Jewish Agency would later press on for a full vote in the general assembly, a move strongly opposed by Arab member states.

> The Jewish Agency's spokesmen at Flushing Meadow declined to comment yesterday on the new American position. They indicated that they might find voteless representation on Committee 1 acceptable but would reserve a decision on any other solution that might be presented.[53]

U.S. officials hastily tried to position their increasingly frequent acquiescence to the lobby's demands as "nothing more than a shift, certainly not a reversal in policy," and of course not orchestrated by pressure focused on the White House. In reality, the groups applying the most intense pressure to the Truman administration were the American Zionist Emergency Council (the umbrella speaking for six organizations including the Zionist Organization of America and Hadassah), the American Christian Palestine Committee,[54] the American Jewish Conference, and the Political Action Committee for Palestine.[55] The American Zionist Emergency Council led the charge for voting status before Truman and the U.S. delegation at the United Nations and released a statement:

> The American Zionist Emergency Council, speaking for six affiliated Zionist groups, telegraphed "emphatic protest" to President Truman that Arab views were being presented adequately while the Jewish viewpoint was barred, "owing mainly to the attitude taken by the American delegation."[56]

The Jewish Agency leadership met daily in a brownstone close to the UN headquarters. Nachum Goldman led the Jewish Agency, while Abba Hillel Silver (1893-1963) represented the Jewish Agency's American Section; Emanuel Neumann spoke for the Zionist Organization of America. Rose Halprin represented Hadassah, Chaim Greenberg the Labor Zionists, and Rabbi Max Kirshblum and Wolf Gold the Religious Zionists. During the next 40 months, Isaiah Kenen would act as press liaison and spokesperson for the Jewish Agency for Palestine and liaison with the United Nations Special Committee on Palestine. Kenen would again travel to England, Palestine, Egypt, France, Switzerland, Germany, and Austria between June and August 1947, in his capacity as a Jewish Agency press representative.[57]

On October 3, 1947, Truman's former business partner Edward Jacobson was carefully briefed and prepped to lobby the president for a favorable UN outcome. Kenen noted Jacobson's singular utility as he was deployed by the cause:

Truman had a Jewish partner, Eddy Jacobson, and many people thought that Jacobson influenced his decision in favor of Israel. Like many other B'nai B'rith members of the day, Jacobson was not a Zionist. But he did have an impact, for it was he who insisted that Truman receive Weizmann, who, more than anyone else, persuaded Truman to overrule his Arabist advisers and to recognize the State of Israel.[58]

But Kenen's ostensibly representative umbrella organization was still dealing with more than apathetic non-Zionist members of B'nai B'rith. The highly active American Council for Judaism again registered its disagreement with the nationalist movement for the creation of Israel. Presenting a 27-page memorandum to the Committee of Inquiry on Palestine, ACJ president Lessing J. Rosenwald now simultaneously attacked the Herzl vision, the Balfour Declaration, and modern U.S. Zionist efforts to set up a state as an "anti-Semitic racialist lie that Jews the world over were a separate, national body." Rosenwald's UN memorandum protested references to the "historic connection of the Jewish people with Palestine." It also stated that ignoring Christians' and Muslims' equivalent historic and religious connection with Palestine had served to reattribute national characteristics of ambiguous loyalty to Jews of the world. The American Council for Judaism called for treating the issue of displaced persons as a larger problem affecting people of all faiths and attacked the Jewish Agency for assiduously cultivating the notion that it was an authorized spokesperson for "the Jews." Rosenwald stated bluntly a refrain he would repeat decades later: that the Jewish Agency was not qualified to be the political spokesman for Jews in either the United States or the Soviet Union, "where 70 percent resided."[59]

Truman concurred in a July 21, 1947 diary entry detailing conversations with former Treasury secretary Henry Morgenthau[60] (1891-1967) that the Zionist lobbyists had "no sense of proportion nor do they have any judgment on world affairs." Although thoughts on the impending election also loomed in the entry, Truman's diatribe excoriated the "selfishness" of those lobbying him who "care not how many Estonians, Latvians, Finns, Poles, Yugoslavs or Greeks get murdered or mistreated as DP as long as the Jews get special treatment."[61] He was philosophical about the loss of empathy and candor of any national or religious group after rising to power and influence, especially in the U.S. Congress, noting, "They all come from DPs."[62]

Kenen and the American Zionist Council felt that any lengthy debate, especially such an open one about which bodies represented the "Jewish Cause," was unnecessary and dangerous. By having pro-Zionist executives grouped under the Jewish Agency's unified banner, Kenen could stress that these groups alone should be heard at the UN due to the Jewish Agency's official status under the Mandate. Kenen put out his first press release on behalf of the Jewish Agency expounding on this legitimacy. In spite of the lingering terror campaigns against the British in Palestine, Kenen worked to tarnish the image of Arab delegations in the UN. He characterized the same release as noting that "the Egyptians had never lifted a fez to help win World War II."[63] But even that was a more generous and balanced position than the effective public relations effort to "Nazify" the entire Arab position at the UN.

Leaked U.S. State Department documents were circulated in the United Nations and Congress revealing that the Mufti of Jerusalem, like the Irgun, had attempted coordination with the Nazis—only the Mufti had attempted to stem Jewish immigration to Palestine. David Niles warned Truman of the leak in an urgent May 12, 1947 memo:

> You have received a copy of Documentary Record submitted to the United Nations. This contains very confidential material that is in the files of the State Department.
>
> I think it is important to find out how it got out. It is very damaging evidence that the Arab representatives now at UNO were allies of Hitler. There is also included in this material the diary of the Grand Mufti, which Justice Jackson [Robert H. Jackson (1892-1954)] found at Nuremburg. Copies of this document have already gone to all the Members of Congress.[64]

Truman was America's first White House victim of this type of orchestrated Israel lobby leak, which would later become a mainstay of interaction between U.S. administrations and AIPAC. Truman scrawled an angry handwritten message to Niles about the lobby's tactics and usurpation of foreign affairs powers through the acquisition and distribution of classified documents:

> I knew all about the purported facts mentioned. And of course, I don't like it. We could have settled this Palestine thing if U.S. politics had been kept out of it. Terror and Silver[h] are the contributing causes of some, not all, of our troubles. The document referred to could have been used by us for the welfare of the world had not our political situation come into the picture. I surely wish God Almighty would give the Children of Israel

---

[h] Rabbi Abba Hillel Silver.

an Isaiah, the Christians a St. Paul, and the Sons of Israel a peek at the Golden Rule. Maybe he will decide to do that.[65]

But the lobby did have an Isaiah, who was bubbling over with pride at the lopsided version of history. Kenen was proud that the Mufti's diaries had been effectively circulated on to the broader public via *The Nation* magazine.

> The Nation Magazine's Associates, headed by Freda Kirchwey and Lillie Shultz, had circulated a document indicting the pro-Axis activities of the ex-Mufti of Jerusalem, who had joined Hitler in Berlin—coincidentally, on December 7, 1941, the 'Day of Infamy'—to broadcast calls for the 'final solution'.[66]

Clumsy Arab efforts in the United Nations to counter the campaign simply reinforced growing negative views. Kenen noted that the Arab delegation's attempt to respond was as damning as the leaked diaries: "After that polemic, the Committee defeated Arab proposals which called for immediate Palestine independence...Silver, Sharett and Ben-Gurion summarized the Zionist case in less than eighty minutes."[67] The effort to "Nazify" the broader Arab case at the UN and in the press was successful. Countervailing documents revealing that Irgun and Stern (which were later integrated into the Israeli Defense Forces) had also approached the Nazis would not surface until decades later and would never receive much recognition.

UNSCOP recommended that the British mandate over Palestine finally be ended with the territory partitioned into two separate states, over the strident objections of Arab leaders. By October, the Arab League Council member states were moving troops to Palestine's border. Meanwhile, President Truman began framing his grudging support for the Jewish colonists and newly arrived refugees from war-torn Europe as being in line with Roosevelt's principles of "self-determination and self-government." Truman ordered the reluctant U.S. State Department to support the UN partition plan. The UN General Assembly passed the partition plan on November 29, 1947.

Truman Recognizes Israel

Truman's recognition of Israel in May of 1948 occurred as a uniquely isolated executive decision made under intense lobbying. It was on the eve of a presidential reelection campaign to be funded by "friends in New

York." Truman released his hand-corrected draft recognizing the new state to the press without consulting either the U.S. State Department or other key government agencies.

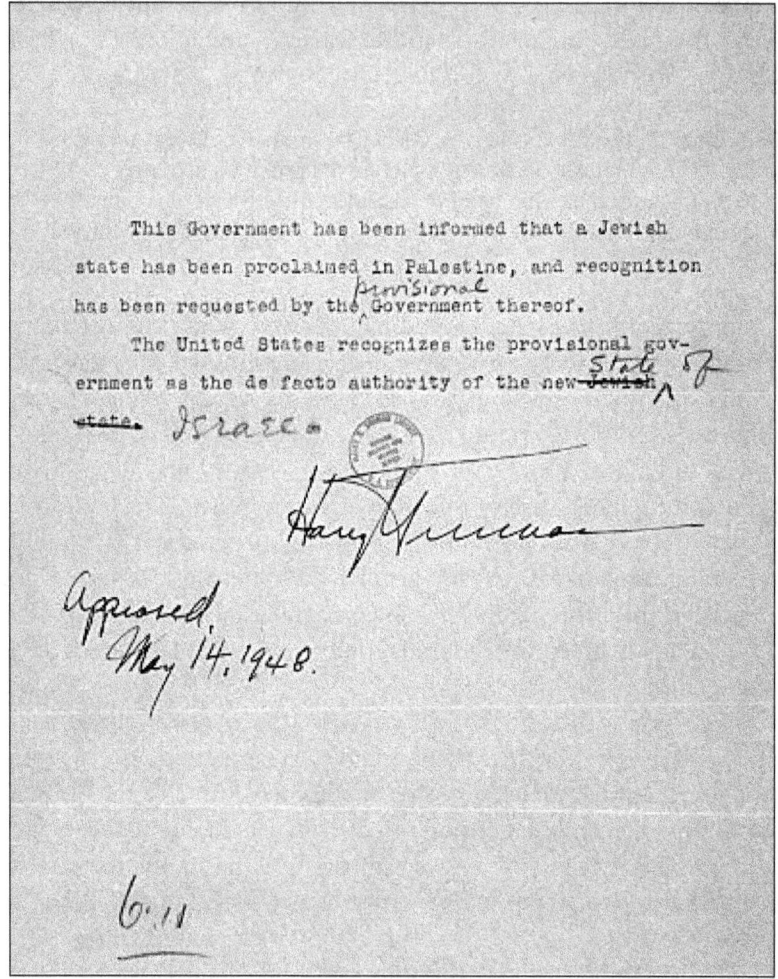

Figure 2 Truman recognizes Israel, May 14, 1948.

In outraged response, Secretary of State George C. Marshall threatened to campaign against Truman in the upcoming November elections. The harsh State Department view of Truman's political expediency was summed up by Gordon P. Merriam (1900-1999), a member of the Policy Planning Staff in July of 1948:

We have no long-term Palestine policy. We do have a short-term open-ended policy which is set from time to time by White House directives.[68]

The government agency revolt against Truman also revealed structural weaknesses of the government: bureaucratic indecision and an inability to present attractive and actionable alternative recommendations. It meant that the U.S. government agency and legitimate Arab and Palestinian concerns were steamrolled. The Zionist case, tempered by Nazi atrocities in WWII, was pointed, simple, and professionally executed. Meanwhile, Truman's State Department and Joint Chiefs of Staff advisors continued to send detailed, lengthy, hand-wringing position papers through May of 1948. While accurate and well documented, they failed to present a simple, actionable, and unified plan for tackling the issue in a way that would adequately represent U.S. interests and provide closure to the issue. Public relations effectively marginalized the legitimacy of Palestinian concerns, a factor that has continued for many decades.

Truman's agency heads were simultaneously charged with the more important tasks of winding down a global war, developing new policies toward the Soviet Union, and rebuilding Europe. Of course, the government bureaucracy had no solution that would or should contribute to Truman's immediate desire for reelection. The U.S. Department of Justice was not yet aware of or attempting to rein in an intense global lobby as it surged forward into domestic U.S. affairs.

To this day, most history students remember little of the 1948 presidential campaign except a photo of Truman jubilantly waving a newspaper that incorrectly proclaimed his rival, Governor Thomas Dewey, the winner. The campaign's financial history is useful and more relevant but was completely unknown to American voters when it mattered most. Contemporary news accounts provided no clue as to how Truman suddenly managed to raise massive funds to stage a comeback, but serious historians now know it would not have happened without Abraham J. Feinberg (1908-1998). Cash infusions into Truman's reelection campaign from the elite financial arm of the nascent Israel lobby directed by Feinberg averted Truman's almost certain defeat. This also consummated a prerogative of secretive and growing "one-on-one" relations between the Israel lobby and U.S. presidential administrations.

On May 25, 1948, a vital initiative of the reelection campaign began when Truman received Chaim Weizmann, Israel's first president, as a state guest and discussed lifting an embargo on arms sales. They chatted about U.S. foreign aid to Israel in the $90-100 million range. Truman had no way of knowing that his embargo had long been lifted by the Haganah (a paramilitary force in Palestine, predecessor of the IDF), the Jewish Agency, and a network of arms smugglers covertly rushing stolen and illegally reconditioned WWII surplus weapons to Palestine and later Israel in violation of U.S. law.

Truman appointed James G. McDonald (1886-1964), an accomplished New York publicist and former *New York Times* editorial staffer, as his first ambassador to Israel on June 22, 1948. Before his appointment, McDonald traveled overseas on a sponsored trip, but he lost no time excoriating the United Nations upon returning to the U.S.:

> Last night at his home in Bronxville, James G. McDonald declined to comment on his new diplomatic duties, saying that such information should come from the State Department. However, on arrival here on June 7 from a visit to South Africa, where he was a guest of the Jewish community, he was quoted as having expressed a lack of faith in the ability of the United Nations to settle the Palestine problem. "The United Nations are almost futility personified," he said.[69]

In the meantime, Truman sat down with Abraham Feinberg to discuss his reelection campaign's financial problems.

Feinberg Factor

Abraham J. Feinberg rose through entrepreneurial grit from humble surroundings to become the chairman of Kayser-Roth Corporation, a New-York-based apparel manufacturer. Later he would become chairman of the American Bank and Trust Company, acquired in 1978 by Bank Leumi.[i] Upon his death in 1998, Feinberg was serving as chief executive for a major Coca-Cola bottler in Israel.[70] Many attribute these concessions to his dedicated and always well-financed public and private initiatives for Israel. Feinberg was instrumental in operations funneling arms to the Haganah and later arranging financing for Israel's clandestine nuclear weapons program.[71] Feinberg's understanding of Truman, Kennedy, and Johnson campaign realities and his own role was succinct:

> My path to power was cooperation in terms of what they needed—campaign money.[72]

---

[i] Bank Leumi was founded at the Second Zionist Congress and incorporated in London in 1899 as the financial instrument of the Zionist Organization; it later became a commercial bank.

As a member of the Democratic Party's campaign finance committee, Feinberg was summoned to the White House for a meeting with Truman, who was now drumming up campaign support in earnest buoyed by his role in recognizing Israel. Although accounts of the historic meeting vary, Feinberg remembered Truman saying, "If I had to bet money, I'd bet on myself—if I could go across the country by train." In the meeting, Truman aides presented an estimated price tag of $100,000 for the national whistlestop tour (around $1.2 million in today's dollars). Feinberg brashly guaranteed the money would be raised within two weeks, on his own behalf as well as that of Kay Jewelry Company owner Ed Kaufman. Not only did he come through on the pledge, Feinberg also arranged to have Jewish delegations meet and "refuel" the whistlestop campaign, providing additional cash contributions all along the way.[73] Feinberg estimated that the total donations to the reelection campaign reached $400,000. He received and cherished a personal seven-page letter of thanks from Truman. Truman also offered to make him U.S. ambassador to Israel, which he turned down. Later, in his personal memoirs, Truman frankly noted the quid pro quo basis this special interest placed upon him to provide a U.S. diplomatic and even military umbrella to Israel:

> Top Jewish leaders in the United States were putting all sorts of pressure on me to commit American power and forces on behalf of the Jewish aspirations in Palestine.[74]

The central, all-important role of Feinberg and the budding Israel lobby's financing in Truman's victory was a closely guarded secret at the time. Contemporary press accounts of the famous whistlestop campaign in 1948 and most campaign historians simply could not link Feinberg or Israel lobby funds to the Truman election campaign. This operational security about donors was critical to the campaign's public image. The hidden financial and logistical operations and closed-door deal-making for political appointments would not emerge until it was irrelevant. Throughout his career Feinberg was content to remain in relative public obscurity, which he knew guaranteed his effectiveness. However, when the Truman Library was founded, Feinberg consented to an interview that confirmed some activities.

Feinberg worked closely with both Eddie Jacobson and Isaiah Kenen to "open doors" with the Truman administration and Congress. Feinberg observed that claiming huge strength in numbers and managing Jacobson, who had a much longer history with Truman, was critical:

> Anyway, Truman was receptive for several reasons. Coincidental with my gradual approach to him, Eddie Jacobson became much more important than I in his usefulness, since he was an active member of the B'nai B'rith, which had a large political following. The B'nai B'rith embraced then, I think, about 400,000 people. He had been a partner of Truman and a very close friend. Eddie was a wonderful man. He was not a creator. He was a follower of ideas, which were presented to him to present to the President. But he did that job very well and he was able, obviously because of his association with the President and with the knowledge of the President that there was political muscle behind this organization.[75]

According to Isaiah Kenen, Feinberg was also indispensable for jump-starting his own early access to bipartisan power and political fundraising:

> Later, in 1951, when I began to lobby for economic aid to Israel, Feinberg was indefatigable. Just as he had established a warm relationship with Truman's aides, he made it a point to know many senators and their aides and he would call them on the telephone to ask them to see me. And he would call me from time to time to make certain that we were maintaining a balance between Republicans and Democrats—between both sides of the House and the Senate.[76]

But Kenen and Feinberg's measured words masked the ever-present threat of politically oriented violence inherent in the movement. British Secretary of State for Foreign Affairs Ernest Bevin (1881-1951) presented an uncompromising challenge to the growing lobby that could have cost him his life. In a lengthy 1975 interview for the Truman Presidential Library, Feinberg put a soft spin on one potentially violent confrontation occurring between Zionist organizations and the United Kingdom at the end of WWII:

> Now, the business with Palestine and then Israel was front page news in the world largely because of [Ernest] Bevin and Bevin's attitude, which was impossible. Even when the concentration camps were liberated, he refused to let any numbers of the survivors go to Palestine, which was then a British protectorate. I, meanwhile, was deeply involved in the preparation of Israel for self-defense.[77]

The UK policy led by Bevin did not support the creation of a Jewish homeland in Palestine and worked actively toward future reintegration of displaced persons (DPs) within Europe. Bevin supported an Arab-ruled state in western Palestine and blocking armed Jewish groups turning toward terrorism; he even called for forcefully returning Jewish Holocaust survivors trying to enter Palestine to DP camps in Europe. Bevin was critical of the U.S. refusal to welcome and issue more visas to DPs, even as the UK offered, then withheld 100,000 of its own visas. However, the political reality of Britain's burgeoning indebtedness and dependence on the United States at the close of WWII meant that the UN, and especially the U.S., would ultimately decide the matter. Bevin voiced his strong objections to the creation of Israel largely on principle:

> The majority proposal is so manifestly unjust to the Arabs that it is difficult to see how we could reconcile it with our conscience.[78]

Contemporary newspapers broke sketchy stories that this opposition had made Bevin and London targets for terrorist retaliation. However, as with the Feinberg/Truman election financing, the relevant details surrounding Zionist terrorism have only recently emerged. In 2003, the UK's National Archives released intelligence reports about advanced planning for a terrorist assassination attempt on Bevin coordinated by Zionist groups active in Palestine and the UK, and the U.S.:

> Jewish terrorist groups plotted to assassinate Ernest Bevin, the Foreign Secretary in the post-war Labour government, as part of a bombing campaign on the British mainland inspired by the IRA.
>
> MI5 warned Clement Attlee, the prime minister, that the Stern Gang and Irgun intended to establish five terrorist cells in London to mount a bombing campaign aimed at driving Britain out of Palestine. Bevin, who was opposed to the creation of the state of Israel, was a prime target.
>
> Security Service files also contain details of an outlandish plan by the followers of an American Zionist rabbi to bomb London from the air. Details of that plot have been heavily censored. The warnings came in 1946 from James Robertson, head of the Security Service's Middle East Section.
>
> He wrote: 'Our Jerusalem representative has received information that the Irgun and Stern groups have decided to send five cells to London to work on IRA lines. To use their own words, the terrorists intend to 'beat the dog in his own kennel".
>
> 'The Stern group has been steadily recruiting in recent months and may

now number 600 followers, most of whom are desperate men and women who count their own lives cheap.'

'In recent months it has been reported that they have been training selected members for the purpose of assassinating a prominent British personality. Special reference has been several times made to Mr. Bevin.'

The plot to bomb the capital from the air was said to be the product of followers of one Rabbi Korff.[79]

While Israel's emergence as a modern state in the aftermath of the Holocaust has been broadly lauded, the hidden lobbying, arms smuggling, covert election finance, threats of violence and thwarted law enforcement attempts in the United States clearly don't fit within the commonly promoted consensus narrative. That Israel was also born in a crucible of Zionist terrorism is usually only a brief footnote or ignored entirely in high-profile histories. However, according to historian Paul Johnson, the distinguishing characteristic of the "on the ground" formation of Israel was the unprecedented, timely, and highly effective deployment of terrorism:

> If British evacuation had been postponed another year, the United States would have been far less anxious to see Israel created and Russia would almost certainly have been hostile. Hence the effect of the terror campaign on British policy was perhaps decisive to the entire enterprise.[80]

The Truman administration possessed, but did not act on, Central Intelligence Agency reports about illegal arms smuggling and clandestine false-flag flight operations to Palestine that broke the Neutrality Act. While mysterious reports of war surplus bombers moving between North America and the Mediterranean sporadically appeared in the mainstream press,[81] the role of fundraisers and Haganah operative groups active in arms smuggling within the U.S., like the terrorist charges, would be only lightly investigated and seldom prosecuted. We discuss the newly declassified connections between the U.S. fundraising groups, Czech arms merchants, Latin American dictators, and organized crime in Chapter 4.

Throughout 1948, Zionist groups and Isaiah Kenen made it a point to constantly broadcast lobbying muscle claims in the mainstream press. In a major 1948 article titled "Zionist Groups are active in the U.S.: Eight Major Parties here Claim 700,000 Members among the country's 5,000,000

Jews" by Ira Freeman, little data about the alleged scope and reach of the lobby was left to the imagination of politicians:

> With the fulcrum of Zionism shifted dramatically to the new state of Israel, the power arm of the international movement to settle the Jews in Palestine now definitely is in the United States.
>
> The 5,000,000 American Jews constitute the greatest concentration of population and wealth of their co-religionists in the world today. In Eastern Europe, formerly the area of densest population, the Jews were reduced from 9,000,000 to about 3,500,000 by Nazi and Fascist extermination and incidental war deaths between 1933 and 1945.
>
> Not all Jews in the United States are Zionists. Of the 5,000,000, Zionists like to estimate that four-fifths are "sympathetic" to their cause, a guess that anti-Zionists strenuously contradict. In any case, only a little more than 1,000,000 Jews in America bought "shekels" (ballots) to vote in the election of delegates to the last World Zionist Congress in 1946.
>
> The aggregate claimed membership of the eight Zionist parties in the United States is under 700,000. Each of the political parties here is an American, or American Canadian, or, in a few cases, a Western Hemisphere affiliate of an international Zionist party. Invariably, the national headquarters of each American party is in New York, which has the largest Jewish population of any city in the world as well as the lion's share of wealth and influence possessed by Jews...[82]

From the perspective of critics and Jewish anti-Zionist opposition groups, Truman's recognition of Israel also largely removed the welcome mat of frequent access to opinion editorial space and reporters at elite newspapers such as the *New York Times*.[83] Paid foreign propaganda and a massive foreign financed public relations campaign soon began filling the void.

Israel Lobby Legacy

Examining the creation of Israel from Harry S Truman's point of view yields several insights that provide valuable context for understanding the Israel lobbying that continues to operate to this day in the United States.

While Truman lamented the domestic foreign interest pressure on his policy, he appeared to have little appreciation for the vast and growing international coordination capabilities of the Israel lobby. When he was lobbied as a Senator to support a "Jewish Army" in Palestine, he had no way of knowing that the front organization in Washington represented Menachem Begin's Irgun Z'vai Leumi, which was in contact with the Axis while it was winning. He also did not know that in spite of his explicit ban, U.S. military equipment was being purchased, refurbished and stolen for shipment to Jewish fighters in Palestine. As U.S. president, he was stepping in front of a movement already creating facts on the ground over which he had little or no control. He could only get in front and later leverage them for political gain. This was, of course, the very essence of Herzl's negotiorum gestio.

The timely leaks about the Mufti of Jerusalem's collaboration with the Nazis and subsequent UN smear campaign against the legitimacy of Palestinians and all Arab governments were highly effective, and the lobby continues to excel in such tactics. In that particular campaign, Israel lobby operatives leveraged friends in the U.S. media, which included *The Nation* magazine. Though, as Kenen noted later, that particular channel was ultimately "lost," others soon replaced it. Many media and academic figures were place under contract as we'll see in Chapter 10. Leaking explosive, closely held, and sometimes classified information at precisely the right moment would become a commonplace Israel lobby tactic.

The Israel lobby developed an insatiable acquisitiveness for U.S. classified documents that administrations and the State Department hoped to use to U.S., as opposed to Israel's sole, advantage. U.S. Department of State investigation files reveal the American Israel Public Affairs Committee's (AIPAC) director received classified U.S. national defense information. In 1975 the Ford administration tried to sell improved Hawk anti-aircraft missiles to Jordan and duly sent notification containing classified Department of Defense data to the Senate Foreign Relations Committee and House Foreign Affairs Committee. AIPAC's Director Morris Amitay reviewed the classified document after being informed "secretly by aides of Senator Clifford P. Case, Republican of New Jersey, and Representative Jonathan B. Bingham, Democrat of New York" according to the New York Times.

According to criminal investigation files released on January 20, 2012, this disclosure to AIPAC was "unauthorized" and included the dollar amounts and quantitative configurations of the missile system. The State Department considered "The specific details of Jordan's military equipment needs are information provided us in confidence by that government. The classification of the documents in question was, in our view, substantively proper."[84]

Amitay and AIPAC quickly mounted a massive campaign in opposition to the missile sale, telling constituent public pressure groups that the weapons were capable of "providing cover for offensive operations against Israel." Jordan subsequently considered acquiring a similar system from the Soviet Union. According to the U.S. Department of State, "Had Jordan actually entered into such a major arms-supply relationship with the Soviets, this would have had a significant adverse impact on U.S. national defense interests and on U.S.-Jordanian relations." The Defense Department letter is still classified.

The U.S. State Department advised the Justice Department on the feasibility of criminally prosecuting Amitay. "With the public disclosure of the information having already occurred, the authorization of its release for the purpose of prosecution would not be expected to cause damage with our relations with Jordan." However, Amitay was never charged and continued to serve as director of AIPAC until he resigned 1980 to establish an Israel-oriented political action committee in Washington.

In 1984, the FBI found AIPAC in possession of secret International Trade Organization documents that the U.S. was using to negotiate a favorable free trade agreement with Israel. The subsequent agreement signed would be uniformly disadvantageous to U.S. industry, yielding a $182.25 billion loss to the U.S. between 1989 and 2018.[85] In a campaign to toughen U.S. policy toward Iran, two AIPAC executives, along with a colonel at the U.S. Department of Defense, were indicted in 2005 for obtaining and distributing classified U.S. national defense information in violation of the 1917 Espionage Act. These are not coincidences.

The Truman experience in the 1948 presidential elections established a constant race for Israel lobby political campaign contributions, implicitly given to secure foreign interests. This race is euphemized in the U.S. mainstream media as a quest for the "Jewish vote," a framing coup Kenen would be proud of but an upsetting overgeneralization for American Jews who disapprove of Israeli and U.S. regional policies. Even as Truman's era of unrestricted, unmonitored cash contributions came to an end under campaign finance reform and openness laws, the importance of campaigning on a "pro-Israel" platform soon became a "no-brainer" for politicians. Since 1948, presidential candidates, with few exceptions, have competed to "out-Israel" their opponents to secure access to funding. Moderates are effectively and simply branded as "anti-Israel".

This dependence on campaign contributions severely limits both presidential foreign policymaking in the Middle East and political capital for warranted law enforcement actions against key contributor groups at home. As John F. Kennedy would later lament, the exchange was implicit: reelection funds in exchange for control of policymaking and critical political appointments vetted and promoted by the Israel lobby. While insiders and elite political operatives knew about the driving force behind much U.S. policymaking in the region, the American public remain largely in the dark.

Truman's personal correspondence on the matter extensively quoted in this chapter did not come to light until it was declassified by the government and released by the Truman Library in 1975. Feinberg granted an interview in 1973 about the whistlestop campaign to the Truman Presidential Library, which then did not release it until 1984. If the American public had an accurate and immediate juxtaposition of the lobbying for the creation of Israel against Feinberg's campaign finance coordination, it is entirely possible that they would have thought it as unseemly as the Pendergast machine and chosen not to elect Truman president in 1948. Truman had no fallback strategy. Secrecy was therefore paramount to the whistlestop campaign's success.

Since the 1940s, the secrecy pervading the U.S.-Israel relationship, Israel's U.S. lobbyists, and Middle East policymaking has only become more pronounced—so much so that historians are only beginning to understand the specifics of what was truly driving regional policy and policymaking. Declassification ultimately provides some relevant information to the public. But the ongoing shift from paper to digital files may mean the days of enduring records are ending. The Bush administration destroyed email correspondence and backups of key digital communications relevant to its decision to invade Iraq in 2003. This ability to permanently delete documentary evidence about behind-the-scenes decision making influence may become the norm rather than an anomaly. Similar secrecy has been vital for shielding from public examination how in the face of numerous Israel lobby violations, FARA has been tied into its own scabbard at the expense of the American people. No example has been as clear as the case of the Justice Department's FARA registration order to the American Zionist Council declassified in 2008.

It is hereby declared to be the policy and purpose of this Act (Title 22, 611 et seq) to protect the national defense, internal security, and foreign relations of the United States by requiring public disclosure by persons engaging in propaganda activities and other activities for or on behalf of foreign governments, foreign political parties, and other foreign principals so that the Government and the people of the United States may be informed of the identity of such persons and may appraise their statements and actions in the light of their associations and activities. —The Foreign Agents Registration Act as amended in 1942

Chapter 3: Foreign Agents Act

The rise of the American Emergency Committee for Zionist Affairs (AECZA) began one year after the passage of a law specifically aimed at curbing foreign influence over the U.S. government. The Foreign Agents Registration Act (FARA) was enacted in 1938. FARA's purpose was to limit the influence of foreign agents and propaganda on American public policy through agent registration and public disclosure. FARA defined a "foreign agent" as any person acting as a lobbyist, PR professional, or lawyer for a foreign principal or any domestic organization subsidized by a foreign principal.

In June of 1934, a special House committee started to investigate "the extent, character and object of Nazi propaganda in the U.S. and the diffusion within the U.S. of subversive propaganda." For three days, the committee grilled foes of Nazi Germany as well as some of Germany's contract public relations agents operating in the U.S. In 1934, *Time* magazine exposed details of German payments to the nation's top PR firm, Carl Byoir & Associates:

> Carl Dickey is a member of the Manhattan press-agent firm of Carl Byoir & Associates. Carl Byoir, onetime publisher of the Havana Post and Telegram, developed to his full stature under George Creel in wartime propaganda service. From Publicist Dickey the committee learned that in 1933 the Byoir agency had received $4000 from Consul Kiep to "explain" Hitlerite anti-Semitism in publicity releases. Since then the

firm has handled a $6,000-a-month campaign publicizing German Railways, travel in Germany. Of the $6,000 monthly fee, said Mr. Dickey, $1,750 went to George Sylvester Viereck.[86]

George Sylvester Viereck (1884-1962) would later face prosecution and prison time for his publicity role, while Carl Byoir & Associates were cleared. The firm became somewhat more discriminating in handling foreign public relations jobs. But one personality involved in the German propaganda was less one-dimensional than *Time* magazine portrayed him. The trajectory of the "Consul Kiep," whose full name was Otto Karl Kiep, ended heroically. After returning to Germany from his stint as consul general in New York Kiep joined the resistance and was implicated in the July 20, 1944 bomb plot against Adolf Hitler. Kiep was hanged that very year in Berlin.[87]

Although later analysis (and the legal counsel of the Jewish Agency in congressional testimony) claimed the intent of FARA was primarily to preempt Nazi activity in the United States, in reality the framers of the act purposefully wrote it broadly to encompass any "propaganda designed to popularize various alien political faiths." No clear-cut filters for distinguishing "friends" from "foes" were embedded in FARA. One country on the mind of U.S. legislators was certainly the Soviet Union: Soviet Communism was clearly covered by FARA, even after Russia declared war on Germany in WWII. Years of congressional investigations prior to 1938 by the Fish and later the McCormack committees had examined subsidiaries of Amtorg, an agency of the Russian government. The Associated Press correctly trumpeted FARA as a broad new initiative against all foreign "isms" on October 7, 1938:

> Representative Dies of Texas urged President Roosevelt today to recommend legislation outlawing "any organization which is under the control of a foreign government."
>
> "There are several hundred organizations in this country that are under the influence of Soviet Russia, Italy and Germany," said a statement by Mr. Dies...He urged also that the President back a proposed bill requiring organizations which are disseminating foreign "isms" to make an accounting of their funds and contributors. This, he said, would keep "many good people from joining the organizations and being used as 'dupes.'"

President Roosevelt's remarks at Hyde Park today were seconded by officials there, who said that foreign spies had been trying hard to get details of the new American defense program.[88]

The very first criminal trial over the law involved not agents of Nazi Germany, but Soviet propagandists. The criminal prosecution commenced half a year before the U.S. entered the Second World War.[89]

Disclosure is the mechanism that allows the enforcement of FARA. Before the "sunshine" provisions of 1946 lobbying disclosures, campaign finance laws, or the 1966 Freedom of Information Act (FOIA), FARA was pioneering transparency as a tool for better public policymaking. It provided that FARA registration disclosures would be "public records and open to public examination and inspection at all reasonable hours."[90] The act has been updated several times since 1938. (See the Appendices for the text of the original 1938 act and the amended version from 1942. These were the FARA statutes in force over the period covered in this book.)

The law was therefore designed not to directly restrict foreign propaganda, but to provide total public transparency over the operations of foreign agents in the U.S. Mandatory disclosure and fear of punishment would deter the most effective foreign propaganda campaigns, those which were launched as grassroots "American" initiatives. By 1942, FARA would ensure that propaganda was properly labeled as being paid for and distributed bearing the name and address of the registered foreign agent.[91] **The secondary core purpose of FARA disclosure has always been to shield the U.S. Congress and the president from foreign-influenced grassroots lobbying shaping policy, legislation and lawmaking.**[92]

As with all U.S. laws, the actual enforcement of FARA depends on the U.S. Department of Justice's "prosecutorial discretion." This, in turn, is shaped by the priorities of the president. Faithful execution of FARA has been tempered by little-understood drivers as presidential appointees in the Department of Justice, especially the attorney general, interpret the changing political realities of the administration and country.

U.S. State Department Enforces FARA

Foreign agents are compelled to file detailed activities reports, including declarations of receipts and disbursements of all funds in support of their activities, every six months. All such reports were originally filed with the U.S. Department of State, which was charged with administering FARA. In 1938, the U.S. State Department drummed up press coverage warning that foreign agent filings were due by October 6 and that referrals to the Department of Justice and possible penalties and imprisonment would be in store for violators. The State Department felt compelled to encourage registration through moral suasion due to low initial volumes of responses to its own mailings and outreach efforts:

> The department is doing everything possible to impress upon all agents of foreign principals the advisability of a careful study of the Act of June 8, 1938...[93]

Later in the month, the State Department was forced to go on a diplomatic offensive to smooth the ruffled feathers of foreign agents who felt that their "patriotism and their loyalty to American principles had been impugned."

> The department takes this opportunity to point out that registration under the act requiring the registration of agents of foreign principals is designed merely to show the exact nature of the connection of such an agent to his foreign principal.
>
> The act is broad in its terms and imposes the duty to register on many American citizens, companies and organizations whose work is of a wholly unimpeachable character. The mere fact of registration under the act affords no ground for assuming that any person so registered is engaged in unpatriotic activity.[94]

By March 28 of 1939, the State Department was able to announce 317 FARA registrants, including Marine Safety Devices, representing Dutch, German and British commercial firms; the American Express Company affiliate in Rome; Helen Black of the Soviet Literary Agency; and Joseph Brainin of the Jewish Agency for Palestine.[95] By November 11, 371 foreign agents had registered. The *New York Times* headline blared ominously that there were "no prosecutions yet," but there were "several investigations under way."[96]

Soon FARA's epicenter shifted from the State Department's role in generating registrations to greater law enforcement emphasis at the U.S. Department of Justice. In December of 1939, the first criminal indictments under FARA targeted Soviet propaganda:

> Two Russian citizens, officers of Bookniga, Inc. a Soviet propaganda agency, were fined in Federal district court here today after pleading guilty to willful omission of material information from a registration

statement filed with the State Department under the Foreign Agents Registration Act.[97]

Specifically, the Russians pled guilty to "willful omission of material information" on their FARA registrations. They had failed to mention in their FARA registrations the structure of their foreign compensation and names of acting foreign principals. They were summarily returned to Russia and their inventories of magazines, books, and other materials were ordered disposed of "as quickly as possible." However, two Russians who had since become naturalized American citizens and the secretary of Bookniga, Inc. stood trial in 1941.

> There will be three defendants in the trial, which opens here two weeks from Monday, Raphael Rush and Morris Liskin, Russian-born naturalized Americans, and Norman Weinberg, a native American citizen.
>
> They were indicted as long ago as December 16, 1939, charged with having served as agents of Mezkniga, a Soviet organization with headquarters in Moscow, which is the official literary agency of the Soviet Government.[98]

In July of 1939, a German news organization was also prosecuted. The U.S. government charged Transocean News with being "a propaganda arm of the Nazi government." Ten years later, two managers of the American branch were released under terms of a diplomatic agreement.[99] Russia again came under the spotlight as Amtorg Trading Corporation officials were indicted for alleged violations of FARA. Although Amtorg functioned primarily as a purchasing company for the Soviet Union, Attorney General J. Howard McGrath (1903-1966) charged that it had been collecting information, disbursing funds, and "otherwise acting as an arm of the Soviet Government in this country."[100] Amtorg's activities and the documented Jewish-Agency-financed U.S. operations examined later are strikingly similar—except that one organization was dismantled, while the other flourished, expanded, morphed, and formed subsidiaries.

Department of Justice Takes Over FARA

On April 29, 1942, FARA was vastly strengthened as wartime threat perceptions spurred Congress to augment the penalties and to initiate a crackdown on violators. Prison terms for violations were increased. Given the location and U.S. jurisdiction over registrant agents, the enforcement of FARA was transferred from the secretary of state to the attorney general at the Department of Justice.[101] Registrants would no longer be hearing awkward pronouncements in the American press from the U.S. State Department. Records had to be transferred, stipulated by a revision to the act ordering that all "property, books and records heretofore maintained by the Secretary of State with respect to his administration of said act of June 8, 1938 are hereby transferred to and vested in the Attorney General." The attorney general was required to keep the State Department "in the loop" by providing copies of all registration statements, although this close communications mandate would later break down. The attorney general was vested with the creation of forms and enforcement policies.

FARA as amended in 1942 would not be revised again until 1966. Key clauses within the act made it clear that a simple agreement to act as a foreign agent, or a person who "holds himself out to be" an agent whether a contract was present or not, was enough for an individual or organization to come under the jurisdiction of the law:

> Except as provided in subsection (d) of this section, the term "agent of foreign principal" includes—
>
> any person who acts or agrees to act, within the United States, as, or who is or holds himself out to be whether or not pursuant to contractual relationship, a public-relations counsel, publicity agent, information-service employee, servant, agent, representative, or attorney for a foreign principal;
>
> any person who within the United States collects information for or reports information to a foreign principal; who within the United States solicits or accepts compensation, contributions, or loans, directly or indirectly, from a foreign principal; who within the United States solicits, disburses, dispenses, or collects compensation, contributions, loans, money, or anything of value, directly or indirectly, for a foreign principal; who within the United States acts at the order, request, or under the direction, of a foreign principal.[102]

The likelihood of "indirect" contributions to finance a foreign agent became poignant; in 1963, Senator James William Fulbright (1905-1995) would uncover how hidden and ongoing "subventions" from the quasi-governmental Jewish Agency in Israel were being used to offer free newsletter subscriptions to influential Americans, including senators. The conflict over a huge flow of payments for public relations and lobbying as well as Isaiah Kenen's status as a foreign agent culminated in a major public showdown in the Senate, and a private battle with the Department of Justice

The 1942 amendments took care to exclude news or press services "organized under the laws of the United States" engaged in "bona fide news or journalistic activities." This was predicated on majority U.S. ownership and no "subsidy" provided by foreign principals. This clause raised questions about whether Soviet news services and Eastern Bloc publications would be allowed into the U.S., even if registered. It also impacted the Jewish Telegraphic Agency, which provided news and bulletins to community newspapers across the United States but was owned by the Jewish Agency.[103]

More troubling for Isaiah L. Kenen were the 1942 strictures covering public relations, public policy, and politics:

> (g) The term "public-relations counsel" includes any person who engages directly or indirectly in informing, advising, or in any way representing a principal in any matter pertaining to political or public interests, policies or relations.

The 1942 amendments also broadened the definition of foreign principals to include agencies of sovereign groups, foreign political parties, and even bodies of insurgents vying for control of a state. The law also focused on defining "political propaganda" subject to FARA oversight as any expression and communication that:

> is reasonably adapted to, or which the person disseminating the same believes will, or which he intends to, prevail upon, indoctrinate, convert, induce, or in any other way influence a recipient or any section of the public within the United States with reference to the political or public interests, policies, or relations of a government of a foreign country or a foreign political party or with reference to the foreign policies of the United States or promote in the United States racial, religious, or social dissensions...

These strictures were enforced. Two San Francisco publicists, Frederick Vincent Williams and David Warren Ryder, were convicted in June 1942 for violating FARA. They were charged as unregistered foreign agents of the Japanese government because they worked for Japan's San Francisco Consul General.[104] The prosecutions spurred other registrations. By December of 1942, 330 registration statements for entities had been filed, covering more than 2,000 individual foreign agents. One-third represented allied or "friendly" nations.[105]

Viereck Goes to Prison

Allied and friendly governments were given a holiday from strict FARA disclosure during WWII to reduce their paperwork burdens and facilitate the war effort. President Roosevelt was concerned that representatives of allies would be inconvenienced during frequent travels to the U.S. However, on October 8, 1946, U.S. Attorney General Thomas Campbell Clark (1899-1977) announced that henceforth, a complete and timely FARA registration from any foreign agent would be expected by the Department of Justice. This cancellation of the wartime ally exemption was personally directed by President Harry S Truman.[106] Until the Truman cancellation, no registration disclosure was required beyond foreign country principals providing the names of their agents. This courtesy was extended only to countries "the defense of which the President deems vital to the defense of the United States." Given the unpredictable nature of world war, the U.S. did reserve the right to terminate this special reduction in red tape at any time.[107]

A great deal of press attention was devoted to the saga of the wartime FARA conviction of George Sylvester Viereck. During pre-FARA House committee hearings in 1934, Viereck had been unrepentant about his reporting on Germany, personal beliefs, and public relations contracts with the regime. *Time* magazine detailed his testimony:

> Mr. Viereck ran a paper called *The Fatherland* during the War to counteract Allied propaganda in the U.S. Of late he has been writing and speechmaking, "interpreting" the New Germany to his adopted land. When he heard his name mentioned at the committee hearing he loudly declared; "There is not the slightest touch of impropriety in the contract between Byoir & Associates and the German railroads nor in my connections with that distinguished firm…If it is right for the Russians to hire Mr. Ivy Lee, why is it wrong for the German railroads to employ Mr. Carl Byoir and Mr. Carl Dicky? It was specifically understood that the work involved no propaganda and no anti-Jewish activities…I always regarded it almost as a consecration to interpret the land of my fathers to the land of my children…"[108]

Viereck was convicted in March of 1942, but his case was remanded by the Supreme Court after he had served a year in prison. This reversal came at the Supreme Court's finding that he was not compelled to report activities falling outside those strictly pursued as a foreign agent. This same issue of "overbroad" indictments and unsubstantiated claims would also cause problems later: a similar 1960s FARA enforcement attempt to rein in a rogue FBI agent turned foreign agent for the Dominican Republic was also overturned.

Viereck was again found guilty on July 16, 1942 on six FARA charges of failing to list foreign principals and failing to detail to the U.S. State Department a comprehensive statement of activities, as was required before the 1942 amendments. The presiding justice, Bolitha J. Laws (1891-1958), emphasized during instructions to jury members that Viereck had a right to act as a foreign agent "even for the German Reich," as long as he properly registered with the State Department.[109] Viereck was sentenced and returned to prison. He received early parole in 1947 with 18 months of his sentence remaining.[110]

1946 Lobbying Reform

In 1946, Wisconsin Senator Robert M. La Follette, Jr. (1895-1953) spearheaded the Legislative Reorganization Act to modernize Congress and make it more efficient. In addition to reducing and streamlining standing committees, this act required lobbyists to register with Congress for the very first time. Like foreign agents, lobbyists were also required to file periodic disclosures of their activities. La Follette hoped that the opaque yet effective tactics of lobbying and "buttonholing" would become more transparent to the public:

> The term itself, which is peculiar to the United States and not used generally elsewhere, apparently has its origins from the practice of seeking contact with legislators in the waiting rooms or lobbies, near the legislative chamber where the public is permitted. It is picturesque, just as the associated term to "buttonhole" a legislator, which is duly listed in Webster's dictionary with the definition: "to hold by the button or buttonhole, as for conversation." It is doubtful how effective the literal application of the term may be; but "buttonholing" in the more general sense is in fact lobbying in its simplest and sometimes most effective form.[111]

Although the U.S. State Department was no longer the agency charged with enforcing FARA, it did receive negative overseas feedback for a few Department of Justice investigations. In March of 1947, King Ibn Saud of Saudi Arabia summoned ambassador J. Rieve Childs to Riyadh to complain about an FBI FARA investigation of the Arab office in New York.[112] During that year, a group called the Non-Sectarian Anti-Nazi League circulated a brochure in a PR campaign against Arab governments. The group's director, Herman Hoffman (1884-1962), submitted a complaint to the United Nations. Hoffman charged that the Arab League and its associated agencies had deliberately provoked internal trouble and racist tension in friendly countries and stimulated propaganda against the admission of Jews to Palestine.[113] It would be among the few FARA complaints filed by Zionist or dominant Israel lobby groups in America. Top-tier organizations also complained and called on the Department of Justice to investigate Irgun front group leader Peter Bergson (Hillel Kook). As discussed in Chapter 2, Bergson's brash publicity campaigns and successful lobbying diluted and damaged their unified message and leadership on the issue in the 1940s.[114] But the lobby's own vulnerability to FARA made pursuing it against enemies, at least directly, largely untenable.

A broad "pushback" against FARA became visible in the number of registrations. By the close of 1952, there were only 234 active registrations, 137 less than in 1941. While there were 58 new registrations in 1953, 40 registrations were terminated, bringing net active registrations to only 252. As detailed in an attorney general report to Congress, most of the registered agents listed their primary activities as concentrated in conducting "propaganda." Sixteen persons also registered under a section of the law requiring disclosure of training received for espionage or sabotage tactics, though none claimed to be simultaneously engaged in representing a foreign principal.[115] Many of these interesting details would be lost to the public domain when agents terminated their filings.

Practically speaking, when foreign agents filed declarations that they were no longer active, they could request that their names be struck from public registries and information formerly available to the press or public watchdog groups. Many files vanished into largely inaccessible archives and remote storage facilities. Detailed registrations and copies of brochures, press releases, and other materials used in foreign agent PR campaigns were then subject to agency retention and destruction policies. Classified non-public administrative files compiled by FARA enforcement officials have seldom been released. While some of the history of foreign agent lobbying propaganda in America can be found in files at the Library of Congress and National Archives and Records Administration, much is simply lost to history. Fortunately, the files on Isaiah Kenen and the American Zionist Council were not.

FARA Enforcement Malaise

FARA's impulse for transparency was matched by other disclosure initiatives. In 1955, the U.S. Treasury Department began working with Congress to pass legislation allowing public inspection of applications for tax exemption made by nonprofit corporations. Undersecretary H. Chapman Rose (1907-1990) testified before the House Information Subcommittee that increasing transparency would stem nonprofit abuses that had been examined in closed hearings. Rose revealed that the Secretary of Treasury had been considering such a move "for some time," although the Treasury was then not considering allowing public access to any of the 30,000 tax-exempt returns already filed.[116] Later, all applications and partially censored tax-exempt organization returns would become publicly accessible, by written request to charities. Today most are directly accessible over the Internet through the designated website ProPublica.[j] Public disclosures are considered an important check that charities are in fact performing legitimate activities. But FARA was never perfect and did enable government abuse. Ominously, FARA was once interpreted as a license to censor materials sent through the U.S. mail.

During the same 1955 hearings, the U.S. Postmaster General was called to testify about FARA-related mail interceptions. He refused to discuss a secret program that had been in place since 1950. Many subscribers to Soviet publications simply never received their bulletins, magazines, and newsletters, which had been seized and burned. By 1956, the Post Office did let some material it deemed unlikely to be used for propagandistic purposes through to libraries and universities. In 1960, a Senate subcommittee investigated the practice and found that the postal service had intercepted fifteen million pieces of mail it considered "Communist or subversive." From 1958 onward, many citizens received United States Post Office notices that literature with "foreign political propaganda" was being held under the Foreign Agents Registration Act. They were asked to sign and return a card within fifteen days attesting to the fact that they had ordered it. Many refused, fearing that their names and interests in overseas publications would be referred to the FBI. Others, such as an irate sociologist from Chicago, sued the Post Office for their withheld mail.

---

[j] Nonprofit corporations are not required to (and usually don't) publicly disclose the identities or itemized contribution amounts of their largest source of contributions: individual donors. This effectively shields any revelatory analysis of the identity and relative influence of donors and the true breadth of public support of any given nonprofit.

The Post Office was operating under enforcement policies enacted in 1940 by Attorney General Robert H. Jackson. Jackson interpreted the term "agent" in FARA included foreign publishers and that "foreign propaganda mailed into the U.S. was both illegal and hence non-mailable" unless the foreign sender registered under FARA. The ACLU and legal experts launched three lawsuits to challenge the First Amendment implications of mail censorship and "intimidation" effect of the return cards.[117] By the following year, the State Department, the Justice Department, and the Post Office unanimously recommended the elimination of the program.[118]

The Department of Justice itself suffered another black eye when former FBI agent John Joseph Frank was convicted in 1957 on four counts of acting illegally as a foreign agent. But, as in the Viereck case, the prosecution team initially meandered beyond strict FARA limits, stating that Frank was also linked to the mysterious disappearance of a critic of the Dominican Republic's Trujillo regime. On March 12, 1956, regime critic and Columbia University professor Jesus de Galindez disappeared during a visit to the Dominican Republic. Gerald L. Murphy, an American pilot who claimed to know what happened to Galindez also mysteriously disappeared the following December 3. This prompted a federal grand jury investigation to which Frank was called to testify.[119]

On October 20, 1958, the conviction was reversed on appeal based on the prosecution's remarks alleging, but not definitively proving, links between Frank and the disappearances.[120] The Dominican Republic case was nevertheless a stain on the FBI and enforcement of FARA that would reemerge. It foreshadowed the slippery slope of influence peddling that could and did reach high into the other two branches of government. The Dominican Republic case would surface again as a warning to all observers of just how politically explosive FARA enforcement could be, even as the Senate Foreign Relations Committee began a serious investigation into FARA enforcement in 1962. However, FARA enforcement was never intended to be "optional" or used as a political cudgel against an administration's perceived enemies.

The president is required by the Constitution to make sure "the Laws be faithfully executed." Presidents who allowed FARA to be only selectively enforced, particularly Truman and Johnson, highlight a grave weakness in constitutional checks and balances that has become even more apparent ever since. If a president's chosen U.S. attorney general tacitly understands that certain laws are not to be uniformly applied, the rule of law and the viability of the entire nation are undermined. In modern times, the mechanism for undercutting the Constitution is euphemistically called "prosecutorial discretion" within the Department of Justice. Entities under investigation, such as the American Zionist Council, call it "prosecutorial power" that should always consider "special circumstances." Such discretion virtually guarantees that the least politically enfranchised will face the maximum law enforcement attention, even while their position in society is further eroded by inattention to elite crime. Classification, secrecy, and backroom understandings have been vital to preserving this prerogative. Understanding how FARA has been only selectively applied provides an important context for how it completely failed against two of its most egregious violators: the Jewish Agency's American Section and AIPAC's antecedent, the American Zionist Council. This is revealed in Israel's claims on U.S. military aid which began in illicit channels before receiving official support.

There can be no kind of discussion of a voluntary reconciliation between us and the Arabs...Any native people...view their country as their national home. They will not voluntarily allow, not only a new master, but even a new partner...Colonization can have only one goal. For the Palestinian Arabs this goal is inadmissible. This is in the nature of things. —**Vladimir Jabotinsky**

Chapter 4: Arms Smuggling

FARA investigations and prosecutions after 1938 and cases targeting the influence of the Dominican Republic through 1958 seem like a drop in the bucket when contrasted against the violations of U.S. law inherent in the arms smuggling activities of the Jewish Agency and Haganah and the violence of paramilitary groups associated with the Irgun. These secret activities involving foreign agents and principals are still only gradually coming to light, in end-of-career disclosures by individuals who were directly involved and a trickle of document releases by U.S. intelligence agencies. One dossier released by the CIA in 2005 titled "The Objectives and Activities of the Irgun Z'vai Leumi" attempted to summarize the objectives, activities, and reach of the organization:

> The Irgun Z'vai Leumi is an underground, quasi-military organization with headquarters in Palestine and branches in Poland and other European countries. Its members are fanatical Zionists who wish to convert Palestine and Transjordan into an independent Jewish state and who advocate the use of force against both the Arabs and the British to achieve this maximal political goal. In the past Irgun was responsible for organizing illegal Jewish immigration into Palestine. It has conducted since February of this year periodic raids on government buildings as a protest against the British White Paper policy. Irgun activities have been condemned by the rest of the Palestine Jewish community as irresponsible, misguided and harmful to the Zionist cause.[121]

The 1944 intelligence report detailed how Irgun was originally intended to serve as the military arm of the Revisionist Party in Palestine, but broke away. Recruits were drawn from the Revisionist youth movement, which provided pre-military training that Irgun could later build upon. The intelligence report noted the leadership role of "Eri Jabotinsky" (Vladimir Yevgenyevich Zhabotinsky, 1880-1940) who was in charge of the "Bitar Immigration Department 1938-1940 and force estimate of 3-4000 members in Palestine." It also noted the Irgun's preferred use of terrorist violence and intimidation after the British imposed immigration restrictions.

The intelligence report categorized another Irgun activity as more similar to that of modern-day coyotes (human smugglers who help undocumented immigrants cross the U.S.-Mexico border in exchange for money) than a rescue operation designed to transport European Jews to Palestine.

> The organization of illegal immigration proved to be a lucrative venture, since in addition to charging the prospective immigrants what the traffic would bear, Irgun representatives in the U.S. and elsewhere collected funds for the support of their "humanitarian" undertaking. These funds have largely been used to train and equip with arms the members of the society and to defray the costs of terrorist activities. [122]

The physical document released by the CIA also contains a hand-scrawled note—"Bergson?"

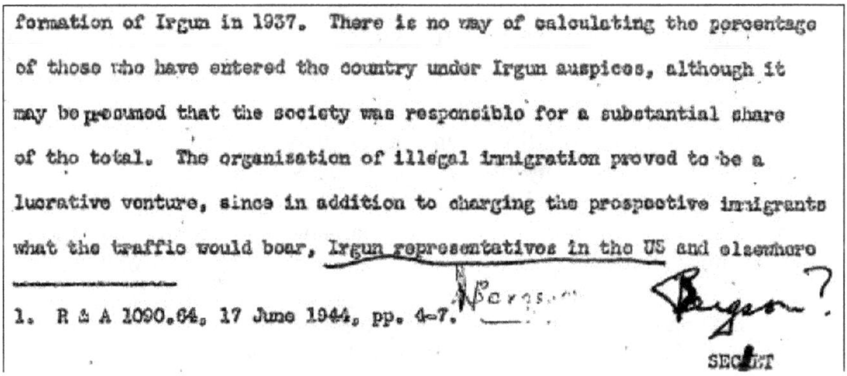

formation of Irgun in 1937. There is no way of calculating the percentage of those who have entered the country under Irgun auspices, although it may be presumed that the society was responsible for a substantial share of the total. The organization of illegal immigration proved to be a lucrative venture, since in addition to charging the prospective immigrants what the traffic would bear, Irgun representatives in the US and elsewhere

1. R & A 1090.64, 17 June 1944, pp. 4-7.

Bergson?

SECRET

Figure 3 "The Objectives and Activities of the Irgun Z'vai Leumi," page 5.

This referred to the same Peter H. Bergson who was lobbying Congress and Truman while conducting public relations for the formation of a "Jewish Army" in the Middle East. The report also noted that Irgun had created a protection racket in Palestine—the Jewish Front Tribute that collected funds under threat of violence if "ordinary solicitation proves ineffective." [123]

Even the intelligence reports released so far belie the true scope and reach of Irgun activities in the United States. Bergson's allies stretched high into the U.S. Treasury Department, facilitating his use of State Department cables to coordinate with overseas allies. One key Irgun leader, Jabotinsky, would die peacefully in a Catskills Betar[k] militant training camp in New York after a long reign of terror in Palestine.

Irgun and the U.S. Treasury Department

Vladimir Jabotinsky was a major figure in the World Zionist Organization and put together a force of 5,000 soldiers as the organization's contribution to the British conquest of Palestine during WWI. In 1920, he organized the Haganah, the precursor to the Israeli Army, and held a position in the WZO World Executive for his leadership role. He resigned to build his own far-right-wing Zionist-Revisionist World Union in 1925, which opposed WZO president Chaim Weizmann's vision. Jabotinsky's was to "revise" the British decision to separate Trans-Jordan[l] from territory allotted to become the "Jewish National Home" after WWI in the Balfour declaration. Jabotinsky also wanted to "revise" the British decision to disband the Jewish legion. His views evolved over time toward supporting the absolute necessity of violent armed displacement of Arabs in Palestine. This was frankly encapsulated in his 1923 "Iron Wall" manifesto:

> There can be no kind of discussion of a voluntary reconciliation between us and the Arabs...Any native people...view their country as their national home. They will not voluntarily allow, not only a new master, but even a new partner...Colonization can have only one goal. For the Palestinian Arabs this goal is inadmissible. This is in the nature of things. To change that nature is impossible...colonization can therefore, continue and develop only under the protection of a force independent of the local population—an iron wall which the native population cannot break through. This is, in toto, our policy toward the Arabs. To formulate it any other way would only be hypocrisy.[124]

---

[k] Betar (also spelled Beitar) was the last standing Jewish fortress in the second century-AD Bar Kochba revolt and was destroyed by the Roman army. Accounts of the event are prominent in the Talmud.
[l] A large expanse of Ottoman territory incorporated into the British Mandate of Palestine in 1921.

Jabotinsky established his paramilitary Betar youth group in 1923 in Palestine and other countries. Menachem Begin joined in 1929 in Poland, rising to head the national unit that became Betar's largest branch.

Jabotinsky's organization grew rapidly. At the 1931 World Zionist Congress it was the third largest faction, holding 25 percent of the delegates. The Revisionists demanded that the WZO formally call for a Jewish state on both sides of the Jordan River with a majority Jewish population. Jabotinsky's phalanx of brown-shirted Betar Youth bodyguards alienated other constituencies of the World Zionist Organization in 1933. At the time, the WZO was attempting to come to grips with the rise of Hitler. During the conference, WZO leadership met with Baron Leopold von Mildenstein of the Nazi SS in Palestine. The WZO's Chaim Weizmann asked the Nazis for permission to go to Berlin to negotiate for the transfer and financial facilities for immigration to Palestine under a formal "Transfer Agreement."

The Transfer Agreement (Ha'avarah Agreement) was signed between the Nazi administration and organizations representing German and Palestinian Jews in 1933. Herzl's stated vision to form a company in which a "Jewish Company will be the liquidating agent of the business interests of departing Jews" is reflected in the Transfer Agreement, except that the agreement was signed under extreme coercion and threat of Nazi violence. The agreement did facilitate an orderly and legal transfer of sequestered German-Jewish wealth to Palestine, but it came at another horrible cost. The real tradeoff was between strengthening immigration to Palestine and breaking highly effective grassroots international boycott movements against trade with Germany led by such U.S. groups as the Jewish War Veterans. Between 1933 and 1936, Nazi power was at its weakest trajectory and Reich leaders sought every possible trade and financial advantage for accelerated economic recovery. The deal cemented a new level of trade between Palestine and the Third Reich. It was also a vehicle for the Reich to leverage the Transfer Agreement to build trade ties throughout the Middle East through bilateral treaties. These Reich precursors to "free trade agreements" were struck with 25 nations in the years leading up to 1939.[125] Under the terms of the agreement, 60,000 Jews and $100 million in assets were transferred to Palestine.[126] But the agreement itself was so controversial and the documents so diffuse that few popular historians could comprehensively deal with it until the mid-1980s.[m]

Jabotinsky decried these official elite Zionist accommodations of the Nazis and the WZO's simultaneous attempts to compel member organization adherence to WZO doctrine. Edwin Black, author of *The Transfer Agreement*, detailed the key meeting with Nazi leader Hermann Wilhelm Göring (1893–1946) to overcome the boycott:

> But Zionism's threatened status in Germany changed instantly following the March 25 meeting in Goering's office with Jewish leaders. It was after Kurt Blumenfeld's utterance that only the Zionists possessed the international organization capable of stopping the anti-Nazi movement that the Nazi view changed. From that moment on, the Third Reich realized it could exploit the Zionist movement against the Jews. At the same time, Zionists became convinced that they could exploit the Nazi movement for the benefit of future generations of the Jewish people.[127]

Jabotinsky lampooned fascists in his early writing, but ultimately sided with the rising fascist dictatorship in Italy under Benito Mussolini (1880–1940). By 1934, Betar was training cadets in Italy with Mussolini's permission. Jabotinsky formed the "New Zionist Organization" and entirely broke with the WZO in 1935. Italy's surprise attack and conquest of Ethiopia in 1935 inspired Betar members to adopt brown shirt uniforms similar to those of Mussolini's fascists.

Jabotinsky's many followers, such as Bergson, identified with and were committed to the vision of a Jewish homeland carved out and defended by a Jewish Army. The lobbyist for a Jewish Army Peter H. Bergson, born in Lithuania and raised in Palestine, was strongly influenced by Revisionist Zionism while studying at Hebrew University in Jerusalem. He joined the Irgun Z'vai Leumi paramilitary organization in Palestine in the 1930s, which worked to smuggle 40,000 European Jews in spite of the restrictions of the British White Paper.

It was April of 1940 when Bergson came to the United States to meet up with Irgun associates already working to gain support for the Jewish Army, including Vladimir Jabotinsky. Jabotinsky had arrived in March

---

[m] In the introduction to his seminal 1984 book *The Transfer Agreement*, Edwin Black noted the intense personal nature of writing about the issue. "When I told my parents, my mother threatened to disown me and my father threatened to personally to strangle me if I would dare lend any credence to the notion of Nazi-Zionist cooperation. This was done against a background of anti-Semitic and anti-Israel attempts to somehow link the Nazi regime with Zionists."

thinking the U.S. was the only place where recruitment of a truly formidable new Jewish Army might be possible. [128]

By this time, Jabotinsky's Irgun had much more blood on its hands than even the CIA would document four years later. Jabotinsky's efforts to form paramilitary training camps for deployment to Palestine also included efforts to cooperate with anti-Semitic elements in Poland. Between 1933 and 1936, Jewish immigration to Palestine had reached 164,267 or 29.9 percent of the population. Arab Palestinians, sensing their own eventual displacement, began revolting against Jewish immigration in 1936. The WZO's Haganah, dominated by Labor Zionists, had worked jointly with the British to quell the uprising as their "settlement police." The Revisionist paramilitary, which split from the Haganah in 1931, was placed under the command of Jabotinsky in December of 1936. Although they were originally committed to "self-restraint," by November the Irgun forces were actively engaging in terrorism, including the use of milk-can bombs that would also be deployed a decade later against the British in the King David Hotel.

> Earlier in September, 13 Arabs were killed supposedly in retaliation for the death of three Jews. Several Irgunists were determined to act on their own, but the Irgun Command headed them off by organizing a wave of operations, beginning on November 14, that resulted in 10 dead and numerous wounded. The Irgun's campaign of attacks on purely civilian targets reached its high point in the summer of 1938. On July 6, a bomb in a milk can went off in the Arab market in Haifa, leaving 21 dead and 52 injured. On July 15, an electric mine in David Street in the old city of Jerusalem killed 10 and wounded 30. On July 25, another bomb in the Haifa market left 35 dead and 70 wounded. On July 26, a bomb in Jaffa's market killed 24 and injured 35.[129]

In America Jabotinsky roamed freely, for a short time. On August 2, 1940, he was examined by a doctor who suspected that he had heart trouble. Jabotinsky then made his way to a Betar camp in Greene County in the Catskill Mountains, 130 miles from New York City. After reviewing an honor guard, he collapsed and died. But Bergson and the remaining Irgun men fought on through press, politics, and some well-placed friends at the U.S. Department of Treasury.

They formed the Committee for the Jewish Army in the fall of 1941. It was headquartered in New York with local councils in eight other cities. They not only published a monthly magazine but staged theatrical productions and sponsored rallies. But they had sharp elbows. Jewish

Army newspaper advertisements and radio broadcasts targeted other Zionist groups when calling attention to their cause. By 1943, as the situation in Europe worsened, Bergson was working for direct rescue and evacuation operations rather than the army and immigration to Palestine. Bergson's new approach was consciously designed to avoid alienating Western governments over the Palestine question and Zionist political goals by focusing on immediate rescue. Bergson opened a Washington office dedicated to this objective, and was soon signing up honorary committee chairmen, including publisher William Randolph Hearst, Herbert Hoover, and Interior Secretary Harold Ickes. He also lined up the U.S. Treasury Department after being rebuffed by the U.S. State Department.

Treasury Secretary Henry Morgenthau Jr. strongly identified with Bergson's rescue efforts and sought to remove evacuation matters from the jurisdiction of the State Department. He commissioned his own assistants, Josiah Dubois, John Pehle, and Randolph Paul, to compile a report on rescue opportunities and failures, which he presented to President Roosevelt on January 16, 1944. It roundly castigated the State Department and recommended that Roosevelt "remove the hands of men who are indifferent, callous and perhaps even hostile." He also threatened to launch a public relations attack on the State Department as a bastion of anti-Semitism. It was a charge, he said, that "will require little more in the way of proof for this suspicion to explode into a nasty scandal."[130]

Roosevelt, not wishing to face such a scandal in an election year, issued Executive Order 9417 establishing the War Refugee Board (WRB). He named Morgenthau, Secretary of State Cordell Hull, and War Secretary Henry Stimson to head the board. John W. Pehle, who as Assistant Treasury Secretary had spent much of his time working to produce evidence of State Department procrastination on refugee efforts, became director of the WRB. Josiah Dubois affirmed that the work of Bergson was effective in "generating an atmosphere conducive to its formation...we were seeking the same goals." Earlier, Pehl ordered that Bergson be allowed to utilize State Department cables to communicate with Jabotinsky, and facilitated Jabotinsky's movements to Turkey.[131] The WRB was now authorized to establish refugee absorption centers in neutral countries, but was unable to lead by example. By late July of 1944, the WRB was only able to secure infrastructure for 1,000 refugees at Fort Ontario in Lake Oswego, New York. This number was unimpressive to other countries being lobbied to absorb refugees, and the entire effort was largely a failure.[n]

Haganah Arms Smuggling in the United States

The U.S. Treasury Department was not the only agency being diverted to Israel's cause. A temporary wartime institution, the War Assets Administration, was covertly being harvested by the Haganah for arms and military gear for Palestine. The War Assets Administration (WAA) was established within the Office for Emergency Management on March 25, 1946 under Executive Order 9689 by President Harry Truman. Truman also invoked the Neutrality Act on December 14, 1947, officially banning weapons shipments to either side of the Zionist-Arab conflict. The Haganah blithely ignored Truman's order.

U.S. demobilization after WWII presented Haganah agents with massive opportunities to illicitly acquire a wide variety of advanced U.S. weaponry and military equipment and divert it to Palestine. WAA regulations required that all weapons be rendered inoperable and converted to scrap. But public newspaper accounts and CIA, FBI, and U.S. Customs Service incident reports soon revealed the tentacles of a massive smuggling operation encompassing the U.S., Europe, Caribbean and Latin America, all moving illicit arms shipments to Palestine. This enormous network is detailed in Leonard Slater's tell-all tribute *The Pledge*, published in 1970. It is substantiated by more recently declassified CIA reports. The Jewish Agency and its foreign agents in America (some registered at the FARA Office) were intimately involved.

Slater's book chronicles a key meeting between Rudolf Goldschmidt Sonneborn (1898-1986), Henry Montor (1906-1982) of the United Jewish Appeal, David Ben-Gurion of the Jewish Agency Executive, and 17 prominent Jewish-American fundraisers active in finance, law, and retail businesses on July 1 of 1945. The group operated under the cover of a fake charity supposedly dedicated to the relief of European Jews called the Sonneborn Institute (also known euphemistically as Materials for Israel).[132] This separate legal entity gave the Jewish Agency and the

---

[n] The parallels with later efforts to replace a designated agency's authority with more effective "outside expertise" are notable. In 1976, George H. W. Bush ordered the CIA to deliver raw CIA intelligence to an outside group led by Paul Wolfowitz. The group produced wildly inaccurate overestimations of Soviet weapons and capabilities. A couple of decades later, Douglas Feith's Office of Special Plans would do the same with intelligence about Iraqi weapons of mass destruction.

Haganah their letter of marque and operational "plausible deniability" if any of the autonomous cells of the arms smuggling operation were uncovered. Some were, but overall, it worked.

Rabbi Irving Miller was instrumental in coordinating higher-level issues concerning arms smuggling and finance even as he served as the chairman of the Jewish Agency American Section, according to Teddy Kollek, a Haganah and Jewish Agency operative based in New York who later became mayor of Jerusalem.[133] Miller went on to chair the American Zionist Committee. Kollek described his own hands-on role coordinating a wide spectrum of agents and rogues:

> My work touched on weapons production...speculations on ship purchases, dealings with factories and junkyards, liaison with spies, mobsters, movie moguls, statesmen, bankers, professors, industrialists, and newspaper men; and no lack of illegalities, from petty to international...Deals were made with South American governments to buy tanks and innumerable other things and ship them on to Palestine.[134]

Kollek cohort Yehuda Arazi, an arms smuggler active in Europe-Palestine arms smuggling since 1938, had contacts in Poland. Another associate, Leonard Weisman, was a scrap machinery magnate with numerous trading and development companies. Another node of the smuggling network, Sam Sloan, continuously scanned WAA lists of war materiel for desirable arms. By studying how weapons were rendered inoperable at different WAA facilities, a highly non-standardized process, Sloan was able to acquire and assemble fully operational arms with components purchased or stolen from different scrap facilities.

Haganah operative Elie Schalit in New York was responsible for clandestine shipments from shell companies set up by Nahum A. Bernstein, a lawyer and founder of "Americans for Haganah."[135] The litany of nonprofit corporations used as fronts for the actual arms smuggling included "Materials for Palestine," a warehouse front for illicit goods and itself an umbrella organization for the nondescript "Eastern Development Corporation," which exported machinery and "Inland Machinery and Metal Company," which exported weapons components and weapons-making equipment disguised as civilian machine tools. "Oved Trading," a mining operations exporter, provided cover for buying and shipping explosives. Yet another front, "Land and Labor for Palestine," chartered as a youth group, recruited WWII combat veterans to fight in Palestine.º

One Haganah arms theft operation involved the scrap yard of Nathan Liff, who had acquired a WAA contract for scrapping surplus arms in Honolulu. Liff notified Sonneborn about his scrap yard and access to surplus war planes during a visit to New York. Al Schwimmer was a wartime TWA flight engineer who worked in an aircraft reconditioning and air freight business in Burbank, refitting C-46 and Constellation transports as well as B-17 Flying Fortresses for shipment to Palestine. Schwimmer sent Haganah West Coast coordinator Hank Greenspun to Hawaii to look over Liff's inventory and, if possible, procure functioning surplus aircraft engines.[136]

Greenspun noticed brand-new crated .30 and .50 caliber machine guns in a section of the yard with other stock that had not been rendered inoperable. The crates were still owned by the military and actively patrolled by U.S. Marines. Greenspun observed the sentries' timetable and then used a forklift to steal 58 crates containing 500 machine guns. He replaced the new stock with crates of guns already rendered inoperable from Liff's side of the yard.[137] Greenspun then sent them to Los Angeles for transshipment to Palestine via Mexico. He almost lost the 35 tons of machine guns just out of San Pedro harbor while employing civilian yachts for the Los Angeles-to-Acapulco leg of the smuggling operation, but the machine guns arrived in Israel by October of 1948.[138]

Kolleck also established front operations with Latin American dictators including Anastasio Somoza to buy operable WAA stock for reshipment to Palestine in exchange for a 3.5 percent kickback on the purchase. Haganah operatives coordinated with gangster boss Sam Kay to traffic arms through Cuba and Panama.[139]

Schwimmer used Panama as a base to avoid Civil Aeronautics Administration airworthiness requirements and escape the FBI. The FBI prevented Schwimmer from acquiring U.S. licenses to operate a fleet of military transports made up of twelve C-46 Commando aircraft and three Lockheed Constellations; Schwimmer transferred legal ownership of the aircraft to the Panamanian national airline LAPSA and flew the wing to Panama and then on to Czechoslovakia in May of 1948. From there, the

---

º Similar practices continue. Between 2002 and 2003 lobbyist Jack Abramoff purchased and shipped $44,000 worth of sniper equipment and other military gear to the illegal West Bank colony of Beitar Illit through a US nonprofit corporation called the Capital Athletic Foundation.

planes ferried disassembled surplus Messerschmitt Bf-109 fighter planes and other arms purchased in Czechoslovakia to Palestine to fight the Arabs upon the declaration of the state of Israel. The Haganah also acquired B-17 bombers in the U.S. through a front company and illegally flew them to Palestine, after stealing one back that had been impounded by U.S. government officials at an airbase in Tulsa, Oklahoma. They bombed Cairo on the way to Palestine and operated against Arab ground forces in 1948.

The CIA detected the smuggling operations centered on the Czechoslovakian airbase at Zatec. Schwimmer's new "Service Airways," denied U.S. licenses for his fleet in America, was operating the planes through countries allied with the U.S. His crews wore U.S. military uniforms to deceive foreign airport officials in one of the first of many documented Israeli false flag operations.

CIA Detects False-Flagging in Europe

The U.S. Central Intelligence Agency filed a top-secret report with the Secretary of Defense on May 28, 1948 titled "Clandestine Air Transport Operations." R.H. Hillenkoetter, Rear Admiral of the U.S. Navy and Director of Central Intelligence, indicated in a report cover letter a new danger to U.S. interests in Europe and the Middle East:

> U.S. National security is unfavorably affected by these developments and that it could be seriously jeopardized by continued illicit traffic in the "implements of war."[140]

The report, declassified and released on September 21, 2001, detailed Schwimmer's false-flag operations with the C-46 Commandos and the obliquely named "Service Airways":

> The history of a single operation undertaken by an aircraft owned by Service Airways is here cited as typical of the traffic which has now grown to large proportions. A C-46 air transport carrying a Jewish American crew departed from the U.S. for Italy early in March, 1948. The crew obtained clearance for the aircraft and U.S. visas for themselves by false statements and the exhibition of letters from their company. This correspondence implied that a contract existed with an Italian aircraft manufacturing concern for the conversion of several aircraft from cargo to passenger accommodation. The aircraft took off from a New Jersey airport and was next reported at Geneva, Switzerland, having flown the route by way of Greenland, Iceland, and France. The

crew, dressed in U.S. Army uniforms without insignia, permitted only the Swiss airport superintendent to board the plane. Secrecy evidenced by the crew, and the fact that they were wearing uniform caused the Swiss official to believe that this was a U.S. Air Force operation and no inquiry was made other than to learn that the aircraft's next destination was Rome.

The Swiss official reported seeing cargo of small arms and commented on the unusually large number of crew members. Taking off from Geneva on 11 March with a full load of gas, the aircraft proceeded to land at Castiglione del Largo, near Perugia, Italy. Its arrival was evidently anticipated by Italian customs officials who were dispatched to the airfield. They stated later that flight clearances and "all documents for the aircraft" were in order. No report was made of the cargo, although the aircraft was later seen to have been unloaded. The aircraft eventually took off without clearance for Catania, Sicily, where, on arrival, the crew declared their intention to return to Castiglione del Largo. Instead, having left behind certain members of the crew, the aircraft took off for Paris where it was last seen on 6 May at Orly field.

No modification of the aircraft, it is now learned, was undertaken by the Italian concern (Societa Aeronautical Italiana). This company, furthermore, denies that any contract exists between the owners of the aircraft for such work. Orders have been issued by the Italian authorities to impound the aircraft involved in this incident should it return to Italian territory.

The Italian Government apparently has cooperated with Service Airways, believing it to be engaged in bonafide operations. The behavior of minor Italian officials, however, in failing to report the C-46 incident to American authorities in Italy and in apparently expediting the aircraft's movements, indicated that the cargo of arms probably was unloaded and disposed of with their knowledge and collusion. Since this operation took place prior to the Italian elections, it was suspected at first that its purpose was to aid the Communists. Sufficient evidence is now available, however, to attribute the activities of the crew of this aircraft to illegal traffic in arms for the Jewish underground...Two crew members of this aircraft who, with some others, did not accompany the aircraft to Paris, were later held in custody by Greek Police, having landed at Rhodes for gasoline. These men were cooperating with British pilots engaged in flying four Anson aircraft to Palestine to join the nucleus of the Zionist air force. [141]

An annex to the CIA report on false-flag arms smuggling, labeled "Example B," detailed the offshore arms smuggling operations of Ocean Trade Airways out of North Carolina.

Ocean Trade Airways, Inc. This irregular carrier operates from an airfield at Laurinburg-Maxton, North Carolina, about twenty-five miles from Pope Field (U.S.AF base). Ralph Cox of New York, owner of the airline, and most of the operating personnel, are employed by American Airlines on a part-time basis. When working for Ocean Trade Airways, crews wear American Airlines uniforms with the company insignia removed. The airline apparently has a heavy schedule of commitments and is flying DC-3's as well as C-54's on missions to South America and Europe.

A C-54 transport plane owned by the company landed with an American crew at Prague, Czechoslovakia on 31 March. It was immediately surrounded and isolated by Czechoslovak security police and 35 cases weighing a total of 14,000 pounds were loaded onto the aircraft from two large trucks. The plane took off immediately without obtaining the necessary clearances from airport officials. Their protests, however, were overruled by the Chief of Security Police who stated that this was a government operation. The aircraft returned the following day and the pilot and crew were interrogated at the U.S. Embassy. In a sworn statement, Seymour Lerner admitted being in charge of the flight and revealed that Ralph Cox of New York owns and operates a charter airplane service under the name of Ocean Trade Airways. The plane was chartered in Paris by Lerner to a British subject named Cooper, without the knowledge, but under the authority given by Cox and Lerner to carry freight while in Europe to "various destinations". The pilot stated his cargo to have been "hand tools and surgical instruments" which he flew in a non-stop flight to Beit Daras, Palestine.[142]

Israel's growth into a regional military hegemon counted on such smuggling, clandestine international coordination, and the cover provided by many organizations claiming to be charities. The public relations, fundraising, and lobbying activity that made much of it possible is most effectively observed at the level of a single individual. Tracing Isaiah L. Kenen's public and private activities as he transcended obstacles utilizing ever-morphing lobbying groups while dodging government prosecutions provides one illuminating path through a murky history.

"The Washington [IOI] office is a goodwill and intelligence outpost for the [Israeli] government. It is not an office of information in the sense of production and distribution. . —Federal Bureau of Investigation

Mr. Isaiah L. Kenen, Director of Information for the Government of Israel's Mission to the United Nations and one of the officers of the Israeli Office of Information, visited my office on January 17, 1951 to discuss his possible obligations under the Foreign Agents Registration Act in the event he terminates his present activities and establishes his own public relations business.

Mr. Kenen stated that his first client would probably be the Government of Israel and consequently I told him that he should file a new registration statement on Form FA-1. I explained to Mr. Kenen the registration statement of the Israeli Office of Information and the necessity for the filing of a new statement. Mr. Kenen stated that he would file a new statement as soon as he commences his activities on behalf of the Government of Israel. Suitable forms were given to Mr. Kenen. —Internal U.S. Department of Justice Foreign Agent Registration Section memo filed by Nathan Lenvin, 1/17/1951; declassified and released 3/10/2008

Chapter 5: Israel Office of Information

By the late 1940s, Isaiah Kenen was actively probing the Department of Justice FARA unit for weaknesses he could exploit. By the late 1950s and early 1960s, Kenen and his front organizations were driving truckloads of tax-exempt foreign cash and lobbying influence across the spans of deception erected over the U.S. Department of Justice and around public scrutiny.

Isaiah Kenen worked closely with Abba Eban, Israel's ambassador to the United Nations, in the late 1940s. Eban soon became Israel's ambassador to Washington and would later rise in various Israeli government ministries. Kenen was charged once again with heading press relations, only now on behalf of the Israeli embassy's Office of Information, an organization specifically established, registered, and funded to distribute Israeli government propaganda within the United States. Kenen's tendencies toward non-disclosure and misleading filings (which had landed other foreign agents in jail) during his tenure at the Israel Office of Information in New York City are only now apparent.

The Israel Office of Information's first FARA filing (Form FA-2) and the Department of Justice's responses, released under the Freedom of Information Act in March 2008, are a case in point. (See appendix) The form was originally received and date-stamped by the Department of Justice FARA section on October 12, 1948.[143] On October 26, 1948 the FARA office acknowledged receipt of the filing and offered the Israeli Embassy the courtesy of choosing mid-year and year-end calendar reporting dates. The Israeli Embassy responded, availing itself of June and December reporting deadlines.[144]

After an internal review, on June 17, 1949, the FARA office cited the initial filing as "deficient" and notified the Israel Office of Information's Washington office.

> An examination of your registration statement, filed on October 12, 1948, reveals certain deficiencies which are noted below. It is requested that these deficiencies be corrected in filing the next supplemental statement.[145]

Internal Department of Justice working papers and the official notice reveal that the Israel Office of Information not only omitted four required supplementary exhibits, including detailed propaganda dissemination reports, but also neglected to mention the existence of an entirely separate "information office" already up and running in California.[146] The FARA form required disclosure of "all branches and local units of registrant and all other component or affiliated groups or organizations."

The required exhibits[p] the IOI failed to file would have given the FARA a clear picture of the organization's geographical span, its contractual agreements with the Israeli consulate, and the terms under which Israel Office of Information material was entering the U.S. "news stream" via

---

[p] Exhibit B—a copy of the agreement, arrangement, or authorization (or if not in writing a written description thereof) pursuant to which Registrant is acting for, or receiving funds from, each foreign principal named.

Exhibit D—If Registrant is a non business organization, a copy of its charter, constitution, bylaws or other instruments of organization.

Exhibit F—A copy of the agreement or arrangement (or if not in writing, a written description thereof) between the Registrant and each business firm or other organization named.

continuous press relations, suggested newspaper articles, paid placements, and magazines.

During the Israel Office of Information's startup period, the FARA section was rarely given complete information about agent lobbying, the specific content of important radio addresses and appearances, or the public relations efforts targeting prominent journalists that Kenen pursued mainly from behind the scenes.

But the FARA section review could not detect other far more deliberate omissions by Isaiah Kenen that would have presented an accurate and early picture of the network of contacts of the IOI's most important individual foreign agent and his early lobbying.

Deficient Declarations

As a co-director of the IOI, Kenen was required to file his own individual foreign agent declaration (Form FA-1, called a "short form") with the Department of Justice. In his declaration, Kenen neglected to disclose the most important data sought by FARA: his close working relationships with Israeli government officials such as Eban and scores of others.[147] Kenen's own writing about these relationships many decades later, after he retired, fills in important historical records about the founding of Israel and its initial lobbying forays.

The Israel Office of Information's two declared offices in New York City and Washington, DC were modest. 2210 Massachusetts Avenue is northwest of DuPont Circle, nearly four miles from Congress. In 2008, the building housed the Embassy of Sudan. (This can be contrasted with AIPAC's present office at 440 1st ST NW, which is two minutes from the Capitol and eight minutes from the White House.) The IOI New York office, close to Central Park and less than two miles from the UN building, last sheltered a treatment center for patients with obsessive-compulsive disorder.

The IOI's first FARA declaration in 1948 understandably did not include overall budget information or payments from foreign principals, since this was still being worked out from the budget of the overall Israel mission. Nevertheless, its overall budget from the Israeli Ministry for Foreign Affairs grew to almost $50,000 per month by 1950 (about half a million in today's dollars) for New York, Washington, and Los Angeles offices.[148] Kenen came to understand the burdens of FARA compliance, as he personally signed off on the Israel Office of Information's FARA declaration for January 1–June 30, 1950 for all three offices.[149] Kenen listed himself as in charge of the New York office, Minna Davidovitch as running the DC office, and Shirley Brostoff Lewis as heading up the Los Angeles operation.

Kenen listed Y. H. Rosenkranz at the Israeli embassy as a new Israel Office of Information Press Advisor. Rosenkranz, formerly a captain of the Israeli army and foreign editor of the *Palestine Post*, was then pressing an urgent PR campaign against the internationalization of Jerusalem.[150] The Israel Office of Information reported that Moshe Pearlman at the Ministry of Foreign Affairs in Israel was its solitary "foreign principal."

Kenen listed Rita Grossman as another New York IOI office employee on the declaration. Indeed, Grossman had accompanied Kenen from the Jewish Agency on to the United Nations delegation, and then to the Israel Office of Information. From there, she would follow Kenen all the way to AIPAC lobbying and other public relations activities on behalf of Israel. Kenen remembered her first day fondly:

> When the United Nations opened its special session to determine the fate of Palestine in 1947, I was besieged by the press and I urgently needed an assistant to handle the office while I was at the U.N. In the meantime, Jesse Lurie of the Jerusalem Post served as my temporary assistant....
>
> ...That was a momentous day for me too because on that day Gromyko made his astonishing speech endorsing partition and because Rita Grossman became my first assistant—a post she filled brilliantly for about 18 years. She worked for me at the UN, and then in Washington. She was my indispensable aide at political conventions and fundraising meetings across the country...[151]

Grossman continued working for Kenen until 1965, a traumatic year for the AZC and important moment for AIPAC. As Kenen reviewed and edited the mandatory annexes to FARA reports, he strategized how to lay claim on U.S. taxpayer dollars through direct foreign aid from the government, as opposed to the scattered charitable donations and investments from individuals that were the mainstay of "Israel bond" campaigns attended by members of the Israel Office of Information. Kenen's filing divulged cursory details of the IOI's Israel bond campaign meetings and community fundraising gatherings at regional Hadassah and ZOA chapters, as well as film and radio clip distribution and cultural outreach activities.[152] But his public relations activity disclosure provided few additional details.

Kenen did list himself as the top broadcast PR "producer" of the Israel Office of Information. While he made only 22 formal speeches, three less than Ruth Goldschmidt, Kenen delivered 83 separate radio broadcasts in six months. No other Israel Office of Information officer listed any.

Yet even as IOI activity ballooned throughout the early 1950s, IOI declarations continued to be cited as deficient by the FARA section office. For every proper listing of a new or departing employee (such as research assistant Mordecai Chertoff, the uncle of the George W. Bush administration's Department of Homeland Security director, who resigned on February 2, 1951)[153] or activities disclosure, the FARA office cited missing employees, missing copies of the actual Israeli government propaganda distributed, or propaganda circulated without a proper FARA disclosure label. The FARA section's recommended label, when affixed to material, left little to the reader's imagination:

> A copy of this material is filed with the Department of Justice where the required statement under the Foreign Agents Registration act of (your name and address) as an agent of (name and address of your foreign principal) is available for public inspection. Registration does not indicate approval of this material by the United States Government.[154]

All publicly circulated Israel Office of Information communications had to bear such onerous declarations. Kenen's writings reveal acute insights about the attributes of effective public relations. IOI FARA disclosures gave him firsthand experience about how revelatory, and thus restrictive, the filings could be in their listings of people, expenditures, locations and topics of public or private events, and required duplicates of images, recordings, and print documents. This would not do.

Marching orders from Mossad

During 1949 Kenen drafted a confidential strategy report about how the Israeli Ministry of Foreign Affairs could implement Israeli policy initiatives and PR most effectively in the United States. This "Kenen Report" described how the New York IOI processed Israeli government information into news releases. IOI N.Y. "disseminates documents" into the U.S. news stream for the "general public." This is known because the FBI was closely monitoring Kenen's activities.[155] Early references in FBI files noted IOI founder Kenen had become a member of the Communist Party in 1937 while working as a newspaperman at the Plain Dealer in Cleveland, though he was never the subject of an investigation. The FBI noticed Kenen because he interacted with so many U.S. and foreign nationals who were targets of espionage, foreign counterintelligence, and domestic security investigations such as Abraham Feinberg, Israeli diplomats, and assorted Mossad and other Israeli intelligence officers. Kenen's movements appear as cross-references in hundreds of pages of FBI documents only declassified and released in 2012. [156]

One IOI Public Relations Board meeting held in the Israeli Consulate General in New York on May 9, 1949, pushed U.S. media initiatives aimed at boosting Israel's economy. The IOI wanted to "place a series of pieces in from eight to twelve top magazines" including *Reader's Digest* and *Cosmopolitan* by "making funds available for important propaganda programs." The New York IOI focused on "U.N., Organizations (Jewish), and the press emanating from New York" while the IOI Washington office covered "other embassies, Congress, Washington Press, and the National Press Club" according to the FBI. [157]

During a July 18, 1949 meeting Israeli Counsel Reuven Dafni informed Isaiah Kenen and others that Foreign Minister Moshe Sharett in coordination with Mossad founder Reuven Shiloah and Israeli ambassador to the United States Eliahu Elath had recently conducted a strategy session about public relations and "thrashed out" everything except for the question of funding. Kenen reported that his New York IOI was ready to go. The FBI description characterizes the IOI as functioning more like a Mossad intelligence outpost for collection and foreign propaganda distribution than a press office. IOI New York was responsible for receiving information cables from Israel. "One member of the staff spent much of the day decoding and stenciling" the cables. IOI offices established secure communications crisscrossing the U.S. Dafni "reported that his [Kenen's] office and the Washington IOI worked out a code so that classified messages could be translated." [158]

The FBI noted in September 1949 that Kenen had initiated "the distribution of a weekly news service…sent to Anglo-Jewish newspapers, Jewish organizations, and individuals." The FBI also noted Kenen's strategy of having the Israel lobby media apparatus pay for favorable coverage of Israel. "The report further states that frequent conferences were held with representatives of the Jewish agencies and the American Zionist Council to discuss public relations policies and techniques. It states how 104 National Jewish Agencies in New York receive releases and constantly ask for news editorial advice, feature material, and photographs and had cooperated in helping produce some of the more important publications by buying and distributing large quantities."

Kenen described core IOI functions, while foreshadowing his impending move to Washington. "He collects intelligence, meeting press attaches of other embassies, publicity men of national political parties, Congress and government officials.... Washington is a city of personal contact. The Washington office is a goodwill and intelligence outpost for the government. It is not an office of information in the sense of production and distribution."

Like the AIPAC of today, IOI was highly attentive to Israeli military objectives. In January 1950 the IOI strategized how to effectively quash U.S. arms sales to Arab states. IOI Press Relations Board coordinator Moshe Keren "had discussed with Jewish organizations the serious situation arising out of Egypt receiving arms; that the balance of power in the Middle East was completely changed by this move and it would be advisable to contact the major papers." Kenen agreed with the Foreign Ministry and Mossad strategy but differed on tactics. Kenen highlighted the advantages of a more indirect approach, suggesting that action instead be initiated at the U.N. Security Council or that an explosive news story be leaked that could overturn U.S. arms-sale policy in a way not traceable back to IOI. Kenen thought it might be dangerous to directly fight U.S. Cold War objectives of buying friends in the Middle East through arms sales. According to Kenen, it "would be difficult to get support from the papers since the question of armaments was part of the East-West complications."

The FBI report frankly categorized Kenen's exchange as an example of "efforts being made by the Israelis to change the policies of the United States State Department." In 1953, the director of the FBI finally filed a classified internal report to Assistant Attorney General Warren Olney III alleging that the Israel Office of Information was not properly labeling all of the propaganda it was circulating.

On June 2, 1953, Olney responded that the propaganda filed at his office did bear the proper disclosure stamps. Whether the FBI had goofed and sent the wrong source documents in its communication or misinterpreted the labeling requirements, the matter ended. Since Olney found that an original copy of the propaganda had in fact been filed in the FARA section, no further action to see whether propaganda circulating on American streets bore the proper label was taken.[159] The DOJ exhibited tolerance for the ongoing irregularities, but Kenen would remain on the Department of Justice radar for many more years, despite his best efforts.

Kenen Makes a Clean Break

Kenen's writings reveal that as he chafed under FARA registration, he came to believe that the degree of disclosure required to lobby on behalf of the Israeli embassy as a foreign agent would never allow him to win the level of unconditional aid and influence he felt Israel deserved. The IOI's open approach was encapsulated in its mission:

> The purpose of the Israel Office of Information is to provide accurate and up-to-date information in the United States on all aspects of the State of Israel, including political, economic, cultural, social, and other activities.[160]

Kenen knew as a public relations practitioner that FARA would never allow him to properly "frame" issues in a sophisticated way that transformed and sold their presentation from Israeli needs to perceived American interests. Kenen's own preference for stealth can be seen on his personal 1948 FA-1 "short form" declaration. A cursory review of Kenen's personal registration statement as director of the New York IOI office, filed with the Department of Justice on October 12, 1948, would have revealed it was unacceptable (see Appendices). Rather than disclose the titles and subjects of publications he had circulated in the previous six months at the Jewish Agency and UN, as required, Kenen simply noted that any he personally deemed covered under FARA had already been "filed" at his discretion.[161]

In reality, Kenen's personal discretion was quite forgiving. He never let his position as a foreign agent of the Israeli government keep him away from Capitol Hill, noting in his biography that he actively lobbied Congress to provide arms for Israel in 1950.

> I spent a week in Washington in January 1950 to voice concern to friends on Capitol Hill.[162]

Kenen never disclosed this crucial congressional lobbying foray or documents delivered in his FARA declarations. The FARA section never discovered the omissions or investigated it. Kenen's brevity included even his own name: in the first FARA disclosure form question, Kenen stated that his full name was "Isaiah Leo Kenen." To a subsequent question regarding "all other names ever used and when each was used," Kenen responded simply, "None."

Today, even with modern computer keyword search and data retrieval, it is difficult to find any of Kenen's writings or associations by searching for "Isaiah Leo Kenen." That is because most of his articles since the Ohio newspaper days were filed under the byline "IL Kenen." Indeed, Kenen usually abbreviated his first and middle names to initials in his signature. His nickname among friends was written "Si" or alternately "Sy."

Any Department of Justice investigator following up on Kenen's public relations activities in the 1940s and early 1950s, limited to index card files and print reference guides to major newspapers, would not have been able to find Kenen's articles or locate any of his associates. But Kenen's connections to the fledgling Israeli government after serving at the Jewish Agency and the United Nations were legion.

As mentioned, among Kenen's closest associates was the legendary Aubry "Abba" Eban, who served with Kenen at the Jewish Agency and later the UN delegation while simultaneously acting as ambassador to the U.S. He was a brilliant orator, and Kenen reveled in the honor of working with him:

> For a decade I was privileged to work with Eban, both at the UN and later in Washington.[163]

At the UN, Kenen also worked closely with delegation leader Moshe Sharett, who later became the first foreign minister of Israel. In 1946, he traveled to Palestine from Paris at the direction of David Ben-Gurion to help spring Sharett from jail. He was being held on arms smuggling charges.

> David Ben Gurion, who led the struggle to establish the Jewish state, was responsible for my first visit to Palestine, in 1946. BG then lived at the Royal Monceau Hotel in Paris and I had a room nearby. He was in Paris because he had left Israel to escape arrest and detention by the British. He directed activities of the Jewish Agency and of the Haganah—Israel's Defense Forces—from his hotel room. I was then in Paris representing the American Jewish Conference, which, along with major constituent organizations, was meeting to consider the future of the surviving Jews in Europe.
>
> One Saturday morning there was the alarming report that the British had arrested leaders of the Jewish Agency, accusing them of smuggling arms in anticipation of an impending struggle with both the British and the Arabs. Moshe Sharett was one of them....I knocked on Ben Gurion's

door. He was furious. "There has been a pogrom," he shouted at me. "Go there. Go there at once. You can help them. You are a newspaperman."[164]

Kenen traveled to Palestine, where he then nearly died at the hands of Menachem Begin. By 1946 Ben-Gurion had agreed that the Haganah could cooperate with Menachem Begin's Irgun fighters against the British. Begin planned the 1946 terror bombing of the King David Hotel targeting British military units stationed there. Kenen recalls his near brush with death at the hands of these terrorist-to-be-statesmen:

> After two weeks in Israel, I felt it was time for me to return to Paris. A rickety single engine plane that shuttled between Cairo and Jerusalem was scheduled to leave Jerusalem around 11:00 AM. I thought I should use the time to visit the barbershop in the King David Hotel. But the manicurist was not there; it was a Saturday. And so I walked to Ramallah to board the tiny plane, which, it seemed to me, was tied together by shoelaces. An hour or so later I picked up a newspaper in Cairo, at Shepherd's Hotel, and read that some 96 British soldiers and civilians had been blown into eternity. Two years later I learned that Eban had stopped at the King David that day to get a haircut. We almost met that day—in eternity.[165]

The Zionist terrorists who bombed the British headquarters at the King David Hotel also attempted to false flag—they dressed as Arabs and disguised explosives in milk churns. Ninety-one people, only 28 of them British, were killed in the attack.

Despite his near-death experience at the hands of one, Kenen had reservations about reporting his tightening ties with legendary Israeli government officials like Ben-Gurion to the U.S. Department of Justice. In Kenen's FARA declaration, a question demands "List all of your connections, not fully described above, with all foreign governments, foreign political parties, or officials of agencies thereof." It provides space for both officials' names and connections; Kenen simply wrote "None." Kenen then clumsily scrawled his entire first name on the signature line, though he dropped that inconvenience and returned to "IL Kenen" in his subsequent FARA declarations.

Also revealing is Kenen's response to "Furnish the following information as to all amounts received by you, as compensation or otherwise, during the 3 months preceding the filing of this exhibit, directly or indirectly from the Registrant or Agent or from any foreign principal of yourself or of the Registrant or Agent." In June and July of 1948, Kenen received a monthly salary of $916.66 from the Jewish Agency, the equivalent of roughly $8,200 today. In August and September, he also received $916.66 each month from the "Government of Israel."

When he left the service of the Israel Office of Information in 1951, Kenen would state in a letter to the Department of Justice that he was actually more of a public relations "advisor" than an actual employee. Still later, he would be forced to explain to both the Federal Bureau of Investigation and Senator Fulbright why he was still receiving funds from the Jewish Agency in Israel well into the 1960s, in amounts much greater than his old monthly salary of $916.66.

By December of 1950, Kenen was charting his departure from the Israel Office of Information for a more effective, less visible organization. He made no pretext that this new initiative was anything but a response to the demands of the Israeli government.

> Israelis began looking for a lobbyist to promote the necessary legislation...would I leave the Israeli delegation for six months to lobby for aid on Capitol Hill?
>
> There were other questions. Should I continue my registration as an agent of the Israel government? Was it appropriate for an embassy to lobby? Embassies talked to the State Department, and American voters talked to their congressmen...[166]

Kenen's multiple, overlapping leadership positions in major Zionist organizations and his growing ties to entities and political parties in Palestine and later Israel were all covered by FARA. Other visitors to Palestine in 1946 included Abba Hillel Silver, president of the Zionist Organization of America and co-chair of the American Zionist Emergency Council. Dr. Stephen Wise (1874-1949) was another co-chair, joining Louis Lipsky, former president of the Zionist Organization of America and career Zionist leader. All were simultaneously members of the Jewish Agency Executive, the World Zionist Organization's core financing and colonization entity.[167] Kenen's FARA filings disavowed his relationships with all these major leaders of foreign quasi-governmental organizations.

The omissions in his filing occurred at a point in time when the Justice Department was very actively enforcing FARA. It is reasonable to deduce from Kenen's later writings that in 1948, his position as a quasi-diplomat for Israel may have led him to believe that he had a future in Israel's fledgling diplomatic corps. If he left the jurisdiction of the U.S. legal system, his FARA declarations would simply no longer matter. The general climate under the Truman administration was also highly favorable. But a critical visit to Israel after a lobbying victory in Congress irrevocably changed his career plans and left him scrambling to purge his FARA records at the U.S. Department of Justice.

Israel's American Lobbyist

Kenen began coordinating with the Israelis to undertake stealth lobbying as a purely domestically registered lobbyist late in 1950. On January 17, 1951, Kenen met with Nathan B. Lenvin of the FARA section. In a Department of Justice office memorandum summarizing the meeting, Lenvin filed an internal memo stating that Kenen told him he would be leaving the Israel Office of Information and setting up a public relations business, ostensibly with the Israeli government as his main client. Given Kenen's trajectory in the press and public relations, this was certainly a plausible career move. Lenvin nevertheless advised Kenen that he'd still need to keep filing as a foreign agent and even provided him with additional registration forms:

> Mr. Isaiah L. Kenen, Director of Information for the Government of Israel's Mission to the United Nations and one of the officers of the Israeli Office of Information, visited my office on January 17, 1951 to discuss his possible obligations under the Foreign Agents Registration Act in the event he terminates his present activities and establishes his own public relations business.
>
> Mr. Kenen stated that his first client would probably be the Government of Israel and consequently I told him that he should file a new registration statement on Form FA-1. I explained to Mr. Kenen the registration statement of the Israeli Office of Information and the necessity for the filing of a new statement. Mr. Kenen stated that he would file a new statement as soon as he commences his activities on behalf of the Government of Israel. Suitable forms were given to Mr. Kenen.[168]

Kenen clearly had no intention of ever filing another disclosure with the FARA office. He finalized his actual plans coordinated in December of 1950 with the Israelis to lobby Congress from the tax-exempt U.S. nonprofit American Zionist Council.

> On January 31, 1951, it was decided that I should leave the Israeli government and spearhead the lobbying campaign for the Zionist Council.[169]

Kenen noted that the American Zionist Council had already started a fledgling "education" campaign for aid to Israel, but that "no legislation had been projected." He quickly got to work, noting that:

> On February 13, [1951] I notified the Department of Justice that I was withdrawing as an agent of a foreign principal, and I then filed with the Clerk of the House and the Secretary of the Senate in conformity with domestic lobbying law.[170]

The full text of the actual letter Kenen sent to the Department of Justice, referred to so briefly suggests a complete severance from any ties to the Israeli government, but he mentioned nothing to the Department of Justice about his plans to domestically register and lobby in Washington. Although it was then on the verge of a period of enforcement malaise, the Department of Justice would have undoubtedly asked Kenen for a new FARA registration. But Kenen made every effort to give the FARA office no grounds for following up with him about any further registration requirements, even downplaying his role leading three Israel Office of Information offices as a paid employee of the Israeli government to that of a mere "advisor."

> This is to inform you that, effective today, I have resigned from the service of the Government of Israel.
>
> I have been registered on an exhibit A form, as part of the registration of the Israel Office of Information.
>
> Since January 1st, I was retained by the Government of Israel in an advisory capacity in the field of public relations. However, I have now changed my plans and severed my relations with the Israel Government. I would, therefore, request that my name be removed from your lists.[171]

Kenen was no doubt familiar with the FARA statutory language covering withdrawal when he wrote his termination letter to the FARA section. There is also little doubt that his desire to be "removed from your lists" was in earnest. However, that decision was up to the attorney general, not Isaiah Kenen.[q]

---

[q] The applicable statute read: "The Attorney General may withdraw from public examination the registration statement and other statements of any agent of a foreign principal whose activities have ceased to be of a character which requires registration under the provisions of this subchapter."

The Department of Justice never removed Kenen from their lists and internal files. In turn, Kenen never stopped coordinating his lobbying or receiving payments from Israeli-government-related entities. Using funds laundered from Israel into the U.S. to jump-start lobbying and propaganda, he soon began incorporating a series of nonprofit front organizations under the guise of elite domestic lobby umbrellas that would ultimately merge into the domestically funded, secretive, self-sustaining powerhouse that is AIPAC.

From his perspective, Kenen's timing was fortuitous. The mid-to-late 1950s were a period of FARA enforcement malaise, with registrations below the level of the early 1940s when the law was fresh on the books. The U.S. State Department, formerly in charge of FARA enforcement and zealous about comprehensive registration of agents, was now mostly out of the picture and anyway not in tight FARA oversight coordination with the Department of Justice. Truman had opened the door for productive U.S.-Israel relations and direct lobby-elite-to-president contacts. Barring any mistakes, Kenen could quietly build his lobby's political power base to a point where not even the appointed attorney general, much less the FARA section, would want to publicly challenge it. There were two exceptions: Dwight D. Eisenhower and John F. Kennedy.

The lobby for Israel, known as the American Israel Public Affairs Committee (AIPAC) since 1959, came into existence in 1951. It was established at that time because Israel needed American economic assistance...—*Isaiah L. Kenen*

Chapter 6: American Zionist Council

The American Zionist Council traced its roots to the American Zionist Emergency Council, formed in 1939 and led by Dr. Abba Hillel Silver, Stephen S. Wise, and Louis Lipsky. In 1944, their very first major lobbying initiative ended in disaster due to factionalism and Hillel's counterproductive pressures on the Senate Foreign Relations Committee. The American Zionist Emergency Council was publicly positioned as a "joint political action agency." Today it would be called simply an umbrella organization.

At that time, the American Zionist Emergency Council united 26 representatives from several key organizations: the Zionist Organization of America, Hadassah (the women's Zionist movement), Poale Zion (Zionist workers), and Mizrachi (the Reform movement). A summit was called at the American Zionist Emergency Council headquarters at 342 Madison Avenue, a few blocks from the UN. The AZEC was pushing hard for a Senate resolution calling for the U.S. to obtain free entry for Jews into Palestine and reaffirm the establishment of a Jewish commonwealth in Palestine.

The Senate failed to pass the resolution on December 11, 1944 under the guidance of the U.S. State Department, which urged that passage "at the present time would be unwise from the standpoint of the general international situation." The AZEC suffered fallout as its leaders agonized over how hard to push for a tough U.S. line on Palestine with the UK.[172] But few would take a soft line on the State Department from this time forward.

Stephen Wise was opposed to pressing the resolution on tactical grounds and cautioned patience for a "more auspicious moment." After the resolution failed, the Council fell to squabbling, alternately calling for a censure of Hillel and the resignation of all executives to clear the way for new leadership. The Wise and Silver factions generally opposed the confrontational approach of pressing both the United Kingdom and U.S. favored by Hillel.[173]

As an elite umbrella organization, the AZEC was only functional as long as key fundraisers and donors were convinced of its cause, leadership, and effectiveness. Donors found Hillel's use of threats too abrasive and unprofessional to secure results. Abraham Feinberg clarified the new approach:

> FEINBERG: I was dissatisfied with the routes that the Jewish organized community was using, through the Zionist organization, in presenting its case to the President or the Secretary of State. I felt that the use of threatened pressure was not going to be productive...
> QUESTION: You felt that many of the organizations were using this tactic?
> FEINBERG: Yes. They were, largely because the leader of the Zionist movement at that time in America was a Republican by the name of Dr. Abba [Hillel] Silver, who was a Rabbi, a very arrogant, brilliant speaker, and a despotic type of leader. He was a very close friend of Senator [Robert] Taft. And so his innate feelings toward Roosevelt were inimical. I felt that he was directing the whole movement in the wrong way and if one could establish a man for man relationship with the President and then subsequently the Secretary of State, you could reason things out without threatening. Any President worth his salt will not respond to political blackmail.[174]

Kenen also reflected that Hillel might have actually set the Zionist cause back with his incessant finger-wagging at both Roosevelt and Truman:

> On the one hand, there were the State Department Arabists; the anti-Zionists—both Jews and non-Jews; the oil and defense lobbies, which had always influenced FDR; and the missionaries, who regarded the Jews as interlopers.

> On the other hand, there were overwhelming pressures from the Zionists. Like FDR, Truman cordially welcomed the flexible Stephen Wise. But he was furious when the inflexible Abba Hillel Silver pressured him for recognition, demanding an affirmative reply as he pointed his finger at

Truman's face, as he was wont to do with adversaries and as he did when he and Wise met FDR with a similar demand a few days earlier.[175]

In 1946, the American Zionist Council's predecessor suffered additional blows from the U.S. State Department. Kenen and other lobby leaders would see this as cause for discrediting and seeking the elimination of State Department influence on all matters concerning Palestine and later Israel. Building a unified movement in the U.S., able to take direction, funding, and coordination from Israel, but defensible as a purely "American lobby"—the core proposition of AIPAC—began in earnest in 1951. There was much work to do.

Kenen found out personally that while Truman continued to be an ally, he still resisted the lobby's core public relations issue frames, as he had in the 1948 declaration of recognition—most importantly, the references to a "Jewish State" against a subtle background of divine intervention. Truman subsequently downplayed his unique individual role in Israel's creation. Kenen labored mightily to put the proper doctrine into Truman's mouth:

> President Truman stressed the extent of public support in a 1952 speech to a Jewish audience in New York. The sponsoring organization had asked me to suggest a text. "I take great pride in the fact that I was selected by destiny to be the first to recognize the new Jewish state," I wrote.
>
> I doubt whether Truman ever saw that draft, for his speech bore no resemblance to it. On the contrary, he almost seemed to be arguing with me when he declared: "I take no special credit for recognizing the State of Israel on the day it was born. I did what the people of America wanted me to do."[176]

By 1952, the American Zionist Council was positioning itself, with Kenen's vital expertise, as the "public relations arm of the Zionist movement." The Council touted itself as uniting and tapping political and financial support from the largest and most powerful Zionist organizations in the United States. The reality was somewhat less grandiose and seamless, given the different organizational objectives, leadership, and overlapping areas of concern. Uniting and exerting influence was contentious and not always successful. Kenen lamented the turf wars that greeted his arrival as a lobbyist:

> I encountered many difficulties. There was Elihu Stone of Boston, a veteran of the Zionist Council staff stationed in Washington. He strongly

> resented my coming to Washington to supersede him. He argued that I was a public relations counsel and contended that I should do my job in New York rather than on his beat.
>
> And there was some resentment in the Israeli Embassy because the diplomatic corps led by Eliahu Eilat and Moshe Keren contended that they could do it all by themselves and that I was an intruder....
>
> In addition there was Hadassah, which had inspired and assisted me for many years. But Denise Tourover, who represented Hadassah in Washington, insisted that she knew Washington much better than I did and she constantly complained to the New York Hadassah leadership that I was an interloper.
>
> To sum up all my difficulties; I was the unwanted man. Keren and Stone did not want me in Washington working for the American Zionist Council. Unger did not want me in New York because that was his turf. But the adamant Lipsky did not want me to have anything to do with the Embassy; he wanted the job done by the American Zionist Council.[177]

This all began shaping up when harsh new orders came in from abroad and squabbling heads were cracked together. On November 23, 1952, former Jewish Agency executive, now Prime Minister David Ben-Gurion met with leaders of the four major American Zionist groups in Jerusalem. On the table was the issue of how to transfer important activities from the Jewish Agency, the executive arm of the World Zionist Organization, to the American Zionist Council. This move was meant to bolster the appearance of "indigenous American control." Ben-Gurion's vision was for an "all-embracing territorial federation" with which individuals or groups such as synagogue congregations could affiliate themselves. Ben-Gurion's overall objective was to remove legal and organizational barriers to the growth of Zionism, and the final resolution of the conference vastly broadened the functions of the American Zionist Council.

By design, the Jewish Agency's U.S. subsidiary, the American Section in New York, would now "confine its activities to control of fund campaigns, economic activities, and purchasing." The American Zionist Council could drive forward with establishing a definitive plan for structuring itself, coordinating subtle and effective public relations, and its most important tasks: broader grassroots and executive-level lobbying in support of Israel.[178]

By 1954, the new AZC leader Rabbi Irving Miller had entered his second term as executive director of the organization. Miller largely replaced the combative Hillel finger-wagging approach with expert public relations firepower. The Council was also gathering funding and other resources to execute a formal plan to "enlarge its activities here."[179] In 1954, the American Zionist Council proclaimed a total constituent organization membership of 750,000. The lead organizations under the American Zionist Council umbrella continued to be Hadassah and the Zionist Organization of America. But Ben-Gurion's mandatory reorganization had not revoked the Foreign Agent Registration Act, and the AZC soon ran into trouble.

American Israel Public Affairs Committee Born

Kenen regarded his ascension to the American Zionist Council in 1951 as the true beginning of AIPAC, as he wrote in his chapter "We Begin to Lobby." In private, Kenen made no pretense that this lobbying was in any way related to American interests:

> The lobby for Israel, known as the American Israel Public Affairs Committee (AIPAC) since 1959, came into existence in 1951. It was established at that time because Israel needed American economic assistance...[180]

As mentioned, by the early 1950s Kenen had crafted and implemented the American Zionist Council's new public relations issue framework. This frame has been further refined by AIPAC and is still in widespread use today. Rabbi Miller voiced it aloud in 1954, though he clumsily revealed that it was in fact a public relations strategy to change American public opinion. He made this during an introspective "meta-analysis" gaffe Kenen himself rarely committed. The American Zionist Council and its constituent organizations were now publicly pursuing "American interests."

> Rabbi Miller underscored the council's need of "informing public opinion of the great issues which are at stake for America and for our way of life in Israel's struggle to build a secure, progressive and democratic society in the Middle East."[181]

Blurring the distinctions between Judaism and Zionism and anti-Semitism and anti-Zionism was also a keystone for Israel lobby issue framing. In the background of every battle over policies to benefit Israel, loomed the prospect that opponents would face a barrage of charges of anti-Semitism fired by lobbyists purposefully blurring the line, as Joe Stork and Sharon Rose lamented in 1974:

> The fight against anti-Semitism can be carried out first and foremost by being absolutely clear about the difference between anti-Semitism and anti-Zionism, between Judaism and Zionism. The Zionist establishment wishes to blur those differences every time it serves their purposes. Therefore Zionist interests are served every time that distinction is not made.[182]

While the issue reframing was underway early in 1952, Kenen became nervous. Would his continued contact and receipt of funds from the Israeli government create problems at the Department of Justice? The FARA section was presumably still waiting for his personal declaration as a private-sector public relations consultant to Israel. This issue was made all the more urgent since the nascent Israel lobby's greatest benefactor, President Truman, was on his way out. Kenen's lobby was among the first to receive this privileged and vital information from Abraham Feinberg, who consulted directly with the president.

Feinberg was carefully observing Truman in 1952 and was among the very first to realize he would not be running for reelection. He was so close to Truman that he functioned as a kind of press secretary to reporters in Washington on the crucial issue of reelection, as noted in Feinberg's 1998 *New York Times* obituary:

> In the political world, he led many Democratic fund-raising drives. His family said he played an important role in providing financial support for President Harry S Truman's successful whistle-stop campaign for reelection in 1948. In 1952, while the country was waiting to see whether President Truman would run again, Mr. Feinberg visited him at the White House and then told reporters the President had not made up his mind.[183]

In the end, Truman running for reelection was only wishful thinking, and his departure temporarily suspended Israel's special direct access to the White House. For Kenen, the danger of exposure and legal liability under FARA intensified exponentially once Truman left office. In late 1951 through early 1952, Kenen's activities in Israel and return to the U.S. proceeded quietly. Then, on February 29, 1952, the *New York Times* broke a short story detailing his movements in Israel and the U.S., titled "I.L. Kenen in Zionist Unit Post":

The appointment of I.L. Kenen, former director of information for the Jewish Agency in Palestine, as the Washington representative of the American Zionist Council, the public relations arm of Zionist groups in this country, was announced yesterday by Louis Lipsky, chairman of the council. Mr. Kenen, who also had served as director of information of the Israel delegation to the United Nations, recently returned from Israel.[184]

The FARA section actively monitored the media and filed relevant press clippings in its central files. Kenen had to respond. On March 14, 1952, Kenen wrote a convoluted letter to the FARA section about his employment at the American Zionist Council, still without revealing any Israel lobbying activity. In it, he stated that he had joined and then temporarily resigned from the American Zionist Council for a precise period between October 1951 and January 1952. During that short time, he had visited Israel and received money from the Israeli government, only to return and pick up the reins of the American Zionist Council. He disclosed no material details about his actual activities in Israel. Kenen did reveal how urgent he felt it was to establish on record that since he was not sending propaganda back to the United States "during this trip," he should not be required to file as a foreign agent:

> At the outset I should like to refer you to my letters of February 13, 1951, in which I advised you of my receipts and expenses in connection with personal services rendered to the Government of Israel prior to February 14, 1951.
>
> Following that date I took a position with the American Zionist Council. That appointment expired in October 1951.
>
> On November 1951, I went with my wife to Israel as guests of the Government of Israel. I was not an employee of the Government of Israel. However, the Government of Israel did pay for my passage and also a sum to cover expenses, amounting to approximately $2518.00, calculating Israeli pounds at the tourist rate.
>
> During this trip to Israel, I did not publish or transmit to the United States any documents, printed or propaganda material, whatever.
>
> In January 1952, after returning from my trip to Israel, I again reverted to the American Zionist Council where I am presently employed.

I do not believe this is required to be filed under the Foreign Agents Registration Act, but am submitting this information to you to avoid any possible question.[185]

Lacking relevant details of Kenen's actual lobbying activities, the chief of the FARA section, William E. Foley (1911-1990), responded that if Kenen was not engaging in propaganda, there would be no need to file.[186] Fatefully, Foley did not ask about Kenen's specific contacts or the substance of the meetings with Israeli government officials. If he had, he would have discovered that Kenen did not need to send propaganda back to the United States: the United States, in the form of key members of Congress, went to Israel to receive it. During his trip, Kenen had been formally tasked by the Israeli government with lobbying and feting these members of the United States Congress on Israel's behalf.

Perhaps tellingly, the Department of Justice did file Kenen's March 14 letter with all of Kenen's previous foreign agent registrations. Decades later Kenen presented his leadership role in the American Zionist Council as seamless and uninterrupted:

> Between 1951 and 1953, I had been the Washington Representative of the American Zionist Council, a tax exempt organization...[187]

In Kenen's shorter final personal account published by Near East Research in 1985 he asserted that Israeli sponsorship of the trip was an inadvertent diversion and that he had actually intended to initiate immigration. The trip was undertaken just after Israel won an unprecedented aid package from the U.S. Congress, worth over half a billion in today's dollars. According to Kenen:

> When Congress adjourned, I resigned my post with the American Zionist Council and Bebe and I flew to Israel to see how the $65 million was to be spent. But we had another reason. When I became a member of the Israeli U.N. delegation, I agreed to go aliyah (settle in) to Israel after my work at the U.N. had ended. Moreover, I wanted to perfect my Hebrew and to enter an ulpan (school) for that purpose. I was traveling at my own expense and so Bebe and I had to take a modest room at the Moriah Hotel. This was a cooperative run by eight Yugoslavians—five men and three women—who came there in 1948.[188]

Reading between the lines of his two autobiographical accounts, it seems likely that Kenen did dream of becoming a permanent citizen resident of Israel, which probably contributed to his recklessness in filing deceptive FARA declarations. If he'd permanently left the U.S., it would not have mattered much. But reality and the ongoing need to lobby the U.S. Congress soon dissipated his lifelong dream of life in Israel. Kenen was joined in Israel by U.S. Congressmen eager to be feted in a "victory lap" for their efforts winning foreign aid on Capitol Hill. He was drafted by the Israeli government to conduct them on tours and pass out favors. His government handlers and Kenen no doubt realized that his maximum future value could only be achieved if he returned to Washington.

If Kenen had honestly disclosed his activity in Israel with members of Congress to the FARA section, they probably would have recognized it for what it was: a massive lobbying junket paid for by a foreign principal. Much later, Kenen details how he became aware not only that there wasn't enough free cash flow in Israel to properly finance street signs, but that he was probably becoming too old to serve as an official diplomat for Israel.

> But I was not the only visitor to Israel to find out how Israel intended to use the $65 million. Congressmen, naturally, were interested. On December 6, the Israel Foreign Ministry called to tell me that I must leave the ulpan to meet a delegation consisting of Representatives Fugate and Barrett, members of the House Banking and Finance Committee, who were part of an official sub-committee checking on loans made by the Export Import Bank. ...
>
> That was just the beginning. Many more Congressmen were scheduled to arrive, for there was widespread doubt that Israel could survive. Celler was first and I escorted him around Jerusalem and its historic shrines.
>
> Javits kept me busy for the next 18 hours. He had another project. His mother, Ida Littman Javits, was born in Safed. I went to Safed to urge the mayor, Rabbi Podhoretz—father of the editor of Commentary[r]—to name a street after her. He demurred because, he explained, there was no budget for street signs. Safed used the alphabet instead of street signs. In Jerusalem, I asked the Israel Foreign Ministry to paint the sign. But it too demurred. There was no money—either for signs or for paint. I promised to pay the bill....
>
> During ensuing weeks I continued to escort visiting Congressmen: Ribicoff, Fugate, Keating, O'Toole, Barrett and Fein.

---

[r] Norman Podhoretz, the former editor of *Commentary Magazine*, lobbied the George W. Bush administration to bomb Iran before the end of his term. Podhoretz's son-in-law Elliot Abrams worked as Bush's national security advisor.

> It soon became evident to me that I could be more useful in Washington than in Israel. Moreover, I became aware that youthful diplomats were being trained in Israel for overseas assignments. What would become of me?
>
> So Bebe and I returned to Washington and I resumed my work on Capitol Hill.[189]

The trip had a major impact on the visiting members of Congress, who toughened their line about supporting Israel upon returning to the U.S. When Democratic Representative Emanuel Celler of Brooklyn returned to New York, he immediately began deploying standard Kenen and lobby talking points in a sharp denunciation of the United Nations. He also charged that the UN Mediator for Palestine, Dr. Ralph Bunche, was taking "orders veiled as suggestions" from the U.S. State Department. Celler failed to make common cause with Truman's consular appointee to Israel and erstwhile ally John McDonald; he charged McDonald with taking direction from the United Nations, since he also functioned as the chairman of the United Nations Truce Commission and had a role requiring correspondence with Arab states. Celler declared:

> I shall make it my studied purpose to keep him out of Israel and the Near and Middle East if not out of service.[190]

As one of the original proponents of the Foreign Agents Registration Act, Celler was an invaluable ally to the Zionist cause, Israel, and Isaiah Kenen. Celler is famously quoted as stating that the intention of the FARA was to be a "pitiless spotlight of publicity,"[191] but he never pressured his own army of Israel lobby supporters to register and subject themselves to that spotlight. Celler's double standard included issuing humorless, offhand death threats to effective dissidents, as Rabbi Elmer Berger and Lessing Rosenwald experienced during a 1944 House Committee on Foreign Affairs session. Berger noted years later:

> By 1944 we anti-Zionists were a vocal presence at most of the forums where the political future of Palestine were discussed. We testified at "Hearings" held by the House Committee on Foreign Affairs. The "Hearings" were inspired by a Zionist resolution requesting American support for an effort to ease immigration restrictions imposed by the 1939 British White Paper. We supported the appeal on purely humanitarian grounds, but argued vigorously against the Zionist addendum urging endorsement of a "Jewish Commonwealth" which was

the real purpose of the Joint Resolution for which the "hearings" were held. It was a stormy session. The House Committee was fairly evenly divided and the Zionist witnesses were as nervous as the proverbial cats. After our witness had finished their testimony and Mr. Rosenwald and I were standing at the elevator in the House Office building waiting to leave, Emanuel Celler, a Congressman from New York and a committed Zionist, came by. "They ought to take you bastards out and shoot you," he said.[192]

But despite Celler's and his own best intentions, Kenen's move from employee of the Israeli government to stealth lobbyist did not go entirely unnoticed by the U.S. State Department. The Israel trip was a legal exposure he needed to quickly paper over at the FARA section. After returning from Israel, Kenen also came under growing scrutiny and challenges from FARA's former enforcement agency. He noted:

> Now, however we heard that the State Department was busily comparing my critical 1953 memoranda with those circulated by the Israeli Embassy.
>
> "Shouldn't Kenen register as an agent of a foreign government?" a desk officer indignantly demanded of an Israeli journalist, Eliahu Salpeter of *Haaretz*, who called me to sound the alarm.[193]

Kenen would enjoy many similar tidbits of timely inside intelligence and warnings from foreign and U.S. sources when threats to his lobbying initiatives gathered. But the U.S. State Department, no longer in charge of enforcement, could do very little. Even in the face of such alarms, Kenen's American Zionist Council lobbying was beginning to pay huge dividends: on February 27, 1952, the U.S. agreed to sell weapons to Israel, partly as a result of Kenen's ongoing Capitol Hill lobbying for arms that began while he was still on the payroll of the Israeli government's Information Office.

However, Kenen's slipping the restraints of FARA oversight did not prevent Eisenhower administration officials from detecting the pressures emanating from his growing stealth grassroots lobby. The Department of Justice Internal Security Division began compiling a file on American Zionist Council activities and financial operations. The Eisenhower administration then privately threatened to crack down, leading to a crisis at the American Zionist Council, as chronicled by Kenen:

> Then, late in December 1953, a Republican member of our Executive Committee, who worked in Washington, told our Committee that I might be a target…[194]

Beyond the issue of failing to file a FARA registration, a glaring violation was that the American Zionist Council operated within a category of nonprofit corporations that was "subject to strict limitations on the amount of time its employees were permitted to lobby members of Congress."[195] Devoting most of its time and resources to lobbying with tax-exempt funds was unlawful, then as it is now. The Eisenhower administration attention also threatened exposure of the American Zionist Council's undisclosed activities as its grassroots lobbying pressures began challenging the administration's regional strategic and peace initiatives. Kenen reflected upon the American Zionist Council's resolution to its tax-exemption problems:

> Our acrimonious clashes with the Eisenhower-Dulles regime over arms and water led to rumors that the American Zionist Council faced investigation. The rumors were ill-founded but they were persistent and could not be ignored. We reorganized and established a lobbying committee—the forerunner of the American Israel Public Affairs Committee (AIPAC).
>
> Between 1951 and 1953, I had been the Washington representative of the AZC, a tax-exempt organization. A government agency had ruled that only an insubstantial portion of AZC funds had been used for lobbying.[196]

Kenen and the administration quietly came to an agreement that the American Zionist Council would no longer lobby with tax-exempt funds.[s] Kenen then incorporated yet another Israel lobbying front group. It had all of the same donors and officers, but now operated under the pretext that because no further tax-deductible contributions were to be used for lobbying, it was a legitimate operation in spite of FARA.

> Nevertheless, because of the possibility that we might be subject to attack, we organized a new and separate lobbying committee in 1954,

---

[s] Many years later, another complaint would be filed against AIPAC with the Federal Elections Commission (FEC), alleging that AIPAC was illegally coordinating political action committees and functioning as a PAC in violation of its nonprofit status. The FEC found that this was "not the major purpose" of AIPAC, triggering an appeal against the FEC to Federal District Court in 1992.

independent of AZC control and financing and thus impervious to challenge. It was named the American Zionist Committee for Public Affairs (AZCPA). There was no change in leadership or membership, but we stopped receiving tax-exempt funds from the AZC. Instead, we solicited contributions which would not be deductible from income tax.[197]

The overriding issue of FARA registration, the AZC's true foreign principal, using Israeli funds transferred from the Jewish Agency into the United States was thus successfully delayed for an entire decade. Not until the early 1960s would the Senate begin to investigate whether U.S. aid sent overseas and other funds were being secretly laundered back into the U.S. to obtain political influence and additional foreign aid; in 1963, a close examination of Isaiah Kenen's financing revealed that entirely foreign funds were creating an "American lobby." This investigation was prompted by a crescendo of calls for enforcement made to the Department of Justice by the American Council for Judaism.

American Council for Judaism Dissents

The American Zionist Council faced highly vocal internal opposition in attempting to unite disparate Jewish-relief-oriented groups into a more unified and dependable bloc lobbying for Israel-oriented legislation. This even led founder Louis Lipsky to threaten to resign, as it was "impossible to cope with the confusions of functions and authority that prevail in the Zionist movement in the United States." He cited lack of coordination among constituent organizations of the AZC, which took stands on issues affecting the Zionist cause without consulting the other council members or giving them an opportunity to weigh initiatives in relation to the Zionist program as a whole.[198]

One of the most powerful opposition voices continued to be Rabbi Elmer Berger, executive vice president of the American Council for Judaism, who feared that the work of Kenen and others would "envelop American Jews in political blocs." In particular, Berger was worried that the "nationalist character" of the Zionist movement around the cause of Israel would break with the "universal, ethical and moral principles" of Judaism. Berger also felt that militant Zionism would reverse the integration of Jews into society and rekindle self-segregation.

> It is precisely enjoyment of liberty and the successful integration of Jewish communities that pose today's central problem of the Jewish people.[199]

Berger felt that these were painful but necessary questions that needed to be openly debated even after the creation of Israel.

> [That] we persist in raising these questions and suggesting answers—as does the Zionist mechanism—does not mean we are opposed to Israel, even if we are opposed to many answers to these unresolved questions offered by the Israel-Zionist mechanism.[200]

This threat to the enormous public relations value of the concept that Kenen and other Israel lobby groups somehow "represented American Jews" had been around since before statehood. In 1945, Lessing J. Rosenwald sternly dismissed as "propaganda" the idea that in spite of public mobilizations, "all Jews were united in support of the Zionist plan to establish Jews as a nation and to make Palestine a Jewish commonwealth." The press covered it fully, and for Kenen, excruciatingly:

> This is simply not true...No one possesses the authority or the right to speak in the name of all Americans of Jewish faith...In behalf of the American Council for Judaism, an organization of Americans of Jewish faith [who] oppose Jewish nationalism, refuse to participate in a political organization of Jews, and oppose the creation of a Jewish state, we call attention to the divergence of opinions among Jews on this subject. We draw public attention to our program which seeks to maintain the only identity of Jews as individual adherents of a Jewish religion. We seek one thing only for Jews: a status of equality of rights and obligations throughout the world.[201]

On the subject of the status of Palestine, in 1945 the American Council for Judaism urged aid without discrimination or privileged status conferred on any.

> We favor the earliest possible acquisition of self-government in Palestine in which all, Moslems, Christians and Jews, fulfilling the requirements of citizenship shall participate equally.
>
> We deem it particularly important to draw attention to the fact that an overwhelming body of American Jews hold this view by virtue of their principles as Americans of Jewish faith. We reject all those self-appointed spokesmen who presume to make their partisan claims in the name of all Americans of the Jewish faith.[202]

Clearly, as leading spokesmen and advocates for the newly created state, Kenen and Zionist movement leaders had to deal with the American Council for Judaism. But the American Zionist Council could never credibly unleash their most potent weapon—insinuating that opposition leaders were "anti-Semitic"—against the American Council for Judaism. Indeed, the ACJ even turned the table by calling out groups and surrogates of the American Zionist Council who smeared legitimate American opponents with that label. Rabbi Elmer Berger explored the lobby's smear tactic targeting U.S. and UK government institutions charged with foreign policy in a lengthy 1953 speech:

> The logic of the Zionist-Israeli contention that the national interests of Zionism and Israel, on the one hand, and of the United States, on the other hand, are inseparable and the same, is wearing thin; increasing numbers of Americans wonder about the 40,000,000 people in the area.
>
> The Zionist Israeli axis is attempting to isolate the Department of State from the Eisenhower Administration and the American people as the Zionist campaign in England, for a decade, attempted to isolate the British Foreign Office.
>
> American Foreign Service officers and other Americans who know there are more states in the Middle East than Israel...[203]

Berger contended that these State Department officials had been labeled as anti-Semites by Zionists. He also went on to reject the notion that such views could not be expressed in public:

> We have rejected not only the theory but the practice of medievalism which regards Jews as some kind of an exclusive fraternity, with family linen on public issues which should not be washed in public. This kind of fantastic, medieval logic can serve only—as it has—to support the medieval suspicion that Jews are precisely such a fraternity.[204]

Berger also lamented the transformation of Jewish relief organizations that fought to prevent "infraction of the civil and religious rights of Jews, in any part of the world" into Zionist "apologists for, and defenders of, the national aspirations of the State of Israel."[205]

In his signature lobbying bulletin, the *Near East Report,* Kenen would labor mightily to minimize the ACJ as a mere fringe group. But Kenen's minimization of his opponent's power was soon debunked by events. The

American Zionist Council's corporate entity would be destroyed by the American Council for Judaism when Berger and others took their case directly to the Department of Justice to force the American Zionist Council to register as an agent of a foreign power in the early 1960s.

NEAR EAST REPORT A Washington Letter on American Policy in the Near East—*Cover Logo 1957*

Chapter 7: Near East Report

Isaiah Kenen owned and edited the *Near East Report*, a professional lobbying bulletin published in Washington, DC beginning in 1957. Between June 1957 and May 1959, Kenen churned out 48 issues. The positioning and mandate of the newsletter appeared in a print issue shortly after it commenced publication. Tellingly, Kenen's public relations framework was now so highly developed and subtle that it made no mention at all of its core concern, the State of Israel:

> In the last decade, the Near East has attained international significance in contemporary history. Always a center of religion, culture and philosophy, the Near East is now of primary concern in our "cold war" world. Events shaping the destiny of this crucial region are playing a decisive part in the arena of world politics—and propaganda in both a new mouthpiece to rewrite the past and a deadly weapon to determine the future.
>
> Two years ago, the *Near East Report* was established as a Washington newsletter reporting and interpreting American foreign policy in the Near East. Our purpose, then and now: to sift out the propaganda and to clarify the facts. Our policy: to provide a lucid analysis of developments as they occur. Our aim: to contribute to a positive, constructive policy which will enlarge and strengthen the circle of American friendship in the Near East.[206]

The *Near East Report* was absolutely vital to Kenen's lobbying efforts, counting votes and spurring U.S. military sales and aid to Israel. As in his abortive attempt at writing a book, Kenen kept a tight binary tally of what he categorized as "anti-Israel" votes in Congress and the UN. His expanded serialized criticism of members of Congress who attempted to craft more broadly representative Middle East policy was phrased in a lofty and disembodied third person-plural voice. The prose was geared to instill a sense of an observant, omnipotent, and unified Israel lobby. Kenen also threw out hunks of red meat to drum up opposition phone calls, letters, and impassioned responses in key congressional districts. Early on Kenen went after Senator J. W. Fulbright, printing articles bearing lofty titles such as "We Differ with Fulbright" that chastised the senator for reaching out to Arab countries. Kenen also reprinted letters from activists and allies that appeared in leading regional and national newspapers.

The *Near East Report* also published many timely and detailed media monitoring reports from the Arab press and radio broadcasts, which appeared in the Comments section. Kenen seemed to be instantly privy to expansive in-region foreign press monitoring, though no information about sources and collections methods appeared in the *Near East Report*.[†]

Somewhat ironically, an early mainstay section of the *Near East Report* was the "Propaganda Pressure" corner, which called out and rebuked individuals and entities Kenen considered "enemies of Israel." The *Near East Report* constantly spun down the impact of the American Council for Judaism whenever Kenen felt it had attracted undue attention:

> A discordant note was sounded by the American Council for Judaism, a fringe organization created in 1943 by the dwindling hard core of anti-Zionists to oppose the creation of Israel because they were against the concept of a Jewish state. Despite the fact that it represents only a tiny fraction of American Jewry, the Council does not hesitate to appear at political conventions in an effort to juxtapose itself with a majority in the minds of the American people.[207]

[†] Since 1998, a nonprofit organization called the Middle East Media Research Institute, founded by a former colonel of Israeli Intelligence and two other intelligence officers, has provided free translated content from Arabic and Farsi sources in the Middle East. With a pipeline to many American journalists and media personalities including content prominently featured on Fox News, MEMRI's success has supplanted the fledgling media monitoring found in Isaiah Kenen's newsletter. One critic states, "MEMRI's intent is to find the worst possible quotes from the Muslim world and disseminate them as widely as possible." Scholar Juan Cole hypothesized that MEMRI is fed, and thus subsidized, by Israeli intelligence service press monitors.

Analysis and excerpted statements from Senator J. W. Fulbright appeared under such blaring headlines as "Fulbright Attacks." Kenen must have seen Fulbright as attempting to expose and pull up the tender roots of his growing Israel public relations network in the U.S. In mid-May of 1960, Fulbright conducted a sweeping five-day tour of the Middle East. In his June edition of the *Near East Report*, Kenen printed an excerpt of Fulbright's pre-trip announcement in which the senator seemed to strike back at the very heart of the Israel lobby's U.S. public relations campaign.

> I have a feeling that we don't appreciate the Arab point of view. I think our press generally presents it in a way that makes it appear that he is just being arbitrary.[208]

In the early 1960s, the *Near East Report* began to dabble in cartoons and more sophisticated graphics, which generally portrayed Arabs as heavily armed, violent, and incapable of crossing the bridge of modernity. The cartoons became more vicious and stereotypical as time went by (see additional cartoons and analysis in the Appendices).

Figure 4 NER cartoon stereotyping Arabs as hypocrites and terrorists.

One inalterable position of the *Near East Report* was that there should be no "right of return" or reparations payments for Palestinian refugees expelled during the formation of the state. Kenen would often highlight and diametrically oppose Fulbright's argument that the Palestinian refugee issue was at the heart of Arab-Israeli hostility.

> While in Israel, Sen. Fulbright said that the refugee problem was at the root of Arab-Israel hostility. Although he conceded that the constructive solution was resettlement in underdeveloped areas of the Arab countries, he believed that Israel should accept more than a symbolic number. Mr. Ben-Gurion wants the refugee issue considered in Arab-Israel peace talks.[209]

Kenen's own voice on the refugee issue, disembodied and expressed in an omniscient third person-plural "we," countered such analysis. His counterpoints and talking points on Palestinian refugees emphasized the Israeli position as being the only "sensible" and clearly "mainstream" choice for Americans:

> There is growing recognition of the fact that the Arab refugee problem is not the cause of the Arab-Israel war. It is a result of that war and cannot be solved unless and until the war is abandoned.[210]

Fulbright often seemed to be the sole congressional opponent to the new phenomenon of Israel-centric legislative restrictions attached to regional aid programs and unrelated bills. He publicly criticized this tactic of the Israel lobby. Much later Fulbright gradually won over even President John F. Kennedy, an extremely dangerous development for the lobby. The unmovable position probably infuriated Kenen, who printed many Fulbright quotes like the following in the *Near East Report* to mobilize his base:

> I cannot help but believe that a marked improvement in our relations with the Middle East would result from some changes in attitude. A greater recognition of the dignity of newly independent nations and a small dose of humility would be deeply appreciated by most new nations....I am sure, the peoples of the Middle East would appreciate less preoccupation on our part with assertions of our own righteousness and fewer self-judging conditions tied to our aid.[211]

The *Near East Report* attempted to lionize and reward faithful supporters whenever it could. Senator Javit's pithy quotes were sprinkled liberally across many editions. In a section called "File for the Record," Kenen profiled then up-and-coming Senator John F. Kennedy's "correct" views about the need for Arab acquiescence to Israel and its demands on the Palestinian refugee issue. Senator Kennedy called for the new approach in the Middle East in a speech to the Senate on June 14, 1960:

> We must formulate, with both imagination and restraint, a new approach to the Middle East—not pressing our case so hard that the Arabs feel their neutrality and nationalism are threatened, but accepting those forces and seeking to help channel them along constructive lines, while at the same time trying to hasten the inevitable Arab acceptance of the permanence of Israel.[212]

But Kenen was not simply a distant and bombastic Washington political observer promoting Israel and chastising politicians from behind the drapery of a newsletter. Following Herzl's mandate to get "behind our banner and fight for our cause with voice and pen and deed," he also helped draft planks for both major political parties.

Israel's Plank

Kenen traveled to Los Angeles on July 15, 1960 to participate in the formulation of the "Near East" plank at the Democratic Convention, which he reprinted in full in the *Near East Report*:

> In the Middle East we will work for guarantees to ensure independence for all states. We will encourage direct Arab-Israel peace negotiations; the resettlement of Arab refugees in lands where there is room and opportunity for them; an end to boycotts and blockades; the unrestricted use of the Suez Canal by all nations.
>
> We urge continued economic assistance to Israel and the Arab peoples to help them raise their living standards. We pledge our best efforts for peace in the Middle East by seeking to prevent an arms race while guarding against the dangers of a military imbalance resulting from Soviet arms shipments.[213]

For Kenen the propaganda value of highlighting his personal involvement in both Democratic and Republican Party politics was irresistible. He momentarily broke from his usual background role dictated by his tight public relations standards. Kenen provided rare "meta level" analysis of the national and international impact of his participation in the plank formulation to *Near East Report* readers:

> The importance of platforms. Many people are skeptical about political platforms. But skepticism is unjustified. Platform declarations have a positive value in the clarification and implementation of our national policies. They help to mold public opinion at home because they inform and guide candidates, who stand for election on their party's program. They have importance abroad because they transmit to other governments the views of the American people. Sometimes our foreign policy is expressed more forcibly and plainly in a platform than when masked in the language of diplomacy.[214]

In this way, the *Near East Report* also served as a paper-based lobbying mini-seminar to educate and energize donors and activists in each congressional district. Kenen's teachings would multiply as the lobby later began grooming candidates, executing opposition research and smear campaigns, and establishing an archipelago of coordinated stealth political action committees to tip key races. The critical early role of Israeli money in Kenen's publishing venture never made it into the *Near East Report*'s masthead.

Lavon Affair Crisis

As Kenen churned out the newsletter, Kremlinologists in U.S. intelligence agencies were trying to interpret the complex inner workings of Soviet power politics during the Cold War by "reading between the lines." They observed body language and the location of various leaders at Soviet events in Red Square filling in troublesome gaps in hard human and electronic intelligence. Kenen's strange February 1, 1961 *Near East Report* article about the "Lavon Affair" is a contorted masterpiece of misdirection and obfuscation. It is close to being unintelligible without insider information. His article attempted to tell his readership how to react to what outsiders would have seen as merely a distant internal power struggle in the Israeli government.

> The clash between Prime Minister David Ben-Gurion and Pinhas Lavon, secretary-general of Histadruth, Israel's powerful trade union federation, whipped up Israel's gravest political crisis and culminated in Mr. Ben-Gurion's resignation on Jan. 31....
>
> The conflict came to a climax after a "security mishap." The Israel government has never disclosed the precise nature of the incident which forced Mr. Lavon to retire under a cloud in February 1955. At that time—and ever since—Mr. Lavon denied responsibility for the affair, but in the

ensuing inquiry his subordinates in the defense department claimed that the operation was in accord with his instructions...

Censorship, however, creates vacuums which are swiftly filled—and contaminated—by propaganda. Egyptian propagandists identified the 1954 mishap as the 1955 Gaza raid. In 1955, the Israeli army attacked Egyptian military installations at Gaza in reprisal for fedayeen raids. Egyptians always claim that Nasser was forced to ask the Soviet bloc for arms because of their defeat at Gaza. And so they circulated press reports that the Lavon affair was responsible for Nasser's attachment to Moscow. But this propaganda is confounded by the calendar. The Gaza raid took place on Feb. 28—long after the Lavon resignation.

But the 1954 incident, itself, is of little significance today. The Lavon affair of 1954 is far overshadowed by the Lavon affair of 1960. What is important is that Israel's democratic system is now facing its most critical challenge.[215]

What was Kenen tiptoeing around with such care? A scandal that very indirectly tied the Jewish Agency Executive to an Israeli terrorist attack on the United States. In the summer of 1954, Israel conducted a covert false flag operation in Egypt, code-named "Operation Susannah." Israeli agents launched terrorist bombing attacks against U.S.-, British-, and Egyptian-owned targets in Egypt. U.S. Information Service libraries in Alexandria and Cairo were targeted.

Since 1950, it had been U.S. policy to pressure the British to withdraw from the Suez Canal and abandon two treaties: the Anglo-Egyptian Treaty of 1936, which made the canal a neutral zone under British control, and the Convention of Constantinople. Israel feared that a British withdrawal would remove an important check on Egyptian president Gamal Abdel Nasser's military ambitions. After Israel's diplomatic efforts failed to convince the British to stay, Israel unleashed the false flag terrorist operation designed to convince the British that it was too dangerous to leave while framing the Egyptians.

Israel recruited and the IDF trained a group of young Egyptian-born Jews to carry out the terror operations in Cairo and Alexandria. While exactly who ordered the operation and other details remain to this day a closely guarded secret in Israel, it is known that members of the terror cell were apprehended by Egypt in 1954. In December of the same year, they were put on trial. Operatives Max Binet and Yosef Carmon avoided revealing operational details by committing suicide.

Kenen wrote about the scandal caused by the arrest of the group using its Israeli reference, *essek bish* (the mishap). The scant reporting on the "mishap" that appeared in the Western press referred to it as the "Lavon Affair," after defense minister Pinhas Lavon. Lavon strenuously denied that he had ordered the terror operation. As Kenen noted, Lavon was forced to resign his post over the matter in January 1955.[216]

The incident caused a break between Ben-Gurion and Levi Eshkol (1895-1969) in 1961 over Ben-Gurion's insistence on fully investigating and learning lessons from the sordid incident. Up-and-coming political rival Levi Eshkol was insistent that investigating the affair was a waste of time, and he wished to bury it as soon as possible. On December 13, 1964, he addressed the issue before the Mapai Central Committee:

> If I vote in favor of an inquiry into the Lavon Affair...We would be opening a Pandora's box of troubles. It will not end with this affair or with this investigation. We'll be spending the next fifteen years dealing with investigations into various unsolved matters.[217]

The matter was of more than passing historical interest to Kenen. Before becoming Prime Minister of Israel in June of 1963 and engineering the Lavon cover-up, Eshkol[u] sat on the board of the Jewish Agency. Eshkol and other Israelis approved the disbursal of millions in funding from that agency, some laundered through the American Zionist Council secretly subsidized Kenen's public relations efforts, lobbying, and publication of the *Near East Report*. Eshkol clearly felt that Jabotinsky and the Operation Susannah terrorists were quintessential Israeli heroes. This view was later quietly supported by the Israeli military. The surviving members of the terror cell received acknowledgement and military honors in Israel in 2005, as noted by the *Jerusalem Post*:

> Marcelle Ninio, Robert Dassa and Meir Zafran were accorded military ranks Wednesday in recognition of their service to the state and their years of suffering. The three are the last surviving members of Operation Susannah, an Israeli spy and sabotage network.[218]

Kenen, who delighted in publishing cartoons depicting Arabs as the region's only terrorist bomb-throwers, could never portray his foreign principal in the same way when writing about the Lavon affair or Israel's

---

[u] Levi Eshkol also fulfilled Vladimir Jabotinsky's wish that his body be brought to Israel for burial.

creation. By November of 1961, he had downgraded the Lavon Affair to merely an "espionage debacle" in the *Near East Report:*

> Another Explosion. Premier Ben-Gurion may resign in a new political upheaval which has split the dominant Mapai party. He is protesting a cabinet decision which clears his political antagonist, Pinchas Lavon, secretary general of Histadruth, of any responsibility for an espionage debacle in Egypt in 1954. The investigation showed that a senior military officer had falsely accused Lavon of ordering the operation which led to Lavon's resignation as Minister of Defense.[219]

Kenen's and the Jewish Agency's survival of the Lavon Affair required a degree of incuriosity from Congress. Senate investigators briefly compelled verbal testimony from Jewish Agency executives that revealed Eshkol's key position on the Jewish Agency board which was directly funding Kenen's newsletter in the U.S. during 1963 testimony. But they did not (and probably could not) establish Eshkol's link to covering up the bombing of U.S. government property in Egypt, for lack of relevant public and classified U.S. intelligence information. There were also no "Kremlinologists" capable of interpreting Kenen's or any other obtuse press accounts and circumlocutions surrounding the cover-up in the U.S.

Compliments of I. L. Kenen

Copies of the *Near East Report* reached the desks of U.S. media, society, and political elites, often accompanied by a heavy linen bond presentation card reading, "With the Compliments of I. L. Kenen."

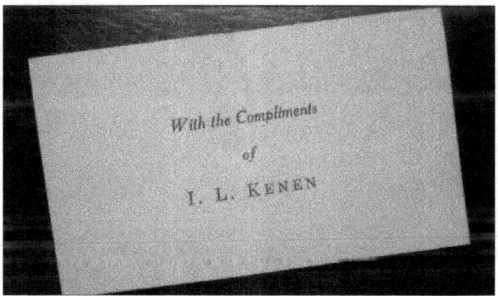

Figure 5 I. L. Kenen presentation card.

In reality, the Israeli-government-funded Jewish Agency was partially footing the bill. Between June 29, 1960 and October 13, 1961, Kenen received $38,000, usually in $5,000 increments, from the Jewish Agency, laundered through the American Zionist Council, to publish the *Near East Report*.[220] The Jewish Agency–American Section in New York filed highly deceptive registration statements with FARA, first omitting the transfers, then disclosing only "lump sum" disbursements to the American Zionist Council, which it called "subventions"[v] for "education". These purposefully vague, non-itemized disbursement declarations were in keeping with Ben-Gurion's intent to amplify the domestic role of the American Zionist Council. As a nonprofit corporation, it did not have to disclose the ultimate destination of funds transferred on to academics, lobbyists, and think tanks. These payments not only allowed Kenen to finance his own startup activities at AIPAC, but also paid for free *Near East Report* subscriptions for every member of Congress, large donors, editors, and allies in the private sector news and information services. Although the term "money laundering" was not used at the time, it is a highly accurate description of how this financial flow thwarted FARA.[w]

Fulbright's investigation created an unassailable public record of the fact that Kenen never formally severed ties to the Israeli government and related foreign principals as he had represented in his FARA correspondence. Yet both Kenen and his supporters would continue to attempt to drown out facts surrounding the critical Jewish Agency startup funding. They played up the supposedly "cleansing" and legitimizing effect of non-tax-deductible funds he later raised in the U.S. as an AIPAC lobbyist, never discussing his critical foreign subsidy. Kenen's defenders at the Fulbright hearings maintained that shell corporation transfers shielded him from foreign agent status. To Kenen, claiming autonomous non-tax-deductible domestic funding, as scarce as it was, was the whole key to stealth. He tried to make this clear to his colleagues, who did not understand why he was even bothering to present himself as somehow severed from the foreign payroll or anything but a foreign agent.

---

[v] A subvention is a grant of money, as by a government or some other authority, in aid or support of some institution or undertaking.

[w] The Financial Action Task Force, a Paris-based multinational group formed in 1989 by the Group of Seven industrialized nations to foster international action against money laundering, agreed to a "working definition" of money laundering that includes legitimate proceeds used with the intent to promote unlawful activity. In this case, tax-exempt charitable donations made by a foreign entity were surreptitiously moved into the US financial system to fund lobbying on behalf of Israel in a way designed to avoid FARA disclosures. All of this came out, painfully and abruptly, in J. W. Fulbright's historic 1963 hearings.

Many could not understand why the Israeli government could not subsidize this modest undertaking; they did not realize that foreign agents were limited in expression and activity.[221]

However, from a strictly cash-flow standpoint, Kenen's early lobbying fundraising was a disaster that would not have survived if he had not tapped his Israeli-subsidized cash flow to the *Near East Report* and even his own funds to meet budgetary gaps. Fortunately, once again, the crisis of war, ever an economic opportunity, came to the rescue in 1967.

> We were always in the red, and I often had to wait a long time for my modest $13,000 a year salary. I frequently had to lend money to the Committee, and I had to dispense with a capable assistant. The budget was not lifted until the Six-Day War.[222]

The United Jewish Appeal would collect more than $100 million in funds based on threats of imminent destruction from a mighty, Soviet-backed Arab army poised to push Israel into the sea.[223] The "Israel in Crisis" fundraising appeal became a mainstay theme after Israel's victory. Not until January 12, 2004 did the U.S. State Department's Office of the Historian declassify internal Johnson administration deliberations and diplomatic cables that debunked many myths about the Six-Day War. These revealed the administration's own assessment that appeals for arms and aid were based on deliberately inflated Israeli intelligence estimates. Johnson's advisors quietly sought to restrain Israel long enough for a visit by the Egyptian diplomatic representative to wind down the confrontation. News of this shuttle diplomacy leaked to the Israelis, who promptly launched surprise attacks on June 5, 1967.

> On June 4, 1967, Secretary Dean Rusk, Secretary of Defense Robert McNamara, National Security Council Special Representative Walt Rostow, and Ambassador Thompson began preparations for the visit of Egyptian Vice President Mohieddin and discussed ways to "hold the Israeli 'tiger'". The Secretary of State informed the Israeli ambassador of Mohieddin's visit.[224]

Kenen went to great lengths to publicly highlight a number of policy differences he allegedly had with the Israeli government as a badge of independence that AIPAC was a domestic entity lobbying for "American interests." But in spite of the Six-Day War crisis and the massive fundraising opportunity it generated, he was candid about his tight coordination with the Israeli embassy on the key issues of arms and aid to

Israel. The Israeli embassy, in turn, was more truthful to Kenen than to the U.S. President, as it pumped the administration for arms.

> I was opposed to a major public campaign for arms because I had been led to believe by the embassy that it would not be necessary.[225]

Kenen's *Near East Report* and burgeoning ranks of allies in the U.S. press supplanted the need for the Israel Office of Information's policy-oriented propaganda bulletins. In turn, the *Near East Report* served as an advocacy training program for others who went on to achieve high-profile mainstream mass media careers entirely independent of Israeli funding. Wolf Blitzer was an editor of the *Near East Report* in the mid-1970s. While at the newsletter he followed Kenen's adversarial style with Fulbright and launched attacks on Capitol Hill opponents. Senator James Abourezk felt Blitzer was extremely one-sided.[226] Blitzer has since moved on to serve as the anchor of *CNN's Situation Room.*

The *Near East Report* was eventually transferred from Kenen's private ownership to an affiliated AIPAC nonprofit shell corporation called Near East Research, housed in the same building as AIPAC's Washington DC headquarters. The Kenen legacy of harsh cartoons of Arabs as puppeteers, violent thugs, and subhuman stunted by inherent psychosis continued after his departure. (see cartoon analysis in the Appendix) Although the newsletter's recent nonprofit annual reports claim that it is now funded through tax-deductible contributions, it is still not clear precisely how or when Jewish Agency funding ceased.

And the device of merely using the American Zionist Council seems to me to be a very thin way of insulating him [Isaiah L. Kenen] from the effects of the Foreign Registration Act. —*Senator J. W. Fulbright, 8/1/1963*

Chapter 8: Senate Investigation

In 1963 the Senate Foreign Relations Committee conducted lengthy hearings on the activities of agents of foreign principals in the United States.[x] Two days of testimony in May and August publicly revealed the massive money laundering operation that had only briefly been investigated a decade before by the Eisenhower administration.

On May 23, 1963, the committee heard testimony and reviewed subpoenaed internal American Zionist Council activity reports and vouchers of payments made to Kenen. Senator Fulbright wondered aloud why Kenen was not registered as a foreign agent with the Department of Justice. Fulbright would receive few satisfactory answers to that question during the hearings. A transcript of sworn testimony details Senator Fulbright grilling two representatives of the Israeli entity responsible for channeling overseas funds to Kenen. Maurice Boukstein and Isadore Hamlin of the Jewish Agency grudgingly revealed to Fulbright how hidden "subscription" payments for Kenen's *Near East Report* subsidized his lobbying activities well into the early 1960s. Later, in his memoirs, Kenen would insinuate that Senator Fulbright was a product of such rural isolation he was susceptible to anti-Semitism:

> While a strong majority of Congress supported us, one man conspicuously led the opposition. He was Senator J. W. Fulbright, an Arkansas Democrat. There were few Jews in that state, most of them—

---

[x] Portions of this chapter are from the book *Foreign Agents: The American Israel Public Affairs Committee from the 1963 Fulbright Hearings to the 2005 Espionage Scandal.*

a handful—in Little Rock, and he had little opportunity to learn about Jews and their interest in Israel. Understandably, he was susceptible to the anti-Semitic doctrine that Jews were guilty of dual allegiance.[227]

Kenen's Jewish-Agency-financed attacks on Fulbright had reached a crescendo in his *Near East Report* by the early 1960s. Given the buildup, it is a mystery that Kenen was completely unprepared for an investigation into the financing of his activities.

Kenen's Flight to Iran

When Kenen caught wind of Fulbright's pending investigation in 1961, he promptly fled the country for a safe haven, as he detailed in *All My Causes*:

> In 1961, it was rumored that Fulbright intended to investigate foreign agents. I was subjected to a barrage of inquiries from friends and foes wherever I went, and while I was confident that I would survive the attack I decided to vanish from the scene. Coincidentally, I was invited that year to visit Iran as a guest of the Iranian government. I accepted the invitation and from there I flew on to Africa to learn more about the people of that continent. I was happy to find most African countries friendly to Israel and I was more relaxed in Africa than in Mr. Fulbright's Washington.[228]

Kenen had two valid reasons for worry. First, the Department of Justice was privy to the Senate investigation and about to go on record that it was dead serious about allegations that the American Zionist Council was operating as an unregistered foreign agent. It issued a blunt public statement in March of 1963 before the Senate hearings began:

> The American Zionist Council's relationship with the American section of the Jewish Agency for Israel has raised the question of whether the council has an obligation to register under the Foreign Agents Registration Act.[229]

Second, Kenen could not successfully counter the formal investigation by the Department of Justice and Senate as a "pogrom" instigated by "anti-Semites." Once again it was the American Council for Judaism leading the charge against the American Zionist Council. Fed up, the ACJ had taken its case directly to the Department of Justice, as noted in the *New York Times*:

The Justice Department said today it was studying whether the American Zionist Council should be required to register as a foreign agency.

The acknowledgement, in response to reporters' queries, was the first statement of the department on differences between the Zionist group and the American Council for Judaism.

The Council for Judaism has publicly urged that the Zionist Council be required to register as a foreign agency that promotes immigration to and advances the political policies of Israel.[230]

The American Council for Judaism's public demands provided added impetus and a bit of political cover for the deep and probing Senate investigation that followed. The group's objections about how tax-exempt funds raised in the United States were being used to finance politics in Israel as well as the U.S. stemmed from a quiet power struggle. The unprecedented disclosure of how United Jewish Appeal and international funds were actually being used in America was a rumbling aftershock to the earth-shifting Zionist takeover of Jewish relief fundraising in the United States.

Jewish Relief Fundraising Coup

Between 1921 and 1930, Zionist organizations active in the United States collected approximately $15 million in contributions from the public. Between 1931 and 1940, this amount only rose to $25 million, but in the period from 1941 to 1948, the amount suddenly ballooned to $287 million. The replacement of general philanthropic, humanitarian, and relief-oriented leaders at the largest fundraising organizations with dedicated Zionists was premeditated and caused a wholesale redirection of these private tax-deductible financial flows.[231]

The United Jewish Appeal was established in 1939. IRS treatment of UJA funds as tax-deductible contributions has been uninterrupted since then, though it was briefly threatened by the Eisenhower administration and placed in jeopardy by the non-exempt activities of groups such as the American Zionist Council. The war for control and direction of the funds raised by the United Jewish Appeal and related organizations led to a series of ugly battles between Zionist and non-Zionist stakeholders, as chronicled by Rabbi Elmer Berger:

> Some years earlier, Rosenwald and Rabbi Morris Lazaron had fought against merging the United Palestine Appeal (the central Zionist fund

raising effort in the United States) with the American Jewish Joint Distribution Committee. The "joint" was dominated by "non-Zionists." Its beneficiaries ran to practically every country where there were Jews in need. In an over-simplified formulation its philosophy was to provide assistance to Jews in countries in which they lived, hoping to facilitate their eventual integration into those societies. The United Palestine Appeal restricted its beneficiaries to Palestine and Zionist propaganda designed to condition contributors to support building "the national home."

Of the two major funds, the JDC had consistently enlisted the greater support—proof again that on its own, Zionism had no firm hold on the grass-roots of American Jews. Never at a loss for maneuver—or dissembling—however, the Zionist managers persuaded the "big givers" that a "united campaign" would be more efficient than the competing, double campaigns. Ideology was deliberately subordinated to "expediency" and, after a long series of negotiations and several "trial marriages" and separations, the Zionists succeeded again in forcing the "philanthropists" to confront the issue of a joint campaign. Rosenwald and Lazaron were leaders of the opposition and the battle established a kind of friendship. But they lost and the United Jewish Appeal was established.[232]

Candidly and much later, Kenen was very succinct about the need to establish umbrella organizations that would consolidate power and ongoing fundraising resources into the hands of a few relatively nontransparent elites who could maintain cohesion through urgent issue advocacy and appeals to the funding base:

American Jews have a multiplicity of organizations serving diverse religious, philanthropic, cultural, and educational views and needs, but they have never created one permanent national Jewish organization to express the views of the totality. The American Jewish Conference came the closest. It was conceived in 1942, and its liquidation, in 1948, came after it helped to win its major objective—the restoration of a Jewish state. It died in success—perhaps because of it.[233]

Between 1951 and 1960, approximately $18 million of United Jewish Appeal money raised in the United States was transferred to the Jewish Agency in Israel and then on to Israeli political parties. In 1954, American Zionist groups affiliated with Israeli political parties were the dominant means for participating in the movement, though none registered as foreign agents.

Zionist Groups are now quasi political bodies affiliated more or less with the political parties in Israel. A Zionist sympathizer can become a member of the World Movement only by joining one of these constituent groups.²³⁴

The $2 million per year allocation (2 percent of the agency's $100 million budget) kept political parties from directly conducting unsightly political fundraising campaigns within the United States.²³⁵ However, FARA statutes in force at the time (see Appendices) strictly defined and applied to even these hidden aggregate connections to foreign political parties without proper disclosure.ʸ U.S. funding flows to politicians in Israel continue to create problems. In 2008 Israeli Prime Minister Ehud Olmert was forced to resign over a corruption scandal involving U.S. based donors.

No U.S. based Zionist organization faced prosecution for dodging FARA statutes covering ties to foreign political parties. However, in 1959, Treasury Undersecretary Fred Scribner (1908-1994) warned Zionist organization leaders that they needed to restructure and alter their U.S. fundraising operations to keep the administration, the IRS, and the Department of Justice from prosecuting them for criminal violations. In a wide-ranging 1960s reorganization, the Jewish Agency then transferred Zionist activities to the American Zionist Council's management, including youth immigration to Israel, propaganda, and Zionist cultural activities in the U.S..²³⁶ But funding commingled with contributions from other countries and even from the Israeli government continued to flow back into the U.S. from entities directed by Israeli principals.

The Jewish Agency created a new executive board of 21 members in control of all UJA dollars going to Israel—what one critic called "another paper operation intended to satisfy a legalism in Washington."²³⁷ This allowed Kenen and like-minded Zionists to obliterate the financial influence of opponents like the American Council for Judaism. Chairman

---

ʸ The relevant section states "f) the term "foreign political party" includes any organization or any other combination of individuals in a country other than the United States, or any unit or branch thereof, having for an aim or purpose, or which is engaged in any activity devoted in whole or in part to, the establishment, administration, control, or acquisition of administration, control, or acquisition of administration or control, of a government of a foreign country or a subdivision thereof, or the furtherance of or influencing of the political or public interests, policies, or relations of a government of a foreign country thereof..."

Lessing J. Rosenwald quickly saw through the reorganization and complained loudly in May of 1960:

> For a time, these past few months, non-Zionists and anti-Zionists had the opportunity to recover control of the vast fund-raising mechanism. Despite some honorable efforts to make a basic change in the system, the Jewish nationalist movement once again rode roughshod over non-Zionists and anti-Zionists alike.[238]

The reorganization successfully channeled funds raised in the U.S. through conduits under the exclusive control of Zionist activists. But it also legally exposed the Jewish Agency and the American Zionist Council as they surreptitiously moved tax-exempt funds raised in the U.S. and overseas into non-tax-deductible FARA-regulated propaganda operations, including Kenen's lobbying newsletter. This operation was uncovered in 1962 and vividly revealed by Senator Fulbright in hearings. Behind the scenes, on a parallel track, the Department of Justice moved to register the AZC as a foreign agent.

AZC Funding from the Jewish Agency

The Senate Foreign Relations Committee's research team, led by Walter Pincus,[z] went to work in 1962 subpoenaing Jewish Agency and American Zionist Council documents and deposing witnesses. The Senate investigators personally visited the offices of the Jewish Agency–American Section in New York to rifle through filing cabinets, an insult that Kenen blasted in the *Near East Report*.

---

[z] A longtime reporter at the *Washington Post*.

The hearings immediately revealed the American Zionist Council's lack of independent fundraising capabilities in the U.S. In spite of its status as an official Israeli-sanctioned umbrella organization for powerful Zionist organizations, even in 1963 the American Zionist Council had so little direct non-tax-deductible U.S. funding that it all but completely relied on the Jewish Agency for support. The AZC was forced to admit this in a deposition to Fulbright:

> The American Zionist Council is composed of local Zionist groups in the United States and is affiliated with the World Zionist Organization with headquarters in Geneva.
>
> The American Zionist Council has received virtually all of its operating funds from the Jewish Agency for Israel, via the American Section. Approximately 40 per cent of the total budget of the Jewish Agency for Israel, in turn, is contributed from the United States through the United Jewish Appeal. The Government of Israel also contributes to the Jewish Agency's budget.[239]

Ben-Gurion's vision for the American Zionist Council as a U.S.-based successor organization to the Jewish Agency did not inspire much direct funding from Jewish-relief-oriented donors. The AZC should have seen where the threat to this laundering operation would come from; it was another direct result of disgruntled Jewish organizations who resented the Zionist funding power grab and black-box decision-making championed by Kenen and lobby elites. The Jewish Agency's corporate veil was about to be lifted by the ACJ's demands.

Initially in the May 23, 1963 Fulbright hearings testimony about the American Zionist Council's funding from the Jewish Agency in Israel ran into a wall of offshore opacity. The Jewish Agency's New York legal "architect" and long-serving registered agent was Maurice Boukstein[aa] (1905-1980). He issued a complicated set of wire diagrams of both on- and offshore entities. He hoped they would convince the Senate investigators that the Jewish Agency was highly complex, somewhat inscrutable, and mainly engaged in "resettlement", education and "relief" operations. Whenever testimony approached formal contractual arrangements with the Israeli government, articles of incorporation, and bylaws, the

---

[aa] Boukstein also served as the director of a group called the American Economic Committee for Palestine in the late 1930s, a leading member of the Claims Conference delegation to the Hague negotiations for Holocaust reparations, and served as a legal advisor to the World Zionist Organization.

"architect" became vague and evasive. All of that was safely ensconced offshore, beyond the reach of the Senate. Or was it? Fulbright, a former Department of Justice lawyer in the anti-trust division attempted to penetrate the veil.

> Senator Fulbright: Do you execute and prepare the registration? [FARA registration]
> Mr. Boukstein: Mr. Chairman, as I am the expert on the subject, having acted for the Agency as counsel. The constitution defines the function of the Executive. There is no document that I am aware of that lays down the working rules, such as we would in this country refer to as bylaws of the Executive. They act by resolution.
> Senator Fulbright: Well, do they act under majority rule?
> Mr. Boukstein. They act under majority rule by resolution.
> Senator Fulbright: Do they have subcommittees?
> Mr. Boukstein: They have subcommittees which they appoint ad hoc or sometimes continuing subcommittees, Mr. Chairman. But we shall search—but I am aware of the existence of no document which would be the equivalent of rules or bylaws.
> Senator Fulbright: Do they have minutes of meetings?
> Mr. Boukstein: Yes, they do.
> Senator Fulbright: Could you supply us with copies of the minutes of their meetings since 1960?
> Mr. Boukstein: Mr. Chairman, I am not so sure that would be a pertinent document. The minutes are in Jerusalem. They relate to all kinds of matters. If you mean excerpts of minutes relating to activities in the United States, we will be glad to furnish them. But I don't think that you have any interest in minutes relating to matters of completely ungermane subjects.
> Senator Fulbright: No; we wouldn't request anything ungermane. It was my understanding from testimony this morning that a very large percentage of the funds of the Executive derive from this country, is that correct?
> Mr. Boukstein: That is correct.
> Senator Fulbright: I will agree that not all of it would be. I was interested in how this Agency operates. I don't know of any precedent of anything like it in any other instance, and I thought it would be interesting to the committee to understand how foreign agents in this particular field operate and what kind of principals they represent.[240]

Boukstein's effort to dodge discussions about offshore operations and the existing "covenant" document between the Jewish Agency and the Israeli government endured, for a while. But during the same May hearing, subpoenaed internal American Zionist Council "activity reports" never meant for public release revealed the extensive, highly developed, and subtle behind-the-scenes effort to plant stories favorable to Israeli initiatives via a select and growing group of volunteer and paid public relations specialists based in New York. The FARA section of the U.S. Department of Justice was dumbfounded by testimony illuminating the extent of the operations divulged in the internal documents:

> The American Zionist Council's Public Relations Advisory Board was reported by Mrs. Epstein to be "our newest Committee which has only had its first meeting, and, therefore, it is difficult to know how it will develop. One of the more important public relations men in this city was invited by the Government of Israel to introduce a course on public relations at the University of Tel Aviv and to help the Government map out better procedures for its own public relations effort. Israel was delighted with the contribution which this man made, and he, in turn, came back excited and deeply interested in Israel and everything for which it stood. We were asked to approach him to build up a committee of public relations men who could be called on when and if problems arose which needed the technical know-how and assistance which only such people could give. Mrs. Epstein approached him, found him most responsive. He sent out a letter and last week 15 of the outstanding public relations men of this city sat around this table to consider how they could be of help in presenting a positive picture of Israel in the U.S..[241]

A confidential and damning internal strategy report on 1962-1963 public relations was placed into the Senate records (see Appendices for a reproduction of the report, "American Zionist Council Committee on Information and Public Relations"). It was not only shockingly detailed but seemed purpose-built to violate every line of FARA disclosure laws.

The damning documents placed into the Senate record also included a field report filed on October 23, 1962, by Mrs. Judith Epstein, chair of the American Zionist Council's Department of Information. Her budget had fallen from $750,000 to $175,500 since part of the work of the American Zionist Council had, in her words, "now been taken over by the Kenen Committee, which was charged with political action, formerly in the province of the American Zionist Council. All approaches on the Hill to the political parties, etc. are now the responsibility of the American Israel Public Affairs Committee whose funds are not tax-exempt. Thus, the greater emphasis is now put on the more subtle approach, which, through positive presentation of Israel's accomplishments, aims and purpose, and by counterattack of the many enemies of Israel and the Zionist movement."[242]

Epstein mentioned the American Zionist Council Information Department's efforts to prepare responses to what they considered hostile anti-Israel reports appearing in *Cosmopolitan, The Columbia University Quarterly Forum,* and *Editor and Publisher.* These were among "25 responses to newspapers or magazines that are written or sent" in an average month.[243] The American Zionist Council was "following closely" the "Arab States with their numerous embassies and consulates, the Arab Information Office, the American Friends of the Middle East, and the American Council for Judaism," but urged that "local Councils be strengthened throughout the country so that we may be kept informed of anti-Israel activities."[244] The Middle East Institute in Washington, DC was also being closely monitored for "anti-Israel propaganda of a subtle nature."[245] The department formed a campus watch group[bb] called the Inter-University Committee on Israel, which expanded from its base in New York to place favorable articles in "leading academic publications" in the U.S..[246]

The American Zionist Council also established a "Magazine Committee" chaired by a "man who holds a key position on the editorial level in the magazine business. He knows everyone in the trade, has important contacts and exploits them on behalf of Israel."[247] This unnamed editor led a committee composed of "15 writers and editors who are eminent in their respective fields" that "built up a 'bank of ideas' for freelance writers who go to Israel in search of articles and has provided the Israelis with a better idea of the kind of material which is acceptable to the American reading public and magazine editors. We cannot pinpoint all that has already been accomplished by this committee except to say that it has been responsible for the writing and placement of articles on Israel in some of America's leading magazines."[248] For broadcast media placements, the "TV-Radio Committee" had secured the services of "the director of creative projects of an important TV chain" to arrange for "talks and interviews on radio and TV; submits ideas for possible programs to stations and networks so as to give a better and more sympathetic understanding of Israel to the viewing American public; and takes steps to counteract hostile propaganda in these media. In view of the many

---

[bb] In 2002, Daniel Pipes, leader of the neoconservative think tank Middle East Forum, founded a group called Campus Watch. Like the AZC unit, it is charged with monitoring academia for professors who speak against Israel or content that reflects negatively on Israel. They originally published critical "dossiers" on individual professors on the Internet.

millions of Americans who daily watch TV and radio, this is one of the more important media in which we must expand our work."[249]

The Department of Information Speakers' Bureau did 2,240 engagements in 1961 with an "absurdly small staff." Targeting multiple community venues, one speaker in a single day would make four to seven appearances: "a Rotary Club, a World Affairs Council, a church group, a high school assembly or college group, a woman's club, a TV or Radio appearance, a background session with a local editor or commentator, etc." with the majority of "engagements before non-Jewish groups."[250]

According to the field report, the American Zionist Council Research Bureau "analyzes books and articles that deal with Israel or the Middle East. When a book is favorable, it is recommended. When it is unfavorable, it is analyzed and distortions are pointed up by providing the factual data required, so that our local councils will be prepared to react to the impact which these books have on the communities."[251]

The Research Bureau also interjected itself into high school textbook content: "The Inter-University Committee has been preparing textbook material as a guide to social science teachers in the junior and senior high schools on the subject of Israel. It would be impossible for these busy academicians to do the painstaking research required..."[252] The Research Bureau developed centralized policy positions, now commonly referred to as talking points, for "informing local Zionist Council leaders and Jewish community leadership as to our recommended position and steps for action on issues such as the Arab refugee problem, the Soblen case,[253] the Jordan water dispute, etc. Similarly, we distribute material and advisories for special occasions such as the celebration of Israel's Anniversary, the tenth anniversary of Weizmann's passing, etc."[254]

The American Zionist Council in New York was quick to put out memos and templates for stories to be submitted to local newspapers from local councils across the United States. Propaganda quality control was a key concern. A February 27, 1963, American Zionist Committee memo from Harry A. Steinberg urged that "enclosed herewith suggested material which can be used by you in preparing replies to the Max Freedman articles, in the event they have appeared in one of your local papers. It is not necessary to use all of this material in your own letters to the editor. Use the portions which you feel will make the most impact on your editor and the readership of the paper. We request also that you do not use this material in the submitted form, but that you rewrite it so that letters submitted in various parts of the country do not appear to be identical..."[255]

Influencing Christian religious groups was also a key objective of the American Zionist Council. The AZC's Commission on Inter-Religious Affairs was responsible for "effort in gaining friends in the Protestant and Catholic religious communities." In addition to bringing together Orthodox, Conservative, and Reform rabbis, the committee concerned itself with "monitoring the Christian church press, stimulating articles presenting Israeli and Zionist ideology, and answering the hostile attacks very often found in the publications of the Protestant and Catholic Church, as well as cultivating key religious leaders and editors."[256]

The commission held seminars that in Boston alone attracted 50 Catholic priests, and documented the successful seminar approach in a "Manual for Rabbis giving the know-how of establishing these seminars, steps to be taken and the scope of the subject matter, approach, etc." The commission's work was seen as one of the "great possibilities for the future since one cannot underestimate the impact of public opinion of churchmen in this country."[257] The successful fusion of the power of evangelical Christian groups with the Israel lobby a generation later would prove this analysis to be entirely correct.

The range of Department of Information activities described in the American Zionist Council field report, and the fact that they were being financed with Jewish Agency funds, raised Senator Fulbright's ire. Isadore Hamlin (1917-1991) was appointed executive director of the Jewish Agency–American Section in 1961. In sworn testimony, Hamlin was evasive about the massive public relations campaign underway in the United States and the central role of Isaiah L. Kenen.

> Senator Fulbright: Now, let us see. Was this report furnished to the Jewish Agency–American Section by the American Zionist Council?
> Mr. Hamlin: Sir, this handwriting on this memorandum indicates to me that it was sent to one of the members of our Executive, who is a member of one of the governing boards of the American Zionist Council. It happens to be a member of one of the governing boards of the American Zionist Council.
> Senator Fulbright: But he is also a member of the Jewish Agency?
> Mr. Hamlin: Yes.
> Senator Fulbright: Does this report accurately describe the type of activities of the American Zionist Council which were being financed by the Jewish Agency–American Section?
> Mr. Hamlin: I cannot answer that question honestly, sir, I do not know.
> Senator Fulbright: Who would know about that?
> Mr. Hamlin: Sir?
> Senator Fulbright: Who would know about that?

Mr. Hamlin: I presume the staff members of the American Zionist Council.
Senator Fulbright: You are not very familiar with what the American Zionist Council does?
Mr. Hamlin: I am in a general way, but I am not an officer there, or an employee, so I cannot vouch for these activities.
Senator Fulbright: Do you approve of the budget that they submit to you?
Mr. Hamlin: No, sir.
Senator Fulbright: Who does?
Mr. Hamlin: The treasurer did in this period.
Senator Fulbright: Who is the treasurer?
Mr. Hamlin: Mr. Louis A. Pincus.
Mr. Boukstein: Mr. Chairman, I think there was a misunderstanding. You did not mean him personally. You mean "you" in the sense of the organization?
Senator Fulbright: Yes, the Jewish Agency.
Mr. Boukstein: He took it to mean, does he personally approve the budget.
Mr. Hamlin: Yes, I did.
Senator Fulbright: Does the Agency approve the budget?
Mr. Hamlin: Yes, sir.
Senator Fulbright: This was a period in 1962 in which, as you have testified before, the Agency is contributing approximately 80 percent of their budget, and it would be quite natural that you would examine and approve or criticize, or what you like, the budget, would it not? I mean not you, in every instance, but I mean the Agency.
Mr. Hamlin: Yes, the organization, certainly. Now, the treasurer of the Jewish Agency was requested by the Executive to negotiate this allocation.
Senator Fulbright: Who did he negotiate with?
Mr. Hamlin: With Rabbi Miller and Mr. Bick, the treasurer of the Council.
Senator Fulbright: That is right.
Mr. Hamlin: Yes, sir.
Senator Fulbright: Take the second paragraph of that memorandum, the report, I guess you would call it. I quote, "At that time the department had a budget of $750,000." What is "the department"?
Mr. Hamlin: Did you ask at what time?
Senator Fulbright: What does "the department" mean?
Mr. Hamlin: The Department of Information.
Senator Fulbright: Department of Information?
Mr. Hamlin: Yes.
Senator Fulbright: (reading) "Today the budget is $175,450 with an obligation to carry on a comprehensive, diverse and complex project which demands personnel and funds. However, she pointed out that the part of the work of the original council had now been taken over by the

Kenen Committee, which was charged with political action, formerly in the province of the American Zionist Council. All approaches on the Hill to the political parties, etc. are now the responsibility of the American Israel Public Affairs Committee whose funds are not tax-exempt. Thus the greater emphasis is now put on the more subtle approach, which, through positive presentation of Israel's accomplishments, aims and purpose, and by counterattack of the many enemies of Israel and the Zionist movement."

Was direct political action of the unsubtle type at one time in the province of the American Zionist Council?

Mr. Hamlin: I have no personal knowledge of this, Senator.

Senator Fulbright: What do you mean by the "Kenen Committee"? I have not heard it referred to as a committee before.

Mr. Hamlin: The "Kenen Committee" is the American-Israel Public Affairs Committee.

Senator Fulbright: I thought he was known as some kind of reporter up to now. What did he—

Mr. Boukstein: It was brought out, Senator, he was in two capacities. He is the owner and publisher of a—what is it called—*Near East Report*. But in addition, he is also the director of the American-Israel Public Affairs Committee.

Senator Fulbright: And that is what this is?

Mr. Boukstein. Yes.

Senator Fulbright: Well, we will just place the report in the record.[258]

The documents that Fulbright placed into the Senate record reveal that the assertion that AIPAC was only receiving "non-tax-exempt funds" from American donors was not accurate. $574,550 (former budget of $750,000 minus the then-current budget of $175,450) mysteriously disappeared from the Department of Information budget around the same time that the "Kenen Committee," or AIPAC, was ramping up its activities. The Jewish Agency's legal counsel refused to affirm what seemed obvious to Fulbright and the Senate Foreign Relations Committee: Kenen was lobbying Congress with overseas funds. The earlier lobbying with tax-exempt funds became untenable after the meeting with Fred Scribner and warnings of impending investigations. New artifices were erected to hide activities while the AZC continued the effort with UJA relief and Israeli government funds from the Jewish Agency. Based on budget analysis, it seems highly likely that the formation of AIPAC was an effort that temporarily sapped the "Department of Information" as startup funds were channeled to Kenen and his activities through various hidden conduits. But the "subvention caveat" discussed in Chapter 9 means Americans will probably never know for sure. The FBI, ready to raid AZC offices for records, remained leashed, and the Justice Department accepted a FARA registration that omitted the critical period when Isaiah Kenen received most of his foreign funding.

The Jewish Agency and the American Zionist Council initially claimed that they had an "arm's-length" subscription-based relationship with Isaiah Kenen. However, their own internal reports and handwritten notes revealed that their payments were directed by the foreign principals in Jerusalem specifically to subsidize Kenen.

> Senator Fulbright: Well, I now show you an undated handwritten note and signed "OK. I. Hamlin," and ask you if you signed and approved the payment set forth in this note?
> Mr. Hamlin: Yes, sir. This is my signature.
> Senator Fulbright: The main part of the note deals with "HK Subventions," but I call your attention to the line reading "Kenen (paid 1/14 5,000)" which has a line drawn through it and the initials "OK" next to it, and ask you if this refers to I. L. Kenen?
> Mr. Hamlin: Sir, I will have to look, try to find out what happened in this case. But it is possible that when we made the payments to the Council for Kenen we may have, that is, for the purpose of these subscriptions of the *Near East Report*, which was done by the American Zionist Council, for the sake of bookkeeping, for the sake of our internal records, it may have been designated as "Kenen," just as in the case of these memorandums I designated "Shwadran"[cc] just to save time.
> Senator Fulbright: I am just trying to clarify the record on this. Could you file for the record the payments that you made through the American Zionist Council to Mr. Kenen?[259]

In a lengthy grilling of the Jewish Agency's American foreign agent, Isadore Hamlin, during the August 1, 1963 Senate Foreign Relations Committee hearings, Fulbright attempted to clarify Kenen's employment status as well as exactly how the Jewish Agency was financing the *Near East Report*. As mentioned, Kenen provided copies to the Senate Foreign Relations Committee and the rest of Congress free of charge. Fulbright's interrogation of Hamlin about Kenen was dogged and revealing:

> Senator Fulbright: Here I would gather he says he is an employee, or was, of the American Zionist Council; he is not an independent

---

[cc] Benjamin Shwadran ran one of the precursor Israel lobby "think tanks" funded by the Jewish Agency. For a complete history of the strategic evolution of these entities, see *Foreign Agents: The American Israel Public Affairs Committee from the 1963 Fulbright Hearings to the 2005 Espionage Scandal*.

entrepreneur the way you described a moment ago, according to his letter.

Mr. Hamlin: Sir, I don't know the relationship between Mr. Kenen and the American Zionist Council. But the letter is clear, that he performed certain services to the American Zionist Council. Now, what we are discussing is my answer to this question is a subsequent period to this relationship and refers only to subscriptions to the *Near East Report*.

Senator Fulbright: Well now, this change in status came about approximately the same time as you reorganized your whole operation in America, did it not?

Mr. Hamlin: Yes, it did.

Senator Fulbright: Now, was this change of Mr. Kenen's status part of the reorganization, so instead of paying him directly, you now buy enough subscriptions to pay him?

Mr. Hamlin: It would not, sir.

Senator Fulbright: Why not? Doesn't he perform very much the same function as he did before? He serves the same purpose.

Mr. Hamlin: No, sir, not at all.

Senator Fulbright: Why not?

Mr. Hamlin: He was performing speaking services during that earlier period. We were giving the American Zionist Council a money grant for subscriptions for the *Near East Report*.

Senator Fulbright: Doesn't he speak anymore?

Mr. Hamlin: To my knowledge, he has no connection now, no arrangements with, the Zionist Council.

Senator Fulbright: But he writes these letters, doesn't he?

Mr. Hamlin: Pardon me?

Senator Fulbright: He writes the *Near East Report*.

Mr. Hamlin: Yes, sir, he does.

Senator Fulbright: And he sends them to all sorts of people free of charge, doesn't he?

Mr. Hamlin: I am sorry, sir?

Senator Fulbright: He sends them all around free of charge.

Mr. Hamlin: Free of charge? I don't know.

Senator Fulbright: Well, you pay for them. I mean the arrangement is that you, through the Council pay for them and they send them to a list who do not subscribe, is this not correct? I can see from my own experience. He sends me one, and I don't pay for it.

Mr. Hamlin: Sir, the Council provided the funds—

Senator Fulbright: Is it me or the committee? Maybe I do him an injustice but we get one; maybe it is the committee.

Mr. Boukstein: Mr. Chairman, it is obvious from what the witness said that a large number of recipients of the bulletins don't pay for it.

Senator Fulbright: That is right.

Mr. Boukstein: The American Zionist Council pays for a number of them.

Senator Fulbright: That is right.

Mr. Boukstein: But nevertheless, the impression should not be left that that is the bulk of the majority or the major part of the recipients of the publication. My information is that it isn't so, and while you permit me, Mr. Chairman—

Senator Fulbright: I missed that, wait a minute. What is not so?

Mr. Boukstein: That the number of people receiving—that the people receiving bulletins are—what is it called, the *Near East Report*—which are paid for by the American Zionist Council, are not the majority of recipients. I don't know the exact percentage, but it is only a part of the number published and distributed. Now, while I am at it, Mr. Chairman, I would like to say one more word so that you will have the information. I personally in my capacity as counsel had a great deal to do with the reorganization which took place in 1960. I participated in many meetings. At no time, Mr. Chairman, did the services or functions of Mr. Kenen enter into a discussion which had anything to do with the reorganization or the purposes for the reorganization. I am saying this simply so that the record be clear and so that no unfair inferences may be drawn as to the payments being made to Mr. Kenen.

Senator Fulbright: I am reminded, Mr. Kenen in his own letter says that these subscriptions, from the Zionist Council, average about 23 percent of the total circulation expired in 1962. You do not regard Mr. Kenen, for practical purposes, as an employee of the Agency?

Mr. Hamlin: Definitely not.

Senator Fulbright: Do you find his policies in disagreement with yours?

Mr. Hamlin: I know Mr. Kenen as a director of the American Israel Public Affairs Committee, which is composed of distinguished citizens of this country. He travels around, they have a fundraising campaign. These are not tax-exempt funds which Mr. Kenen carries on his activities as a director of that committee.

Senator Fulbright: What are his activities in Washington? Are you familiar with it?

Mr. Hamlin: Not in detail, no, sir. But he is a registered lobbyist in Washington in his capacity as a director of the American Israel Public Affairs Committee.

Senator Fulbright: He is a registered lobbyist under the domestic lobbying law?

Mr. Hamlin: That is right, sir.

Senator Fulbright: Why do you think he shouldn't register under the Foreign Agents Registration Act?

Mr. Hamlin: Excuse me. I can't comment on that, Mr. Chairman.

Mr. Boukstein: I am not acting here for Mr. Kenen, Mr. Chairman.

Senator Fulbright: Well, maybe we ought to ask Mr. Kenen. Do you think he would be competent to answer that question?

> Mr. Boukstein: I assume he would be. My offhand opinion would be that he does not have to register under the Foreign Agents Act, not from the facts as disclosed in this, in the executive session, or at this hearing.
> Senator Fulbright: Not as disclosed, but from the facts as you know them?
> Mr. Boukstein: Let me go further. From the facts as I know them, he would not have to register.
> Senator Fulbright: Mr. Boukstein, I would not hesitate to challenge your opinion about whether he should register or not, but for the life of me I can't understand why a person who received such a large subsidy from a foreign agent indirectly, because it goes through the American Zionist Council, should not have to register, whereas if he received it directly, I think you would agree he would have to register, wouldn't he?
> Mr. Boukstein: He—
> Senator Fulbright: And the device of merely using the American Zionist Council seems to me to be a very thin way of insulating him from the effects of the Foreign Registration Act.
> Mr. Boukstein: Mr. Chairman, he is selling a service, he is publishing a bulletin. If there are any debts or any liabilities, he or his corporation are responsible for them. As a matter of fact, when the American Zionist Council ceased paying him for the bulletin, he ceased sending out copies to the list which they had furnished him. I don't believe he is subject to registration under those conditions.
> Senator Fulbright: I have seen a number of his publications, and if they aren't completely devoted to the promotion of the purposes of your—the same purposes, the Jewish Agency, and the state of Israel, I don't know what is. It is directed to that purpose. I am not criticizing the purpose. You have a right to do it. You do it, and you register for it. I just am not quite clear why Mr. Kenen, who serves the same purpose, and, in fact, in some ways much more directly in his contact with Congress than you are, why he shouldn't have to register? [260]

Widespread evidence that the Jewish Agency, American Zionist Council, and AIPAC were end-running the Foreign Agents Registration Act led to one final showdown over the registration law. Late in the August 1, 1963 hearing, Fulbright put the question directly to the Jewish Agency's legal counsel and engineer of the 1960 reorganization of U.S.-based Zionist organizations, Maurice M. Boukstein:

> Senator Fulbright: Mr. Boukstein, you haven't enlightened me as to how we may deal with this matter because you only confirmed my view that under the existing law and practices, at least, as they are illustrated here, it completely thwarts the purpose of the Foreign Agents Registration Act, because we are not given any information—neither the public or

government—as to the nature of these activities and the nature of these projects for which this registrant here is supplied the money.

Mr. Boukstein: Mr. Chairman, if you would go back to the time when the Foreign Agents Act was made law, in 1938, I think the purpose was altogether different. The language, of course, comprehends everybody; but the purpose at the time was to bring out, into the open, subversive, at that time particularly Nazi activities, and I hope that the law in this respect served its purpose.

But to the extent that it is still law and to the extent that it is to be applied to other purpose, I certainly agree with you that it needs considerable modification and change.[261]

In fewer words, the head of the Jewish Agency–American Section implied that the raw power of the Israel lobby in the U.S. meant that governing laws would have to accommodate the lobby's activities, rather than the reverse. Fulbright attempted to legislate ever more stringent modifications to FARA, and the 1963 Senate Foreign Relations Committee hearings on the agents of foreign principals propelled covert U.S. activities of the Israel lobby to the front pages. Many Americans concerned about Middle East policy sat back, confident that in light of the overwhelming documented violations, the U.S. Department of Justice would soon be issuing indictments or at least demanding foreign agent disclosures in the FARA section.

The FARA section, Department of Justice, and FBI were indeed working in tandem with the Fulbright investigation, but the public record in the press is truncated and provides no closure. This is because the records of the internal DOJ deliberations and actions were classified and unavailable for public review. The files contain valuable insight about the DOJ's battle to enforce FARA over its most egregious violator.

Dear Sirs:
Would you please send me the booklet on subversive organizations? Would you please tell me, in case these organizations are too new to be in your booklet, what kind of organizations they are, if they are communist, etc.?

The American Zionists
The Revisionists

It would be so helpful to real Americans if they could know which organizations are communistic, as there are so many which are just fronts. Whenever I read about an organization, I sometimes wonder, sometimes I am able to realize that they are, and reading about what they do or who is in it, or what "big" people lend their name of support to it, and the real American columnists tell about them, and then we know.

I am anxious to get this information as soon as possible, thank you, I remain,
Yours Truly —Birdie Segal Voerg, letter to the U.S. Department of Justice, Internal Security Division, June 6, 1960

Chapter 9: Fighting Justice

News of the foreign agent investigation reached Isaiah Kenen in 1961. Fulbright's team investigated in 1962, rifling through Jewish Agency filing cabinets and analyzing proprietary financial data. The Senate Foreign Relations Committee held hearings about Israeli foreign principals in May and August of 1963. The looming threats of the investigation forced the Jewish Agency–American Section to file slightly more detailed declarations: the American Section began revealing, but not itemizing, substantial payment flows to the AZC in the fall of 1962.[262] Senate testimony and preliminary committee reports soon made their way into the public domain in 1963. But the fate of the AZC has always been something of a mystery. The relevant internal documents revealing a secret Department of Justice battle to force the AZC to register as a foreign agent were not released until June 10, 2008, in response to Freedom of Information Act filings. An analysis of the episode sheds light on why the U.S. Department of Justice has subsequently been extremely reticent to prosecute Israel lobby legal violations, even when the evidence of wrongdoing is simply overwhelming.

The Internal Security Division of the U.S. Department of Justice quietly took action on a parallel track to the Senate. On October 31, 1962, Assistant Attorney General and director of the Internal Security Division J. Walter Yeagley[dd] (1909-1990)[263] notified Attorney General Robert F. Kennedy (RFK) (1925-1968)[ee] of a major enforcement move. Yeagley's division was formally demanding FARA registration of the American Zionist Council:

> I think you ought to know that we are soliciting next week the registration of the American Zionist Council under the Foreign Agents Registration Act. In an amendment to a supplemental registration statement filed by the American Section of the Jewish Agency for Israel for the period ending in March 31, 1962, it was reported that the Council received over $32,000 in subventions and over $11,000 as a special grant from the American Section of the Jewish Agency for Israel. Under the Act the receipt of such funds from the Jewish Agency constitutes the Council an agent of a foreign principal as that term is defined in Section 1(c) of the statute. The stated purpose for which these funds were received makes unavailable any exemption from registration…You may be aware that the American Zionist Council is composed of representatives of various Zionist organizations in the United States including the Zionist Organization of America.[264]

Going after a group of powerful nonprofit corporations under the AZC umbrella such as the Zionist Organization of America and Hadassah was no trifling matter. John F. Kennedy had courted and won over key figures in the Israel lobby in his campaign for president. Although the aftermath of the Cuban missile crisis was undoubtedly requiring most of the administration's attention, RFK brought in Department of Justice Director of Public Information Edwin Guthman[265][ff] to review the strength of the case against the AZC and the exact approach the FARA section chief would take.

[dd] In 1959, Yeagley became the Assistant Attorney General and director of the internal security division. Yeagley had graduated from the University of Michigan and practiced law in South Bend, Indiana before becoming an FBI agent and later administrative aide to Director J. Edgar Hoover.

[ee] Robert F. Kennedy served as Attorney General of the United States from January 20, 1961, through September 3, 1964.

[ff] Guthman served in DOJ public information between 1961 and 1964. He was press assistant to Robert F. Kennedy from 1964 to 1965.

On November 14, 1962, Guthman sent his report to RFK and copied it to Deputy Attorney General Nicholas deBelleville Katzenbach (1922-   ). Guthman, Yeagley, and Nathan Lenvin in the FARA section were confident about the likely response of the American Zionist Council and its constituent organizations.

> I met with Walter Yeagley and Nat Lenvin today in connection with the proposal to require the American Zionist Council to register under the Foreign Agents Registration Act.
>
> The facts as set forth in the attached memorandum from Yeagley and Lenvin should clearly that the American Zionist Council has been receiving substantial amounts of money for two years or more from the American Section of the Jewish Agency for Israel for the express purpose of disseminating propaganda about Israel's position in the Middle East. This money comes from funds raised in America through the United Jewish Appeal.
>
> Nat Lenvin proposes to write a letter to the American Zionist Council indicating that the Council should register. Undoubtedly, representatives of the Council will wish to confer with Nat.
>
> I believe that Nat should go ahead and send the letter and handle this matter as any other registration. I doubt very much that there will be any fuss. I don't think the American Zionist Council is in any position to do so. If, as it appears, the Zionist Council has used for political propaganda purposes money raised by the UJA in America, the Council has compromised its position. This UJA money is generally for charitable work in the United States and Israel. Disclosure that some of the money—even a small part—had been used for political propaganda could hurt the UJA fundraising.[266]

In the ensuing two-and-one-half-year battle, the Internal Security Division would obtain few direct material disclosures of the massive propaganda campaign funded by the Jewish Agency and document no specific international control relationships beyond the damning testimony and documents disclosed in Fulbright's Senate Foreign Relations committee hearings. Understanding JFK's and Lyndon B. Johnson's (LBJ) evolving relationships with the Israel lobby and nonproliferation initiatives is critical for understanding the failure of the Department of Justice's extremely serious attempt to compel the Israel lobby's FARA registration.

John F. Kennedy and the Israel Lobby

Like Harry S Truman, both John F. Kennedy (1917-1963) and Lyndon B. Johnson (1908-1973) learned how to interface with Abraham Feinberg and his cadre of Israel lobby financiers. JFK lamented the realities of the blatant and raw exchange of campaign money for policy control, while the more seasoned LBJ recognized the relationship as essentially unidirectional and non-negotiable.

A decade earlier, Feinberg had elaborated on the power of the Israel lobby and its elite vision for how U.S. politics and regional policy should function. During a frank 1952 discussion when Adlai Stevenson (1900-1965) was looking for support in his presidential run against Dwight Eisenhower, Feinberg briefed him on the realities of vote counting:

> He finally did call me, and we met at the Biltmore Hotel. It must have been five or six weeks after the nomination. And obviously, he was putting his best foot forward. He said, "Abe, I know a lot about you and your interest in Israel."
>
> I said, "Fine, let's get to that right away. What can I do to tell you about the need for continued support of Israel?"
>
> "Well, "he said, "I first have to tell you my problem. I was in Iran for the State Department in 1946 when the Russians made their move into Iran. It was I who activated the United States, through the State Department, to threaten to resist that move. That incident endeared me to the Arabs, and I have many friends in the Arab world."
>
> So I said, "How many votes are there in the Democratic party in the Arab world?" That was the only thing I said, and he understood that I meant he was being impractical. A President should have friends in the Arab world. I think it would be very helpful for a President to have friends in the Arab world to whom he could talk man to man, without being blackmailed with oil, and friends in Israel to whom he could talk, man to man.[267]

Feinberg and his affiliated organizations could muster enough votes and campaign contributions to factor into practical Cold War considerations and purely realist U.S. interests in the region. Feinberg indeed lived long enough to see the beginning of an implementation of the neoconservative vision for the U.S. This vision advanced to include U.S. military control of Middle East oil supplies and further institutionalized the ever closer "man-to-man" U.S.-Israel ties championed by such figures as Paul Wolfowitz, Richard Perle, and Douglas Feith.

Abraham Feinberg met John F. Kennedy through Connecticut Governor Abraham Ribicoff (1910-1998), Kennedy's floor manager at the Democratic convention. Ribicoff, also Isaiah Kenen's confidant, arranged a meeting between Kennedy and Feinberg at the Hotel Pierre where Feinberg lived. Feinberg invited about 20 prominent financiers and businessmen to the meeting.

Kennedy was grilled about his father's controversial views on Jews in general and Adolf Hitler in particular. The next morning, Kennedy visited Charles L. Bartlett, a close friend and newspaper columnist, and blew off steam. Bartlett recalled Kennedy's anger:

> As an American citizen he was outraged to have a Zionist group come to him and say: "We know your campaign is in trouble. We're willing to pay your bills if you'll let us have control of your Middle East policy." "They wanted control," Kennedy told Bartlett.[268]

But after becoming president, Kennedy duly expressed gratitude to Feinberg and made several sensitive political appointments that appeased the Israel lobby. In October of 1961, Kennedy pardoned Hank Greenspun, caught smuggling military hardware to Israel and convicted of violating the Neutrality Act in 1950.[269] Kennedy appointed Myer (Mike) Feldman, a campaign aide, to be the presidential liaison for the "Jewish and Israeli Affairs" group in the White House. One day after Kennedy's inauguration, Feldman was given authorization to monitor all secret U.S. State Department and White House cable traffic pertaining to the Middle East. This node created bureaucratic chaos as national security and State Department officials attempted to route sensitive information around Feldman. One U.S. ambassador insisted on sending his most sensitive reports directly to Kennedy.

At the time, Feldman's and Feinberg's support for Israel's nuclear program was the polar opposite of Kennedy's nuclear nonproliferation treaty initiatives. Israel's nuclear program would prevail as the JFK administration came to a cataclysmic end.[270]

DOJ Forces AZC to Register as a Foreign Agent

On November 21, 1962, J. Walter Yeagley sent a two-page letter (signed by Nathan B. Lenvin, Chief of the Registration Section) and foreign agent registration forms to the American Zionist Council by certified mail (see Appendices).[271] The letter cited the section's finding that because it received Jewish Agency funds for propaganda purposes, the AZC had to register. The Jewish Agency–American Section received advance notice that such a request was imminent. On October 31, 1962, even as Yeagley notified RFK of the pending registration request, Maurice Boukstein, the Jewish Agency's New York legal counsel and architect of the 1960 Zionist reorganization, conferred with Lenvin about a potential AZC registration. According to Lenvin's files, Boukstein broke the ice with a topic he probably knew was of little interest to the FARA section before getting down to the business at hand.

> On Wednesday, October 31, 1962, I conferred with Mr. Maurice Boukstein in regard to a problem he wished to discuss which may involve the application of the Foreign Agents Registration Act. Mr. Boukstein stated that the American Section of the Jewish Agency was thinking of financing a number of academic grants for Bar Mitzvah girls and boys to study in Israel with particular emphasis on Jewish culture and education. The question had been raised as to whether this grant, if made to the association handling the Bar Mitzvah grants, would be required to register. I expressed the view to Mr. Boukstein that in my opinion such activities would come within the purview of the exemption from registration provided by Section 3 (e) of the statute and there would not be a requirement for registration.[272]

Boukstein then inquired about whether the recent and more detailed Jewish Agency–American Section FARA disclosures would trigger any Department of Justice action. Lenvin stated that the matter was "still under consideration," but then turned the question around and asked Boukstein whether the AZC would likely protest a FARA registration demand. Boukstein said the matter had already been discussed internally and outlined a possible strategy the AZC might tender to avoid registration. He also speculated about RFK's likely reaction if the registration issue moved forward, laying groundwork through the term "bona fide," which would resurface prominently as the DOJ finalized the case file in 1965:

> Mr. Boukstein replied that in his view it was doubtful that any great protest would be made since in the discussions he has had with the

various officials connected both with the Zionist Council and the Jewish Agency he had made it clear that in his view an agency relationship would result which may well require registration.

He hazarded a view that perhaps the most that would be sought would be a non-pressing by A. G. of any request for registration on the basis of bona fide representations that the Jewish Agency no longer would contribute funds to the American Zionist Council. I did not express any opinion as to what action the Department would or would not take in this regard.[273]

J. Walter Yeagley wrote in the margin of Lenvin's file memo that he "would expect this" same non-pressing of registration. But the magnitude of Jewish Agency disbursements to the AZC was not yet known within the U.S. Department of Justice. When they were later disclosed in Fulbright's hearings, the Justice Department's insistence on registration became absolute.

Rabbi Irving Miller of the American Zionist Council, in a December 6, 1962 letter to Lenvin, politely acknowledged receipt of the FARA registration forms but contested the basis of the Justice Department's request:

> The request for registration contained in your letter raises various questions of fact and of relationships which first must be resolved by us before compliance can be made. Therefore, it is requested that you be good enough to grant us a delay of 120 days to consider these matters and to take appropriate action.[274]

The American Zionist Council immediately hired Simon H. Rifkind (1901-1995) of the powerhouse law firm Paul, Weiss, Rifkind, Wharton & Garrison LLP[gg] as its outside legal counsel to deal with the Department of Justice. Rifkind was a shrewd choice. Between 1941 and 1950, he had been a federal district court judge in New York City. In March of 1961 he was appointed chair of the Presidential Railroad Commission, having taken over from Secretary of Labor James P. Mitchell. Rifkind chaired the commission on behalf of President Kennedy until it terminated with the publication of its final report on February 28, 1962.[275] He also continued to provide valuable political cover to JFK over the fallout with railroad labor groups generated by the abolishment of their formerly sacred work rules.

[gg] As of July 2008, Paul, Weiss, Rifkind, Wharton & Garrison LLP employs more than 500 lawyers, according to its website.

On March 5, 1962, Rifkind proclaimed to the news media that labor concessions were the only option for avoiding a "moribund" economy.[276]

On January 23, 1963, Rifkind, an unrecorded member of his law firm, and two representatives of the AZC sat down with Nathan Lenvin and his executive assistant Thomas K. Hall in what could have been an intimidating and contentious confrontation. Rifkind's opening gambit was in line with Boukstein and Yeagley's initial expectations: he positioned himself as if he were above the fray and delivering a considered opinion from the bench.

> Judge Rifkind indicated that he had carefully reviewed the facts and the pertinent provisions of the Foreign Agents Registration Act and had concluded that while the situation is fraught with considerable doubt he had advised his client to discontinue completely the agency relationship and cut off the receipt of any additional funds of this nature. This action he stated on the part of this client became effective on January 18. He stressed the fact that his client and its activities fall within the purview of the so-called educational or cultural exemption of the Act. There were, however, certain activities such as the dissemination of publications and the use of mass media as to which it could conceivably be argued they were non-exempt. In the light of this he deemed it advisable that his client terminate the relationship in its entirety.[277]

This "we didn't do it and certainly won't do it again" stance, now fairly common in corporate crime investigations and non-prosecution agreements, didn't initially work out. Lenvin's meeting notes also record Rifkind's frank assessment that the Jewish Agency funding cutoff would be an enormous financial sacrifice:

> In regard to the latter point, Judge Rifkind pointed out that rather than incur any possible obligation to register, the subject had arrived at a decision that it would no longer accept any funds from the Jewish Agency and that it would attempt to continue its activities by raising its own funds within the United States, which would be a task of considerable difficulty.[278]

Rifkind's comment substantiates how weak Zionist fundraising, as opposed to general Jewish relief fundraising, continued to be in the United States at the time. It was this debility that necessitated the elaborate international financial conduits through Boukstein's various shell corporations. Senator Fulbright referred to this often in the hearings as simply "rigmarole."

Lenvin wasn't sympathetic to the AZC's self-imposed penalty of future direct U.S. Zionist fundraising. He wouldn't back down before Rifkind.[279] He indicated that the alleged termination of Jewish Agency funding did not absolve the AZC of an obligation to retroactively register for the period when an agency relationship clearly existed and foreign subsidized activities were being carried on across the U.S. Rifkind objected on the grounds that the AZC would have carried on such activities anyway, without, it should be noted, explaining precisely how they would have been financed. Possibly realizing the inconsistency of that case with the dearth of direct funding, Rifkind then suddenly changed course and made an impassioned "good vs. evil" plea for special treatment using violent metaphorical language:

> ...it would not benefit the government at this time to obtain such a registration and the disclosure involved; that registration would place a noose around the neck of his client, a long-standing organization of excellent repute and important to the national interest of the United States and thus choke the very life out of it; that registration would furnish a weapon to anti-Zionist groups, a spokesman of which is alleged to have said he would pay a half million dollars to get AZC registered as a foreign agent. He further stated that he was not urging that we should not enforce the statute solely because of the disastrous consequences but because it was a reasonable and permissible canon of construction to give it a meaning dispensing with registration by AZC thus applying it in a manner that would do good rather than promote evil.[280]

Lenvin and Hall reasserted the FARA section's position that the request for registration represented an official interpretation of the act, which was applied on an equal basis to all. They then suggested that Rifkind submit a brief to Yeagley outlining his legal argument, and Rifkind agreed.[281]

Conveniently for Rifkind, a news item drawing on this closely held information appeared the very next day. It was probably released by AZC insiders. Titled "AZC Gives Up $ to Avoid Foreign Agent Registration," it appeared in the *National Jewish Post*. The clipping duly made its way to the Internal Security Division and was docketed in the FARA section files on April 8, 1963.[282]

Meanwhile, the American Council for Judaism was ecstatic. In a February 19, 1963, bulletin to members celebrating its own upcoming 20-year anniversary, the ACJ broke the FARA registration news and trumpeted the imminent fall of the AZC:

> The American Zionist Council (coordinating political-action arm of all U.S. Zionist organizations) was asked last month by the Justice Department to register as a "foreign agent" of the State of Israel.[283]

On March 6, 1963, Tony Lewis of the *New York Times* telephoned the FARA section seeking verification of the AZC registration order, but Lenvin, who normally handled inquiries from Lewis, was not available to receive the call. Edwin Guthman was still working out a communications strategy for dealing with such calls in the interim.[284]

On March 21, Nathan Lenvin received a cover letter individually signed by each partner of Paul, Weiss, Rifkind, Wharton & Garrison and a brief outlining why the AZC could not be complied to register under FARA.[285] Another face-to-face meeting was called.

On April 1, 1963, Hall and Lenvin met with Rifkind and other members of his firm at their 575 Madison Avenue law office in New York City. Lenvin stated that based on the Jewish Agency FARA registration, "the facts did not bear out" the firm's objections to AZC registration based on claims that it was no longer an agent of a foreign principal or that the material disseminated was only educational in nature. Lenvin said he believed there was an inherent agency relationship created by the funding flows and communications, and bluntly stated that he would recommend litigation over the matter. The meeting ended with Lenvin promising to deliver reproductions of the relevant Jewish Agency–American Section FARA registration documents to Paul, Weiss, Rifkind, Wharton & Garrison. For its part, the AZC promised to produce copies of its informational materials to prove its contention that only exempt "cultural" material was ever disseminated.[286] Lenvin had clearly rattled the law firm.

Yeagley, meanwhile, wanted the entire matter "concluded" and wrote a memo to Hall on April 5, 1963 asking if the relevant Jewish Agency FARA registration disclosure had been sent to the AZC's legal counsel.[287] But the matter was far from concluded, and the clock was ticking toward the Senate hearing. Rifkind abruptly escalated his appeal directly to Yeagley's boss.

On May 2, 1963 (only two weeks before Fulbright's first formal Senate hearings on the agents of Israeli foreign principals), Deputy Attorney General Nicholas Katzenbach, J. Walter Yeagley, and Nathan B. Lenvin met at the New York City offices of Paul, Weiss, Rifkind, Wharton & Garrison for a major dressing down by Rifkind composed of blanket denials, accusations, appeals for clemency, and raw political calculations. The FARA matter simply had to be shut down. Lenvin detailed the meeting in a three-page internal file reviewed and verified by both Yeagley and Katzenbach:

> Judge Rifkind opened the discussion by explaining to Mr. Katzenbach something of the nature of the composition and activities of the American Zionist Council. He explained that the Council is composed of representatives of the various Zionist organizations in the United States and that it thereby, in effect, represents the vast majority of organized Jewry within this country. He also mentioned the existence of the... [American Council for Judaism], which is an anti-Zionist organization, and briefly touched on the conflict which exists between the Zionist groups and the... [American Council for Judaism].[hh] He placed particular stress on the proposition that for the Department to insist upon the registration of the Council would do it incalculable harm without any corresponding benefit to the government. He touched briefly upon the points raised in the brief previously submitted by his law firm in support of the argument that the Council was not under an obligation to register. He stated that regardless of what technical agency relationship may have resulted as a consequence of the subventions received by the Council from the American Section of the Jewish Agency for Israel, nevertheless, this agency relationship had now been terminated since the Council had arrived at a decision that it would not incur any vestige of possible obligation to register by cutting off all funds from the American Section and that it would continue its program through the raising of funds from domestic sources. Judge Rifkind went on to state that even though an agency relationship may have been created by the receipt of funds, the general over-all program of the Council was such that it could come within the purview of the cultural exemption from registration as contained in Section 3 (e) of the Foreign Agents Registration Act, and even though the Council did disseminate some publications which conceivably through a broad interpretation of the definition of political propaganda would fall within that category, Judge Rifkind stressed the fact that these activities were a very minor portion of the entire program for which funds received from the Jewish Agency were utilized. He emphasized that the Council used most of these funds for Hebrew education, youth movements, charitable purposes and other cultural activities related to the Jewish people.
>
> Finally, Judge Rifkind raised the point, after emphasizing the disparity of numbers between the... [American Council for Judaism] and the American Zionist Council, that the vast number of Jews who adhered to the principles of Zionism could not understand how "our administration" could do such harm to the Zionist movement and impair the effectiveness of the Council by insistence on registration. He appealed to the

---

[hh] Lenvin probably meant to reference the American Council for Judaism.

discretionary power of the Department which he claims it has in all criminal cases by stating that the Department generally makes a judgment as to which cases it will pursue and which it will not, pointing out in this connection that not all traffic violators, for instance, are given tickets, but that other circumstances must be taken into consideration.

Mr. Katzenbach replied to this observation that it was a matter of proper administration of justice to use discretion and judgment in the exercise of prosecutive powers, but that he wanted to make the point to Judge Rifkind that the laws of the United States were not only to be enforced against Republicans, but were to be enforced impartially.

After Judge Rifkind completed his outline of his position—and in this connection it is noted that he did not go into any detail as to the controlling facts upon which the request for registration was based—Mr. Lenvin outlined for Mr. Katzenbach's benefit the principal facts upon which the request for registration was predicated. [288]

Deputy Attorney General Katzenbach then offered a very clever, but ultimately fatal, accommodation to Rifkind: additional disclosure from the AZC in exchange for DOJ reconsideration of the entire FARA registration order.

After hearing these facts, Mr. Katzenbach asked Mr. Rifkind whether the receipt of the funds from the American Section of the Jewish Agency was considered to be confidential and the reply was negative. Mr. Katzenbach then asked whether information as to how these funds were expended was considered to be of a confidential nature, and again Judge Rifkind replied in the negative. Mr. Katzenbach then noted that if the Council made a full disclosure of the receipt and expenditure of the funds it received from the Jewish Agency so that such information would then be available for public inspection the purposes and objectives of the Registration Act might well be accomplished and very likely there would be nothing further for the Government to do. Mr. Katzenbach made it clear that he was not at this time committing the Department to accepting this procedure, but that we would examine the material filed by the Council before reaching a decision. In the event this was the eventual solution, it should be understood that the information submitted would be a matter of public record, the same as a registration statement filed under the Act. Judge Rifkind indicated the Council quite likely would submit all of the information to the Department.[289]

As the true volume of Jewish Agency payments was registered in the Senate record in 1963, Rifkind and the AZC would alternately delay, reinterpret, flood the section with irrelevant data and ruthlessly exploit this "Katzenbach concession" to avoid filing the requested information. This lasted until the cover provided by the JFK administration was suddenly and violently destroyed forever.

The battle was soon joined at the grassroots level as constituents across the U.S. entered the fray. Attorney General Robert F. Kennedy and the Congress were bombarded with outraged constituent letters and telegrams after the first major media confirmation that the Department of Justice was working on an AZC FARA registration. This appeared in a curious *Wall Street Journal* article on June 28, 1963:

> FEDERAL LAWYERS near decision on whether to require the American Zionist Council to register as an agent of the Israeli government. High Justice Department officials weigh the risk of offending Jewish opinion in the U.S. Senate Foreign Relations Chairman Fulbright also eyes the council's activities.[290]

The article had no byline, and subtly echoed the threat Rifkind explicitly made to Katzenbach in early May. It produced an immediate flurry of public outrage. Among the first of many protests to arrive on RFK's desk was a letter from L. Edward Tonkon of the Dallas, Texas-based Tonkon Millinery Company.

> As an American of Jewish faith, I feel a deep affinity religiously with people of my faith in Israel and elsewhere in the world. However, I could not in keeping with my loyalty to my country, the United States, countenance our Justice Department's failure to enforce the law against any one person or organized group of persons, simply because of a religious belief and the grossly misinterpreted "mythical" concept in this instance of such a thing as a "Jewish" vote. However, if the highly organized, well financed and pressure force of the satellites of the Israeli government in this country, under many names and guises, has convinced our present government that there is such a thing as a "Jewish" vote (which they assert exists in strategically large electoral vote areas in the East and California) I am hopeful an honest government, with honest officials, fulfilling the complete oath of their office, will not succumb to such pressures and enforce the law of the land.[291]

The record reveals that Tonkon's hopes were initially well placed. But Tonkon was prescient in seeing that resisting years of grinding pressure from all sides would be the DOJ's true challenge. Only one official would survive the onslaught. The sentiments expressed in copies of other letters and telegrams filed at the Internal Security division were similar:

To Senator Ralph Yarborough: "Urge your influence to insure [FARA decision] not be determined on religious or political grounds..." Marjorie and Raymond Arsht

To Senator Douglas and RFK: "You would do grave injustice to five million American Jews, should you make any decision affecting the welfare of our country in order to risk offending a supposed Jewish opinion." Jane Dreyfus

To RFK: "I am unaware of any provision in the statutes of such a criterion for this legal determination of facts. I am also unaware of any provision in the fabric of American national political life for the necessity to consider the 'opinion' of any so-called national minority group in the formulation of policy decisions affecting the national security." Richard L. Hoffman

RFK: "As a Jew I urge decision based on legal considerations only. I doubt that most Jews support Zionism and none should oppose complying with U.S. laws." Resident of Highland Park, IL

RFK: "We wish to practice our religion of Judaism without any involvement with a political subsidiary of any foreign state, therefore, we urge you as Attorney General look seriously at the American Zionist Council for political involvement with the State of Israel and thus necessitating it to register as a foreign agent." Mr. and Mrs. Harvey Lanero[292]

Illinois Congressman and future Secretary of Defense Donald Rumsfeld also wrote RFK about the marked influx of constituent concerns over the Wall Street Journal article. Rumsfeld asked that RFK "report as to the policy of the Department of Justice will follow in determining this question."[293] The letters and requests for responses from members of Congress continued to flow in through late summer of 1963. If there were any constituents lobbying for the DOJ to consider political calculations in its law enforcement process, they were clearly using other avenues and representatives: no letters making an opposing argument appear in the FARA section file.

Meanwhile, Adrian W. DeWind[ii] and another lawyer from Paul, Weiss, Rifkind, Wharton & Garrison submitted a stack of publications and papers to Nathan Lenvin on June 28, 1963. When Lenvin asked whether the

---

[ii] Adrian W. DeWind is listed as legal counsel at the Paul, Weiss, Rifkind, Wharton & Garrison tax department according to their company website as of June 28, 2008.

submission included papers in compliance with the Rifkind-Katzenbach agreement, including receipts and expenditures, DeWind indicated that he had not attended the meeting, but did not think the papers delivered included expenditures. Lenvin briefed DeWind on what he understood were the terms of the Katzenbach concession before leaving:

> We would examine the submitted publications, and if it was decided that the exemption from registration was not available, the Department would insist that the receipts and expenditures of the Council be furnished for public inspection. It was understood in the meantime that records regarding receipts and expenditures would be made available to the Department.[294]

Lenvin's interpretation clearly provided no motivation for the AZC to risk delivery of highly sensitive public relations and lobbying disclosures. Under the agreement, these could later be made public by the department. Yeagley's handwritten notes on the file outlined a possible special registration deal for the AZC: "It was my understanding they were to give us in effect a full disclosure but not on a registration form."

On July 17, 1963, Nancy Fahrnkopf filed an internal content analysis memorandum to Nathan Lenvin. She first outlined the corporate objectives of the AZC to "create and maintain a climate of opinion favorable to Israel" through the efforts of the "Department of Information and Public Relations" and reviewed approximately 40 samples of literature delivered by DeWind. She found that "a substantial portion of this material contains support for specific domestic and foreign policies of the Israeli government" and that "memos to the Local Zionist Chairmen and key community leaders included reprints of favorable articles, instructions for countering unfavorable articles, recommendations of books and articles, comments on the Syrian-Israel crisis..." Fahrnkopf's summary was conclusive: "the bulk of the materials and programs offered by the various departments of the AZC are intended to promote a favorable attitude toward Israel" and that the "Department of Information and Public Relations is clearly the most 'political' of its activities." Fahrnkopf included an extensive distribution list from Rabbi Jerome Unger dated August 27, 1962 outlining public relations market channel segmentation, segment size, and materials to be distributed.[295] (see Appendices for the complete original 1962-1963 Committee on Information and Public Relations strategic communications plan summary.)

Yeagley telephoned Rifkind on July 17, 1963 about the absence of itemized financial information in the DeWind submission.[296] Rifkind claimed to be "embarrassed" that the AZC had not delivered any information on receipts and expenditures and said he understood from DeWind that everything "had been settled." He promised to get back to Yeagley "right away."[297] On July 22, Yeagley also responded to Donald Rumsfeld. He confirmed that the AZC FARA registration matter was under consideration, but clarified that the *Wall Street Journal* article was not an accurate representation of the way the Department of Justice did business.

> You may wish to advise your constituents that the implications they found in the Wall Street Journal article represent neither the views nor policies of the Department of Justice. The question of whether the American Zionist Council should be required to register under the Foreign Agents Registration Act is presently under consideration by this Department. I am sure that your constituents will be interested in knowing that our ultimate determination will be based on the law as applied to the facts in this particular case and not on any consideration of its effect on the public opinion of the Jewish community in the United States.[298]

Senator Fulbright's second hearing on the Jewish Agency was scheduled for August 2, 1963. On Friday, July 18 at noon, Nathaniel S. Rothenberg, representing the AZC, was logged[ii] telephoning Nathan Lenvin at the FARA section. He advised Lenvin that Mr. Bick, the treasurer of the AZC, was out of town for two weeks. The controller was hospitalized due to a heart attack. Rothenberg requested a two-week extension for the submission of the registration statement data. Lenvin replied that he would discuss it with Yeagley, but that the registration was expected not later than the first week or so in August. Rothenberg asked how detailed the statement should be and Lenvin replied that the "statement should be detailed and complete in every respect." Rothenberg said he wanted to stress that "we are working on it" and ended the call.[299] By July 30, on the eve of the Senate hearings, Katzenbach wrote to Yeagley that "Rifkind should be needled, but much depends on Fulbright, too."[300]

On August 14, 1963, the FARA section had received nothing from the AZC, but was immersed in digesting the deluge of highly incriminating information from testimony and documents divulged in the Senate

---

[ii] Only as "Mr. Rothenberg."

Foreign Relations Committee hearings. Yeagley asked Thomas K. Hall for an update: "Mr. Hall, is it time to write Rifkind—or send a memo to AG, or send in FBI?" he scrawled. Hall wrote a derisive internal memo to Lenvin about the AZC's filing status: "Judge Rifkind has had ample time to respond to our request for information in this matter. It appears to me that as in the past he is stalling hoping that time will resolve the difficulties faced by the AZC. Immediate action in my opinion is necessary...we should go on record with the AG (copy to the Deputy) outlining the posture of this matter and indicate the need for more drastic action..." Yeagley ordered Nathan Lenvin to prepare another memo on the matter.[301]

On August 16, 1963, Rabbi Jerome Unger sent Lenvin two reports of income and expenditures, which Irene Bowman of the Internal Security Section rejected as inadequate in light of the newly public information from the Senate Foreign Relations Committee. On August 20, 1963, Lenvin responded with an internal memo to Yeagley outlining how the records of the May and August Fulbright hearings had disclosed a much broader and deeper array of AZC activities than the FARA section was previously aware of.

> ...this testimony reveals that the Council's actions have been much more widespread in the propaganda area than was heretofore realized or disclosed during the course of our meetings with counsel for and representatives of the Council...
>
> While some of the activity of the Council may well fall within the educational or cultural exemption from registration, it is clear that the principal objective of the Council is to create by means of propaganda and other devices a favorable picture of the State of Israel and the Zionist movement. In addition, despite the disclaimers of representatives of the Jewish Agency that the Agency is separate and distinct from the State, it is also clear there is a close affinity between the two. Consequently, it appears to me that there is no alternative but to require the American Zionist Council to do no less than file a full and complete registration statement and to make a public disclosure through a registration statement of its activities on behalf of the Jewish Agency, Jerusalem, and/or the American Section of the Jewish Agency. There is attached hereto a proposed letter to Judge Rifkind implementing this recommendation.[302]

This "close affinity" mentioned by Lenvin would later provide grounds for a direct Department of Justice challenge to the Jewish Agency–

American Section. George Washington University law professor W. T. Mallison Jr. and Rabbi Elmer Berger of the ACJ would ask the DOJ to force the American Section to disclose its true agency relationship with the Israeli government. It would ultimately do so, but not for almost another decade, after Lenvin was dead.

On August 22, Yeagley forwarded the Lenvin memo and an AZC material and hearings analysis to Deputy AG Katzenbach, suggesting that a letter to the AZC be copied to Rifkind demanding a complete public AZC registration statement. FBI director J. Edgar Hoover had asked Yeagley on August 14 whether he needed the bureau's assistance regarding the AZC matter. Yeagley responded:

> This is to advise you that the registration of the American Zionist Council was originally solicited by letter dated November 21, 1962, as a result of disclosures made in the registration statement filed by the American Section of the Jewish Agency for Israel....pending a determination as to whether a further letter should be written insisting on registration no investigation will be required. You will be kept advised of developments in this matter.[303]

On October 9, 1963, Nathan Lenvin and Irene Bowman from the FARA section met once again with Rifkind in the firm's offices. Lenvin advised Rifkind that Nicholas Katzenbach was in agreement: due to new facts emerging from the Fulbright hearings, the department must insist that the AZC file a complete FARA registration statement using official forms immediately. The Katzenbach concession was canceled. Lenvin also suggested that Rifkind could file a statement indicating the registration was made under protest, if he so desired.

Rifkind asked Lenvin what exactly had arisen in the hearings that had not been previously disclosed. Lenvin cited a Jewish Agency payment to the AZC of $197,500, another for $712,000, and a $100,000 AZC loan taken at Bank Leumi and left on the AZC's books. Repayment was guaranteed by the Jewish Agency. He also discussed the AZC's propaganda activities in "cultivation of editors," letters to editors and approaches to Capitol Hill. Lenvin summed it up by stating that since the American Section of the Jewish Agency was itself just a conduit, the AZC should name the Jewish Agency in Jerusalem as its true foreign principal. He also rejected the summary report submitted by the AZC on August 16, 1963, as "bald statements" that precluded any previously discussed exemptions to registration tendered by Katzenbach.

Rifkind asked if there were any special registration forms and Yeagley responded affirmatively. Rifkind said he "believed the statement should be filed as of the date of dissolution of the AZC, January, 1963."[304] On October 10, 1963, Yeagley and Lenvin sent a terse one-page letter to Rifkind, again including FARA registration forms, insisting on a response within 72 hours.

Four days later, the AZC had still not complied with the deadline, but instead called another meeting. Yeagley detailed this summit between Katzenbach, Rifkind, and DeWind, at which Simon Rifkind was apoplectic:

> Judge Rifkind then made the plea for no registration, stating that it was the opinion of most of the persons affiliated with the Council that such registration would be so publicized by the American Council for Judaism that it would eventually destroy the Zionist movement....Mr. DeWind thought there were no differences between its situation and a hypothetical situation such as the NAACP receiving grants from some group in England but continuing its same program and functions...[305]

Katzenbach held his ground and told Rifkind that he did not have any discretion in the case, and that it "seemed clear to the government that the Council came squarely within the provisions of the Act and would have to register." Rifkind countered that he thought requirements could be covered by filing materials amounting to disclosure, but Yeagley replied that materials submitted so far by the AZC had not been relevant.

Rifkind claimed he had already consulted with the AZC member organizations and believed they could supply all the information required of the "average registrant," but he did not believe his clients would file any papers indicating that the organization was the agent of a foreign principal.[306]

The FARA section was pressing a very strong case against the AZC. It had compiled documentary evidence of agency through the Fulbright hearings. With Rifkind now talking about the "dissolution of the AZC," it seemed as though a transparent, publicly disclosed FARA disclosure of relationships and activities, however historical it might be, was at hand. FARA was also being reinvigorated with new resources after years of institutional malaise, falling registrations, and declining prosecutions. This was due to the efforts of Senator Fulbright and the Foreign Relations Committee preliminary 1962 reports with their warranted criticism of the DOJ and U.S. State Department's implementation of FARA. Both played major roles in restoring FARA enforcement, for a time. But events favored Rifkind.

The unity of purpose of the Department of Justice under RFK was about to be shattered by a cataclysm that would forever shift the advantage back to the AZC: the assassination of President John F. Kennedy on November 22, 1963, less than one month in the future.

FARA Ascendant

The Senate Foreign Relations Committee's damning report alleged that FARA was enforced only "sporadically" and selectively. It was usually directed at members of Communist countries. The report depicted foreign agents for a vast array of other countries, most of them U.S. citizens, as free to propagandize and lobby without disclosure of activities:

> With the growth of foreign Government representation in the public relations field, the amount of disguised political propaganda disseminated has greatly increased...though the act contemplated control of just this type of activity through its labeling provisions, these particular provisions have been all but erased from the law books through non-application.[307]

The initial report cited registration statements with obvious omissions and verifiable evasions, suggesting that the Justice Department was not devoting sufficient resources to monitoring registrations, policing and enforcing FARA. The report's citation of the Department of Justice's own statistics seemed to support charges that FARA enforcement had largely stalled. In the first six years of the act, nineteen indictments were brought, with eighteen convictions. Between 1945 and 1955 only two indictments were lodged, and only nine between 1955 and 1962. Most damning, according to the report, was that since 1945 all cases were for failure to register, rather than failure to list all activities, expenses, and other required data:

> The requirement for full and accurate completion of the various forms has been only sporadically enforced by the Justice Department.[308]

The Department of Justice was also failing to be proactive about keeping the U.S. State Department in the loop about foreign agents' activities, according to the report:

In almost every case, the initial statement becomes the first and last time that State receives official information on a registered agent and his activities. Six-month supplemental statements, dissemination reports and any additional short-form statements...are normally not circulated to the State Department. [309]

A Justice Department spokesperson countered that there was some cooperation with the State Department and indicated that they could provide more information on a regular basis if desired. The Senate report, meanwhile, mandated a further inquiry into the five categories of foreign agents investigated by the committee:

Lawyers, who handle everything from purchasing an embassy, lobbying a bill through Congress, drawing up a peace treaty and supervising public relations activities;

Public relations men, who, through the mass media, try to establish the United States public image desired by their client country;

Economic consultants, whose activities range from drawing up development plans for their client countries to helping promote the United States Government loans that put such plans in operation;

Purchasing agents, who, for their foreign clients, deal in anything from light machinery to heavy armaments;

Influence peddlers, who, because of their Washington contacts, are hired to advance their foreign client's interests at the highest and lowest levels of the United States Government.[310]

By early February 1963, the Department of Justice announced that sixteen additional lawyers were being put to work reviewing active foreign agent files just as the Senate Foreign Relations Committee began holding hearings. The Department of Justice reviewed 510 paid agents for foreign principals, and additional information was requested of 70 more. Twenty-two were asked for additional details of expenditures. Other inquiries pertained to proper labeling of foreign government propaganda circulated in the U.S. Although he had already privately agreed to force the AZC to register as a foreign agent, Deputy Attorney General Nicholas E. B. Katzenbach publicly agonized during the hearings over the political consequences of going after the nation's elites:

I think this committee can appreciate the problems involved for indicting, for example, a prominent attorney or a prominent public relations firm for a failure to report expenditures in great detail where the expenditures were for entirely legitimate activities.[311]

Committee chair J. W. Fulbright responded that the committee felt that Americans acting as foreign agents had done things "inimical to the interests of our government" and that both the U.S. State Department and Department of Justice had been "very casual" in enforcement and compliance. Senator Bourke B. Hickenlooper concurred in particular with investigating whether foreign aid money was being cycled back to U.S. agents "to lobby in behalf of more foreign aid."[312] Fulbright was clearly thinking about Israel's U.S. lobby and the activities of Isaiah L. Kenen, the ballooning demands for aid and opaque foreign financial flows.

But as the Senate Foreign Relations Committee went on to subpoena witnesses in 1963, a case against a foreign agent for the Dominican Republic was also slowly and painfully unwinding. It verified Katzenbach's intuitions about how politically explosive even seemingly straightforward FARA prosecutions could become as they unraveled hidden webs connecting elite members of the U.S. press corps, public relations firms, and politicians, including the president.

Dominican Republic

John F. Kennedy faced his own minor FARA-related trouble, compliments of the First Lady's couturier, just as Fulbright's Senate Foreign Relations Committee issued an initial Foreign Agents report in 1962.

In 1960, the Eisenhower administration had severed diplomatic relations with the Dominican Republic, which was still ruled by the aging dictator Rafael Trujillo (1891-1961). The Organization of American States found that Trujillo agents had tried to assassinate the president of Venezuela. Between 1960 and 1961, the loss of preferential sugar exports to the U.S. cost the Dominican Republic almost $28 million per year. Until his own assassination in May of 1961, Trujillo labored mightily to restore ties through public relations, diplomacy, and lobbying in Washington.

The succeeding Dominican Republic government attempted to exploit a Cuban gambit by convincing the Kennedy administration of the threat of a potential Castro-type revolution with Soviet backing in the Dominican Republic.

Igor Cassini, an elite society columnist for Hearst whose column was syndicated worldwide in 150 newspapers, claimed credit for inventing the popular term "jet set". He picked Jacqueline Bouvier (the future First Lady Kennedy) as "debutante of the year" in 1948. His younger brother Oleg Cassini was a fashion designer and became her official couturier when she became first lady.[313] Igor Cassini started the public relations firm Martial & Company in the late 1950s. He leveraged his friendship with Porfirio Rubirosa, a fellow "jet-setter" in charge of inspecting Dominican embassies, into three six-figure public relations contracts for a related firm domiciled in Zurich, Switzerland. Cassini then parlayed the threat of overthrow to President Kennedy to win approval for an official secret mission to Santo Domingo toward restoration of trade and diplomatic ties.

Subsequent political turbulence in Santo Domingo led to the public release of Cassini's lobbying contracts. The Kennedy administration denied knowledge of Cassini's lobbying ties. In 1963, Cassini pled no contest to charges of violating FARA, which saved the administration further embarrassment. Cassini also paid a $10,000 fine for failing to register and was sentenced to six months' probation.[314] He subsequently lost his job at Hearst and most of his public relations clients. He then lost his wife to an overdose of sleeping pills.[315] FARA violations could deliver harsh consequences.

Nonproliferation and Dimona

Kennedy had bigger worries than tawdry scandals surrounding the Dominican Republic—namely the Cold War and countering nuclear proliferation. Israel suddenly loomed large on the second front. When the existence of Israel's secret nuclear reactor abruptly became public, Isaiah Kenen carefully broadcast the Israeli government line that the Dimona nuclear reactor was being built for research and peaceful purposes in his January 2, 1961 issue of the *Near East Report*:

> New Reactor. Israel is building a nuclear reactor high in the frontier town of Dimona, east of ancient Beersheba and overlooking the southern tip of the Dead Sea. The French are assisting in the project which will be completed in three or four years...
>
> Mr. Ben Gurion denied published rumors that Israel intended to produce an atomic bomb. Ambassador Avraham Harman informed the Department of State that Israel would welcome visits by students and

scientists of friendly countries when the reactor is completed, to demonstrate its peaceful character.

> ...reports of Israel's new reactor created a furor and a temporary U.S.-Israel rift because of the secrecy which attended them...Israel government spokesmen then denied that they could or intended to produce the bomb and gave that assurance to Secretary of State Christian A. Herter upon his return from a NATO conference. But U.S. officials were vexed because they had not been kept informed.[316]

When reporting on particularly sensitive matters such as the Israeli nuclear weapons project, Kenen carefully selected and highlighted clips from mainstream U.S. news sources that downplayed the issues or supported the Israeli government's line on them. Kenen's work with the American Zionist Council cultivating a cadre of PR professionals and opinion columnists often paid off in such moments of crisis, when he would print exonerating quotes from "outside experts" and "reliable sources" in the *Near East Report*.

> No Bombs Possible. Meanwhile, many asked whether the Israel reactor could really produce sufficient plutonium, a nuclear weapon component, to construct a bomb. Science editor William L Laurence of the New York Times deflated these reports, on Dec. 25, when he wrote that "the plutonium produced in a small nuclear reactor of 24,000 thermal kilowatts is very minute indeed...and 'completely useless for bomb material.'" The basic facts, if fully understood, would make it clear why only great industrial nations, particularly the United States and Soviet Russia, can be full-fledged members of the "atomic club."[317]

Kenen's fellow travelers at the venerable business magazine *Barron's* also managed to get off a broadside at the State Department about Dimona which he reprinted in the *Near East Report* :

> Against this background, observers ask why a non-military reactor caused such a violent explosion in Washington. Barron's, the business weekly, caustically commented on Dec. 26, "The U.S. State Department once more placed itself in a ridiculous posture by accusing Israel of conspiring to build atomic weapons. The project was a subject of common gossip in the coffee houses of Tel Aviv (where American diplomats venture)..."[318]

The U.S. administration's firm internal consensus was that the facility would indeed be used to produce nuclear weapons. President Kennedy privately sent a top-secret ultimatum to the new Israeli Prime Minister through American ambassador Walworth Barbour about U.S. concerns over Dimona on July 5, 1963. Kennedy demanded that Israeli Prime Minister Levi Eshkol submit to periodic U.S. inspections of the facility to verify claims that it was only for research:

> It gives me great personal pleasure to extend congratulations as you assume your responsibilities as Prime Minister of Israel. You have our friendship and best wishes in your new tasks. It is on one of these that I am writing you at this time.
>
> You are aware, I am sure, of the exchange which I had with Prime Minister Ben-Gurion concerning American visits to Israel's nuclear facility at Dimona. Most recently, the Prime Minister wrote to me on May 27. His words reflected a most intense personal consideration of a problem that I know is not easy for your Government, as it is not for mine. We welcomed the former Prime Minister's strong reaffirmation that Dimona will be devoted exclusively to peaceful purposes and the reaffirmation also of Israel's willingness to permit periodic visits to Dimona.
>
> I regret having to add to your burdens so soon after your assumption of office, but I feel the crucial importance of this problem necessitates my taking up with you at this early date certain further considerations, arising out of Mr. Ben-Gurion's May 27 letter, as to the nature and scheduling of such visits.
>
> I am sure you will agree that these visits should be as nearly as possible in accord with international standards, thereby resolving all doubts as to the peaceful intent of the Dimona project. As I wrote Mr. Ben-Gurion, this Government's commitment to and support of Israel could be seriously jeopardized if it should be thought that we were unable to obtain reliable information on a subject as vital to the peace as the question of Israel's effort in the nuclear field.
>
> Therefore, I asked our scientists to review the alternative schedules of visits we and you had proposed. If Israel's purposes are to be clear beyond reasonable doubt, I believe that the schedule which would best serve our common purposes would be a visit early this summer, another visit in June 1964, and thereafter at intervals of six months. I am sure that such a schedule should not cause you any more difficulty than that which Mr. Ben-Gurion proposed in his May 27 letter. It would be essential, and I understand that Mr. Ben-Gurion's letter was in accord with this, that our scientist have access to all areas of the Dimona site and to any related part of the complex, such as fuel fabrication facilities or plutonium separation plant, and that sufficient time to be allotted for a thorough examination.

Knowing that you fully appreciate the truly vital significance of this matter to the future well-being of Israel, to the United States, and internationally, I am sure our carefully considered request will have your most sympathetic attention.[319]

JFK's administration was later proven correct in believing that Dimona was a nuclear weapons facility. Disclosures by Israeli whistleblower Mordechai Vanunu revealed that the reactor would ultimately be configured and cooled to operate at 120-150 megawatts, capable of producing enough enriched materials for up to twelve nuclear bombs per year. In March of 1968, the Mossad surreptitiously acquired 24 tons of uranium ore from West Germany, ostensibly bound for an Italian company, but illicitly diverted by sea to Israel.[320] By 1969, Israel had quietly emerged as a full-blown nuclear power.[321] In 1979, the Israelis even tested a low-yield nuclear artillery shell, which was detected by an American spy satellite despite the cloudy conditions.[322] But not until 2008 would a former U.S. president publicly confirm for the first time that Israel had developed an arsenal of 150 nuclear weapons.[323]

Kennedy's insistence on international inspections of Dimona and his evolving position on Palestinian refugees had him falling out of favor with Kenen's lobby late in 1963. He joined Senator Fulbright in vocal criticism of the Israeli prerogatives constantly being written into foreign aid bills at the urging of AIPAC. Kenen's November 19, 1963, *Near East Report* alerted the lobby to Kennedy's sudden and dramatic reversal under the shrill banner "President Kennedy Opposed":

At his November 14 press conference, President Kennedy criticized Congress for denying the foreign aid funds he requested and for putting restrictions on their expenditure.

He did not think that the language of the anti-aggression amendment, which required him to make an "extremely complicated" finding, "strengthens our hands or our flexibility" in dealing with the UAR. "In fact, it will have the opposite result," he declared.

He described the Arab countries as nationalist, proud, and "in many cases radical." Threatened with suspension of aid, they would be tempted to say, "Cut it off."

President Kennedy did not think that "threats" from Capitol Hill produced hoped-for results. He said that cutting off the Aswan project had not "brought the UAR to follow us."[324]

Kennedy was assassinated one week later. Kenen's next issue of the *Near East Report* briefly mourned JFK's passing before moving on to the business at hand. The Department of Justice subsequently lost all of the political cover necessary to force the Israel lobby to register under FARA.

> "AIPAC, as previously noted, was registered as a domestic lobby to work on legislation and public policy that enhance the U.S.-Israel relationship. As such, it may engage in an unlimited amount of congressional lobbying and is free to exchange information with Israeli leadership in carrying out that function. At the same time, it retains full autonomy in deciding when and how to act." *Jewish Polity and American Civil Society*, 2002.

Chapter 10: Secret Deal

News the death of John F. Kennedy changed everything, especially at the Department of Justice. It meant that RFK's remaining days as attorney general were numbered. RFK began looking at a run for a New York Senate seat (Jacob K. Javits held the other) early in 1964. Although Nicholas Katzenbach succeeded RFK as attorney general in September of 1964, there was no longer any White House support for directly confronting the Israel lobby. The reelection question loomed large with Lyndon B. Johnson, like it had with his predecessors.

Investigative reporter Seymour Hersh chronicled Abraham Feinberg's inroads with the Lyndon Johnson administration as his crowning achievement. The older, more experienced Feinberg now had booming business concessions in Israel, which turbo-charged his financial and lobbying acumen to ever higher velocities.

> There is no question that Feinberg enjoyed the greatest presidential access and influence in his twenty years as a Jewish fund-raiser and lobbyist with Lyndon Johnson. Documents at the Johnson Library show that even the most senior members of the National Security Council understood that any issue raised by Feinberg had to be answered....By 1968 the government of Israel had rewarded Feinberg for his services by permitting him to become the major owner of the nation's Coca-Cola franchise. It would quickly become a multi-million-dollar profit center.[325]

The exemption of Israel from Kennedy's nuclear nonproliferation regime was confirmed after his death by President Lyndon Johnson in a telephone call to Clark Clifford (1906-1998). Clifford replaced Robert McNamara as secretary of defense. In 1968, as the Israelis ramped up processing at their Dimona facility while denying to the U.S. that there was a weapons program, Clifford placed an urgent call to Johnson:

> "Mr. President, I don't want to live in a world where the Israelis have nuclear weapons." Johnson's reply was definitive: "Don't bother me with this anymore." And he hung up. [326]

Johnson would go on to celebrate the signing of the Nonproliferation Treaty with 50 nations as "the most difficult and most important of all the agreements reached with Moscow." But Johnson soon learned that even though the Israel lobby had been granted an unofficial preliminary exemption to the Nuclear Nonproliferation Treaty and even U.S. agreement not to acknowledge its arsenal, this could not buy support for the war in Vietnam. None of his Israel lobby backers would (or more likely, could) push top-down policy mandates into the grassroots organizations for whom they claimed to speak. In particular, Johnson simplistically pandered for more "Jewish support" for the war in Vietnam. He colorfully recalled to Israeli Foreign Minister Abba Eban the lack of horse trading on the issue during one delegation's visit:

> A bunch of rabbis came here one day in 1967 to tell me that I ought not to send a single screwdriver to Vietnam, but on the other hand [the U.S.] should push all our aircraft carriers through the Strait of Tiran to help Israel. [327]

Johnson suffered an excruciating public scolding in 1966 when his entreaties for "Jewish support" were leaked to the press. Johnson was upbraided by the American Council for Judaism for believing in the "top-down power myths" of his circle of elite campaign financiers and or that American Jewish views were somehow monolithic and homogeneous:

> ...critical of the meeting held at Mr. Goldberg's apartment last week at which the United States Representative to the United Nations reportedly defended President Johnson from charges that he had ascribed a single view on Vietnam to all Jews and linked the Administration's Vietnam policy with United States aid to Israel....
>
> For 20 years, Mr. Korn said, American Zionists have given the impression that all Jews automatically support Zionist policy.
>
> President Johnson, Mr. Korn stated, should ignore such claims. American Jews, he said, face a fundamental problem when their interests are linked with the national interests of Israel. American Jews, he

charged, have permitted "a handful of self-appointed spokesmen to wheel-and-deal in the name of the 'Jews.'"[328]

Although applying FARA to the Israel lobby was swept off the table by the Johnson administration, pursuit of FARA violations related to other small countries remained active. But the fact remains that any deep FBI or FARA investigation into Abraham Feinberg concerning Israel's nuclear weapons program would have created presidential campaign contribution chaos. Indeed, the volume of Feinberg's cash campaign contributions became a flashpoint when a Johnson administration staffer was caught up in a sordid sex scandal.

On October 14, 1964, Johnson's top administrative assistant Walter Jenkins was arrested in a public restroom and charged with sexual solicitation. It was less than three weeks before the 1964 presidential elections, and panic ensued. At least $250,000 in cash that Abraham Feinberg had raised was secured in Jenkins's office safe. Johnson telephoned his trusted aides Bill Moyers and Myer Feldman to retrieve the money. They successfully moved the cash, contained in a heavy briefcase, to a safer location.[329]

Heavies Pull Out of AZC Registration Battle

After JFK's assassination, the AZC immediately went into an offensive posture on the FARA battlefront. Rifkind promptly and unequivocally notified the FARA section on December 11, 1963 that "our client is not prepared to register as an agent of a foreign principal, or to concede that it is subject to the registration requirement." But Rifkind also included an attachment of AZC payroll records, an income statement, and a schedule of AZC payments made between November 1, 1962, and January 18, 1963. This, he stated, "represents the date when the mode of financing of the American Zionist Council was modified and after which date no further subventions were received from the Jewish Agency." Rifkind then made an additional request for special treatment of the disclosure: "We request, however, under the circumstances, that these papers be kept in files of the Department not available for general public inspection."[330]

On December 13, 1963, Yeagley examined the submission and noted to Nicholas Katzenbach that for FARA purposes it was deficient:

> There is no statement as to activities. The lengthy payroll serves no useful purpose for disclosure purposes. The figures supplied are described as "typical" although greater sums were received at other

periods. The figures show $173,000 received from the Jewish Agency for Israel over the three months. Although this is far less disclosure than they made to the [Senate Foreign Relations] Committee, they ask it not be available to public inspection.

I suggest I write Rifkind—or better—the Council, with a copy to Rifkind advising it is not only not in compliance with the law—but not fulfillment of his representations at the meetings in your office.

This Division would then recommend prosecution of the Council and possibly some top officials to the Attorney General. P.S. Some months ago De Wind brought in some publications and other printed material.[331]

Katzenbach, more attuned to shifting winds in the political stratosphere, suggested a different approach. Yeagley listened and then instructed Nathan B. Lenvin to prepare a letter to Rifkind in a "friendly, rather than a hostile tone and rather brief, generally to the effect that the material be[ing] submitted is not satisfactory or not what we expected, or etc. and adding if Judge Rifkind is going to be in Washington in the near future he hopes he will come in to see him." It was to be signed by Katzenbach, not J. Walter Yeagley.[332] On January 10, 1964, the letter was dispatched to Rifkind, dryly noting that "of course there is no disclosure unless the data is available for public inspection."[333]

On January 31, 1964, Nathan Lenvin attended a meeting with Rifkind and Nathaniel S. Rothenberg at Rifkind's New York law office. Rothenberg presented Lenvin with his business card. The card listed his business address at 55 Liberty Street in New York City. A handoff ensued.

Rifkind kicked off the meeting by showing Lenvin a pamphlet being circulated by the American Council for Judaism, which "contained charges that the Zionists were acting as propaganda agents for the State of Israel and that the Jewish Agency was being used as a conduit for funds to Zionist organizations in the United States." Rifkind was "concerned that any disclosures which were to be made by the subject organizations should not be such as to substantiate these charges made by the American Council."

In discussing the adequacy of previous filings, Rifkind indicated the fact of a high-level conversation with Katzenbach and Yeagley on January 30, 1964. Rifkind characterized Katzenbach as now "relaxed" about the overall FARA issues. He also portrayed Katzenbach as wanting the registration section to work out an "acceptable formula" with respect to the type of information disclosed and what AZC information would be open to public inspection. Lenvin pressed back that too much detail on payrolls and other data was being submitted and not enough data was itemized on expenditures, their destinations, and their purposes. Rifkind countered that Katzenbach had indicated that the Justice Department "did not wish the American Zionist [Council] to go to undue expense and trouble in providing this information, and that the Department would be reasonable in regard to the period and details which this statement would contain."

As if to punctuate that the AZC registration issue was now merely a low-level technical matter that would be resolved with preferential treatment, Rifkind announced that he would personally "not need to participate in the future" and officially delegated attorney Nathaniel S. Rothenberg as the new key contact before the Department of Justice on the matter.[334] On the way out, Rothenberg stressed to Lenvin "one caveat, that they would have to be sure that anything they submitted would not ultimately prejudice the organization in the eyes of the public." Lenvin promised to deliver copies of relevant May and August 1963 Jewish Agency–American Section FARA testimony before the Senate Foreign Relations Committee to Rothenberg.

Rothenberg had his work cut out for him. At one time he was secretary of the United Palestine Appeal,[335] he was likely highly qualified to interface with organizations making expenditures and then trace how they were channeled back into U.S. programs, if compelled to do so. But now the only question was how much the AZC wished to disclose. The answer was not very much.

Rothenberg's assignment as AZC's lead lawyer before the Department of Justice underscored the power shifts in the final phase of the registration attempt. Simon Rifkind was out of the picture. Katzenbach was now the insider attorney general candidate and would be named AG in less than a year. The tough "72 hours or else" stance for an accurate FARA declaration was dissipating as the AG scrambled to extend the more conciliatory line of the Johnson administration. Lenvin, in providing Senate transcripts to the AZC, was now functioning more like the DOJ's duplication and typing pool. He was also being forced to respond to Rifkind's assertions of privilege derived from a January 30, 1964 Rifkind-Katzenbach-Yeagley discussion for which no available DOJ minutes exist. As a meticulous note taker dedicated to the accurate conveyance of facts, Lenvin must have feared the return of the amorphous, seemingly multipurpose Katzenbach concession. The FARA section staff was now fighting a losing battle, armed only with facts, evidence, and the law.

Caveat

Lawyer Irene Bowman of the FARA section read the January 31 meeting notes and was livid. "I don't see how we can accept a caveat that an organization won't submit information that might prejudice it publicly. I hope Nathan made clear to Mr. Rothenberg that is not the test. I think we should advise Rothenberg that the worst that the Council can do publicly is to stall and delay in submitting the financial information which the law clearly requires."[336] In a February 10 memo to Yeagley, Edwin Guthman relayed Bowman's concerns verbatim. By going over his head, Bowman signaled she no longer seemed to trust Lenvin.

Yeagley responded on the 17th to Guthman, Bowman, and Nathan Lenvin: "I don't think the above is quite justified since I did not indicate that we would accept any 'caveat'. But let's wait and see what is submitted."[337] The very same day, February 10, Yeagley sent a letter (signed by Nathan Lenvin) to Nathaniel Rothenberg at his Liberty Avenue offices. It requested detailed expenditures from "April 1, 1960, to the date of the Council's dissolution, if such request is too burdensome, the statement should cover the last two years, 1961-1962." Their request again made clear that the Justice Department was not interested in expenditures related to "Hebrew education and culture," but rather expenditures by the "Department of Information and Public Relations, so as to include the specific dates payments were made, the name of the person or organization to whom payment was made, the purpose for which payment was made and the amount of the payment."[338]

Rothenberg responded on March 16, 1964. He suggested that the request for income and expenditures from the AZC fiscal year 1962 and the ten months ending January 31, 1963 "merely duplicated the information already furnished you by the American Zionist Council." Rothenberg then raised the "Katzenbach concession":

You are familiar, I know, with the agreement reached between Judge Rifkind and Mr. Katzenbach, in the presence of Mr. Yeagley, with regard to additional information to be furnished your Section. Such agreement was reached, as I understand it, in the realization by Mr. Katzenbach that with the present size of the staff of the Council it would be indeed burdensome to furnish your department with itemization of expenditures of the past two years. A sample itemization was therefore forwarded to you for a period of approximately three months. The basis of such agreement still obtains and your request with regard to the expenditures of the Department of Information and Public Relations would certainly impose that burden which it was felt and agreed could be avoided. However, for the purpose of showing the good faith of the American Zionist Council, the Council would be prepared to submit to you a detailed statement of expenditures for the Department of Information and Public Relations for a sample period of three months. Such a period would, I am sure, be representative of the expenditures for the entire period requested.[339]

Rothenberg's hardline position that the AZC would provide only pro forma "samples" drawn from any period it wished rather than providing actual itemized expenditures generated sharp internal debate. The Rothenberg proposal letter crossed paths in the mail on March 16 with an outbound letter from the new acting head of the FARA registration section, James L. Weldon, demanding action. Weldon's letter was drafted by Yeagley, who noted, "the attached outgoing letter is for your information. We requested this info better than a month ago and I see no justification for delaying our attached letter or reminder. I believe our last para[graph] is more polite than is warranted, however, I'm aware of the scope of interest within the Department on this matter."[340]

But the larger question remained unresolved. What exactly were the strictures of the "Katzenbach concession" made to the AZC? Only one person could answer. Yeagley forwarded the Rothenberg correspondence to Nicholas Katzenbach under a confidential memo cover: "Nick, This is the most blatant stall we have encountered. Do you mind suggesting what we do next because all of us here would call their records before a grand jury."[341]

Katzenbach wrote to Nathaniel Rothenberg. Three-month samples were not sufficient. But the deputy attorney general's conciliatory response failed to clarify any tangible limits to his earlier concession made to Rifkind. "While we have endeavored to make our requests as reasonable as possible, we cannot accept your suggestion since the information offered is not in compliance with the Act or what we thought our understanding was with Judge Rifkind."[342]

The AZC dispatched yet another raft of irrelevant documents to the FARA section, analyzed internally by Irene Bowman on October 20, 1964. She found the expenditures were:

> ...lumped into general headings with no dates or recipients mentioned....Under the heading entitled "Department of Information & Public Relations" there are 17 subheadings such as "Grants to Foundations & Kindred Organizations" ($54,020); "Pamphlet, Newspapers, Books & Written Materials" ($7,119.68); "Radio, TV & Films" ($1,503.34) and "Speakers Fees and Expenses" ($17,856.49). As another illustration under a separate heading titled "Special Services & Events" there is an item called "Allocations to Constituent Zionist Organizations" ($83,871.06).[343]

The AZC positioned itself as simply another node in the network, either unwilling or incapable of disclosing the ultimate destination and use of the transferred funds. Bowman again noted the attribute plaguing previous AZC submissions:

> This sample itemization of payments was deemed deficient in that it did not cover a sufficient period of time and the itemization set forth insignificant items in great detail while failing to focus attention to payments by the Department of Information and Public Relations.[344]

Bowman then attempted, possibly in desperation, to outline how the previous FARA requests for itemized disclosures actually fell within the limits of the "Katzenbach concession":

> The above request [FARA Section] appears to be in line with Mr. Katzenbach's position in this matter as expressed in his meeting on May 2, 1963, with Judge Rifkind in which he said if the Council made a full disclosure of the receipt and expenditure of the funds it had received from the Jewish Agency so that such information would then be available for public inspection, the purposes and objectives of the Registration Act might well be accomplished. Mr. Katzenbach made it clear that he was not at that time committing the Department to accepting this procedure, but that we would examine the material filed by the Council before reaching a decision.[345]

But the AZC no longer had to risk full and potentially public disclosure to the Justice Department. On October 22, 1964, Katzenbach briefly attended his last formal meeting on the AZC matter with Rothenberg, Yeagley, and Lenvin. The meeting was the beginning of a cascading series of capitulations to AZC demands for special treatment. Katzenbach then became acting attorney general in September when Robert F. Kennedy resigned from the Department of Justice to begin his run for a New York Senate seat.

Katzenbach's Capitulation

Nathan Lenvin outlined the October 22, 1964, meeting by noting the scarcity of Katzenbach's time and submission to AZC demands for material and temporal disclosure limits. "Mr. Katzenbach had to excuse himself because of urgent business elsewhere, but before he left he made clear to Mr. Rothenberg that, in response to the latter's assertion that to submit all of the financial information we had previously requested for a two to two-and-a-half year period would be a great burden on the subject, we would accept a statement as to a typical three month expenditure projected for the entire period concerned."[346] Katzenbach was now accepting a "projection" as opposed to comprehensive actual declaration filing over the period in question for the FARA section.

Katzenbach was even more conciliatory in allowing the AZC to choose which period it would like to report, as noted by Lenvin: "Mr. Rothenberg replied to Mr. Katzenbach that the Department could take any three month period it wanted, but Mr. Katzenbach made it clear that it was their responsibility to pick a three-month period that would reflect by projection the true state of the expenditures made by the Public Information Department of the American Zionist Council."[347]

After Katzenbach left the meeting, Rothenberg contested the point that actual itemized rather than representative data would be required. Lenvin's notes continue:

> ...he did not entirely appreciate the ruling which Mr. Katzenbach had made in this matter, to-wit that we would not accept a typical three-month period, which was what Mr. Rothenberg seemed to think Mr. Katzenbach had requested, but we would have to have this typical three month period projected so that it would reasonably reflect all of the expenditures of the Public Information Department of the subject during the period concerned. Mr. Rothenberg then stated that he understood and would attempt to accomplish this result. [348]

Rothenberg pressed for an additional major concession from the Department of Justice—that the names of public speakers contracted by the AZC who received indirect compensation from the Jewish Agency not be made public. Lenvin noted that this core public disclosure in the proposed three-month filing was going to be ruled on by Katzenbach:

> Included among the items which we advised Mr. Rothenberg we would want in the breakdown of expenditures were payments made to lecturers who were retained by the subject to make speeches or talks on behalf of the subject. Mr. Rothenberg claimed that this could well be embarrassing, particularly to individuals such as university professors who would not want to make it part of a public record that they received fees or expenses from the subject for this type of activity. Mr. Yeagley indicated that he would present this view to Mr. Katzenbach to determine whether he would be willing to modify the financial statement we were expecting so that the names of these particular individuals would not have to be included.[349]

Katzenbach apparently agreed. In handwritten notations to the meeting memo, Yeagley noted that this type of confidentiality for the speakers was "OK, in view agency is terminated and speakers did not realize Council was a foreign agent." Yeagley further proposed a novel technical treatment of the speakers list: a non-public file to be held in the FARA public registration office. He made this handwritten notation on the second page of Lenvin's meeting notes file: "They are to include the names for confide[ntial] info. of Dept. [of Information and Public Relations] not for public file."[350]

On November 4, 1964, Nathaniel Rothenberg advised Nathan Lenvin that he would provide detailed expenditures from the AZC Department of Information and Public Relations for the period of April, May, and June 1962. The list was to contain administrative expenses, meetings and speakers' fees, written materials, television radio and film, subventions, and visitors to Israel. Rothenberg affirmed that the period chosen "is a fair representation of the expenditures of this Department for any and all other three-month periods, and that the items set forth, when projected over a yearly period, would approximate the annual costs for each item."[351]

Yeagley responded to Rothenberg on November 18, 1964 that "it was intended, however, that the reporting period would be the entire period with which we are concerned, for example January 1960 to April, 1962. Mr. Katzenbach agreed, however, that the report for the full period could be prepared by projecting a typical three month period and that as long as you were satisfied that the sample period selected was representative of the entire period and would result in a reasonably or substantially accurate report, he would be willing to accept it in that form."[352] The Department of Justice had now capitulated, via Yeagley, on any right to compare the three-month expenditures to an actual year of true income and expenses. On November 23, 1964, Rothenberg returned a short letter stating, "In accordance with our understanding, I have asked the American Zionist Council to proceed with the preparation of the report. It will be forwarded to you at the earliest possible moment."[353]

Yet by January 19, 1965, no AZC declaration had yet been received in the FARA section. Irene Bowman alerted Nathan Lenvin to his responsibilities: "To date to my knowledge no such report has been submitted. It may be that you would like to bring this matter to Mr. Yeagley's attention. It appears that a follow-up letter is in order."[354]

Then, on January 28, 1965, President Lyndon B. Johnson suddenly ended months of speculation by appointing Nicholas Katzenbach as attorney general.[355] The AZC registration issue soon began to move rapidly toward closure.

Subvention Recipient Caveat

Nathan Lenvin spoke with Rothenberg on February 25, 1965, about the delayed filing. Rothenberg asserted that it was caused by "the inability to collect all of the information we wanted in the detail it was indicated the Department desired; however, he assured me this material had now been collected and was in the process of being put into proper form..." Lenvin then invoked the name of the new attorney general in double negative scolding: "I told Mr. Rothenberg we had depended to some extent on his good faith in assuring us that the material would be coming in, and that I would not like to believe that he did not intend to adhere to the assurances he gave to Mr. Katzenbach during the course of the above referred meeting."[356]

On March 2, 1965, Harry A. Steinberg, Executive Director of the American Zionist Council forwarded an itemization of disbursements for the Department of Information and Public Relations for the period April 1, 1962 through June 30, 1962. Itemized payments were numerically coded to a separate list of speakers, organizations, and foundations, but Steinberg cautioned it was to be handled with the utmost care: "Mr. Rothenberg has requested of you that this listing be kept separate and apart from the record of disbursement in any public files of your Section."[357]

The Department of Information and Public Relations disbursements for the period totaled $37,986.92 in payments for administration, speakers' fees, written materials, broadcast media, subventions, and visitors to Israel. The secret list of speakers and payments for publications, as probably intended, is somewhat unremarkable. It did not divulge any of the payments to Isaiah Kenen that the Jewish Agency had specifically slated for the *Near East Report*. Those incremental payments, totaling $38,000 disclosed in the Senate hearings were made much earlier—between June 29, 1960, and October 13, 1961.[358] The itemized payments disclosed were for a period long after the American Section and AZC already knew of an impending investigation. Nevertheless, the disclosure matched to the secret coded list is of some interest.

Mortimer J. Kroll, the desk operations manager at the *New York Times* radio station WQXR and later with *The New Yorker* magazine in 1963, appears on the AZC payments list. He received $350 for "press and publicity" from the AZC.[359] If this payment had been disclosed in 1965 it might have surprised Senator Fulbright, who had cautiously and somewhat humorously exonerated the *New York Times* and other major publications during testimony about Kenen's *Near East Report* in the August 1, 1963 session:

> Mr. Boukstein: Mr. Chairman, this is not the only publication which is favorable to Israel in the United States; there are others.
> Senator Fulbright: I have no doubt of it. Certainly, the *New York Times*, the *Washington Post*, I could name a hundred of them, I guess, they are very favorable and I am not suggesting they are in your employ. I am suggesting that Mr. Kenen is receiving far more of his funds from the Jewish—the Israel Government directly and indirectly than is the *New York Times*. They are doing it strictly on their own, at least as far as I know.
> Senator Fulbright (continued): I really shouldn't speak authoritatively because we haven't looked at it, but it is quite clear Mr. Kenen has been, for practical purposes, as he states himself, up to a certain point of your reorganization, he was on your payroll. Then, in order to insulate him, you took this indirect way of paying him by buying his product and paying him in that way. I am only trying to understand how this is done. I don't know why he shouldn't register.[360]

The publications may not have been on the AZC/Jewish Agency's payroll, but some reporters and media personalities were certainly contractors. Among the other names appearing in the key word index were Reverend Karl Baehr of the American Christian Association for Israel ($500 for "meetings" and "written materials") and Jacques Torczyner, president of the Zionist Organization of America ($142 for "travel expenses"). Academics include Harvard Ph.D., professor, and author John Stoessinger ($210 for "fees and expenses") and Dr. Nasrollah Fatemi ($234.97 for "travel expenses"). Fatemi served as Iran's delegate to the United Nations in the 1950s and later became Director Emeritus of the Graduate Institute of International Studies at Fairleigh Dickinson University in New Jersey.[361] Among the smaller payments itemized (as little as $0.72 for a booklet) was a disbursement to Joseph B. Schechtman (1891-1970). But the payment is nonetheless noteworthy.

Schechtman was a founder of the World Union of Zionist Revisionists and became a prolific author after moving to the U.S. in 1941. His many books include *The Arab Refugee Problem* (1952), *The Life and Times of Vladimar Jabotinsky: Rebel and Statesman: The Early Years* (1956), *On Wings of Eagles: the Plight, Exodus, and Homecoming of Oriental Jewry* (1951), *Jordan: A State that Never Was* (1968), *Arab Terror: Blueprint for Political Murder* (1969), and *Israel Explores Deir Yassin Blood Libel* (1969). Though he only received $12 as a "speaker's expense" on the AZC coded disclosure, he was already serving on the executive committee of the Jewish Agency at the time.[362] Like other individuals listed in the "disclosures," the AZC probably felt that Schechtman could fend for himself if he was "outed" as an AZC contractor. Few of the organizations and individuals selected for the short AZC filing would generate undue problems, or even interest, if discovered. They never were. Their "public" disclosure was classified.

Bona Fide Dispute

Nathan Lenvin must have exhaled a somewhat self-satisfied breath of relief to Irene Bowman:

> Apparently my visit with Mr. Rothenberg has had at least some concrete results. If we can reasonably find that this is in substantial compliance with the understanding reached between Messrs. Rothenberg and Katzenbach in regard to what this organization would report, then I believe we should try to write "finis" to this at least for the time being. If you do find this fairly satisfactory, then we should make an effort to gather the other material which has been submitted including the

propaganda material and, if possible, make one file which would then be available for public inspection should such an occasion arise.³⁶³

Now on the spot, Bowman momentarily crumbled. She filed a neutral, almost mechanical memo recapitulating Katzenbach's earlier acceptance of a sample reporting period and the AZC's submission of material without indicating any tangible approval or disapproval. She did raise one final outstanding issue: Would Steinberg's request for recipient secrecy actually be granted by the DOJ? If it was, how would the FARA section handle a non-public, public disclosure? Bowman once again appealed to Lenvin's superiors, writing, "In the covering letter to the Department Mr. Harry A. Steinberg, Executive Director of the American Zionist Council, states that Mr. Rothenberg has requested that this listing be kept separate and apart from the record of disbursements in any public files of this Section....It is suggested that the sufficiency of this material as a registration statement should be passed upon by either Mr. Yeagley or Mr. Katzenbach." But then, in cursive handwriting across the bottom of the memo appears Bowman's obtuse, initialed capitulation. Later documents indicate her additional clarification was produced under duress. "I agree with the conclusion that I recommend that the material be accepted and put into form for public examination."³⁶⁴

Bowman's actual position, truer to her previous form, is illuminated in a file entry detailing the utter inadequacy of the AZC material as a FARA registration. It is dated the very next day (March 24, 1965). Her resentment at being forced to synthesize and approve a statement conjured up from disparate documents and projections shines through in her memo, now coolly addressed to the department "files" rather than to Nathan B. Lenvin:

> While it appears possible to make up a registration statement from documents furnished by a prospective registrant, these documents should furnish all of the information required by the Act to be stated in a registration statement. The above material, none of which is executed under oath, fails to provide the following information for the purpose of the Act: The identification of the foreign principal, the Jewish Agency, American Section, Inc. and whether the agency relationship still exists; the agreement or terms of the agreement, if oral, between the Jewish Agency and the AZC; a detailed itemization of the expenditures for the period, April, 1960—to the date of dissolution from the Department of Information and Public Relations; a comprehensive statement regarding the funds received from the foreign principal from 1960 including the purpose for which received; and a concise statement of the activities taken on behalf of the foreign principal. In addition no short-form

registration statements have been filed by responsible officers of the AZC.

It should also be pointed out that the Department has apparently agreed to accept the report of expenditures submitted by the Department of Information and Public Relations without the listing of the names of the recipients of the subventions, the problem with which Senator Fulbright was concerned during his inquiry regarding the administration of the Foreign Agents Registration Act. It is the writer's view that the report without this listing does not comply with the Act and is meaningless.

For the foregoing reasons the writer is opposed to the acceptance of the material submitted by the AZC as a registration statement.[365]

Bowman was the last bastion defending the rule of law in the FARA section, but time had run out and she was about to be overruled internally. In an exasperated March 31, 1965, memo to Yeagley, Lenvin noted, "At this stage in the game, our only alternative would be to institute prosecutive proceedings. Since in my view this would be impractical, I recommend that the material submitted be accepted as a registration statement and put into such form as would be available for public inspection in the event such an occasion should arise."

Readers of the internal DOJ record may accurately interpret the word "impractical" as a euphemism for "completely lacking necessary political capital." The clock had run out, and rule of law now had to take a back seat as Lenvin approved Rothenberg's assertion that "no useful purpose would be served by including these names in the material which would be made available for public inspection." Lenvin hinged his final recommendation that the section accept the filing as a FARA registration on a tenuous tidbit from a preliminary legislative report draft divulged by a staffer on Fulbright's Senate Foreign Relations Committee:

In connection with our original basis for requesting the registration for the AZC, it is interesting to note that the contemplated report of the Senate Foreign Relations Committee as shown me by Mr. Norville Jones, a staff member of the Committee, states that the receipt of a subsidy from a foreign principal without direction or control by the foreign principal would, in the view of the Committee, not create an obligation to register. In the event it was determined that prosecution should be instituted and such prosecution was initiated subsequent to the issuance of the report, such a statement by the Committee indicating the intent of Congress in regard to coverage of the Foreign Agents

Registration Act would, in my view, seriously militate against any successful prosecution.[366]

Yeagley, who was apparently now eager for the section's blessing of the highly unorthodox registration, noted, "Also the relationship terminated a couple of years ago, at least." Beneath Lenvin's typed justification for not making public the names of fund recipients, Yeagley handwrote, "OK, I would like to see how the file is set up." Both Internal Security Division executives had now conveniently repressed the Jewish Agency's documented direction of funds to Isaiah L. Kenen, among many other contrary findings.[367] Powered by this voluntary amnesia, the AZC's unique non-public registration was gathering momentum. However, the FARA section would be forced to endure a final and precisely timed humiliation. It revealed how lost Yeagley and the others had truly become in convincing themselves that the essence of the foreign principal-U.S. lobby relationship had ever, or would ever, terminate.

AZC's Secret FARA Registration

The majority of the Internal Security Division now seemed anxious to close the AZC file "finally and forever."[368] The Bowman reversal on principal coupled with Katzenbach's newer and higher responsibilities meant only one thing: Yeagley needed to formalize the AZC's special joint public-secret filing at the FARA section.

Nathan Lenvin had already worked out an internal procedure for public inquiries. He circled back to the phrase used by the Jewish Agency's Maurice Boukstein on October 31, 1962, having probably read through his earlier records before crafting his final major memo. Lenvin downgraded the entire affair to the level of a "bona fide dispute."

> The material filed by the American Zionist Council (AZC) was filed in accordance with an understanding between the Department and the AZC and was filed as a result of a bona fide dispute between the parties as to whether registration was, in fact, required under the Foreign Agents Registration Act. Neither party was inclined to test the applicability of the statute in a criminal proceeding. Thus it was agreed that the material would not comprise a registration statement but would supply basic information regarding the activities of the AZC financed in part by the Jewish Agency, American Section, Inc. This material is available for public inspection.[369]

Lenvin built up his earlier tentative rationalizations about the AZC while simultaneously devaluing the real power and institutional prerogative of the Department of Justice to act in the interest of the American people. In retrospect, the only "party" capable of initiating a "criminal proceeding" was the Internal Security Division, which had relatively recently contemplated taking the AZC file to a grand jury and sending in the FBI. The "bona fide dispute" branding now characterized the affair as a squabble between curiously equal parties. J. Walter Yeagley quickly adopted Lenvin's "bona fide dispute" phraseology when he formally closed the case with the FBI, though he wisely dropped Lenvin's references to "testing the statute." May 14, 1965 was the date of Yeagley's last formal contact with the FBI on the entire AZC matter.

> Reference is made to the Division's memorandum to your Bureau dated August 23, 1963, captioned as above, in which you were advised that the registration of the American Zionist Council (AZC) had been solicited under the Foreign Agents Registration Act and that discussions were being held between Departmental officials and representatives of the AZC regarding its obligations under the Act.
>
> For your information the AZC has submitted informational material which is available in the Registration Section for public examination. This material was filed in accordance with an understanding between the Department and the AZC and was filed as a result of a bona fide dispute between the parties as to whether registration was, in fact, required under the Act. The material does not comprise a registration statement but does supply basic information regarding activities of the AZC financed in part by the Jewish Agency, American Section, Inc.[370]

Yeagley then coached the rest of the DOJ staffers about where the color-coded AZC material would be located and how to handle any public inquiries:

> The material filed by the AZC was placed in an expandable portfolio to distinguish it in appearance from the registration statements which are filed in manila folders. In the event Mrs. Eldred receives inquiries as to whether the AZC is registered under the Act, she has been instructed to respond in the negative. She is to advise, however, that the AZC has filed information with this Section which is available for public examination.[371]

On a final consolidating memo formalizing the accommodations for the secret section of the AZC file, Yeagley wistfully penned, perhaps for posterity, "Ok. This seems to be what Attorney General Kennedy and the then Dep. AG Katzenbach had in mind. —JWY."[372] His earlier commitment to uphold "law as applied to the facts in this particular case" was now defunct. Robert F. Kennedy, elected and serving in the Senate since January 3, 1965, had long since moved on to other controversies. RFK fell to his assassin, Sirhan on June 6, 1968. Sirhan, born in Jerusalem on March 19, 1944, was convicted for the crime. After years of being denied parole, a two-person panel of the California parole board granted Sirhan parole on August 27, 2021.

AZC Resurgent

No former Department of Justice insider writing a book, investigator or member of the news media ever had the AZC files declassified to reveal a remarkable, if somewhat bureaucratic, saga. Few insiders had anything to gain from it. For some of those directly involved, promising career advances awaited. Others were reaching the end of the line and had no need to "rock the boat." Only one, Irene A. Bowman, seems to have been a likely candidate for disclosing the story.

J. Walter Yeagley went on to become a District of Columbia Court of Appeals judge and died peacefully in West Palm Beach, Florida in 1990.[373] Nathan B. Lenvin, longtime veteran of the FARA section, never left the Department of Justice; he died in his sleep at the age of 58 during a business trip to Chicago to interview potential recruits in 1968.[374] His wife, an English teacher in northern Virginia, died 30 years later, survived by their two children.[375]

Nicholas Katzenbach died in 2012. He is remembered for a legendary 1963 civil-rights-era showdown with Alabama Governor George Wallace, who literally blocked the entry of two black students into the University of Alabama. Katzenbach rose to become U.S. Undersecretary of State from 1966-1969, and his pithy and now declassified Johnson administration analysis is entering the American public consciousness via new Middle East histories, including those covering the 1967 Six-Day War. These histories refute the volumes of orthodox narratives of an "Israeli David pitted against the Arab Goliath." Among the more recent Katzenbach blurbs: "The intelligence was absolutely flat on the fact that the Israelis...could wipe out the Arabs in no time at all."[376]

But whatever became of the AZC? Its public affairs and lobbying functions eventually morphed into the American Israel Public Affairs Committee (AIPAC) and affiliated organizations and think tanks. But the

AZC did settle its score with the FARA section in Kenen's favorite arena: the press.

Among the last items in the FARA section's file on the American Zionist Council is single news clipping from the *New York Times*, dated May 17, 1965. It was not formally logged into the department until two days after Yeagley closed the AZC case. Its headline read, "9 Zionist Groups Agree on Program." The article revealed that the American Zionist Council, contrary to the multiple assertions from Simon Rifkind and Nathaniel Rothenberg about its impending "dissolution," was very much alive and kicking:

> The American Zionist movement took a major step yesterday toward revising its program to strengthen every phase of Jewish religious and cultural life in this country.
>
> Three hundred delegates of nine Zionist groups, which represent varying ideological viewpoints, agreed for the first time on a program of unified action "to safeguard the survival and growth of the American Jewish community."
>
> The action was taken at an all-day planning conference at 515 Park Avenue convened by the American Zionist Council, the representative body of the groups, which have an overall membership of 750,000.
>
> The delegates reaffirmed "Zionist responsibility toward the security and welfare of Israel" and the need for the United States Government "to affirm in unmistakable terms America's commitment to the security and independence of all Middle East nations and its determination to prevent aggression be it military or economic." They urged that there should be no appeasement at the expense of Israel. [377]

Lenvin, Bowman, and Yeagley were probably shocked not only at the story's timing, but at the audacity of the AZC summit's location. It was listed as taking place at the same address where the Jewish Agency–American Section office was headquartered. The AZC meeting also signaled the beginning of a new and even more aggressive phase for the lobby, which would soon challenge U.S. election law enforcement and the sanctity of classified U.S. economic and national security information.

AIPAC would provide a clean corporate shell organization into which the AZC's lobbying and public relations talent and initiative infrastructure could be poured. Still, scattered public resistance continued. The Jewish Agency–American Section would be abruptly forced to shut down. A professor and an activist, the only two members of the public ever logged at the FARA section as having reviewed the public AZC FARA filing analyzed it and mounted legal challenges to the Jewish Agency–American Section. However, just as the AZC was only temporarily inconvenienced before it was reborn within AIPAC, the Jewish Agency–American Section would also rapidly reemerge, somewhat cynically, in yet another orchestrated corporate shell company ballet. Such timely and opportunistic morphing became the lobby's specialty.

For Americans who have wondered about the Department of Justice's reticence to take on the Israel lobby in the face of decades of seemingly clear statutory violations, this inside account provides useful clarity. There is an institutional history behind that extreme reluctance. Few in the DOJ would, or could, discuss the relevant history with outsiders until the day it was declassified. That day has arrived, and perhaps a more informed discussion—and warranted law enforcement—may commence.

And what became of Irene A. Bowman after this showdown? Predictably, Bowman's innate sense of fair play drove her straight into trouble at the Department of Justice. In 1976, at the age of 45, she filed a lawsuit alleging age and sex discrimination in the promotion of women. Bowman was a highly accomplished 1955 graduate of Ohio State University law school and secretary of the law review. She won her lawsuit and received monetary damages. She then went on to work helping other women with sex discrimination appeals from the Equal Employment Opportunity Commission, an agency established via the Civil Rights Act of 1964 to administer and enforce civil rights laws against workplace discrimination. She worked in this new role until six weeks before she died in 1982.

Bowman was clearly the only public official who did not succumb to the pressures outlined by L. Edward Tonkon in his explicit warning to RFK, "I am hopeful an honest government, with honest officials, fulfilling the complete oath of their office, will not succumb to such pressures and enforce the law of the land." Bowman and other dedicated officials at the U.S. Department of Justice briefly stood and fought on America's defense line. They all failed.

...in the long run, a country's income per head rises by roughly 300 percent if it improves its governance by one standard deviation. —The Economist, 2008

Chapter 11: Above the Law

Senator Fulbright won some amendments to FARA in 1966 concentrated on preserving the integrity of U.S. policymaking. These were based on the comprehensive findings of the Foreign Relations Committee hearings, which explored the foreign agents of many countries besides Israel. The 1966 amendments now required any person who was engaged in defined "political activities" to register as a foreign agent. But this vastly narrowed the original FARA, which had not required that foreign agent activities necessarily be "for or on behalf of" the foreign principal.[378]

Fulbright offered another disturbing finding concerning foreign agent campaign contributions drawn from his investigation. John A. O'Donnell was one of two American members of a postwar commission created to arbitrate damage claims under the 1946 Philippine Rehabilitation Act. Ernest Schein was the commission's chief examiner. Fulbright discovered during closed testimony that O'Donnell had agreed to work on further claims for the Philippines less than four months after the commission was disbanded. Together with Schein, he obtained payments of over $1 million through 1960 representing foreign principals without registering under FARA. These payments were in fact derived from U.S. damage awards paid to Filipino Catholic organizations in 1946 and 1952. The awards recycled to the lobbyists from 23 religious clients and amounting to about 10% of awards already received were used to press for further aid. In 1963, Fulbright attached provisions to a $73 million appropriation to the Philippines stipulating that it would be the "final liquidation" of all damage claims and that none could be disbursed to individual claimants.[379] O'Donnell had doled out $7,100 in campaign contributions during the 1960 congressional elections from his lobbying fees. Fulbright sought to ban such contributions outright. However, the case of Abraham Feinberg's expanding exclusive and government-approved business concessions in Israel, even as he continued to be the point person for presidential campaign contributions, reveals that the Fulbright attempt largely failed. Complex and opaque on and offshore financial flows were impossible to monitor.

Lobbyists such as Isaiah Kenen and AIPAC probably followed FARA proceedings directed at other countries closely, even as they were caught up in the Senate foreign agent investigations. But after the preferential AZC registration, the Israel lobby operated under a different set of rules. AIPAC developed a vast, more distributed array of capabilities than the average Latin America lobbyist could muster, though one lesson that clearly emerged from the Dominican Republic's intersection with first lady Jacqueline Kennedy was the age-old utility of "hooking points."

The more involved and ingratiated foreign lobbyists could become in high officialdom, the less likely they were to ever be seriously prosecuted for FARA-related crimes, up to and including espionage. Between 2005 and 2008, this tactic would be tested to the hilt in pre-trial maneuvers defending two AIPAC officials against indictments brought under the 1917 Espionage Act. The defense was finally granted the right to call high-ranking Bush administration officials to testify, a tactic that almost guaranteed presidential pardon or dismissal of the case for lack of witnesses if all invoke executive branch prerogatives not to appear.

Kenen retired from AIPAC in 1974. The same year, a report from the Government Accounting Office[kk] revealed an obvious FARA weakness. The compliance section was almost entirely reliant on the timely, complete, and accurate disclosure of foreign agents' activities. FARA had the power to issue deficiency notices, initiate investigations, and refer violators for possible criminal investigation.[380] But assuming the good faith of foreign agents and the political will of an administration to prosecute violators continued to be FARA's Achilles' heel.

Two high-profile scandals underscored the inherently elite nature of FARA violations and the political difficulties in strict application of the law. Marion Javits, the wife of Senator Jacob K. Javits, filed a deceptively crafted FARA registration designed to cover the legal exposures but mask the true nature of her lobbying for Iran. It nevertheless ended in disaster. Billy Carter, brother of President James Earl "Jimmy" Carter, Jr.,

---

[kk] Later renamed the Government Accountability Office

like Kenen, didn't bother to register at all for his lobbying on behalf of Libya. Both provided comic-tragic theater signaling that the days of FARA penalties for violators were coming to an end.

In 1974, Marion Javits, a retired actress 21 years younger than her husband with little experience in public relations, crafted a $507,500 proposal for the Shah of Iran on behalf of the firm Ruder & Finn. In a *People Magazine* interview the same year, she stressed that her skills were not law or public relations, but rather more people-oriented:

> So I am socially involved in what goes on in my society, but I'm not a social worker, I'm not a lawyer and I don't choose to be an actress. But I'm playing a role.[381]

Senator Jacob K. Javits's role at the time was ranking Republican on the Foreign Relations Committee. Marion was a friend of the Shah's sister, Princess Ashraf Pahlevi. Mrs. Javits suggested that bad publicity about Iran "buying up all the armaments in sight" produced "attitudes that are both real and prejudicial." She proposed an "educational program directed to the opinion makers of this country, to community leaders, political figures, and the national major media and the broad general public." To stem growing U.S. awareness of the brutal repression of the Shah's regime maintained by the Savak secret police, Javits wanted to promote several somewhat mutually exclusive concepts. "The fact is that the Shah, even though he is in a sense an absolute ruler, has highly constructive social goals and that under the conditions that exist in Iran, the only way to accomplish these goals is by tight control, firm leadership, detailed national planning—and he does this with benevolence and compassion."

Parviz C. Raji, an aide to Iranian Prime Minister Hoveida, wrote the prime minister a frank note in May of 1975: "I think the performance of this plan is advisable even if its only result will be to pour money in the pocket of Mrs. Javits." Both Raji and Hoveida understood that the real objective, detailed in a top-secret memo, was to obtain "private access" to Congress, key politicians, governors, Democratic and Republican party leaders, universities, and, above all, the elite press. "Mrs. Javits herself, who has many contacts with America's news media officials and first-class writers, will play a major role," wrote Raji to Hoveida.

The Shah personally approved the contract while vacationing at a St. Moritz ski resort, conspiratorially noting that "because they are Jewish, this should be kept confidential." Princess Ashraf Pahlevi was to announce the good news to Marion Javits at a private luncheon while stressing the absolute need for secrecy in the matter. As an added precaution, the payment would be channeled through Iran Air, the airline owned by the government of Iran

A unit of Savak based in New York immediately detected a fatal blow to the venture. Marion Javits went ahead and registered as a foreign agent for Iran Air with the U.S. Department of Justice. The *Village Voice* quickly reviewed the registration and broke the news "in a disgusting manner," at least according to Savak's U.S.-based agents. In January of 1976, broadcast news networks picked up the story, and Ruder & Finn was forced to terminate the contract in March. Marion Javits resigned as a senior vice president of Ruder & Finn on January 27, and Senator Javits sheepishly expressed his regrets over the sordid matter.[382]

The prime minister and other Iranians involved in the transaction had intended that the PR campaign be "carefully guarded"—or, put another way, done the way Israel did it. Given their agent was Marion Javits, they had every reason to hope for success. Ruder & Finn was a logical stealth partner for the operation: it had quietly begun providing public relations services to the Israel Office of Information in July of 1967. Shortly after the Six-Day War, the Israeli consulate operation massively ramped up PR efforts (and the budget) in the U.S. to create a positive public image of "Israeli heroics" in America.[383] But the damaging details of both sides of the Javits deal soon became public—in Iran, quite unexpectedly. After the Shah was overthrown in the 1979 Islamic revolution, the Ayatollah Khomeini's regime was only too happy to publicly release all of the secret memos on the matter.[384]

The Javits FARA registration and the resultant public scrutiny clearly doomed the entire Iran project, showing that FARA, though imperfect, functioned when foreign agents actually filed. It was this type of spotlight that Billy Carter, brother of President Jimmy Carter, sought to avoid by not filing his dealings on behalf of Libya.

Billy Carter launched his comical lobbying foray during another periodic lull in FARA enforcement. In 1964, even after the outcome of the Fulbright hearings, active registrants only numbered around 400. By 1980, the number had increased to 700, but with no proportionate increase in FARA section staff. Indeed, the Department of Justice's enforcement policies and attitudes seemed to be softening, if not rotting, from within.

The Department of Justice sought future changes to FARA, in particular replacing the term "propaganda" with less pejorative terms such as "information." FARA enforcement was further hobbled by a 1976 court case in which a federal judge, John J. Sirica, ruled that a law firm acting as a foreign agent for Guinea could claim attorney-client privilege over relevant documents. The firm representing the foreign principal, Covington & Burlington, had refused to turn over 1,000 documents the Guinean government did not want released.[385] This overturned a precedent set in 1972 allowing broad latitude for the FARA section to inspect the records of the Irish Northern Aid Committee.[ll] FARA had been amended to permit such inspections, since the "national defense, internal security and foreign relations of the United States" outweighed possible infringements on First Amendment rights to free speech.[386] The Guinea victory meant that no future Senate investigators would probably ever again rifle through a foreign agent's file cabinet like Fulbright's had.

Covington & Burlington's successful challenge to FARA is also ironic. Nathan B. Lenvin urged Judge Rifkin to consider that "registration never hurt Governor Dewey or the law firm of Covington and Burlington," and that there was no "stigma" for proper disclosure.[387] High-profile firms clearly thought otherwise.

A Justice Department filing against Billy Carter stated that he had undertaken a "propaganda campaign" on behalf of Libya's foreign policy objectives and had received more than $220,000 for services rendered. Like the Dominican Republic in the early 1960s, Libya was experiencing a serious diplomatic rift. U.S. diplomats were withdrawn from Libya in 1979, and the U.S. State Department forced the return of four Libyans present in the U.S. for acting as unofficial diplomats. Libya was also actively opposing Carter's Camp David peace initiative between Israel and the Palestinians.

Billy Carter made two all-expense-paid trips to Libya in September and October of 1979; there, he received a ceremonial sword, gold bracelets, and a saddle worth more than $2000, among other lavish gifts. Billy Carter testified that the $220,000 was simply part of a $500,000 "loan" he had requested from Libya, though his lawyers could produce no loan agreements or other written substantiation. After an 18-month investigation, rather than prosecuting, the Justice Department sought civil sanctions forcing the "immediate and full public disclosure" of his activities. Under a consent agreement, Billy Carter registered as a foreign agent for Libya on July 14, 1980, without admitting or denying charges.[388]

[ll] Noraid was formed in 1969 at the beginning of conflict in Northern Ireland. It has been accused by the US and British government of being a front for the Irish Republican Army and the Justice Department won a court case to register it under FARA in 1981.

By the mid-1970s, FARA's full potential criminal sanctions were accurately portrayed as "rarely pursued." But when they were applied, they tended to target parties with little organized domestic political muscle. On February 19, 1976, the Arab Information Center and its director Amin Hilmy were charged with violating FARA for alleged propaganda efforts on behalf of the Arab League. Charges leveled in federal court stated that the center had distributed advertisements in U.S. papers without required notification that it was acting on behalf of a foreign principal. The Department of Justice did not criminally prosecute the Arab Information Center, but asked for an injunction requiring compliance with FARA. The center was asked to notify readers of the Department of Justice's action in new ads, including the proper FARA disclosure.

Another Department of Justice effort to enforce alleged FARA violations begun in 1975 was thwarted by a ruling and case dismissal based on successful statute of limitations arguments. A Michigan-based media entrepreneur received $11 million through a Swiss bank account to purchase U.S. news media interests on behalf of apartheid South Africa. His efforts to purchase the *Washington Star* (now defunct) in order to counter perceived hostile reporting in the *Washington Post* were rebuffed. But in 1975, John McGoff bought a controlling stake in the United Press International television news agency with $1.35 million in funds provided by South Africa's Department of Information. McGoff decried the 1979 FBI and grand jury investigations as a government attempt to "muzzle" his personal views on foreign policy.[389] McGoff ultimately prevailed in a criminal FARA prosecution against him that did not get underway until the mid-1980s. Federal courts dismissed the case after determining that the statute of limitations had run out.[390]

By the 1990s, FARA enforcement was clearly dying a slow death. Undermined by powerful lobbyists, attorney-client privilege, and foreign-influenced domestic interest groups, it would soon only be applied to the weakest of violators working on behalf of out of favor countries. Even then, prosecution would only be launched if it was in line with clear administration foreign policy doctrine. This would guarantee at least a minimal appearance of enforcement, as constitutionally required, while making sure no potentially embarrassing elite political scandals would surface.

Jewish Agency Metamorphosis

The American Section of the Jewish Agency operated out of its New York City office at 515 Park Avenue into the early 1970s. Isadore Hamlin continued to function as the executive director of the American Section and file the required FARA declarations. But the AZC-DOJ confrontation put a spotlight on the Jewish Agency's activities, and the corporate veil Hamlin and Boukstein had woven was finally beginning to slip. On June 9, 1969, Hamlin responded to a FARA question about the nature of the foreign principal he represented and attached an exhibit explaining why that principal was not a foreign government:

> American Section – Jewish Agency for Israel Inc.
>
> The executive of the Jewish Agency for Israel is the executive arm of the world Zionist organization which, through its constituent member organizations throughout the free world, representing Jews from all over the world principally concerned with immigration, rehabilitation, and resettlement of Jewish settlers and refugees in Israel; with cultural activities in Israel and in other countries; the dissemination of information relating to its activities and the welfare of the people of Israel.
>
> The World Zionist Organization is recognized by the State of Israel as the representative body of Jews outside of Israel for the purposes of immigration, rehabilitation, colonization and resettlement of Jewish immigrants in Israel.
>
> A special law to that effect was passed by the Knesset of Israel in 1962 and an agreement setting forth the areas of cooperation between the executive of the Jewish Agency and the Government of Israel in respect of the foregoing functions of the Agency was entered into in July 1953. The Jewish Agency for Israel is not an instrumentality or a subdivision of the State or the Government of Israel.[391]

Hamlin acknowledged that the Israeli government funded the Jewish Agency, but he would not concede any implicit Israeli government control:

> The government of Israel has from time to time made subventions to the Jewish Agency for Israel, particularly in connection with its work in agricultural settlements and immigrant housing. These subventions varied in amounts from time to time. In all cases, control over the

operations subventioned by the Government remained fully with the Jewish Agency.³⁹²

George Washington University law professor William T. Mallison Jr. knew nothing about the Jewish Agency but received an informal evening briefing from the American Council for Judaism's Rabbi Elmer Berger about the legal issues surrounding the plight of Palestinian refugees. Mallison then began focusing a pointed legal analysis on the underpinnings of the foreign agency relationship between the Israeli government and the Jewish Agency. He felt that FARA required far deeper Jewish Agency disclosures than had been previously filed.

> This persistent blinking of the harder and harder evidence we continued to submit, identifying the Zionist apparatus as a supranational tool of the Israeli government, led us to conceive and develop Mallison's second, major study. This argued that the "Status" law and "Covenant" made the Zionist apparatus either an agent of the Israeli government or actually a part of the government...
>
> When Mallison completed this second study slightly different versions were submitted to both the Department of Justice and the Department of State. The facts and law comprising the body of both petitions were identical. The petitions for relief were tailored to the competencies of each department. At Justice we asked that the Foreign Agents Registration Act be enforced against the Zionist apparatus in the United States. At State we contended that the organized, systematic intervention of the Israeli government in the lives of American Jews, using the Zionist apparatus, was a violation of the Treaty of Friendship and Commerce. At two places in that treaty it is clearly stipulated that the parties were enjoined from carrying on political activity in each other's territory.³⁹³

In August of 1969, after he read the Jewish Agency's FARA declaration, Mallison's report pressured the Department of Justice to compel Isadore Hamlin to file the "1953 agreement" entered into between the Israeli government and the Jewish Agency.³⁹⁴ Mallison also signed out and examined the public portions of the American Zionist Council's file on September 3, 1969. The FARA section's internal withdrawal form duly noted this as only a consultation of AZC's "informational material."³⁹⁵ Mallison based his request on the FARA law then in effect, which required registrants reveal how they were "supervised, directed, owned, controlled, financed or subsidized, in whole or part, by any government of a foreign country." Since registering in 1938, the Jewish Agency had entirely evaded filing such documents.

The Justice Department subsequently compelled the American Section to file its "covenant" with the Israeli government as part of its 1969 registration statement. Senator J. W. Fulbright requested such documents from the Executive in Israel during the course of the May 23, 1960 hearings, but both Hamlin and Boukstein successfully steered him away from the actual covenant. (review the Covenant in the Appendix)

The forced filing of the covenant in 1969 for the first time revealed the extraordinary quasi-governmental powers of the Jewish Agency to independently raise tax-preferential funds for its purposes, encourage capital investments in the state of Israel, coordinate Jewish organizations in Israel, establish new institutions as needed, and even review government legislation before it was submitted to the Knesset (see Appendices).[396] By the time Hamlin filed the covenant, the Jewish Agency–American Section Inc. budget was approximately $35 million.[397] However, the Jewish Agency itself, funded by tax-exempt United Jewish Appeal donations from across the U.S. and other worldwide donations, was one of the best-financed organizations in the world. One observer called the Jewish Agency a "shadow government."[398]

However, as was the norm, no fine or penalty for years of deficient filings was sought by the Department of Justice against the Jewish Agency. The added sunshine only led to the "paper" demise of the American Section, but it was quickly and somewhat cynically reborn.

In 1971, the Jewish Agency–American Section, Inc. notified the Justice Department that it would no longer file under FARA. Operations were functionally passed on to a new registrant, the World Zionist Organization–American Section, Inc. No major contemporary news accounts chronicled this quiet FARA-Jewish Agency movement, perhaps because the transition was so quiet and seamless. In fact, Isadore Hamlin did not even bother changing his office address when the new front organization took over.

The World Zionist Organization–American Section, Inc. registered on September 21, 1971 as a foreign agent for the Executive of the World Zionist Organization in Israel. The WZO Executive in Israel claimed to be the parent organization of the Jewish Agency. The WZO claimed not to be owned, directed, controlled, or financed by any foreign government, and this claim in its FARA filings has not been challenged.

Isadore Hamlin, executive director of the Jewish Agency–American Section, subsequently became the executive director of this new FARA registrant. The WZO immediately took over the publication and distribution of the *Israel Digest* and occupied the Jewish Agency's former space at 515 Park Avenue in New York City. W. T. Mallison Jr., the lawyer who pierced the corporate veil with Rabbi Berger, reflected on the elaborate shell game in 1988:

> Until 1971 the Zionist registrant under the FARA was the "American Section of the Jewish Agency for Israel," Registrant No. 208. Its initial and supplementary registration statements did not include the Status Law or the Covenant, and therefore did not meet the requirements of section 2(a)(2). During the period 1968-1970 administrative proceedings were instituted before the Department of Justice to compel compliance, initially on behalf of the American Council for Judaism (then the principal anti-Zionist Jewish organization in the United States) and subsequently on behalf of American Jewish Alternatives to Zionism. In spite of the strenuous Zionist opposing arguments, Registrant No. 208 was compelled to file both the Status Law and the Covenant on August 28, 1969. These two constitutive documents demonstrated that the agent was not the voluntary private organization which it claimed to be.
>
> On June 9, 1970 the Department of Justice also required the filing of the tax Appendix to the Covenant. Subsequent actions of the Zionist Organization/Jewish Agency demonstrated its concern over these developments. In 1971 there was a "reorganization" of the Jewish Agency which resulted in changing its name, for at least some purposes, to the "Reconstituted Jewish Agency." The apparent purpose was to give the appearance of equal control by the Zionist political and the non-Zionist philanthropic operations of the disposition of funds raised by the Jewish Agency and its subordinate institutions. During that same year, the American Section of the Jewish Agency, Registrant No. 208, deregistered under the FARA on the alleged grounds that it was no longer engaged in political activities. Following that action, the Zionist Organization/Jewish Agency registered under the name, "World Zionist Organization-American Section, Inc." as Registrant No. 2278.
>
> Registrant No. 208 had consistently listed its foreign principal as "The Executive of the Jewish Agency for Israel, Jerusalem, Israel," whereas Registrant No. 2278 has consistently listed its foreign principal as "The Executive of the World Zionist Organization, Jerusalem, Israel." In short, the foreign principal of the past and present registrants is identical although the wording is different. The important change in the new registration is that neither the Status Law nor the Covenant, nor the tax appendix has been filed initially or subsequently although the foreign principal is the same as that of the prior registrant and the specifics of the registration statements of the past and present registrants provide persuasive evidence that the foreign agents (the registrants) are the same or substantially the same.[399]

Isadore Hamlin moved some boxes on his organization chart (rather than between cities or even buildings) by reversing the subsidiary and controlling corporate entities. Then, it was business as usual. There was still the urgent need for an entity to continue Jewish Agency operations in the United States. The WZO's 1972 Congress revealed its goal to intensify consistent ideological and public relations guidance from the foreign principal at the regional and country levels:

> Congress instructs the executive that wherever it is represented at international Jewish conventions every effort should be made to put the Zionist point of view forcibly and to ensure that it prevails; and to this end it considers it essential that the representatives of the Executive and the Zionist Movement generally should consult together before and if necessary during such conventions, in order to frame a common line of policy.[400]

There would be no interruption in U.S. operations as the World Zionist Organization also formally asserted the prerogative of Zionists to assume leading positions across all Jewish organizations outside of Israel:

> Zionists are entitled to a privileged position among the Jewish Organizations in the Diaspora and should be given advisory status in the forming of Israel's external and internal politics.[401]

It is useful to again review why the Jewish Agency/World Zionist Organization was involved in financial flows to finance the *Near East Report*, run public relations campaigns, and indirectly finance U.S. lobbying activity when at least one node of the foreign agency network would likely be compelled to register under the Foreign Agents Registration Act.

By centralizing fundraising in the United Israel Appeal and United Jewish Appeal for exclusive conveyance to the Jewish Agency in Israel, top Israel lobby leadership in the U.S. moved the funds "offshore" outside U.S. jurisdiction and also separated control from contentious and often fractious U.S. Jewish humanitarian aid and relief groups. While Kenen's organization, the American Zionist Council, was an umbrella for powerful U.S.-based fundraising groups, the fact that he was unable to tap significant funds directly from U.S. donors early on is telling. Only by moving the tax-exempt funds "offshore" could they sever control and knowledge of the fund's true destination from domestic source groups. They then quietly moved these and other international funds back into

U.S. public relations efforts, think tanks, and lobbying activities. The offshore component enabled Kenen's and Israel lobby operatives total freedom of movement to secretly pursue activities as they saw fit, rather than by the committee consensus that hobbled predecessor organizations.

Once the groups could show lobbying success and document results, direct access to U.S. funding sources was obtained. Indeed, this was the pattern up to the "reorganization" of the Jewish Agency–American Section. By the early 1970s, AIPAC was able to actually lay claim to less risky non-tax-deductible domestic funding and publicize that for each dollar "invested," a large multiple would be sent to Israel, only now as the burden of all U.S. taxpayers.

Trial by fire means that AIPAC wisely no longer claims to be an umbrella group leveraging the collective membership of constituent organizations. In 2008, AIPAC claimed only 100,000 members, a fraction of the 750,000 AZC trumpeted as an umbrella group in 1965 and 76,000 less than Louis Brandeis first assembled in 1919. In retrospective, the core activist Zionist movement of Isaiah Kenen resembles the modern neoconservative movement: razor-thin, smart, extremely well financed, ably diffused in mainstream media, but curiously unrepresentative of any actual American grassroots following. Only the names have changed as Republican mega-donor magnate Sheldon Adelson and Democratic Party Israeli-American media mogul Haim Saban step in to fill the void left by Abraham J. Feinberg.

AIPAC's efforts to display from the mid-1970s onward a quasi-independent public image had many other advantages. The trauma and legal exposures of the AZC and Jewish Agency–American Section could now be avoided. Should the need arise, AIPAC's core assets and its membership database, operating processes, and relationships management could be quickly shifted into a new shell corporation without damaging the image of the ZOA, Hadassah, or other related membership organizations. These hard-learned lessons about agility would loom and provide options when the DOJ debated whether to indict AIPAC as a corporation, rather than singling out key executives, during the 2005 espionage scandal. Fortunately for the Israel lobby, few in Congress were interested or even willing to investigate the ongoing flow of tax-exempt funds from the U.S. to Jewish Agency and World Zionist Organization operations—even when it was discovered in 2005 that U.S. $50 billion had been laundered into financing illegal West Bank settlements.

AIPAC in the 21st Century

By the beginning of the second millennium, sympathetic modern chroniclers of AIPAC announced that the organization had fully emerged from the FARA gauntlet and was now empowered to act freely, secretly, and in unlimited coordination with the Israeli government. Or at least this is the assertion of the authors of the 2002 book *Jewish Polity and American Civil Society*:

> AIPAC, as previously noted, was registered as a domestic lobby to work on legislation and public policy that enhance the U.S.-Israel relationship. As such, it may engage in an unlimited amount of congressional lobbying and is free to exchange information with Israeli leadership in carrying out that function. At the same time, it retains full autonomy in deciding when and how to act.[402]

No other foreign country claims or enjoys similar lobby-enforced prerogatives in the United States. Many supporters also repeat Kenen's mantra that AIPAC and its executives transcended FARA oversight through their use of U.S. non-tax-exempt funds, confident that if an assertion is repeated often and broadly enough, history will be ignored. This refrain is also amplified by the U.S. media, which is now generally loath to discuss AIPAC history or initiatives.

AIPAC, as the descendant of the American Zionist Council and the Jewish Agency–American Section, is now running bigger gauntlets than FARA. It continues to rely on timely danger alerts from friends in the right places. Like the AZC, AIPAC has counted on behind-the-scenes political pressure and appeals for leniency to keep regulators and U.S. law enforcement officials at bay. AIPAC has become entangled in many alleged violations, including possessing classified commercial documents, breaking election laws, and more recently, espionage.

In 1984, the FBI found that AIPAC helped Israel negotiate an extremely unfavorable bilateral trade agreement with the U.S. while it was in possession of stolen classified information that U.S. companies had supplied in confidence to the International Trade Commission. The FBI was persuaded to drop its criminal investigation of AIPAC, and it was not criminally prosecuted.[403] Between the time it was signed and 2019 the balance of trade has shifted from rough parity to a cumulative U.S. $182.5 billion deficit to the United States when adjusted for inflation.[404]

Two former AIPAC directors allegedly rigged the 1986 California Senate race by laundering campaign contributions in collusion with a network of cutout campaign donors. One of them, Michael Goland, served a few months of prison time, but the results of the dirty election went unchallenged, and AIPAC's reputation and power over politicians seeking seats in Congress ballooned.[405]

AIPAC coordinated Political Action Committee (PAC) contributions in violation of its nonprofit status to promote its vetted candidates for Congress and to pick off foes. This was incontrovertibly revealed by damning internal AIPAC memos published in the *Washington Post* in 1988. Two decades later, after reaching the Supreme Court and being sent down to lower courts, a civil case against AIPAC and the Federal Election Commission produced no accountability for violations of rules and statutes over PAC fund donor disclosure.[406]

In 2004 and 2005, AIPAC received leniency from a prosecutor who indicted AIPAC executives Steven J. Rosen and Keith Weissman for alleged violations of the 1917 Espionage Act. Rather than extend his investigation and indictments to the entire corporation, former U.S. Attorney Paul McNulty secretly promised AIPAC's legal counsel that he would do all he could to limit the scope of the FBI's criminal investigation. The specifics are detailed in a February 16, 2005 memorandum between Rosen's lawyer, Abbe Lowell, and Nathan Lewin, AIPAC's legal counsel. Lewin revealed that the U.S. attorney for the Eastern District of Virginia and chief prosecutor in the case, Paul McNulty, "would like to end it with minimal damage to AIPAC." Lewin further told Lowell that U.S. Attorney McNulty was "fighting with the FBI to limit the investigation to Steve Rosen and Keith Weissman and to avoid expanding it."[407] Like Katzenbach before him, McNulty subsequently rose to a higher position in the DOJ. The upper levels of the Justice Department continue to be a bastion of Israel lobby leniency.

Attorney General Michael Mukasey came under concentrated pressure, loudly voiced in the *Wall Street Journal*, to quash the trial of Rosen and Weissman before it began.[408] The Jewish Telegraphic Agency published a thinly veiled call for a popular uprising against the prosecution, titled none-to-subtly in online news sources as "U.S. Jews should 'rise up' against the classified information case the government has brought against two former AIPAC employees."[409] At the time of publication, the charges against the AIPAC lobbyists and Colonel Franklin look to be moving inexorably toward a presidential pardon.

The Jewish Agency and World Zionist Organization came under a renewed spotlight in 2005, when former Israeli prosecutor Talia Sason released a wide-ranging study commissioned by the Israeli prime minister in which she documented a vast international money laundering infrastructure centered within the Jewish Agency and controlled by the World Zionist Organization. These and other allegedly "charitable" organizations had laundered more than U.S. $50 billion into illegal Israeli settlements while systematically expropriating and developing lands that did not belong to Israel. Reporting on the money laundering scheme even reached *U.S.A Today* in August of 2005:

> JERU.S.ALEM (AP)—Israel's effort since the 1967 Mideast war to fill the West Bank and Gaza Strip with Jews has grown from the scattered actions of zealous squatters into a network of 142 towns and villages that house nearly 240,000 people.
>
> Now that Israel plans to spend some $2 billion to dismantle just 25 of the settlements—for which U.S. aid has been requested—it raises the question of how much money has been poured into populating these biblical lands with Jews, and exactly where it came from.
>
> The official answer: No one knows.
>
> Vice Premier Shimon Peres estimates Israel has spent about $50 billion since 1977, when the hard-line Likud government took over from his Labor party. Other former finance ministers and government officials don't discount a price tag—commonly floated but never documented—of $60 billion....
>
> Despite its declared opposition to settlements, Washington only began taking action in the early 1990s, when Israel sought billions of dollars in U.S. loan guarantees. Washington said it would deduct sums that went into settlements dollar for dollar.
>
> In 2003, when Israel was granted $9 billion in loan guarantees over three years, the cut was $289.5 million. Officials familiar with the issue, and speaking on condition of anonymity, say that low figure was reached with the help of the influential pro-Israel lobby, the American Israel Public Affairs Committee (AIPAC).
>
> AIPAC officials refused to discuss the issue on the record, but denied they helped to negotiate the numbers.
>
> Israel also used private U.S. donations for which it secured U.S. tax-exempt status, said David Newman, a political scientist at Israel's Ben Gurion University who researched settlement funding.

> U.S. tax laws don't exempt donations for political activities such as settlements. Israel separated the World Zionist Organization from the quasi-governmental Jewish Agency, a move that allowed donors to inject money into settlements without losing tax exemptions. In reality, the two groups operate under one umbrella, with the same officials, departments and administrators overseeing the activities, Newman said.
>
> Perhaps the grayest area is how Israel expropriated, confiscated or purchased land for settlements.[410]

The Jewish Agency's money-laundering-for-settlements scheme was designed to utilize U.S. tax-exempt funds from donors to accomplish illegal ends overseas. However, the Sason report was not formally raised in the U.S. Congress in 2005. Only a few newspapers, such as *The Forward*, fretted over the implications of the Sason report—most particularly the legal violations covering U.S. charitable fundraising organizations connected to the World Zionist Organization and Jewish Agency via controlling corporate ties:

> Embarrassed leaders of American Jewish organizations were absorbing the news this week that an international body under their control was at the center of a tangled Israeli scheme, detailed in a bombshell government report, to build illegal settlement outposts in violation of Israeli law, policy and international commitments.
>
> The international body, the World Zionist Organization, or WZO, is described in the report as a pivotal player in the scheme, in which midlevel officials in various government ministries secretly channeled funds and resources to the illegal West Bank outposts. Several sources told the Forward that a WZO department, the Settlement Division, was used as a vehicle for many of the illegal activities, in part because its status as a nongovernmental organization shielded it from government oversight....
>
> WZO is a confederation of pro-Israel groups in dozens of countries, including such mainstays as Hadassah, B'nai B'rith and offshoots of the Reform and Conservative movements. American groups control 30 percent of the organization's main governing bodies, including the World Zionist Congress, which is convened in Jerusalem every four years.
>
> Most leaders of American Zionist groups said they had been unaware of the extent of WZO's work in the territories.[411]

The Forward need not have worried too much about the "embarrassed leaders" or subsequent investigations by U.S. law enforcement. On

November 21, 2005, top U.S. law enforcement officials sent representatives to attend a comprehensive briefing on the matter organized by the Council for the National Interest in the Russell Senate Office about how U.S. affiliates of charities such as B'nai B'rith and Hadassah had direct control of the World Zionist Organization and their linkage to the massive money laundering operation mentioned in the Talia Sason report. Department of Justice and Treasury officials were advised about how the money laundering operation is an indirect generator of terrorism against the United States as illegal settlements, low-intensity conflict, and hopelessness generated asymmetric retaliation against the U.S..[412] They were advised that the majority of funds were coming from the United States. Barry Sabin, chief of the U.S. counterterrorism section, formally thanked the keynote speaker (the author of this book) for the presentation, which included straightforward documentary evidence that could have led directly to indictments for money laundering and other violations of the U.S. criminal code prohibiting hostile acts against a people with which the U.S. is not at war. To date, however, U.S. law enforcement officials have visibly done nothing to slow or prosecute the parties responsible for this new (and yet very old) charitable money laundering operation. Two of the officials assigned to attend the briefing were transferred, one to the DOJ's Anti-Trust Division.[413]

In the U.S. Treasury Department, the money laundering issue has in a way been cynically turned on its head. In 2004, AIPAC and its affiliated think tank, the Washington Institute for Near East Policy (WINEP), lobbied for a separate new U.S. Treasury unit to be created, an effort reminiscent of the Irgun-inspired Morgenthau days. The "Office of Terrorism and Financial Intelligence" is headed by AIPAC-vetted leadership, and many OTFI briefings are delivered directly at WINEP's headquarters in Washington, DC. OTFI's secretive financial operations that target Iran and its trading partners are tightly coordinated with Israel's leadership but impenetrable to the American public. Freedom of Information Act requests to this unit requesting details of the director's many trips to Israel and whether the unit was tackling the issue of U.S. charitable money laundering to West Bank settlements were met with ironic stonewalling. The OTFI unit claims it will not respond to FOIA requests in order to be in compliance with the Bank Secrecy Act.[414] Ironically, the Bank Secrecy Act is an anti–money laundering law.

Secrecy and Dissent

AIPAC continues to operate clandestinely and is almost impenetrable to regulatory oversight or the scrutiny of the American public. AIPAC employees sign confidentiality agreements long before leaving the organization.[415] AIPAC's domestic lobbying disclosures filed in the House and Senate clerk offices reveal little relevant information about how legislation is lobbied or funds dispersed. Nor do they reveal precisely which individuals in Congress and government agency officials are being lobbied, or the organization's far-flung coordination with the Israeli government from AIPAC's Jerusalem office.

Indeed, Kenen's and AIPAC's evasions of FARA oversight created a corporate culture enshrining the concept that because AIPAC is so isolated from public scrutiny, it has transcended U.S. laws. Indicted AIPAC executive Steven Rosen waxed poetic when he stated:

A lobby is like a night flower: It thrives in the dark and dies in the sun.[416]

More troubling for Americans, AIPAC's lobbying disclosures, though meager, reveal a major shift beyond its normal focus on lobbying for military appropriations, a huge annual foreign aid package, and punitive legislation against Iran, Syria, and Palestinians. In 2006, AIPAC weighed in on the Lobbyist Reform Act of 2006, which was killed.[417] AIPAC was also active on the Legislative Transparency and Accountability Act of 2006, designed to "provide greater transparency with respect to lobbying activities, to amend the Federal Election Campaign Act of 1971 to clarify when organizations described in section 527 of the Internal Revenue Code of 1986 must register as political committees, and for other purposes." That legislation also never became law.[418] AIPAC also helped kill off the Honest Leadership and Open Government Act of 2006, designed to "provide more rigorous requirements with respect to disclosure and enforcement of ethics and lobbying laws and regulations, and for other purposes."[419]

Isaiah Kenen stopped registering as a foreign agent because compliance with the U.S. disclosure law would have revealed his activities, just as it did those of Marion Javits, Billy Carter, and Igor Cassini. The law, if applied, would tend to thwart AIPAC's core objectives. While there can be little doubt that other lobby organizations have probably also successfully passed through the FARA gauntlet the passage of time and declassification are gradually revealing the damage done by Kenen and the Israel lobby

Since the creation of Israel, the secrecy that veils both government and AIPAC operations usually prevented American citizens from demanding redress. Absent timely, accurate information about what the Israel lobby and its allies in government are doing, oversight and informed consent is impossible. In the history of special interest group politics, this is nothing new. But in this particular case, it is more pronounced by the recurring nature of illegalities and the institutionalized veil of secrecy. An analysis of the release dates of classified government documents, revelations from insiders, and the published works of "forensic historians" cited in this book reveals a stunning fact: on average, critical information about major initiatives and data critical to Middle East policy formulation become publicly available approximately 40 years after the opportunity for response has passed. (See Appendices)

Isaiah L. Kenen also briefly commented on the effect of declassifying documents from his own unique perspective:

> I have often written about the 1947 fall session of the General Assembly, which voted for partition, but it was not until 1975 that I learned the inside story from declassified documents.
>
> That session was a production in double talk on a double stage. Up front, we listened to formal discussion and debate. Backstage, American diplomacy was maneuvering to defeat the partition resolution—to substitute a plan for trusteeship with a tiny Vatican-like Jewish cultural and religious center.
>
> According to custom, the Department of State declassifies and publishes diplomatic correspondence and documents after twenty-five years. The book recording the 1947-48 papers was published a year late, but the declassified documents were available in the National Archives. In the summer of 1975, I wrote a syndicated article describing what went on behind the scenes and disclosing Marshall's startling threat to vote against Truman if he recognized Israel.
>
> Backstage—a caucus of the U.S. delegation on September 15— Marshall warned that acceptance of the UNSCOP recommendations would provoke "very violent" Arab reaction.[420]

Kenen obviously approved of neither Secretary of State Marshall's analysis nor his responsibilities to align U.S. policy with broader national interests. But ironically, not only has Marshall's analysis proven to be largely correct for 60 years, but he is also one of the last secretaries of state with the courage to stand up to the president. In a 60th-anniversary speech on the establishment of Israel before the American Jewish Conference, Secretary of State Condoleezza Rice mentioned Marshall's challenging and threatening Truman as an example of an approach she would never follow.[421] But while Marshall's legacy, encapsulated in the plan for reconstructing Europe after WWII that bears his name, remains fairly secure, Kenen's, as mentioned in the introduction, is treated like a skeleton in AIPAC's dark and deepening closet.

America's Defense Line

When it comes to improving Middle East policy formulation, the U.S. does not need new laws. Simple enforcement of the spirit and letter of important laws long on the books would substantially improve policy and make the government more responsive to broader American interests. But U.S. agencies appear to be moving in the opposite direction.

Additional special waivers covering Israel lobby transgressions have recently been implemented by allies ensconced in government. Sometimes publicly referred to as the "state secrets privilege"[mm] or "threats to sensitive diplomatic relations," these blanket waivers can be applied to trump almost any apparent criminality or violation of U.S., Israeli, or international law, and bail out key members of the Israel lobby when their activities or illicit gains are exposed. As a power claimed by the executive branch, this waiver seems permanent and irrevocable, has little public recourse, and, like presidential pardons, is rarely deeply questioned by mainstream news media. As a shield against foreign "isms," FARA is now only as strong as the target against which it is applied is weak. If the target is successfully entrenched and empowered in the U.S., even by illegal means, FARA is never applied. Like claims of attorney-client privilege, FARA cannot weather a state secrets claim, no matter how blatant the appearance of a cover-up.[nn] Little public reaction to this abuse has been forthcoming.

[mm] The state secrets privilege is a claim derived from a 1953 Supreme Court ruling permitting the government to refuse to disclose classified evidence in civil lawsuits.
[nn] Sibel Edmonds alleges that while she was working as an FBI contract translator high officials linked to the US Israel lobby were involved in stealing nuclear secrets, money laundering, and bribery of public officials. At the request of FBI Director Robert Mueller, Attorney General John Ashcroft imposed a gag order on Sibel Edmonds, citing potential damage to sensitive diplomatic relations and national security.

The beneficiaries of FARA enforcement are diffuse, heterogeneous, and generally unaware of the violations or the negative impact the lack of enforcement has had on them. They are the unaware and under informed majority of Americans. The key perpetrators and beneficiaries of FARA violations are usually elite, connected, and both willing and able to fight back through legal and other means. While they frequently do not serve the interests they claim to represent, they are buttressed by the perception of unchallengeable power and connections. Yet this power can and must be challenged.

Vocal U.S. critics of the lobby are seemingly few in number, highly visible, easy to isolate, and generally their calls for law enforcement or justice fall on deaf ears or are stymied by institutional memories of the "caveat." This elite crime, unlike street crime, is now rarely prosecuted when warranted.

Failing to file an accurate declaration of activity, whether it is a tax return or FARA declaration, is a crime that gradually takes its toll. Lack of prosecution begins to create a serious drag on society and has a corrosive effect on public law abidance. Enforcement malaise causes entities in many sectors, from business to nonprofits to individuals, to question whether they are suckers for paying their fair share, playing by the rules, or disclosing relevant information that being a citizen of the United States sometimes demands.

It is not controversial that the creation of Israel immediately touched off conflicts in the Middle East affecting all Americans. Major questions, and even a common approach toward a solution, remain unresolved to this day. This book makes the case that factors driving key U.S. policies are rarely publicly known when they are actually in play. In this way, the power democracy gives Americans at the voting booth and in Congress has already been largely subverted on all matters related to foreign policy in the Middle East. Unfortunately for everyone, the United States is also a country where grievances building invisibly against large injustices have a way of exploding suddenly and violently after high officials charged with enforcement and justice fail to uphold the law. The cauldron of U.S. Middle East policy, according to Rabbi Berger, has long been building up steam:

> From then on, nothing that developed in American policy surprised me. After twenty years I saw the old, hackneyed pattern being replayed. The decisions would be made on the basis of political considerations by the politicians in the White House. The objective facts, the merits of the

cases of the several parties to the long-festering conflict, sophisticated judgments of American long-range interests in the Middle East would all be "tabled"—or assigned to levels of secondary importance.[422]

Representing a state with no constitution, the WZO, AIPAC, and by extension the entire Israel lobby are able to quickly morph into whatever thin legal structure is necessary to carry out the objective. History reveals that by the time a major effort is made to hold it to account, it will already be operating under a different umbrella.

FARA was one of the most intelligent and noble attempts to codify and enforce the original vision of the Logan Act (see Appendices). With proper resources and, critically, firm political backing from the executive on down, it could have secured broad American interests as envisioned by its framers. Instead, with 70 years of perspective, it is obvious that when FARA faced its biggest challenge, it completely failed the American people. The declassified FARA section memos cited and reproduced in the Appendix provide a Rosetta Stone for translating what has long been only suspected: public officials responsible for upholding the rule of law are actively thwarted on enforcement matters concerning the Israel lobby.

In the 1950s when Kenen was leaving his job as a public relations operative for the Israel Office of Information, his main objective was to bypass the U.S. State Department and direct pressure toward the U.S. Congress via foreign-funded public relations and tenuous claims of grassroots constituents. By 1973, Kenen was able to boast $1 billion per year in U.S. aid to Israel. When Kenen retired in 1974, he still retained his "editor emeritus" title at the *Near East Report*. The spirit of AIPAC's hardball and often illegal tactics continued long after Kenen left the scene, and the results are staggering. At the time of Kenen's death in 1988, U.S. aid to Israel exceeded $3 billion a year, the highest amount given to any country. This would not have been possible absent the AZC's early subventions from the Jewish Agency. An argument can be made that foreign aid extracted from U.S. taxpayers under such circumstances should be returned, with interest. But under the present circumstances, even discussing disgorgement is difficult, because relevant information has been generally unavailable to American citizens. Attempts to seek justice and open debate generate waves of capable opponents. And, as mentioned, the ability to execute "hooking points" by threatening to drag high officials from almost any agency into potential criminal prosecutions while securing "state secrets" and "sensitive diplomatic relations" blankets over its new forays from friends in high places has vastly expanded the Israel lobby's power.

What becomes more obvious with each passing year is that in charting this course toward institutional power, Kenen and the lobby seemed to be following the advice of Julius Caesar: "If you must break the law, do it to seize power: in all other cases observe it." Now that operatives of the lobby Kenen helped create are calling the shots and entrenching themselves ever deeper into all branches of government, they naively expect the humble acquiescence of Americans impoverished by war and angered by the guile, misdirection of resources, and corruption of U.S. government agencies.

American policy malfeasance in the Middle East has caused many to seek out the authors, individual and institutional, of the decades of debacle, war, and debasement of America and how it came to be. This book has provided a few formerly elusive answers to these historical questions.

AIPAC, in its various permutations, has been at the forefront of a great many efforts that directly challenge rule of law and governance in the United States. Fortunately for America, these types of elite threats have a real grassroots corrective. As awareness builds, endemic corruption soon becomes perceived as a public threat to the safety, livelihood, and quality of life of all citizens. Economic studies have long shown that when "governance" (political accountability) and the ability of bureaucracy to enforce the rule of law go into systemic decline, a nation's people literally become impoverished. According to the *Economist*:

> ...in the long run, a country's income per head rises by roughly 300 percent if it improves its governance by one standard deviation. One standard deviation is roughly the gap between India's and Chile's rule-of-law scores, measured by the bank. As it happens, Chile is about 300 percent richer than India in purchasing-power terms.[423]

Although rule of law is laudable for its own sake, poverty is an inevitable consequence of turning a blind eye on decades of depredations. Just as improving the rule of law produces societal and economic benefits, the reverse is also true. The U.S. is now entering a period of decline prompted by disastrous Middle East policies produced by a formulation system that has been thoroughly corrupted. But the long period of public acquiescence may be drawing to a close. The descendants of Senator Fulbright, Lessing Rosenwald, Nathan B. Lenvin, Rabbi Berger, Irene A.

Bowman, and multitudes of disenfranchised citizens across America may be gradually starting to assemble.

Afterword: Now What?

On October 21, 2010, the National Archives and Records Administration finally released Box #1 out of 67 boxes of the sealed U.S. Senate records about the activities of non-diplomatic representatives of foreign governments active in the United States. The formerly classified documents reveal the original rationale for extensive Senate Foreign Relations Committee investigations: it heavily focused on investigating Israel's lobby. The subsequent early 1960s Senate investigation looked into other foreign agents acting on behalf of countries such as the Dominican Republic, as well as top U.S. lobbying firms, public relations consultants and foreign lobbying groups, which were all ordered to submit records under threat of subpoena to Senate Foreign Relations Committee researchers.

But a declassified March 17, 1961, three-page memorandum outlines why the committee focused so intensely on the Jewish Agency, the American Zionist Council and the American Israel Public Affairs Committee (then functioning as the AZC's umbrella lobbying division and public relations group, before incorporating after the 1962 FARA order.[424] See the final appendix image of the original. The memo read:

> "In recent years there has been an increasing number of incidents involving attempts by foreign governments, or their agents, to influence the conduct of American foreign policy by techniques outside normal diplomatic channels.....there have been occasions when representatives of other governments have been privately accused of engaging in covert activities within the United States and elsewhere, for the purpose of influencing United States Policy (the Lavon Affair)."

The "Lavon Affair" referenced in the secret memo is the 1954 Israeli false flag terrorist bombing campaign code named "Operation Susannah" directed against U.S. and other targets in Egypt. It aimed to reverse official U.S. policy of pressuring British withdrawals to revert control of the Suez Canal to Egypt's government. Israeli agents disguised as Arabs to set off the bombs were discovered, arrested and criminally prosecuted in Egypt when their explosives malfunctioned, leading to a crisis in the Israeli government and relations with the U.S. Israeli Minister of Defense Pinhas Lavon (1904-1976) was deemed responsible and forced to resign over the scandal.[425]

Lavon later moved on to serving on the board of the Israeli government funded Jewish Agency, the very same organization providing startup funding to the American Israel Public Affairs Committee. Operatives. An Israeli willing to launch false flag terror attacks to influence United States foreign policy was part of the network that established AIPAC in America.

The Senate Foreign Relations Committee investigative charter mentioned the Lavon affair twice in three pages, while expressing extreme caution about the implications of investigating such sensitive matters. It read, "There would undoubtedly (even with care) be instances which would lead to foreign governmental protests, to violent attacks by special groups in the United States..."

The declassified Senate memo suggested three avenues for Senate investigation. "I. Public receipt of testimony from Department of Justice and Department of State....II. Public receipt of testimony from selected law and public relations firms....III Executive (perhaps public) receipt of testimony on the Lavon Affair, and similar 'grey area' activities..."

The Senate record of the May 23 and August 1, 1963, hearings on Israel lobbying outline covert activities, but many were heavily redacted at the insistence of the Jewish Agency and its allies in Congress. No testimony on the Lavon Affair or any other false flag attacks was ever given during the investigation. To this day the Eisenhower Presidential Library has never released records about the attacks, or even uncovered any. In 2022, the Eisenhower Presidential Library is still claiming it has not even begun to process 168,000 pages of Treasury Secretary Fred Scribner's papers. These papers surely include his 1959 warning to Zionist groups about what they needed to do to avoid criminal charges and problems with the IRS.

This lack of access to historical records, and more blatant coverups, such as the unjustifiably delayed release of the Justice Department records on its attempts to regulate the Israel lobby under FARA, have aided AIPAC. In 2022, AIPAC has been relentlessly deploying dark money to take out U.S. politicians AIPAC believes won't be sufficiently deferential to the Israeli government. American news media, while quick to propagate Israel lobby talking points about Iran and other topics, has failed to discuss even basic history about AIPAC's origins. Hopefully, this series provides some insight into how AIPAC grew to become the most damaging foreign influence operation ever unleashed against America.

Israel spent $61 million making an American lobby

AIPAC has always been evasive about its origin story, for very good reasons. According to its founder, Isaiah L. Kenen, "The lobby for Israel, known as the American Israel Public Affairs Committee since 1959, came into existence in 1951. It was established at that time because Israel needed American economic assistance..." In other words, AIPAC was a response to the needs of a foreign country, not any U.S. charitable purpose. Because Americans are suspicious of foreign meddling AIPAC does everything it can to blend in. Today AIPAC claims it is simply trying to advance the U.S. Israel "special relationship" rather than only serving Israel's government. That framing has worked on most Americans, especially American politicians who receive AIPAC's coordinated political campaign contributions.

Even the Israel lobby's most prominent academic critics Stephen Walt and John Mearsheimer maintained after publication of their book "The Israel Lobby and U.S. Foreign Policy" that although AIPAC played a key role in disastrous policies such as the U.S. invasion of Iraq, "It's as American as apple pie."

But history reveals AIPAC and the Israel lobby's startup funding was certainly not American. We know this because the May 23, 1963 Senate Foreign Relations Committee hearing compelled financial disclosures about how Israel's massive public relations and lobbying campaigns in the U.S. were funded. The numbers were entered into the record.

The key exhibits appear in *Item 8. "Request for a year-by-year accounting of all foreign payments to the American Zionist Council from January 1 of 1955 to December 31 of 1962"* which begins on page 1403 and runs through page 1422 of the Senate record. Adjusted for inflation the total amount of foreign funding was $61 million. [426]

ACTIVITIES OF AGENTS OF FOREIGN PRINCIPALS IN U.S. 1403

rules and regulations governing its conduct, the calling of its meetings, and such other matters as it shall deem advisable, and may from time to time appoint such committees as it shall deem necessary or advisable. It shall have the power to employ, discharge and fix the compensation of all employees. All vacancies in the Administrative Committee shall be filled by the Board of Directors.

Item 8. Request for a year-by-year accounting of all payments to the American Zionist Council. (See p. 1243.)

For the period from January 1, 1955, through March 31, 1960:

For the period from Jan. 1, 1955 to Sept. 30, 1955

Date	Amount	Date	Amount
Jan. 3	$25,000.00	June 29	10,000.00
Jan. 17	25,000.00	July 1	5,000.00
Jan. 24	17,000.00	July 7	5,000.00
Feb. 2	30,000.00	July 14	10,000.00
Feb. 9	10,000.00	July 20	10,000.00
Feb. 15	20,000.00	July 28	10,000.00
Feb. 28	10,000.00	Aug. 5	12,000.00
Mar. 4	10,000.00	Aug. 8	18,000.00
Mar. 8	15,000.00	Aug. 10	13,000.00
Mar. 21	5,000.00	Aug. 16	10,000.00
Mar. 31	35,000.00	Aug. 24	10,000.00
Apr. 5	35,000.00	Sept. 1	10,000.00
Apr. 21	15,000.00	Sept. 8	10,000.00
Apr. 26	15,000.00	Sept. 15	10,000.00
May 3	20,000.00	Sept. 22	10,000.00
May 11	15,000.00	Sept. 29	10,000.00
May 19	10,000.00		
May 24	10,000.00	Subtotal	551,000.00
June 1	10,000.00	Less, cash received from	
June 8	20,000.00	Shekel board	601.50
June 13	6,000.00		
June 14	20,000.00	Total	550,398.50
June 23	10,000.00		

Figure 6 Jewish Agency Payments to AZC

A great deal of the funding was earmarked to Isaiah L. Kenen who as has been noted previously worked for the Israeli Ministry of Foreign Affairs and the Jewish Agency, before setting up "the Kenen Committee" and subsequently the American Israel Public Affairs Committee lobbying division of the AZC before AIPAC replaced the AZC in 1963.

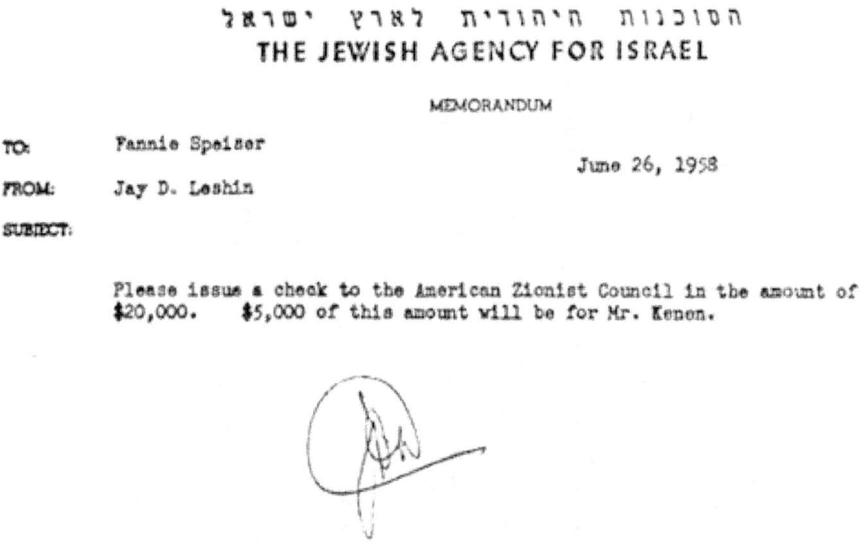

הסוכנות היהודית לארץ ישראל
THE JEWISH AGENCY FOR ISRAEL

MEMORANDUM

TO: Fannie Speiser

FROM: Jay D. Leshin

June 26, 1958

SUBJECT:

Please issue a check to the American Zionist Council in the amount of $20,000. $5,000 of this amount will be for Mr. Kenen.

Figure 7 Jewish Agency payments to AIPAC founder Isaiah Kenen

Confirmation that the funds were not "American as Apple Pie" also came in the form of testimony from the Jewish Agency's longtime executive Gottlieb Hammer who clarified that the funding for lobbying and public relations injected into the U.S. from Israel was "from other Jewish communities throughout the free world as well as income it has from Israel, itself."[427]

SUPPORT OF AMERICAN ZIONIST COUNCIL (AZC)

The CHAIRMAN. Did your organization contribute to the support of the American Zionist Council?
Mr. HAMMER. It did, sir.
The CHAIRMAN. Using the UJA funds paid to your organization?
Mr. HAMMER. No, sir.
The INC. had funds from other sources than UJA, and funds supplied to the American Zionist Council were from these other sources.
The CHAIRMAN. What other funds did it have available?
Mr. HAMMER. Pardon me, sir?
The CHAIRMAN. What other funds did it have available for that purpose?
Mr. HAMMER. Well, the Jerusalem Agency has a budget which is 2.5 to 3 times larger than the amount of American dollars it receives for its work. Its sources of funds include that from other Jewish communities throughout the free world as well as income that it has in Israel, itself.
The amount made available to the American Zionist Council was just a fraction of these other funds.
The CHAIRMAN. Do you know, prior to 1960, approximately how much you supplied to the American Zionist Council?
Mr. HAMMER. My recollection of this—and this is several years ago—my recollection would be somewhere in the neighborhood of around $600,000 to $700,000 prior to 1960.
The CHAIRMAN. Each year?
Mr. HAMMER. Each year; yes, sir.

Figure 8 Jewish Agency chief Gottlieb Hammer testimony to the Senate

The foreign direction and funding led the Department of Justice to order the American Zionist Council to register as an Israeli foreign agent on November 21, 1962. However, Senate investigators and the Department of Justice were at that time unaware of just how closely linked Israel's government was to the Jewish Agency. The Justice Department subsequently compelled the American Section to file the Jewish Agency's "covenant" with the Israeli government as part of its 1969 Foreign Agents Registration Act statement. (See the Appendix)

The forced filing of the covenant in 1969 revealed the quasi-governmental powers of the Jewish Agency (which predated the formation of a country as a "government in waiting," propaganda and arms smuggling network) to independently raise tax-preferential funds, encourage capital investments in the state of Israel, coordinate Jewish organizations in Israel, establish new institutions as needed, and review government legislation before it was submitted to the Knesset.

The massive amount of foreign funding did not entirely escape establishment media scrutiny, which mostly avoided reporting on the Senate hearings investigating the Israel lobby and 1962 FARA order that

AZC register. On May 19, 1970 reporter Mosher Lawrence of the National Observer (Dow Jones), wrote:

> "In 1963 the Senate Foreign Relations Committee investigated the Jewish Agency and uncovered a "conduit" operation run by an organization called the American Zionist Council. Over an eight-year period, this council received more than $5,000,000 from the Jewish Agency to create a favorable public opinion in this country for Israeli government policies. The Senate investigation closed down the conduit, but the extensive propaganda activities still go on."

Until 1963 AIPAC was housed within an Israel lobby superstructure consisting of the Zionist Organization of America, Hadassah (Women's Zionist Organization of America), the Labor Zionist Movement, in total a dozen organizations. The idea, from Israel's objective as documented in here was to have a U.S. "landing pad" for foreign cash infusions for lobbying and direction from the Israeli government.

In 2022, AIPAC's superstructure is largely the same though very much expanded. The ZOA and Hadassah are still there, along with many other organizations that make up the "Conference of Presidents of Major American Jewish Organizations." In AIPAC's bylaws, the chairperson of the each Conference of Presidents member organization has an automatic seat on the AIPAC board of directors. The chief officer of each Conference of Presidents member organization is invited to serve as a member of AIPAC's executive committee. Unlike the dozen organizations that formed the AZC version of the Israel lobby, there are today 102 well-funded member and adjunct organizations.

AIPAC likely believes it is now too embedded in the establishment to ever again become a target of Justice Department regulation under FARA. In 1975 AIPAC used classified information attempting to thwart a US missile sale to Jordan on Israel's behalf. In 1984 AIPAC teamed up with the Israeli Minister of Economics in a joint economic espionage operation in an effort to pass a trade deal giving Israel unrestricted export rights to America. In 2005 AIPAC worked to leak classified Defense Department data in a bid to provoke a U.S. attack on Iran. There were no meaningful consequences for any of these harmful actions.

AIPAC may evade warranted attention from the hapless Department of Justice, but it can no longer escape its history as an Israeli foreign influence operation. The new generations of politicians injected into elected office to serve Israel are only there because of timely and abundant

Israeli funding into what it hoped would eventually become an "American" lobby for Israel in the 1940s-1960s. Today AIPAC is truly "as American as apple pie." But only in the sense that apple pie is a foreign import. Apple pie was conceived in England with influences from France, the Netherlands and the Ottoman Empire. The Americas did not even have "pastry suitable apples" until Europeans arrived.

Appendices

Isaiah L. Kenen Chronology

1905	March 7, Isaiah L. Kenen born in St. Stephen, New Brunswick, Canada.[428] Works as an actor in Toronto.[429]
1917	Forms the first Young Judea Club in Toronto, inspired by Henrietta Szold, founder of Hadassah.[430]
1925	Joins the *Toronto Star* newspaper.
1926	Leaves Toronto for Cleveland, Ohio, where he works as a journalist at the *Cleveland News*.
1933	Helps establish Local One of the American Newspaper Guild.[431] Studies law at night and is admitted to the Ohio Bar Association.
1934	June 8, naturalized as a U.S. citizen in the Northern District Court of Ohio.
1941	Serves as president of the Cleveland Zionist District.
1943	Moves to New York and becomes the executive secretary of the American Emergency Committee on Zionist Affairs in December, lobbying for the creation of a Jewish state in Palestine.[432] Also serves as executive secretary of the American Jewish Conference from December 1 until February 1, 1948.
1947	Named New York information director of the Jewish Agency for Palestine on April 15; serves until May 15, 1948
1948	Appointed as director of information for the Provisional Government of Israel's mission to the UN in June,[433] which becomes the Israeli delegation to the United Nations. By September 1, formally declares to the U.S. Department of Justice that he will become director of information of the Israel Office of Information of the Israeli Embassy to the United States.
1950	In December, travels to Capitol Hill to lobby Congress for arms for Israel while still employed at the Israel Office of Information.
1951	On January 17, visits the FARA office and declares he intends to establish a private public relations firm working for the government of Israel. Advised to re-file as a foreign agent and given forms. On February 13, formally announces to the FARA office that he has "resigned from the service of the government of Israel," then travels to Washington to lobby for U.S. foreign aid and weapons from the American Zionist Council (formerly the American Emergency Committee on Zionist Affairs).
1952	Writes to the FARA office on March 14 to claim he temporarily "resigned" from the American Zionist Council, visited Israeli officials, received payment, and then "reverted" back to the American Zionist Council.
1957	Launches biweekly *Near East Report* newsletter as a private startup.
1961	Hears of potential investigation by Senator Fulbright; leaves U.S. to visit Iran and Africa.
1962	Questioned by the FBI about financing of the *Near East Report*.
1970	In October, the *Near East Report* is published weekly.[434]

1973	Near East Research is incorporated and buys Kenen's investment interest in the *Near East Report*. Eventually, the *Near East Report* is produced within AIPAC's Washington, DC offices.
1975	Retires as chairman of AIPAC and editor of the *Near East Report*, but continues to write a weekly column.
1981	Publishes the book *Israel's Defense Line*.
1985	Publishes the book *All My Causes*.
1988	Dies of a heart attack at his home in New York on March 23.

Organizations

World Zionist Organization

Theodor Herzl founded the Zionist Organization at the First Zionist Congress in Basle, Switzerland in 1897. The Zionist Organization's goals were set forth in the Basle Program: "Zionism seeks to establish a home for the Jewish people in Palestine, secured under public law." The Zionist Organization was renamed the World Zionist Organization in 1960. The right of membership was originally given to individuals who accepted the Basle Program and purchased the Zionist shekel (dues). The Zionist Organization's constitution was passed by the Third Congress in 1899 and amended several times over the years.

When the League of Nations conferred the Mandate for Palestine on Great Britain for the establishment of a Jewish Agency to represent Jewish immigrants in Palestine, the Zionist Organization was given the status of a "Jewish Agency."[435]

The State of Israel has no constitution, but its "basic laws" possess some constitutional characteristics, including having considerably more importance than routine legislation. Israel's basic laws include statutes that implement Zionist ideology and establish the government structure. Status Law, a basic law enacted on November 24, 1952, accorded legal status to the World Zionist Organization (before it was operating on a purely "de facto" basis). Ben-Gurion stated that while Israel was limited in authority to deal with Zionist groups beyond its borders, the JA/ZA was not limited. The statute states that the Zionist Organization "takes care as before of immigration" and that the words "Zionist Organization" (ZO) and "Jewish Agency" (JA) are different names for the same institution. The Executive of the ZO/JA is a juristic body and it "and its funds and other institutions" are exempt from taxes in the State of Israel. In addition to promoting immigration of Jews, the ZO/JA is the designated entity to achieve the "political unity" of Jews outside of Israel to further Zionist objectives. [436]

World Zionist Organization–American Section

The World Zionist Organization–American Section, Inc. registered on September 21, 1971 as a foreign agent for the Executive of the World Zionist Organization in Israel. Isadore Hamlin, executive director of the Jewish Agency–American Section, become the executive director of the new FARA registrant. The WZO–American Section took over the publication and distribution of the Israel Digest and occupied the Jewish Agency's former space at 515 Park Avenue in New York City. The WZO Executive in Israel claims to be the parent organization of the Jewish Agency. The WZO also claims not to be owned, directed, controlled, or financed by any foreign government.

Provisional Executive Committee for General Zionist Affairs

This group was founded on August 30, 1914, when a group of 150 Zionist leaders met in New York City. Louis D. Brandeis was elected president and drove movement membership from 12,000 in 1914 to 176,000 by 1919.[437]

Jewish Agency for Israel

The Jewish Agency began as an unincorporated association founded in Switzerland in 1929. The original name of the organization was the Jewish Agency for Palestine. The agency obtained a mandate from the League of Nations (later the United Nations) to serve as the "representative Jewish authority in Palestine vis-à-vis Britain." Upon the foundation of Israel in 1948, the agency claimed to cease all political functions and operate as a non-governmental body in charge of colonization and settlement. A board of directors called "the Executive" directs and administers the agency. Agency financing comes from worldwide charitable contributions, though the Israeli government also disburses funds to the agency budget. Tax-deductible American contributions were obtained through the United Jewish Appeal and Israel bonds.

David Ben-Gurion served as head of the Jewish Agency Executive between 1929 and his election as prime minister of Israel in 1948. He duly filed a FARA registration form as a foreign agent while working in the U.S.

In 1954, the Jewish Agency and the Israeli government signed a "covenant" that "defines the Jewish Agency's functions in broad terms; immigration, agricultural settlement, land acquisition, development enterprises, private investments, cultural activities and financing." The Jewish Agency, then, functioned as a type of "shadow government" as well as one of the best financed organizations in the world.

American Section–Jewish Agency for Israel

The Jewish Agency for Israel established a representative office in the United States in 1944. After 1948, the American Section was incorporated in New York and registered as the agent of a foreign principal under the control of "the Executive" of the Jewish Agency in Israel, whose 19 members were simultaneously members of the American Section. The mission of the American Section was to "carry out all of the functions of the fiscal agent, purchasing agent, as well as carrying on educational and informational activities in the United States." In August 1969, the Justice Department forced the American Section to file its covenant with the Israeli government as part of its registration statement. In 1971, the American Section notified the Justice Department that it would no longer file under FARA. Operations were functionally passed on to the World Zionist Organization–American Section, Inc.

United Jewish Appeal

The merger of two competing organizations raising funds for Jews in Palestine in the United States (the Palestine Foundation Fund and the Jewish National Fund before 1927) formed the United Palestine Appeal. After 1948, the name was changed to the United Israel Appeal. The Palestine Foundation Fund was an umbrella organization for four groups (the Zionist Organization of America, Hadassah, the Labour Zionist Organization of America, and the Mizrachi Organization).

The United Jewish Appeal emerged in 1938 as the active fundraising organization for the United Israel Appeal and the American-Jewish Joint Distribution Committee. United Jewish Appeal donations are tax-deductible for U.S. donors.

American Zionist Emergency Council

The Council operated between 1943 and 1949 as a "fire brigade" or temporary "pressure group."[438] The primary objective of the organization was securing U.S. support for the establishment of a Jewish state in Palestine. Rabbi Stephen S. Wise was elected chairman of the 24-member body. Voting members were drawn from national executives of the Zionist Organization of America, Hadassah, Paole Zion, and Mizrachi. The organizations claimed a collective membership of 171,132 in 1940.[439]

American Zionist Council

The AZC was established as an IRS tax-exempt organization that was also able to receive tax-deductible contributions. It served as an umbrella organization for eight organizations: the American Jewish League for Israel, B'nai Zion, Hadassah (the Women's Zionist Organization of America), Religious Zionists of America, the Labour Zionist Movement, the Progressive Zionist League (Hashomer Hatzair), the United Labor Zionist Party, and the Zionist Organization of America.

The American Zionist Council was forced to terminate early attempts at lobbying on Capitol Hill in 1954 because its nonprofit status and use of tax-exempt funds did not permit it to devote a substantial amount of resources to lobbying. In the late 1950s and early 1960s, American Zionist Council committees coordinated many activities across the United States, particularly public relations campaigns aimed at swaying American public opinion and building a coalition beyond the core umbrella organization groups. In the early 1960s, the American Zionist Council did not derive major funding from the umbrella organizations, but rather from the Jewish Agency, funneled through its American Section in New York. At times, the Jewish Agency in Israel provided funding directly to the American Zionist Council, and the American Zionist Council provided accounts payable and activity reports to the Jewish Agency.

Conference of Presidents

The Conference of Presidents of Major Jewish Organizations operates as an elite umbrella organization and lobbying group for the presidents of major organizations. It effectively maintains access and lobbies the White House. The group utilized office space at 515 Park Avenue provided by the Jewish Agency–American Section, which also originally covered over half of the Presidents' Conference budget.

American Jewish Congress

A nationalist movement organization founded in 1918 by Stephen Wise, the American Jewish Congress was organized to provide a voice at Versailles for the Jews of Europe whose lives were disrupted by World War I, and to establish a democratic decision-making mechanism for the Jewish community in the United States. More than 350,000 Jews from throughout the U.S. selected delegates to attend the first American Jewish Congress. Among those elected were Judge Louis Brandeis, Judge Felix Frankfurter, and Golda Meier Meyerson from Milwaukee. Wise set forth principles that Jews are entitled not merely to charity, but to justice, and that there exist fundamental rights to which Jews are entitled.

American Israel Public Affairs Committee

The vision of AIPAC was initiated in 1951 to spearhead lobbying for aid and arms in the United States for Israel according to founder Isaiah Kenen. AIPAC assumed a leading position in the Israel lobby in 1963 after the American Zionist Council's functions were transferred to AIPAC following its conflict with the U.S. Department of Justice and compelled nonpublic FARA filing.

AIPAC files IRS form 990 tax returns as a domestic tax-exempt nonprofit corporation. AIPAC registers only as a domestic lobbyist with the U.S. House Office of the Clerk where it files periodic lobbying reports under the Lobbying Disclosure Act of 1995. AIPAC maintains an office in Jerusalem.

American Jewish Conference

Sixty-four national Jewish organizations sent delegates to this August 1943 conference representing more than two million American Jews. The conference sought to "unify American Jewry by the creation of a democratic responsible body which could speak and act authoritatively in meeting the problems confronting the Jewish people." One primary objective was "problems relating to the rights and status of Jews in the post-war world." Although it initially pledged to resist considering issues surrounding a "Jewish state," the conference ultimately adopted a pro-Zionist plank. This created a schism with the American Jewish Committee and American Jewish Labor Council, which thought Zionist groups had "bulldozed" the issue. Non-Zionist groups withdrew in October 1943.[440]

Foreign Agents Registration Act—6/8/1938-4/28/1942

Chapter 11 -- FOREIGN AGENTS AND PROPAGANDA

SUBCHAPTER I – GENERALLY
Sec. 601. Acting as foreign government agent without notice to Secretary of State

SUBCHAPTER II – REGISTRATION OF FOREIGN PROPAGANDISTS
Sec.
611 Definitions
612 Registration statement; filing contents
613 Same; additional statement after 6 months; contents
614 Same; permanent record; public inspection
615 Failure to register; false statement; omission of material facts; penalties
616 Rules, regulations, and forms

SUBCHAPTER I.—Generally
601 Acting as foreign governmental agent without notice to Secretary of State

Whoever, other than a diplomatic or consular official or attaché, shall act in the United States as an agent of a foreign government without prior notification to the Secretary of State shall be punished by imprisonment for not more than ten years and may, in the discretion of the courts, be fined not more than $5000.

SUBCHAPTER II – REGISTRATION OF FOREIGN PROPAGANDISTS
Definitions.
As used in this subchapter-
The term "person" means an individual, partnership, association, or corporation.

The term "United States" includes the United States and any place subject to the jurisdiction thereof;

The term "foreign principal" includes the government of a foreign country, a political party of a foreign country, a person domiciled abroad, any foreign business, partnership, association, corporation, or political organization, or a domestic organization subsidized, directly or indirectly, in whole or in part by any of the entities described in this subchapter;

The term "agent of foreign principal" means any person who acts or engages or agrees to act as a public-relations counsel, publicity agent, or as agent, servant, representatives, or attorney for a foreign principal, and shall include any person who receives compensation from or is under the direction of a foreign principal: provided however, that such term shall not include—

A duly accredited diplomatic or consular officer of a foreign government who is so recognized by the Department of State of the United States; nor

An official of a foreign government recognized by the United States as a government other than a public-relations counsel or publicity agent or a citizen of the United States, whose status and the character of whose duties as such official are of record in the Department of State of the United States; nor Any member of the staff or person employed by a duly accredited diplomatic or consular officer of a foreign government who is so recognized by the Department of State of the United States, other than a public-relations counsel or publicity agent, whose status and the character of whose duties as such member or employee are of record in the Department of State of the United States; nor Any person performing only private, nonpolitical, financial, mercantile, or other activities in furtherance of the bona fide trade or commerce of such foreign principal, nor Any person engaged only in activities in furtherance of bona fide religious, scholastic, academic, or scientific pursuits of the fine arts.

The term "secretary" means the Secretary of State of the United States.

EFFECTIVE DATE OF SUBCHAPTER
Section 7 of act June 8, 1938, cited to text, provided that this subchapter "shall take effect on the ninetieth day after the date of enactment."

612 Registration statement; filing; contents.

Every person who is now an agent of a foreign principal shall, within thirty days after this subchapter takes effect, and every person who shall hereafter become an agent of a foreign principal shall forthwith file with the Secretary a registration statement, under oath, on a form prescribed by the Secretary which shall set forth—the name, business address, and residence address of the registrant;

The name of the foreign principal or other person or organization for which such person is acting as agent; A copy of all contracts of employment under which such person acts or agrees to act as such agent, if written, or a full statement of the terms and conditions thereof, if oral; The date when each such contract was made, the date of commencement of activity thereunder, and the period during which such contract is to be in effect; The compensation to be paid, if any, and the form and time of payment, under such contract; The name of every foreign principal, or other person or organization which has contributed or which has promised to contribute to the compensation provided in such contract; and if the registrant be a partnership, association, or corporation, a true and complete copy of its charter, articles of incorporation, co-partnership association, constitution, and bylaws, and any other instrument or instruments relating to its organization, powers, and purposes.

EFFECTIVE DATE
See note under section 611 of this title.

613 Same; additional statement after 6 months; contents.

Every person who has filed a registration statement required by section 612 of this title shall, within thirty days after the expiration of each period of six months succeeding the first filing, file with the Secretary a statement, under oath, on a form prescribed by the Secretary, which shall set forth with respect to such preceding six months' period—

Such facts as may be necessary to make the information required under section 612 of this title accurate and current with respect to such period;

The amount and form of compensation received by such person for acting as agent for a foreign principal which has been received during such six months' period either directly or indirectly from any foreign principal; and A statement containing such details required under this subchapter as the Secretary shall fix, of the activities of such person as agent of a foreign principal during such six months' period.

EFFECTIVE DATE
See note under section 611 of this title.
614. Same; permanent record; public inspection.
The Secretary shall retain in permanent form all statements filed under this subchapter, and such statements shall be public records and open to public examination and inspection at all reasonable hours, under such rules and regulations as the Secretary may prescribe; Provided, that the Secretary is hereby authorized to withdraw from the public records the registration statement of any person whose activities have ceased to be of a character which requires registration under the terms of this subchapter.

EFFECTIVE DATE
See note under section 611 of this title.

615 Failure to register; false statement; omission of material facts; penalties.

Any person who willfully fails to file any statement required to be filed under this subchapter, or in complying with the provisions of such subchapters, makes a false statement of a material fact required to be stated therein shall, on conviction thereof, be punished by a fine of not more than $1,000 or imprisonment for not more than two years, or both.

EFFECTIVE DATE
See note under section 611 of this title.
616. Rules, regulations, and forms.
The Secretary is authorized and directed to prescribe such rules, regulations, and forms as may be necessary to carry out this subchapter.

EFFECTIVE DATE
See note under section 611 of this title.

Foreign Agents Registration Act—4/29/1942–10/03/1961

Chapter 11 -- FOREIGN AGENTS AND PROPAGANDA
SUBCHAPTER I – GENERALLY
Sec. 601. Acting as foreign government agent without notice to Secretary of State
SUBCHAPTER II – REGISTRATION OF FOREIGN PROPAGANDISTS
Sec.
611 Definitions
612 Registration statement; filing contents
613 Same; additional statement after 6 months; contents
614 Same; permanent record; public inspection
615 Failure to register; false statement; omission of material facts; penalties
616 Rules, regulations, and forms
617 Liability of Officers.
618 Enforcement and Penalties
619 Territorial applicability of subchapter
620 Rules and regulations
621 Reports to Congress

SUBCHAPTER I.—Generally
601 Acting as foreign governmental agent without notice to Secretary of State

Whoever, other than a diplomatic or consular official or attaché, shall act in the United States as an agent of a foreign government without prior notification to the Secretary of State shall be punished by imprisonment for not more than ten years and may, in the discretion of the courts, be fined not more than $5000.

SUBCHAPTER II – REGISTRATION OF FOREIGN PROPAGANDISTS
EX. ORD. NO. 9176 TRANSFER OF REGISTRATION FUNCTIONS FROM THE SECRETARY OF STATE TO THE ATTORNEY GENERAL.

Ex. Ord. No. 9176, May 29, 1942, 7 F R 4127 provided;

By virtue of the authority vested in me by Title I of the First War Powers Act, 1941, approved December 18, 1941 (Public Law No. 354, 77th Congress (Title 50 App., 601 et seq)), and as President of the United States, it is hereby ordered as follows:

All functions, power and duties of the Secretary of State under the act of June 8, 1938 (52 Stat. 631 (section 611 of this title)), as amended by the act of August 7, 1939 (53 Stat. 1244 (section 611 of this title)), requiring the registration of agents of foreign principals, are hereby transferred to and vested in the Attorney General. All property, books and records heretofore maintained by the Secretary of State with respect to his administration of said act of June 8, 1938, as amended, are hereby transferred to and vested in the Attorney General. The Attorney General shall furnish to the Secretary of State for such comment, if any, as the Secretary of State may desire to make from the point of view of the foreign relations of the United States, one copy of each registration statement that is hereafter filed with the Attorney General in accordance with the provisions of this Executive order. All rules, regulations and forms which have been issued by the Secretary of State pursuant to the provisions of said act of June 8, 1938, as amended, and which are in effect shall continue in effect until modified, superseded, revoked or repealed by the Attorney General. This order shall become effective as of June 1, 1942.

Definitions.

As used in and for the purposes of this subchapter—

(a) The term "person" means an individual, partnership, association, or corporation;

The term "United States" includes the United States and any place subject to the jurisdiction thereof;

(b) The term "foreign principal" includes—

A government of a foreign country and a foreign political party; An individual affiliated or associated with, or supervised, directed, controlled, financed, or subsidized, in whole or in part, by any foreign principal defined in clause (1) of this subsection; A person outside of the United States, unless it is established that such person is an individual and is a citizen of and domiciled within the United States or that such person is not an individual, is organized under or created by the laws of the United States or of any State or other place subject to the jurisdiction of the United States, and has its principal place of business within the United States. Nothing in this clause shall limit the operation of the clause (5) of this subsection; A partnership, association, corporation, organization, or other combination of individuals organized under the laws of, or having its principal place of business in, a foreign country

A domestic partnership, association, corporation, organization, or other combination of individuals, subsidized directly or indirectly, in whole or in part, by any foreign principal defined in clause (1), (3), or (4) of this subsection;

(c) except as provided in subsection (d) of this section, the term "agent of a foreign principal" includes—any person who acts or agrees to act, within the United States, as, or who is or holds himself out to be whether or not pursuant to contractual relationship, a public-relations counsel, publicity agent, information-service employee, servant, agent, representative, or attorney for a foreign principal; any person who within the United States collects information for or reports information to a foreign principal; who within the United States solicits or accepts compensation, contributions, or loans, directly or indirectly, from a foreign principal; who within the United States solicits, disburses, dispenses, or collects compensation, contributions, loans, money, or anything of value, directly or indirectly, for a foreign principal; who within the United States acts at the order, request, or under the direction, of a foreign principal; Any person who assumes or purports to act within the United States as an agent of a foreign principal in any of the respects set forth in clauses (1) and (2) of this subsection; and Any person who is an officer or member of the active or reserve military, naval, or other armed forces of any foreign principal defined in clause (1) of subsection (b) of this section, or who is an officer of or employed by any such foreign principal; and proof of any affiliation or employment, specified in this clause, of any person within a period of five years previous to the effective date of this subchapter shall create a rebuttable presumption that such person is an agent of a foreign principal;

(d) The term "agent of a foreign principal" does not include any news or press service or association organized under the laws of the United States or of any State or other place subject to the jurisdiction of the United States, or any newspaper, magazine, periodical, or other publication for which there is on file with the Postmaster General a sworn statement in compliance with section 233 of Title 39, published in the United States, solely by virtue of any bona fide news or journalistic activities, including the solicitation or acceptance of advertisements, subscriptions, or other compensation therefore, so long as it is at least 80 per centum beneficially owned by, and its officers and directors, if any, are citizens of the United States, and such news or press service or association, newspaper, magazine, periodical, or other publication, is not owned, directed, supervised, controlled, subsidized, or financed, and none of its policies are determined by any foreign principal defined in clause (1), (2), or (4) of subsection (b) of this section, or by any agent of a foreign principal required to register under this subchapter; The term "government of a foreign country" includes any person or groups of persons exercising sovereign de facto or de jure political jurisdiction over any country, other than the United States, or over any part of such country, and includes any subdivision of any such group and any group or agency to which such sovereign de facto or de jure authority or function are directly or indirectly delegated. Such term shall include any faction or body of insurgents within a country assuming to exercise governmental authority whether such faction or body of insurgents has or has not been recognized by the United States.

(e) The term "government of a foreign country" includes any person or groups exercising sovereign de facto or de jure political jurisdiction over any country, other than the United States, or over any part of such country, and includes any subdivision of any such group and any group or agency to which such sovereign de facto or de jure authority or functions are directly or indirectly delegated. Such term shall include any faction or body of insurgents within a country assuming to exercise governmental authority whether such faction or body of insurgents has or has not been recognized by the United States;

(f) The term "foreign political party" includes any organization or any other combination of individuals in a country other than the United States, or any unit or branch thereof, having for an aim or purpose, or which is engaged in any activity devoted in whole or in part to, the establishment, administration, control, or acquisition of administration, control, or acquisition of administration or control, of a government of a foreign country or a subdivision thereof, or the furtherance of or influencing of the political or public interests, policies, or relations of a government of a foreign country thereof;

(g) The term "public relations counsel" includes any person who engages directly or indirectly in informing, advising, or in any way representing a principal in any matter pertaining to political or public interests, policies, or relations;

(h) The term "publicity agent" includes any person who engages directly or indirectly in the publication or dissemination of oral, visual, graphic, written, or pictorial information or matter of any kind, including publication by means of advertising, books, periodicals, newspapers, lectures, broadcasts, motion pictures, or otherwise;

(i) The term "information service employee" includes any person who is engaged in furnishing, disseminating, or publishing accounts, descriptions, information, or data with respect to the political, industrial, employment, economic, social, cultural , or other benefits, advantages, facts, or conditions of any country other than the United States or of any government of a foreign country or a foreign political party or of a partnership, association, corporation, organization, or other combination of individuals organized under the laws of, or having its principal place of business in, a foreign country;

(j) The term "political propaganda" includes any oral, visual, graphic, written, pictorial, or other communication or expression by any person (1) which is reasonably adapted to, or which the person disseminating the same believes will, or which he intends to, prevail upon, indoctrinate, convert, induce, or in any other way influence a recipient or any section of the public within the United States with reference to the political or public interests, policies, or relations of a government of a foreign country or a foreign political party or with reference to the foreign policies of the United States or promote in the United States racial, religious, or social dissensions, or (2) which advocates, advises, instigates, or promotes any racial, social, political, or religious disorder, civil riot, or other conflict involving the use of force or violence in any other American republic or the overthrow of any government or political subdivision of any other American republic by any means involving the use of force or violence. As used in this subsection the term "disseminating" includes transmitting or causing to be transmitted in the United States mails or by any means or instrumentality of interstate or foreign commerce or offering or causing to be offered in the United States mails;

(k) The term "registration statement" means the registration statement required to be filed with the Attorney General under section 612 (a) of this title, and any supplements thereto required to be filed under section 612 (b) of this title, and includes all documents and papers required to be filed therewith or amendatory thereof or supplemental thereto, whether attached thereto or incorporated therein by reference;

(l) The term "American republic" includes any of the states which were signatory to the Final Act of the Second Meeting of the Ministers of Foreign Affairs of the American Republic at Habana, Cuba, July 30, 1940.

(m) The term "United States", when used in a geographical sense, includes the several States, the District of Columbia, the Territories, the Canal Zone, the insular possessions, and all other places now or hereafter subject to the civil or military jurisdiction of the United States;

(n) The term "prints" means newspapers and periodicals, books, pamphlets, sheet music, visiting cards, address cards, printing proofs, engravings, photographs, pictures, drawings, plans, maps, patterns to be cut out, catalogs, prospectuses, advertisements, and printed, engraved, lithographed, or autographed notices of various kinds, and, in general, all impressions or reproductions obtained on paper or other material assimilable to paper, on parchment or on cardboard, by means of printing, engraving, lithography, autography, or any other easily recognizable mechanical process, with the exception of the copying press, stamps with movable or immovable type, and the typewriter;

POLICY AND PURPOSE OF SUBCHAPTER

Act Apr. 29, 1942, cited to text, amending generally act June 8, 1938, also cited, added an opening paragraph preceding section I of the latter act and reading as follows: "It is hereby declared to be the policy and purpose of this Act (Title 22, 611 et seq) to protect the national defense, internal security, and foreign relations of the United States by requiring public disclosure by persons engaging in propaganda activities and other activities for or on behalf of foreign governments, foreign political parties, and other foreign principals so that the Government and the people of the United States may be informed of the identity of such persons and may appraise their statements and actions in the light of their associations and activities."

612 Registration

(a) No person shall act as an agent of a foreign principal unless he has filed with the Attorney General a true and complete registration statement and supplements thereto as required by this subsection and subsection (b) of this section or unless he is exempt from registration under the provisions of this subchapter. Except as hereinafter provided, every person who is an agent of a foreign principal on the effective date of this subchapter shall, within ten days thereafter and every person who becomes an agent of a foreign principal after the effective date of this subchapter shall, within ten days thereafter, file with the Attorney General, in duplicate, a registration statement, under oath, on a form prescribed by the Attorney General, of which one copy shall be transmitted promptly by the Attorney General to the Secretary of State for such comment, if any, as the Secretary of State may desire to make from the point of view of the foreign relations of the United States. Failure of the Attorney General so to transmit such copy shall not be a bar to prosecution under this subchapter. This registration statement shall include the following, which shall be regarded as material for the purpose of this subchapter;

Registrant's name, principal business address, and all other business addresses in the United States or elsewhere, and all residence addresses, if any;

Status of the registrant, if an individual nationality; if a partnership, name, residence addresses, and nationality of each partner and a true and complete copy of its articles of copartnership; if an association, corporation, organization, or any other combination of individuals, the name, residence addresses, and nationality of each director and officer and of each person performing the functions of a director or officer and a true and complete copy of its charter, articles of incorporation, association, constitution, and bylaws, and amendments thereto; a copy of every other instrument or document and a statement of the terms and conditions of every oral agreement relating to its organization, powers, and purposes; and a statement of its ownership and control;

A comprehensive statement of the nature of registrant's business; a complete list of registrant's employees and a statement of the nature of the work of each, unless, and to the extent, this requirement is waived in writing by the Attorney General; the name and address of every foreign principal for whom the registrant is acting, assuming or purporting to act or has agreed to act; if the character of the business or other activities of every such foreign principal be other than a natural person, a statement of the ownership and control of each; and the extent, if any, to which each such foreign principal is supervised, directed, owned, controlled, financed or subsidized, in whole or in part, by any government of a foreign country or foreign political party;

Copies of each written agreement and the terms and conditions of each oral agreement, including all modifications of such agreements, or, where no contract exists, a full statement of all the circumstances, by reason of which the registrant is an agent of the a foreign principal; a comprehensive statement of the nature and method of performance of each such contract, and of the existing and proposed activity or activities engaged in or to be engaged in by the registrant as agent of a foreign principal for each such foreign principal;

The nature and amount of contributions, income, money, or thing of value, if any, that the registrant has received within the preceding sixty days from each such foreign principal, either as compensation or for disbursement or otherwise, and the form and time of each such payment and from whom received;

A detailed statement of every activity which the registrant is performing or is assuming or purporting or has agreed to perform for himself or any other person other than a foreign principal and which requires his registration hereunder;

The name, business, and residence addresses, and, if an individual, the nationality, of any person who has within the preceding sixty days contributed or paid money or anything of value to the registrant in connection with any of the activities referred to in clause (6) of this subsection and the amount or value of the same;

A detailed statement of the money and other things of value spent or disposed of by the registrant during the preceding sixty days in furtherance of or in any way in connection with activities which require his registration hereunder and which have been undertaken by him either as an agent of a foreign principal or for himself or any other person;

Copies of each written agreement and the terms and conditions of each oral agreement, including all modifications of such agreements, or, where no contract exists, a full statement of all the circumstances, by reason of which the registrant is performing or assuming or purporting or has agreed to perform for himself or for a foreign principal any activities which require his registration hereunder;

Such other statements, information, or documents pertinent to the purposes of this subchapter as the Attorney General, having due regard for the national security and the public interest, any from time to time require;

Such further statements and such further copies of documents as are necessary to make the statements made in the registration statement and supplements thereto, and the copies of documents furnished therewith, not misleading.

(b) Every agent of a foreign principal who has filed a registration statement required by subsection (a) of this section shall, within thirty days after the expiration of each period of six months succeeding such filing, file with the Attorney General a supplement thereto under oath, on a form prescribed by the Attorney General, which shall set forth with respect to such preceding six months' period such facts as the Attorney General, having due regard for the national security and the public interest, may deem necessary to make the information required under this section accurate, complete, and current with respect to such period. In connection with the information furnished under clauses (3), (4), (6) and (9) of subsection (a) of this section, the registrant shall give notice to the Attorney General of any changes therein within ten days after such changes occur. If the Attorney General, having due regard for the national security and the public interest, determines that it is necessary to carry out the purposes of this subchapter he may, in any particular case, require supplements to the registration statement to be filed at more frequent intervals in respect to all or particular items of information to be furnished.

(c) The registration statement and supplements thereto shall be executed under oath as follows: If the registrant is an individual, by him; if the registrant is a partnership, by the majority of the members thereof; if the registrant is a person other than an individual or a partnership, by a majority of the officers thereof or persons performing the functions of officers or by a majority of the officers thereof or persons performing the functions of officers or by a majority of the board of directors thereof or persons performing the functions of directors, if any.

(d) The fact that a registration statement or supplement thereto has been filed shall not necessarily be deemed a full compliance with this subchapter and the regulations there under on the part of the registrant; nor shall it indicate that the Attorney General has in any way passed upon the merits of such registration statement or supplement thereto; nor shall it preclude prosecution, as provided for in this subchapter, for willful failure to file a registration statement or supplement thereto when due or for a willful false statement of a material fact therein or the willful omission of a material fact required to be stated therein or the willful omission of a material fact or copy of a material document necessary to make the statements made in a registration statement and supplements thereto, and the copies of documents furnished therewith, not misleading.

(e) If any agent of a foreign principal, required to register under the provisions of this subchapter, has previously thereto registered with the Attorney General under the provisions of section 14'17 of Title 18, the Attorney General, in order to eliminate inappropriate duplication, may permit the incorporation by reference in the registration statement or supplements thereto filed hereunder of any information or documents previously filed by such agent of a foreign principal under the provisions of said section.

613, Exemptions.

The requirements of section 612 (a) of this title shall not apply to the following agents of foreign principals:

A duly accredited diplomatic or consular officer of a foreign government who is so recognized by the Department of State, while said officer is engaged exclusively in activities which are recognized by the Department of State as being within the scope of the functions of such officer;

Any official of a foreign government, if such government is recognized by the United States, who is not a public-relations counsel, publicity agent, information-service employee, or a citizen of the United States, whose name and status and the character of whose duties as such official are of public record in the Department of State, while said official is engaged exclusively in activities which are recognized by the Department of State as being within the scope of the functions of such official;

Any member of the staff of, or any person employed by, a duly accredited diplomatic or consular officer of a foreign government who is so recognized by the Department of State, other than a public relations counsel, publicity agent, or information service employee, whose name and status and the character of whose duties as such member or employee are of public record in the Department of State, while said member or employee is engaged exclusively in the performance of activities which are recognized by the Department of State as being within the scope of the functions of such member or employee;

Any person engaging or agreeing to engage only in private, nonpolitical, financial, mercantile, or other activities in furtherance of the bona fide trade or commerce of such foreign principal or in the soliciting or collecting of funds and contributions within the United States to be sued only for medical aid and assistance, or for food and clothing to relieve human suffering, if such solicitation or collection of funds and contributions is in accordance with and subject to the provisions of sections 441, 444, 445, and 447-457 of this title and such rules and regulations as may be prescribed thereunder;

Any person engaging or agreeing to engage only in activities in furtherance of bona fide religious, scholastic, academic, or scientific pursuits or the fine arts;

Any person, or employee of such person, whose foreign principal is a government of a foreign country the defense of which the President deems vital to the defense of the United States while, (1) such person or employee engages only in activities which are in furtherance of the policies, public interest, or national defense of both such government and of the Government of the United States, and are not intended to conflict with any of the domestic or foreign policies of the Government of the United States, (2) each communication or expression by such person or employee which he intends to, or has reason to believe will be published, disseminated, or circulated among any section of the public, or portion thereof, within the United States, is a part of such activities and is believed by such person to be truthful and accurate and the identity of such person as an agent of such foreign principal is disclosed therein, and (3) such government of a foreign country furnishes to the Secretary of State for transmittal to, and retention for the duration of this subchapter by , the Attorney General such information as to the identity and activities of such person or employee at such times as the Attorney General may require. Upon notice to the Government of which such person is an agent or to such person or employee, the Attorney General, having due regard for the public interest and national defense, may, with the approval of the Secretary of State, and shall, at the request of the Secretary of State, terminate in whole or in part the exemption herein of any such person or employee.

614 Filing and Labeling of political propaganda

Every person within the United States who is an agent of a foreign principal and required to register under the provisions of this subchapter and who transmits or causes to be transmitted in the United States mails or by any means or instrumentality of interstate or foreign commerce any political propaganda (i) in the form of prints, or (ii) in any other form which is reasonably adapted to being, or which he believes will be, or which he intends to be, disseminated or circulated among two or more persons shall, not later than forty-eight hours after the beginning of the transmittal thereof, send to the Librarian of Congress two copies thereof and file with the Attorney General one copy thereof and a statement, duly signed by or on behalf of such agent, setting forth full information as to the places, times, and extent of such transmittal.

It shall be unlawful for any person within the United States who is an agent of a foreign principal and required to register under the provisions of this subchapter to transmit or cause to be transmitted in the United States mails or by any means or instrumentality of interstate or foreign commerce any political propaganda (i) in the form of prints, or (ii) in any other form which is reasonably adapted into being, or which he believes will be or which he intends to be, disseminated or circulated among two or more persons, unless such political propaganda is conspicuously marked at its beginning with, or prefaced or accompanied by, a true and accurate statement, in the language or languages used in such political propaganda, setting forth that the person transmitting such political propaganda or causing it to be transmitted is registered under this subchapter with the Department of Justice, Washington, District of Columbia, as an agent of a foreign principal, together with the name and address of such agent of a foreign principal and of each of his foreign principals; that, as required by this subchapter, his registration statement is available for inspection at and copies of such political propaganda are being filed with the Department of Justice; and that registration of agents of foreign principals required by the subchapter does not indicate approval by the United States Government of the contents of their political propaganda. The Attorney General, having due regard for the national security and the public interest, may by regulation prescribe the language or languages and the manner and form in which such statement shall be made and require the inclusion of such other information contained in the registration statement identifying such agent of a foreign principal and such political propaganda and its sources as may be appropriate.

The copies of political propaganda required by this subchapter to be sent to the Librarian of Congress shall be available for public inspection under such regulations as he may prescribe.

For purposes of the Library of Congress, other than for public distribution, the Secretary of the Treasury and the Postmaster General are authorized, upon the request of the Librarian of Congress, to forward to the Library of Congress fifty copies, or as many fewer thereof as are available, of all foreign prints determined to be prohibited entry under the provisions of section 1305 of Title 19 and of all foreign prints excluded from the mails under authority of section 343 of Title 18.

Notwithstanding the provisions of section 1365 of Title 19 and of section 343 of Title 18, the Secretary of the Treasury is authorized to permit the entry and the Postmaster General is authorized to permit the transmittal in the mails of foreign prints imported for governmental purposes by authority or for the use of the United States or for the use of the Library of Congress.

615 Books and Records
Every agent of a foreign principal registered under this subchapter shall keep and preserve while he is an agent of a foreign principal such books of account and other records with respect to all his activities, the disclosure of which is required under the provisions of this subchapter, as the Attorney General, having due regard for the national security and the public interest, may by regulation prescribe as necessary or appropriate for the enforcement of the provisions of this subchapter and shall preserve the same for a period of three years following the termination of such status. Until regulations are in effect under this section every agent of a foreign principal shall keep books of account and shall preserve all written records with respect to his activities. Such books and records shall be open at all reasonable times to the inspection of any official charged with the enforcement of this subchapter. It shall be unlawful for any person willfully to

conceal, destroy, obliterate, mutilate, or falsify, or attempt to conceal, destroy, obliterate, mutilate, or falsify, or cause to be concealed, destroyed, obliterated, mutilated, or falsified, any books or records required to be kept under the provisions of this section.

616 Public examination of official records.

The Attorney General shall retain in permanent form one copy of all registration statements and all statements concerning the distribution of political propaganda furnished under this subchapter, and the same shall be public records and open to public examination and inspection at such reasonable hours, under such regulations, as the Attorney General may prescribe, and copies of the same shall be furnished to every applicant at such reasonable fee as the Attorney General may prescribe. The Attorney General may withdraw from public examination the registration statement and other statements of any agent of a foreign principal whose activities have ceased to be of a character which requires registration under the provisions of this subchapter.

617 Liability of officers
Each officer, or person performing the functions of an officer, and each director, or person performing the functions of a director, of an agent of a foreign principal which is not an individual shall be under obligation to cause such agent to execute and file a registration statement and supplements thereto as and when such filing is required under section 612 (a) and (b) of this title and shall also be under obligation to cause such agent to comply with all the requirements of sections 612 (a) and (b), and 615 of this title and all other requirements of this subchapter. In case of failure of any such agent of a foreign principal to comply with any of the requirements of this subchapter, each of its officers, or persons performing the functions of officers, and each of its directors, or persons performing the functions of directors, shall be subject to prosecution therefore.

618. Enforcement and penalties.
Any person who—
Willfully violates any provision of this subchapter or any regulation thereunder, or

In any registration statement or supplement thereto or in any statement under section 614 (a) of this title concerning the distribution of political propaganda or in any other document filed with or furnished to the Attorney General under the provisions of this subchapter willfully makes a false statement of a material fact or willfully omits any material fact required to be stated therein or willfully omits a material fact or a copy of a material document necessary to make the statements therein and the copies of documents furnished therewith not misleading, shall, upon conviction thereof be punished by a fine of not more than $10,000 or by imprisonment for not more than five years, or both.

B. In any proceeding under this subchapter in which it is charged that a person is an agent of a foreign principal with respect to a foreign principal outside of the

United States, proof of the specific identity of the foreign principal shall be permissible but not necessary.

C. Any alien who shall be convicted of a violation of, or a conspiracy to violate, any provision of this subchapter or any regulation thereunder shall be subject to deportation in the manner provided by sections 155 and 156 of Title 8.

The Postmaster General may declare to be nonmailable any communication or expression falling within clause (2) of section 611 (j) of this title in the form of prints or in any other form reasonably adapted to, or reasonably appearing to be intended for, dissemination or circulation among two or more persons, which is offered or caused to be offered for transmittal in the United States mails to any person or persons in any other American republic by any agent of a foreign principal, if the Postmaster General is informed in writing by the Secretary of State that the duly accredited diplomatic representative of such American republic has made written representation to the Department of State that the admission or circulation of such communication or expression in such American republic is prohibited by the laws thereof and has requested in writing that its transmittal thereto be stopped.

619. Territorial applicability of subchapter.

This subchapter shall be applicable in the several States, the District of Columbia, the Territories, the Canal Zone, the insular possessions, and all other places now or hereafter subject to the civil or military jurisdiction of the United States.

620. Rules and Regulations

The Attorney General may at any time make, prescribe, amend, and rescind such rules, regulations, and forms as he may deem necessary to carry out the provisions of this subchapter.

621. The Attorney General shall, from time to time, make a report to the Congress concerning the administration of this subchapter, including the nature, sources, and content of political propaganda disseminated or distributed.

Israel Office of Information FARA Declaration — 10/06/1948

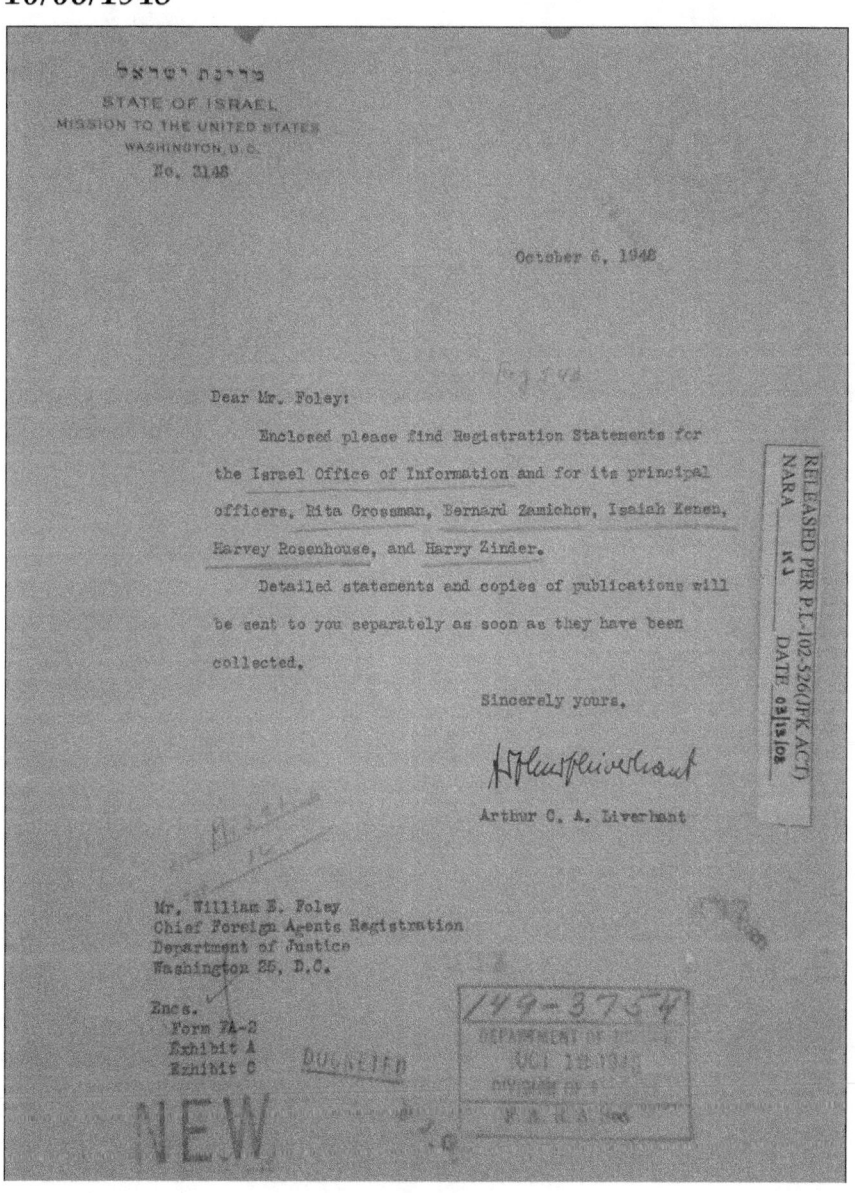

UNITED STATES DEPARTMENT OF JUSTICE
WASHINGTON, D. C.

REGISTRATION STATEMENT

Pursuant to Section 2 of the Foreign Agents Registration Act of 1938, as Amended

1. (a) Name of Registrant. Israel Office of Information

   (b) All other names used by Registrant during the past 10 years and when used.

   (c) Address of principal office. 2310 Massachusetts Avenue, N.W., Washington 8, D.C.
   16 E. 66th Street, New York, New York

   (d) Name of person or persons in charge of principal office. Harry Zinder - Washington, D.C.
   Isaiah Kenen - New York, N.Y.

2. (a) Date when Registrant was organized or created. September 15, 1948

   (b) State or other jurisdiction in which organized or created.

   (c) Type of Registrant's organization.

   Committee _____ Voluntary group _____ Association _____ Partnership _____
   Corporation _____ Other type (specify) Agency of Government of Israel

3. If Registrant is a nonbusiness membership organization, state:
   (a) Approximate number of members in the United States.
   (b) Approximate number of members outside the United States.
   (c) If more than one class of members, specify classes and approximate number of members in each.
   (d) Who may be members and on what terms and conditions.

RELEASED PER P.L-102-526(JFK ACT)
NARA *MS* DATE 3/11/03

APPENDIX

FORM FA-

4. All partners, officers, directors, and similar officials of Registrant.

Name and address of official	Position, office, or nature of duties
Harry Zinder, 2310 Mass. Ave., Wash. 8, D.C.	Director of Information
Isaiah Kenen, 16 E. 66th St., New York	Director of Information

5. All branches and local units of Registrant and all other component or affiliated groups or organizations.

Name and address of branch, unit, group, or organization	Nature of connection with Registrant	Name and address of person in charge

6. Name and principal address of each foreign principal of Registrant.

Name of foreign principal	Principal address
Israel Ministry of Foreign Affairs	Hakiryah, Israel

7. State the nature and purpose of Registrant's representation of each foreign principal named under item 6 and describe fully all activities of Registrant for or in the interests of each such foreign principal.

The purpose of the Israel Office of Information is to provide accurate and up-to-date information in the United States on all aspects of the State of Israel, including political, economic, cultural, social, and other activities.

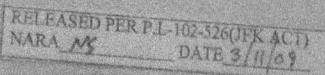

RELEASED PER P.L-102-326(JFK ACT)
NARA _NS_ DATE 3/11/09

FORM FA-8

3

8. Describe briefly all other businesses, occupations, and public activities in which Registrant is presently engaged.

9. All employees and other individuals, except those named under item 4, who render any services or assistance to Registrant, with or without compensation, for or in the interests of each foreign principal named under item 6.

Name and address of employee or other individual	Nature of services or assistance rendered
Harvey Rosenhouse, 6320 14th Street, N.W. Wash, D.C.	Asst. Press Adviser
~~Peter Medzini, 808 Nicholson St., Hyattsdale, Md.~~	~~Secretary~~
Bernard Zamichow, Manhattan Towers Hotel, N.Y.C.	Asst.Dir. of Information
Rita Grossman, 130 East 36th St., N.Y.C.	Administrative Officer

10. Furnish the following information as to Registrant's receipts and expenditures during the 3 months preceding the filing of this statement. The information may, if Registrant desires, be furnished for Registrant's latest fiscal quarter or other latest fiscal period of not less than 3 months.

(a) All amounts received during the period directly or indirectly from each foreign principal named under item 6, itemized as follows:¹

Date funds received	Name of foreign principal from whom funds received²	Purposes for which received⁴	Amount received³

Pending allocation of Ministry of Foreign Officers of separate budget for Israel Office of Information, its expenses are covered out of total budget for Israel Mission and it is therefore difficult to give accurate figures.

¹ Include all amounts so received, whether received as compensation, loans, contributions, subscriptions, fees, dues, subsidies, or otherwise.
² Receipts from a person amounting to less than $100 for the period may be combined with other like amounts, provided the source of the funds is clearly indicated.
³ If here funds were received for various purposes, such purposes shall be listed in reasonable detail.
⁴ Show separately the amount received for each purpose listed under the preceding column.

APPENDIX 235

FORM FA-2

4

(b) All amounts received during the period from other sources to be used directly or indirectly for or in the interests of any foreign principal named under item 6, itemized as follows:[1]

| Date funds received | Name of person from whom received[2] | Purposes for which received[3] | Amount received[4] |

(c) All expenditures made during the period directly or indirectly for or in the interest of each foreign principal named under item 6, itemized as follows:[5]

| Date payment was made | Name of person to whom payment was made[2] | Purposes for which payment was made[3] | Amount of payment[4] |

RELEASED PER P.L.-102-526(JFK ACT)
NARA MS   DATE 3/11/98

[1] Include all amounts so received, whether received as compensation, loans, contributions, subscriptions, fees, dues, subsidies, or otherwise.
[2] Receipts from or payments to a person amounting to less than $100 for the period may be combined with other like amounts, provided the source or disposition of the funds, as the case may be, is clearly indicated.
[3] Where funds were received or paid, as the case may be, for various purposes, such purposes shall be listed in reasonable detail.
[4] Show separately the amount received or paid, as the case may be, for each purpose listed under the preceding column.
[5] Include all transfers of funds to any foreign principal.

FORM ZA-1

11. (a) Speeches, lectures, talks, and radio broadcasts arranged or sponsored by Registrant or delivered by officials or employees of Registrant, during the past 3 months.

Date delivered	By whom delivered	Where delivered	Kind of audience	Subject matter discussed
June	Harry Zinder	Washington	Radio	Palestine
July	" "	"	Hadassah	Palestine
September	" "	Boston	Hadassah	Israel
September	" "	"	Radio	Israel
September	" "	New York	Welfare Board	Israel
September	" "	Washington	Television	Israel

(b) Publications prepared or distributed by Registrant, or by others for Registrant, or in the preparation or distribution of which Registrant rendered any services or assistance, during the past 6 months. (Indicate each type of publication by an "X".)

(1) Press releases X
(2) News bulletins . . . . . . ___
(3) Newspapers . . . . . . ___
(4) Articles X
(5) Books X
(6) Magazines . . . . . . ___
(7) Pamphlets . . . . . . ___

(8) Circulars . . . . . . ___
(9) Form letters . . . . . . ___
(10) Reprints X
(11) Copies of speeches, lectures, talks, or radio broadcasts X
(12) Radio programs . . . . . . ___
(13) Radio scripts . . . . . . ___
(14) Moving pictures . . . . . . ___

(15) Lantern slides . . . . . . ___
(16) Still pictures X
(17) Posters . . . . . . ___
(18) Photographs X
(19) Charts . . . . . . ___
(20) Maps X
(21) Other publications . . . ___

(c) Preparation of publications referred to in answer to (b) above.

Number checked under (b)	Description of publication	By whom written, edited, or prepared	By whom printed, produced, or published
1	Press Releases	H. Zinder	Office
4	Articles	Tel Aviv Office	Mission
10	Reprints	Newspapers	Commercially
11	Copies of Talks	Authors	Scripts

(d) Distribution of publications referred to in answer to (b) above.

Number checked under (b)	Name of distributee	Methods and channels of distribution	Classes or groups of persons to which distributed
1	Israeli Mission	By hand and mail	Newspapers magazines
4	" "	" "	Newspapers magazines
10	Israeli Mission	By mail	General newspapers
11	Israeli Mission	By mail	Radio, newspapers magazines

¹ In case of radio broadcasts, identify the stations from which the broadcasts were made.

RELEASED PER P.L.-102-526(JFK ACT)
NARA _NS_   DATE 3/11/03

FORM FA-1

12. (a) Registrant's affiliations, associations, or other connections, not fully described above, with foreign governments, foreign political parties, or officials or agencies thereof.

Name of government, party, or official or agency thereof	Nature of Registrant's connections therewith
None	

(b) Registrant's pecuniary interest in or control over partnerships, corporations, associations, or other organizations or combinations of individuals, not fully described above.

Name of organization or combination	Nature of Registrant's ownership or other pecuniary interest	Nature of any direction or control exercised by Registrant
None		

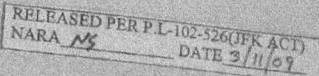

13. (a) Ownership of, or supervision, direction, or control over, Registrant by all organizations, groups, or individuals.

Name of organization, group, or individual	Nature of ownership, supervision, direction, or control
None	

(b) Any subsidy or other financial assistance received by Registrant directly or indirectly from—

Any individual who is a citizen of, or resides in, a foreign country.

Any organization created in, or under the laws of, any foreign country or having its principal place of business in a foreign country.

Any foreign government or foreign political party, or any official or agency thereof.

Name of person from whom subsidy or financial assistance received	Nature and amount of subsidy
None	

12. File the following exhibits with this statement:

Exhibit A.—File an Exhibit A, on the printed form provided therefor, for each person named under items 4 and 9.

Exhibit B.—File a copy of the agreement, arrangement, or authorization (or if not in writing a written description thereof) pursuant to which Registrant is acting for, or receiving funds from, each foreign principal named under Item 6.

Exhibit C.—File an Exhibit C, on the printed form provided therefor, for each foreign principal named under Item 6.

Exhibit D.—If Registrant is a nonbusiness organization, file a copy of its charter, constitution, bylaws, or other instruments of organization.

Exhibit E.—File copies of all printed matter referred to under item 11 (b), except photographs and moving pictures.

Exhibit F.—File a copy of the agreement or arrangement (or if not in writing, a written description thereof) between the Registrant and each business firm or other organization named under item 11 (c) or (d).

RELEASED PER P.L.-102-526(JFK ACT)
NARA NS DATE 3/11/09

APPENDIX

8

FORM FA-3

The undersigned swear(s) or affirm(s) that he has (they have) read the information set forth in this registration statement and the attached exhibits and that he is (they are) familiar with the contents thereof and that such contents are in their entirety true and accurate to the best of his (their) knowledge and belief, except that the undersigned make(s) no representation as to the truth or accuracy of the information contained in Exhibit A insofar as such information is not within his (their) personal knowledge.

(Type or print name under each signature.)

Harry Zinder
(Signature)
Harry Zinder

(Both copies of this statement shall be signed and sworn to before a notary public or other person authorized to administer oaths. The statement shall be signed by the Agent or, if the Agent is an organization, by a majority of those partners, officers, directors, or persons performing similar functions who are in the United States. If no such person is in the United States, the statement shall be signed and sworn to by the duly authorized representative of the Registrant.)

(Signature)

(Signature)

Subscribed and sworn to before me at Washington, D.C. this 7th day of October, 1948.

Adrian Carter
(Signature of notary or other officer)

My commission expires August 31, 1952.

RELEASED PER P.L.-102-526(JFK ACT)
NARA MS   DATE 3/11/08

Isaiah Kenen Personal FARA Declaration—09/01/1948

APPENDIX 241

UNITED STATES DEPARTMENT OF JUSTICE
WASHINGTON, D. C.

EXHIBIT A

TO REGISTRATION AND EXEMPTION STATEMENTS

Under the Foreign Agents Registration Act of 1938, as Amended

Furnish this exhibit for all partners, officers, directors, or similar officials of the Registrant or Agent, as the case may be, and for all employees or other individuals who render services or assistance to the Registrant or Agent for or in the interests of any foreign principal of the Registrant or Agent.

THIS EXHIBIT WILL NOT BE ACCEPTED FOR FILING UNLESS IT IS REASONABLY COMPLETE AND ACCURATE.

1. (a) Full name.

Isaiah Leo Kenen

(b) All other names ever used and when each was used.

none

(c) All present business addresses.

16 East 66 Street
New York, 21, N.Y.

(d) All present residence addresses.

Apartment 62A, 3900 Greystone Avenue, Bronx 63, N.Y.

2. (a) Date and place of birth.

March 7, 1905 St. Stephen, New Brunswick, Canada

(b) Citizenship or nationality.

U.S.

(c) If present citizenship not acquired by birth, indicate when, where, and how acquired.

Naturalization, District Court, U.S.; Northern District of Ohio, June 8, 1934

3. All visits to or residence in foreign countries during the past 5 years.

Name of foreign country	Purpose of visit or stay	Date and port of each departure from and entry into United States
England and France	attendance at International Conferences for American Jewish Conference	left NY Oct.12, 1945 retd.NY Dec. 7, 1945
England, France, Egypt, Palestine, Germany	same	left NY June 20,1946 retd NY Sept.7,1946
England, Palestine, Egypt, France, Switzerland, Germany, Austria	member of Jewish Agency for Palestine liaison with United Nations Special Committee on Palestine	left NY June , 1947 retd.NY Aug.18,1947
France, Israel, countries of transit	member, Israeli Mission to UN	left NY Aug 11, 1948

(Frequent trips to Toronto, Canada, to visit my mother)

RELEASED PER P.L-102-526(JFK ACT)
NARA _NS_ DATE 3/11/93

2

4. All clubs, societies, committees, and other unbusiness organizations in the United States or elsewhere, including any active or reserve military or naval forces, of which you have been a member, director, officer, or employee during the past 2 years.

Name and address of organization	Nature of connection with organization	Duration of connection
Jewish Agency for Palestine	New York Information Director	from April 15,1947, to May 15, 1948
American Jewish Conference	Executive Secretary	from Dec.1, 1943, to Feb.1, 1946
Zionist Organization of America	member	many years
Riverdale Temple	"	since Sept., 1947
Temple Emanuel of Yonkers	"	from Sept. 1944 to Sept. 1946
Jewish National Workers Alliance	"	many years until 1947

5. (a) A full description of all activities of any kind in which you are presently engaged for or in the interests of the Registrant or Agent or any foreign principal of yourself or of the Registrant or Agent.

am now Director of Information for the Government of Israel's Mission to the United Nations, previously having served as Director of Information for the Jewish Agency for Palestine at the United Nations. I am assuming direction of the Israeli Government's Office of Information in New York.

RELEASED PER P.L-102-526(JFK ACT)
NARA NS   DATE 3/11/08

(b) A brief description of all other businesses, occupations, and public activities in which you are presently engaged.

none

6. Furnish the following information as to all amounts received by you, as compensation or otherwise during the 3 months preceding the filing of this exhibit, directly or indirectly from the Registrant or Agent or from any foreign principal of yourself or of the Registrant or Agent.

Date funds received	Name of person from whom received	Purpose for which received	Amount received
June 1	Jewish Agency for Palestine	salary	$916.66
July 1	Jewish Agency for Palestine	salary	$916.66
August 1	Government of Israel	salary	$916.66
September 1	Government of Israel	salary	$916.66

APPENDIX

7. (a) Speeches, lectures, talks, and radio broadcasts delivered by you during the past 3 months.

Date delivered	Where delivered	Kind of audience	Subject matter discussed
none			

(b) All newspapers, magazines, articles, books, pamphlets, press releases, moving pictures, radio programs and scripts, and other publications, prepared or distributed by you or by others for you, or in the preparation or distribution of which you rendered any services or assistance, during the past 6 months.

Description of publication	By whom written, edited, or prepared	By whom printed, produced, or published	By whom distributed
pamphlets and press releases (those requiring registration were filed with Department of Justice)	myself and Miss Rita Grossman	Jewish Agency for Palestine and Israeli Mission to UN	same

8. List all of your connections, not fully described above, with all foreign governments, foreign political parties, or officials or agencies thereof.

Name of government, party, or official or agency thereof	Nature of your office, employment, or other connection	Nature of any subsidy or other financial arrangement
none		

I certify that I have read the information set forth in this exhibit and am familiar with the contents thereof and that the information herein contained is true to the best of my knowledge and belief.

_____
(Signature)

September 1, 1948   Isaiah L. Kenen
(Date of signature)   (Type or print name)

(Two copies of each Exhibit A shall be filed. Both copies shall be signed by the person for whom the information contained herein is given. A third copy should be prepared and retained for future reference.)

RELEASED PER P.L.-102-526(JFK ACT)
NARA MS   DATE 5/11/93

Israel Office of Information Deficiency Notice — 06/17/1949

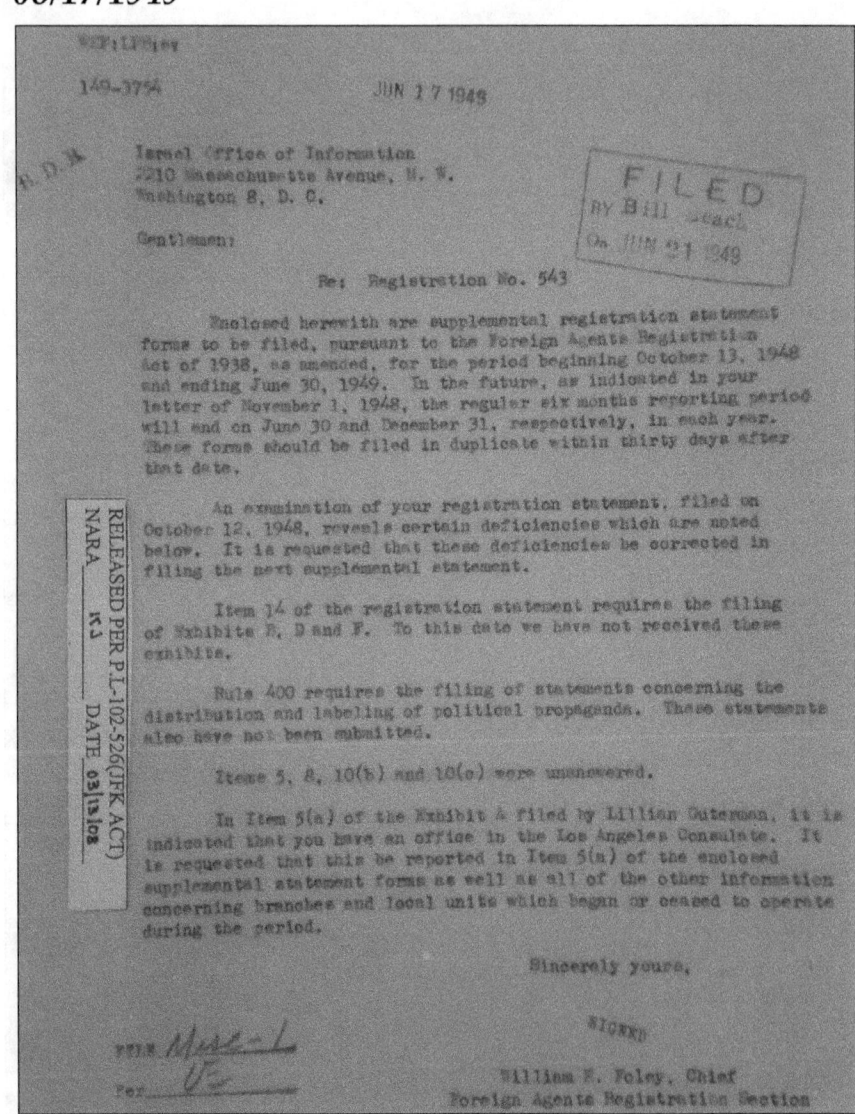

APPENDIX

Israel Office of Information FARA Declaration — 06/30/1950

UNITED STATES DEPARTMENT OF JUSTICE
WASHINGTON, D. C.

SUPPLEMENTAL REGISTRATION STATEMENT

Pursuant to Section 2 of the Foreign Agents Registration Act of 1938, as Amended

REGISTRATION NO. _____

For Six Months Period Ending June 30, 1950
(Insert date)

1. (a) Name of Registrant.

    Israel Office of Information

 (b) All other names used by Registrant during the period.

    None

 (c) Address of principal office.
    1. 2210 Massachusetts Avenue, N.W., Washington, D. C.
    2. 11 East 70th Street, New York, New York
    3. 205 West Eighth Street, Los Angeles, California

 (d) Name of person or persons in charge of principal office.
    1. Minna Davidovitch
    2. I. L. Kenen
    3. Shirley Brostoff Lewis

3. If Registrant is a nonbusiness membership organization, state—

 (a) Approximate number of members in the United States .... None

 (b) Approximate number of members outside the United States .... None

4. (a) All persons who became partners, officers, directors, and similar officials of Registrant during the period.

Name and address of official	Date connection began	Position, office, or nature of duties
I. H. Rosenkranz, Embassy of Israel, Washington, D. C.	May 1, 1950	Press Adviser

(b) All persons who ceased to be partners, officers, directors, or similar officials of Registrant during the period.

Name and address of official	Date connection ended	Reason for ending connection
None		

RELEASED PER P.L-102-526(JFK ACT)
NARA NS   DATE 3/11/69

FORM F.A.C-401

2

3. (a) All branches and local units of Registrant and all other component or affiliated groups or organizations which began to operate during the period.

| Name and address of branch, unit, group, or organization | Nature of connection with Registrant | Name and address of person in charge |

None

(b) All branches and local units of Registrant and all other component or affiliated groups or organizations which ceased to operate during the period.

| Name of branch, unit, group, or organization | | Reason operations ceased |

None

6. All persons who at any time during the period were foreign principals of Registrant.

| Name and principal address | Is person still a foreign principal of Registrant? | If not, give date connection ended |

Moshe Pearlman
Ministry for Foreign Affairs
Hakiryah (Tel Aviv), Israel — Yes

7. Describe fully all activities of Registrant during the period for or in the interests of each foreign principal named under item 6.

Information, news, and statements issued either in the name of foreign principal or Office of Information through press releases, speeches, news bulletins, special statements, pamphlets, documents, and broadcasts

RELEASED PER P.L-102-526(JFK ACT)
NARA NS   DATE 3/11/09

8. Describe briefly all other businesses, occupations, and public activities in which Registrant engaged during the period.

None

9. Furnish the following information as to all employees and other individuals, except those named under item 4, who during the period rendered any services or assistance to Registrant, with or without compensation, for or in the interests of any foreign principal named under item 6:

(a) All such employees and other individuals for whom Exhibits A have previously been filed.

Name and address of employee or other individual	Nature of any changes during period in activities for Registrant or its foreign principals	Has connection with Registrant ended?
I. L. Kenen, c/o Consulate of Israel, 11 E. 70th St., N.Y.		No
Rita Grossman	" " " "	No
Shirley Brostoff Lewis, " " , 208 W. 6th St., Los Angeles, Calif.		No
Minna Davidovitch, 2210 Massachusetts Ave., Washington, D.C.		Yes
Yaaqov Gutman	" "	Yes

(b) All such employees and other individuals for whom Exhibits A have not been previously filed.

Name and address of employee or other individual	Nature of services or assistance rendered	Has connection with Registrant ended?
Ephraim Kaufman 2210 Massachusetts Ave., Washington, D. C.	Reference Service	No
(Lillian Friedman	Secretary	No
(Ruth Goldschmidt	Dir. Ref. and Research	No
(Judith Swet	Research	No
(Catherine D. Saffron	Research	No
(Lillian Outerman	Secretary	No
(Nadine Gherner	Stenographer	Yes
(Idel Pann	Interviewer	No
(Mercia Pearlstein	Interviewer	Yes
(Rachel Mizrachi	Stenographer	Yes
(Hannah Roth	Clerk	No
c/o 11 East 70th Street, New York, New York		

RELEASED PER P.L-102-526(JFK ACT)
NARA NS   DATE 3/11/09

10. Furnish the following information as to Registrant's receipts and expenditures during the period covered by this statement. The information may, if Registrant desires, be furnished for Registrant's latest semiannual fiscal period, provided the period covered is indicated and future statements are furnished on the same basis.

(a) All amounts received during the period directly or indirectly from each foreign principal named under item 9, itemized as follows:

Date funds received	Name of foreign principal from whom funds received	Purposes for which received	Amount received
Middle of each month	Ministry for Foreign Affairs	Information Services	

(b) All amounts received during the period from other sources to be used directly or indirectly for or in the interests of any foreign principal named under item 6, itemized as follows:

Date funds received	Name of person from whom received	Purposes for which received	Amount received

(c) All expenditures made during the period directly or indirectly for or in the interests of each foreign principal named under item 6, itemized as follows:

Date payment was made	Name of person to whom payment was made	Purposes for which payment was made	Amount of payment

See Appendix A

RELEASED PER P.L.-102-526(JFK ACT)
NARA *NS* DATE 3/11/08

APPENDIX 249

FORM FA 5-08

11. (a) Speeches, lectures, talks, and radio broadcasts arranged or sponsored by Registrant or delivered by officials or employees of Registrant, during the period.

Name of person by whom delivered	Number of speeches, lectures, and talks delivered	Number of radio broadcasts delivered
Yaaqov Gutman	1	
Ruth Harshalman	1	
Ephraim Kaufman	5	
Amos Mir	3	
Y. M. Rosenkranz	1	
I. L. Kenen	22	83
Rita Grossman	6	
Ruth Goldschmidt	25	

(b) Publications prepared or distributed by Registrant, or by others for Registrant, or in the preparation or distribution of which Registrant rendered any services or assistance, during the period. (Indicate each type of publication by an "X".)

(1) Press releases . . . X (8) Circulars . . . . . (15) Lantern slides . . . X
(2) News bulletins . . . X (9) Form letters . . . . (16) Still pictures . . . .
(3) Newspapers . . . . . (10) Reprints . . . . . . (17) Posters . . . . . .
(4) Articles . . . . . X (11) Copies of speeches, lectures, talks, or radio (18) Photographs . . . X
(5) Books . . . . broadcasts . . . . X (19) Charts . . . . . .
(6) Magazines . . . . . (12) Radio programs . . X (20) Maps . . . .
(7) Pamphlets . . . X (13) Radio scripts . . . X (21) Other publications . .
                        (14) Moving pictures . . .

(c) Preparation and distribution of publications referred to in answer to (b) above.

Description of publication	By whom written, edited, or prepared	By whom printed, produced, or published	By whom distributed

See Appendix C

(d) Compliance with the filing, labeling, and reporting provisions of Section 4 of the Foreign Agents Registration Act of 1938, as amended, and Rule 400 thereunder.

(1) Were copies or summaries of all communications and publications referred to in answer to (a) and (b) above filed with the Department of Justice and the Librarian of Congress? If not, explain why copies or summaries of any such communications and publications were not filed.

Yes

(2) Were all such communications and publications labeled in accordance with Section 4 and Rule 400? If not, explain why any such communications and publications were not so labeled.

Yes

(3) Were reports of the delivery, distribution, or other dissemination of all such communications and publications made to the Department of Justice in accordance with Section 4 and Rule 400? If not, explain why any such reports were omitted.

Yes

RELEASED PER P.L-102-526(JFK ACT)
NARA NS   DATE 3/11/09

6

12. (a) Any changes during the period, not fully described above, in Registrant's affiliations, associations, or other connections with foreign governments, foreign political parties, or officials or agencies thereof.

Name of government, party, or official or agency thereof *Nature of changes during period in Registrant's connections therewith*

None

(b) Any changes during the period in Registrant's pecuniary interest in or control over partnerships, corporations, associations, or other organizations or combinations of individuals.

Name of organization or combination *Nature of changes during period in Registrant's ownership or other pecuniary interest* *Nature of changes during period in any direction or control exercised by Registrant*

None

13. (a) Any changes during the period in the ownership of or supervision, direction or control over Registrant by any organization, group, or individual.

Name of organization, group, or individual *Nature of changes during period in ownership, supervision, direction, or control*

None

RELEASED PER P.L.-102-526(JFK ACT)
NARA NS   DATE 3/11/09

APPENDIX

FORM FA-1-64

(b) Any subsidy or other financial assistance received by Registrant during the period directly or indirectly from:—

Any individual who is a citizen of, or resides in, a foreign country.

Any organization created in, or under the laws of, any foreign country or having its principal place of business in a foreign country.

Any foreign government or foreign political party, or any official or agency thereof.

Name of person from whom subsidy or financial assistance received	Nature and amount of subsidy or financial assistance
See particulars given under 10(a).	

14. File the following exhibits with this statement:

    Exhibit A.—File an Exhibit A, on the printed form provided therefor, for each of the following persons for whom an Exhibit A has not previously been filed:

        (a) All partners, officers, directors, and similar officials of Registrant.

        (b) All employees or other individuals who during the period rendered any services or assistance to Registrant, with or without compensation, for or in the interests of any foreign principal named under item 6.

    Exhibit B.—File a copy of any changes during the period in the agreement, arrangement, or authorization (or if not in writing a written description thereof) pursuant to which Registrant is acting for, or receiving funds from, each foreign principal named under item 6.

    Exhibit C.—File an Exhibit C, on the printed form provided therefor, for each foreign principal named under item 6 for whom an Exhibit C has not previously been filed.

    Exhibit D.—If Registrant is a nonbusiness organization, file a copy of any changes during the period in its charter, constitution, bylaws, or other instruments of organization.

    Exhibit E.—File a copy of the agreement or arrangement (or if not in writing, a written description thereof) between the Registrant and each business firm or other organization named under item 11 (c), and copies of all changes during the period in similar contracts previously filed.

RELEASED PER P.L-102-526(JFK ACT)
NARA NS   DATE 3/11/09

FORM FA-8-AR

8

The undersigned swear(s) or affirm(s) that he has (they have) read the information set forth in this statement and the attached exhibits and that he is (they are) familiar with the contents thereof and that such contents are in their entirety true and accurate to the best of his (their) knowledge and belief, except that the undersigned make(s) no representation as to the truth or accuracy of the information contained in Exhibit A insofar as such information is not within his (their) personal knowledge.

(Type or print name under each signature)

_____
(Signature)
I. L. KENEN

(Both copies of this statement shall be signed and sworn to before a notary public or other person authorized to administer oaths, by a majority of those partners, officers, directors, or persons performing similar functions who are in the United States. If no such person is in the United States, the statement shall be signed and sworn to by the duly authorized representative of the Registrant.)

_____
(Signature)

_____
(Signature)

Subscribed and sworn to before me at 839 Madison Ave
this 24th day of October, 19 50.

_____
(Signature of notary or other officer)

ROBERT LEWIT
Notary Public, State of New York
Qualified in Bronx ...
Cert. Filed with N. Y. Co. Ch. ...
Commission Expires March 30, 1952

My commission expires ...., 19 ......

RELEASED PER P.L-102-526(JFK ACT)
NARA NS   DATE 3/11/09

Israel Office of Information Personnel—01/01/1951

ISRAEL OFFICE OF INFORMATION
11 EAST 70TH STREET
NEW YORK 21, NEW YORK

APPENDIX B (1)

Personnel - January 1 to June 30, 1951:

Alex Aylat
334 East 82nd Street
New York 21, N. Y.
Research Assistant

Mordecai Chertoff
300 Riverside Drive
New York 25, N. Y.
Research Assistant (Resigned February 2, 1951)

Benjamin Cohen
140-05 Beech Avenue, Apt. 2D
Flushing, N. Y.
Press Archivist

Tisco Frankel
4 West 93rd Street, Apt. 6D
New York 25, N. Y.
Yiddish Secretary

Lillian Friedman
423 West End Avenue
New York, N. Y.
Secretary (Resigned January 15, 1951)

Ruth Goldschmidt
134 West 73rd Street
New York 23, N. Y.
Department Head Assistant

Lillian Guterman
76 Highland Avenue
Yonkers, N. Y.
Secretary

Judith Hershcopf
860 Fifth Avenue
New York, N. Y.
Secretary (Employed March 12, 1951)

Leah Kugelman
166 West 72nd Street
New York 23, N. Y.
Interviewer

Maria Ines Marmor
240 West 98th Street
New York 25, N. Y.
Research Assistant (Employed February 12, 1951)

Rachel Mizrachi
704 East 20th Street
New York 21, N. Y.
Secretary (Resigned March 2, 1951)

Elizabeth Ostrer
16 East 87th Street
New York 21, N. Y.
Secretary-Stenographer

Judith Sert
155 East 77th Street
New York 21, N. Y.
Administrative Secretary

Claire Troob
165 Jerome Street
Brooklyn, N. Y.
Secretary (Employed January 29, 1951)

RELEASED PER P.L.-102-526(JFK ACT)
NARA NS   DATE 3/11/69

FARA Section Memo on Kenen Visit—01/17/1951

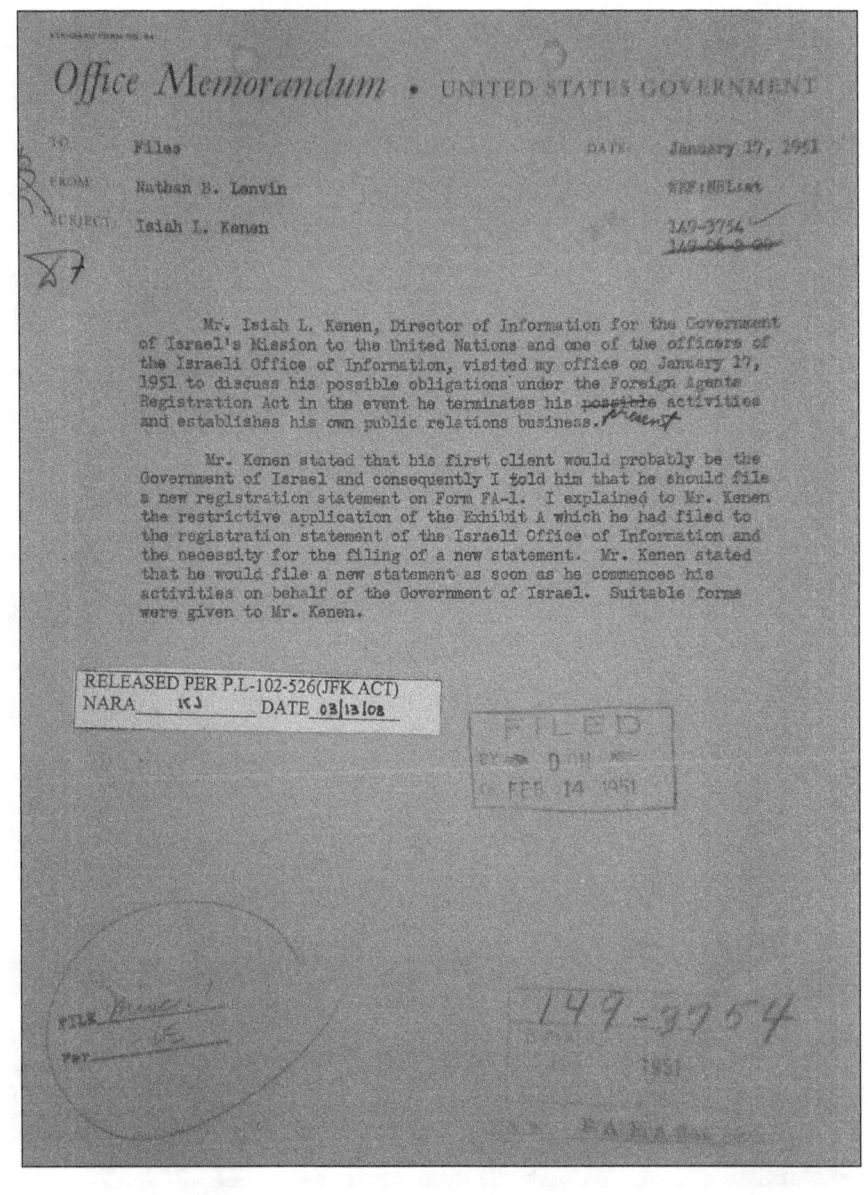

Isaiah Kenen Letter to the FARA Section — 02/13/1951

I. L. KENEN
ROOM 1431
342 MADISON AVENUE
NEW YORK 17, N. Y.

MURRAY HILL 7-1068-9

February 13, 1951

United States Department of Justice
Foreign Agents Registration Section
Washington, D. C.

Dear Sirs:

REGISTRATION NO. 543

This is to inform you that, effective today, I have resigned from the service of the Government of Israel.

I have been registered on an exhibit A form, as part of the registration of the Israel Office of Information.

Since January 1st, I was retained by the Government of Israel in an advisory capacity in the field of public relations. However, I have now changed my plans and severed my relations with the Israel Government. I would, therefore, request that my name be removed from your lists. I will submit a financial statement for the period from January 1st to February 14th, as soon as it is completed. During this period, I published no documents, circulated no printed or propaganda material, and made no speeches.

Sincerely yours,

I. L. Kenen

ILK:SL

Isaiah Kenen Letter to the FARA Section—03/14/1952

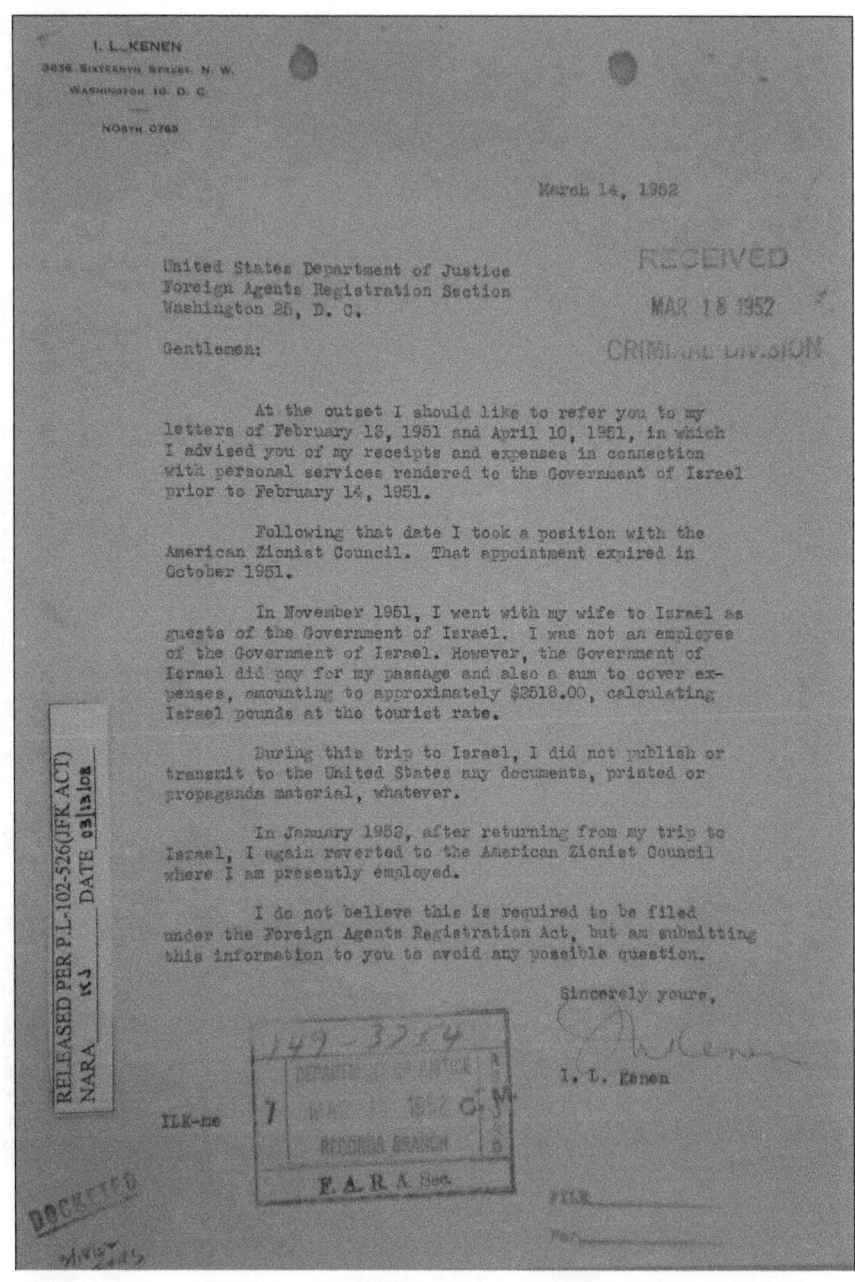

Covenant: The Government of Israel and the Jewish Agency

Covenant between the Government of Israel (Hereafter the Government) and The Zionist Executive Called also the Executive of the Jewish Agency (Hereafter the Executive)

Entered into this day, in accordance with the Zionist Organization–Jewish Agency Status Law, 1952.

Functions of Executive

The function of the Zionist Executive which are governed by this Covenant are: The organizing of immigration abroad and the transfer of immigrants and their property to Israel; participation in the absorption of immigrants in Israeli; Youth Immigration; agricultural settlement in Israel; the acquisition and amelioration of land in Israel by institutions of the Zionist Organization, the Keren Kayemeth Le Israel and the Keren Hayesod; participation in the establishment and expansion of development enterprises in Israel; the encouragement of private capital investments in Israel; assistance to cultural enterprises and institutions of higher learning in Israel; the encouragement of private capital investments in Israel; assistance to cultural enterprises and institutions of higher learning in Israel; the mobilization of resources for financing these functions; the coordination of the activities in Israel of Jewish institutions and organizations acting within the sphere of these functions with the aid of public funds.

Activities under the Law

Any function carried out in Israel by the Executive or on its behalf hereunder shall be executed in accordance with the laws of Israel and such administrative regulations in force from time to time as govern activities of governmental authorities whose functions cover or are affected by the activity in question.

Immigration

In organizing immigration and in the handling of immigrants, the Executive shall act in pursuance of a programme agreed upon with the Government or authorized by the Coordinating Board (see Para. 8). Immigrants will require visas in accordance with the Law of Return 5711-1950.

Coordination between Institutions

The Executive shall, with the consent of the Government, coordinate the activities in Israel of Jewish institutions and organizations which act within the sphere of the functions of the Executive.

Transfer of Functions

The Executive may carry out its functions alone, through its existing institutions, or such as it may establish in the future, and it may also obtain the participation of other institutions in Israel, provided that it may not transfer any of its powers or rights under this Covenant without the consent of the Government; and the Executive shall not authorize any body or institution to carry out its functions, in whole or in part, except upon prior notice to the government.

Mobilization of Resources

The Executive shall be responsible for the mobilization of the financial and material resources required for the execution of its functions, by means of the Keren Hayesod, the Keren Kayemeth Le Israel and other funds.

Legislation

The Government shall consult the Executive in regard to legislation specifically affecting the functions of the Executive before such legislation is submitted to the Knesset.

Coordination Board

For the purpose of coordinating activities between the Government and the Executive in all spheres to which this Covenant applies, there shall be established a Coordination Board (hereafter called the Board). The Board shall be composed of an even number of members, not less than four, half of whom shall be members of the Government appointed by it, and half of whom shall be members of the Government appointed by it, and half of whom shall be members of the Executive appointed by it. The Government and the Executive shall be entitled from time to time to replace the members of the Board by others from among their members.

Its Activities

The Board shall meet at least once a month. It may appoint sub-committees consisting of members of the Board or also non-members. The Board shall from time to time submit to the Government and the Executive reports of its deliberations and recommendations. Subject as aforesaid, the Board shall make its own rules of procedure.

Permits and Facilities

The Government will see to it that its duly authorized agencies shall issue to the Executive and its institutions all permits and facilities required by law for activities carried out in accordance with this Covenant so as to facilitate the Executive's functions.

Relief from Taxes

Gifts and legacies to the Executive or to any of its institutions shall be exempt from Inheritance Tax. All other problems connected with the exemption of the Executive, its Funds and its other institutions from payment of taxes, customs duties and other governmental levies, shall be the subject of a special arrangement between the Executive and the Government. This arrangement shall be formulated in an annex to this Covenant within eight months, as an integral part thereof, and shall be effective as from the date of signature of this Covenant.

Alterations

All proposals for alterations or amendments to this Covenant, or any addition thereto, must be made in writing and no alteration or amendment of this Covenant, or addition thereto, shall be made except in writing.

Notifications

Any notice to be sent to the Government shall be sent to the Prime Minister, and any notice to be sent to the Executive shall be sent to the Chairman of the Executive in Jerusalem.

Date of Coming into Force

This Covenant shall come into force on the date of signature.

IN WITNESS THEREOF, etc.

SIGNED -   Jerusalem

July 16, 1954

AZC Internal Memo on Public Relations 1962-63[441]

AMERICAN ZIONIST COUNCIL

COMMITTEE ON INFORMATION AND PUBLIC RELATIONS

The Committee carries on a major part of its work through highly specialized subcommittees composed of professionals in specific areas of activity who volunteer their services to the American Zionist Council. It is the subcommittee chairmen who have been instrumental, for the most part, in mobilizing these experts to serve with them to help interpret Israel to the general American public. In addition, the AZC staff carries on a number of activities on its own without benefit of these volunteers.

The Committee plans to operate in the following areas during the 1962-63 budgetary year.

1. Magazines

   Cultivation of editors.
   Stimulation and placement of suitable articles in the major consumer magazines.
   Reprinting and distribution of favorable materials which appear in the above publications.
   Stimulation of articles in trade and specialized journals.
   Liaison with writers resident in Israel via a literary agent in New York for ideas and placement.

2. TV, Radio, Films

   The Department arranges for talks and interviews on Radio and TV, and servicing of film requests.
   It also cultivates leading personalities in these media.
   It encourages networks and stations to create programs revolving around Israel.

3. Christian Religious Groups

   Cultivation of key religious leaders and groups.
   Setting up Seminars on Israel for Christian clergy.
   Stimulating of positive articles in the Protestant and Catholic press.
   Counteraction of hostile material in that press.
   Reprints and distribution of favorable materials from the church press.
   Stimulation of suitable articles in the journals of the Jewish religious groups.

4. Academic Circles

   Support of the American Association for Middle East Studies.
   Support of the Inter-University Committee on Israel.
   Cultivation of leaders in the academic community.
   Stimulation of "Israel Day" on college campuses.
   Cooperation with colleges and universities in setting up of Seminars on the Middle East.
   Monitoring and counteraction of material in the campus press.
   Stimulating of articles in academic journals.
   Guidance to student Zionists and other Jewish students on Arab-Israel issues.
   Counteraction of hostile faculty and Arab students.
   Preparation of materials for elementary and high school faculty.

- 2 -

5. Daily Press

   Cultivation of editors.
   Stimulation of positive material via syndicated writers, columnists, etc.
   Counteraction of hostile material.
   Reprinting and distribution of favorable materials.

6. Books

   Assistance to publishers in the promotion of worthwhile books.
   Promotion of reviews of favorable books.
   Distribution of books to public and college libraries.

7. Speakers

   The Speakers Bureau will continue to utilize Israelis, American Christians and American Jews on academic, religious, civic and other platforms around the country for positive presentations on Israel.

8. Liaison with organizations, both on the national and local levels, especially those with an international relations program.
   Special liaison with Negro community.

9. Projects and Issues

   Issuance of special material and guidance on controversial issues such as Arab refugees, Syrian-Israel situation, etc.
   Programming for special occasions such as Yom Haatzmaut, etc.

10. Visitors to Israel

    Subsidization to individual public opinion molders to help provide them with an experience in Israel.
    Inter-University Committee Study Tour to Israel.
    Organize other tours in which public opinion molders will participate.
    Provide suitable arrangements in Israel for handling of American visitors.

11. Counteracting the Opposition

    The monitoring and counteraction of all activities carried out here by the Arabs, American Friends of the Middle East, and the American Council for Judaism.

12. Miscellaneous

    Answering requests for information and providing suitable literature for the many thousands of requests annually received.

* * * *

Alert to AG of Compelled AZC FARA 10/31/1962

TO: The Attorney General

J. Walter Yeagley
Assistant Attorney General
Internal Security Division

SUBJECT: AMERICAN ZIONIST COUNCIL

  I think you ought to know that we are soliciting next week the registration of the American Zionist Council under the Foreign Agents Registration Act. In an amendment to a supplemental registration statement filed by the American Section of the Jewish Agency for Israel for the period ending March 31, 1962, it was reported that the Council received over $32,000 in subventions and over $11,000 as a special grant from the American Section of the Jewish Agency for Israel. Under the Act the receipt of such funds from the Jewish Agency constitutes the Council an agent of a foreign principal as that term is defined in Section 1(c) of the statute. The stated purpose for which these funds were received makes unavailable any exemption from registration. Consequently, it would appear that the Council's registration is required.

  On page 5 of the staff study of the Fulbright Committee it was stated that the registrant for a foreign government that carries on varied fund-raising and public relations activities within the United States showed in its supplemental statement contributions to affiliates of almost $23,000, and grants and subventions of approximately $93,000. The staff study goes on to say that the statement carried no breakdown as to what individuals or organizations shared in this money.

  Upon specific inquiry made by the Registration Section of this Division to the American Section of the Jewish Agency for Israel -- which is the organization referred to in the staff study -- we received the information upon which the request for registration is based.

-2-

You may be aware that the American Zionist Council is composed of representatives of the various Zionist organizations in the United States including the Zionist Organization of America.

FARA Registration Order to AZC 11/21/1962

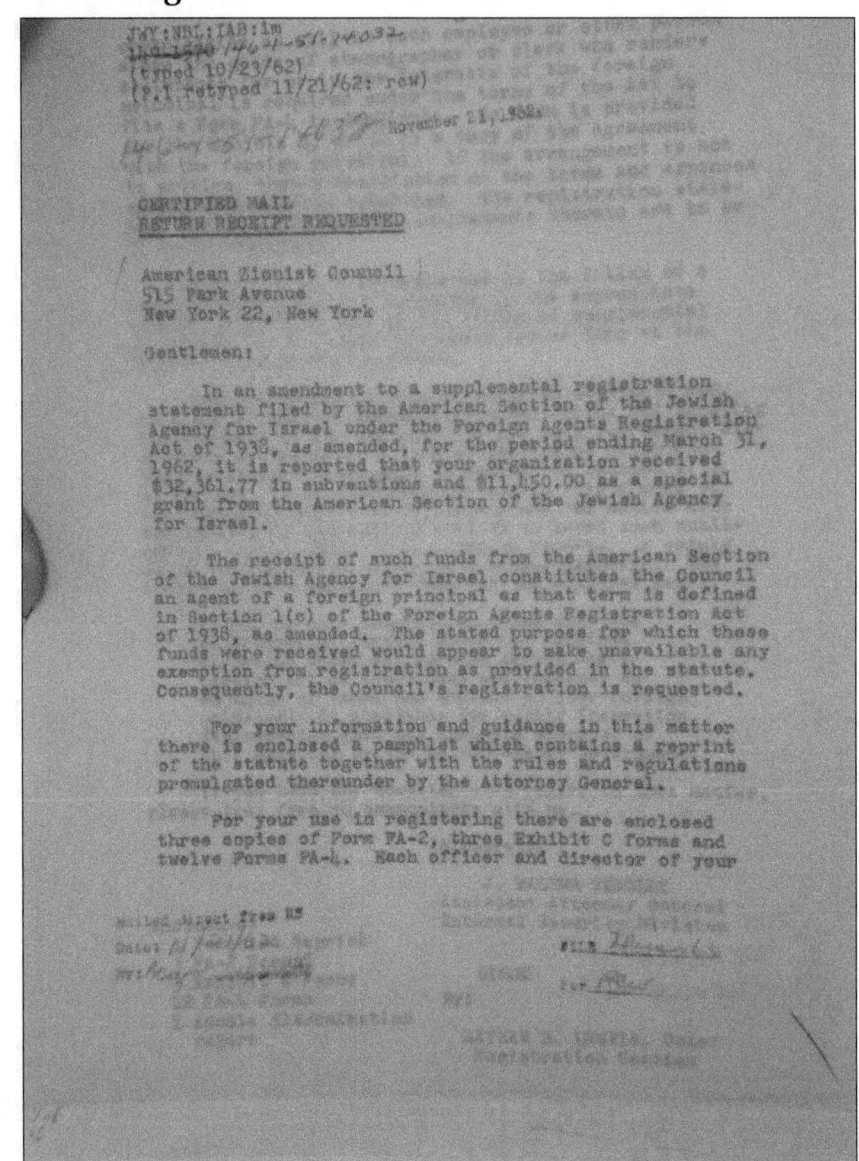

JWY:NBL:IAB:im
(typed 10/23/62)
(P.1 retyped 11/21/62: rew)

November 21, 1962.

CERTIFIED MAIL
RETURN RECEIPT REQUESTED

American Zionist Council
515 Park Avenue
New York 22, New York

Gentlemen:

In an amendment to a supplemental registration statement filed by the American Section of the Jewish Agency for Israel under the Foreign Agents Registration Act of 1938, as amended, for the period ending March 31, 1962, it is reported that your organization received $32,361.77 in subventions and $11,450.00 as a special grant from the American Section of the Jewish Agency for Israel.

The receipt of such funds from the American Section of the Jewish Agency for Israel constitutes the Council an agent of a foreign principal as that term is defined in Section 1(c) of the Foreign Agents Registration Act of 1938, as amended. The stated purpose for which these funds were received would appear to make unavailable any exemption from registration as provided in the statute. Consequently, the Council's registration is requested.

For your information and guidance in this matter there is enclosed a pamphlet which contains a reprint of the statute together with the rules and regulations promulgated thereunder by the Attorney General.

For your use in registering there are enclosed three copies of Form FA-2, three Exhibit C forms and twelve Forms FA-4. Each officer and director of your

- 2 -

organization as well as each employee or other person above the grade of stenographer or clerk who renders assistance for or in the interests of the foreign principal is required under the terms of the Act to file a Form FA-4 in duplicate. No form is provided for the Exhibit B, which is a copy of the agreement with the foreign principal. If the arrangement is not in writing, then a description of the terms and expenses agreed upon must be submitted. The registration statement and all exhibits and supplements thereto are to be filed in duplicate.

Registration is accomplished by the filing of a registration statement supported by the appropriate number of exhibits and by the filing of supplemental statements at six month intervals for as long as the agency relationship continues.

Your attention is also directed to Section 4 and Rule 400 of the Act pertaining to the filing and labeling requirements of the statute. If you as a registrant disseminate any material in the United States which contains political propaganda as defined in Section 1(j) of the Act, it is necessary for you to file a copy of such material with this Department and two copies with the Library of Congress as well as to label such publications and to submit dissemination reports. A sample for a dissemination report is enclosed herewith. The following is a suggested form for the required label.

> A copy of this material is filed with the Department of Justice where the required statement under the Foreign Agents Registration Act of (your name and address) as an agent of (name and address of your foreign principal) is available for public inspection. Registration does not indicate approval of this material by the United States Government.

If you have any question with regard to this matter, please feel free to communicate with me.

Sincerely,

J. WALTER YEAGLEY
Assistant Attorney General
Internal Security Division

Enclosures
1 Pamphlet Reprint
1 FA-2 Forms
3 Exhibit C Forms
12 FA-4 Forms
1 sample dissemination report

SIGNED

By:

NATHAN B. LENVIN, Chief
Registration Section

DOJ Meeting with AZC Legal Counsel 5/2/1963

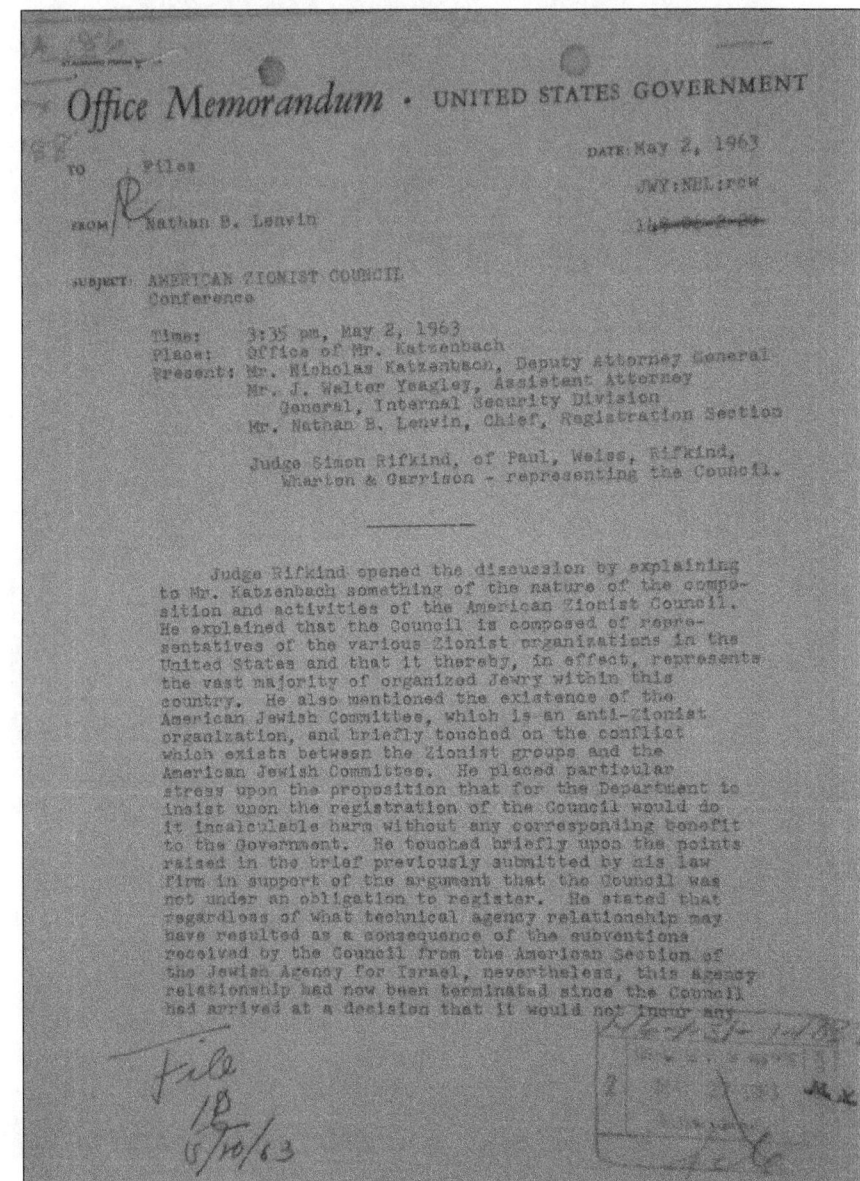

Office Memorandum · UNITED STATES GOVERNMENT

DATE: May 2, 1963

TO: Files

FROM: Nathan B. Lenvin

SUBJECT: AMERICAN ZIONIST COUNCIL
Conference

Time: 3:35 pm, May 2, 1963
Place: Office of Mr. Katzenbach
Present: Mr. Nicholas Katzenbach, Deputy Attorney General
Mr. J. Walter Yeagley, Assistant Attorney General, Internal Security Division
Mr. Nathan B. Lenvin, Chief, Registration Section

Judge Simon Rifkind, of Paul, Weiss, Rifkind, Wharton & Garrison - representing the Council.

Judge Rifkind opened the discussion by explaining to Mr. Katzenbach something of the nature of the composition and activities of the American Zionist Council. He explained that the Council is composed of representatives of the various Zionist organizations in the United States and that it thereby, in effect, represents the vast majority of organized Jewry within this country. He also mentioned the existence of the American Jewish Committee, which is an anti-Zionist organization, and briefly touched on the conflict which exists between the Zionist groups and the American Jewish Committee. He placed particular stress upon the proposition that for the Department to insist upon the registration of the Council would do it incalculable harm without any corresponding benefit to the Government. He touched briefly upon the points raised in the brief previously submitted by his law firm in support of the argument that the Council was not under an obligation to register. He stated that regardless of what technical agency relationship may have resulted as a consequence of the subventions received by the Council from the American Section of the Jewish Agency for Israel, nevertheless, this agency relationship had now been terminated since the Council had arrived at a decision that it would not incur any

-2-

vestige of possible obligation to register by cutting off all funds from the American Section and that it would continue its program through the raising of funds from domestic sources. Judge Rifkind went on to state that even though an agency relationship may have been created by the receipt of funds, the general over-all program of the Council was such that it could come within the purview of the cultural exemption from registration as contained in Section 3(e) of the Foreign Agents Registration Act, and even though the Council did disseminate some publications which conceivably through a broad interpretation of the definition of political propaganda would fall within that category, Judge Rifkind stressed the fact that these activities were a very minor portion of the entire program for which the funds received from the Jewish Agency were utilized. He emphasized that the Council used most of these funds for Hebrew education, youth movements, charitable purposes and other cultural activities relating to the Jewish people.

Finally, Judge Rifkind raised the point, after emphasizing the disparity of numbers between the American Jewish Committee and the American Zionist Council, that the vast number of Jews who adhered to the principles of Zionism could not understand how "our Administration" could do such harm to the Zionist movement and impair the effectiveness of the Council by insistence on registration. He appealed to the discretionary power of the Department which he claims it has in all criminal cases by stating that the Department generally makes a judgment as to which cases it will pursue and which it will not, pointing out in this connection that not all traffic violators, for instance, are given tickets, but that other circumstances must be taken into consideration. Mr. Katzenbach replied to this observation by stating that he appreciated the fact that it was a matter of proper administration of justice to use discretion and judgment in the exercise of prosecutive powers, but that he wanted to make the point to Judge Rifkind that the laws of the United States were not only to be enforced against Republicans, but were to be enforced impartially.

-3-

After Judge Rifkind completed his outline of his position -- and in this connection it is noted that he did not go into any detail as to the controlling facts upon which the request for registration was based -- Mr. Lenvin outlined for Mr. Katzenbach's benefit the principal facts upon which the request for registration was predicated. After hearing these facts, Mr. Katzenbach asked Mr. Rifkind whether the receipt of the funds from the American Section of the Jewish Agency was considered to be confidential and the reply was in the negative. Mr. Katzenbach then asked whether information as to how these funds were expended was considered to be of a confidential nature, and again Judge Rifkind replied in the negative. Mr. Katzenbach then noted that if the Council made a full disclosure of the receipt and expenditure of the funds it had received from the Jewish Agency so that such information would then be available for public inspection the purposes and objectives of the Registration Act might well be accomplished and very likely there would be nothing further for the Government to do. Mr. Katzenbach made it clear that he was not at this time committing the Department to accepting this procedure, but that we would examine the material filed by the Council before reaching a decision. In the event this was the eventual solution, it should be understood that the information submitted would be a matter of public record, the same as a registration statement filed under the Act. Judge Rifkind indicated the Council quite likely would submit all of the information to the Department.

This was seen & approved in draft form by Mr. Yeagly, who advised me on 5/20/63 that the draft has also been seen by Mr. Katzenback.

DOJ 72-Hour Warning to AZC 10/11/1963

JWY:NBL:IAB:tlg
10/10/63

October 11, 1963.

Judge Simon H. Rifkind
Paul, Weiss, Rifkind,
Wharton & Garrison
575 Madison Avenue
New York 22, New York

Dear Judge Rifkind:

Pursuant to our conversation in your office on October 9, 1963, forms are enclosed for the use of the American Zionist Council in registering under the Foreign Agents Registration Act of 1938, as amended. The forms include three copies each of Form FA-2, the basic registration statement filed by organizations, and Exhibit C Form, which calls for information regarding the foreign principal. Form FA-4 (short-form registration statement) should be filed by each officer or director of the Council as well as by all other persons rendering assistance to the registrant in the interests of the foreign principal in other than a clerical or secretarial capacity. No form is provided for the Exhibit B, which is a copy of the registrant's agreement with the foreign principal, or if it is not in writing, a written description thereof. All forms and exhibits are to be filed in duplicate with the third copy being retained for the registrant's files.

Registration is accomplished by filing a registration statement supported by the appropriate exhibits. In accordance with our conference the Department expects a response from you within 72 hours with regard to this matter.

Sincerely,

J. WALTER YEAGLEY
Assistant Attorney General
Internal Security Division

By: SIGNED

NATHAN B. LENVIN, Chief
Registration Section

Enclosures:
3 FA-2 Forms
3 Exhibit C Forms
15 FA-4 Forms

Yeagley Memo to Katzenbach 10/7/1964

Nick —

This is the most blatant stall we have encountered. Do you mind suggesting what we do next because all of us here would call their records before a grand jury.

Walt

Letters answered by Mr. Katzenbach 10-7-64

File grey

CONFIDENTIAL FILE ATTACHED 9/28/64

Mr. Yeagley's office called. They have rec'd another letter from Rothenberg.

APPENDIX

AZC Disclosure 4/1/1962 to 6/30/1962 sent 3/2/1965

AMERICAN ZIONIST COUNCIL -- DISBURSEMENTS OF INFORMATION & PUBLIC RELATIONS DISBURSEMENTS FOR THE PERIOD OF APRIL 1, 1962 to JUNE 30, 1962

Date	Item	Lectures, Speakers Fees & Expenses	Written Materials	Radio & Films	Subventions	Visitors to Israel
April 4	Subvention				$2,000.	
17	Speaker's fee	$50.				
17	Emininger Bros., printer		150.			
17	G.P. Putnam & Sons, purchase of books		102.51			222.19
24	Professional services		200.00	333.33		
24	Professional services & expenses	100.				
24	Professional services	250.	250.			
24	Professional services	125.	350.			300.
24	Professional services					
24	Fee					
	Subvention				2,000.	
May 2	Overseas Press Club-meeting	96.50				
2	Middle East Forum, subscription		5.00			
2	Fee	100.				
2	Misc.	47.77				
2	Misc. Club-meeting					
2	J.R. Atic, subscription		18.			
2	Calif. Jewish Record-cuts		12.36			
2	Bnai Zion-ad-meeting	10.83				
2	Bnai Zion-ad-meeting	6.89				
2	Roman Tours, Inc. plane tickets	447.59				
2	Fee & Expenses	210.				
9	Travel Expenses	234.97				
9	The Liberator - subscriptions		6.50			
9	NY American News-subscription		7.00			
9	Travel Expenses	142.10				
16	Jewish Chronicle-subscription		10.00			
16	Anti Student-subscription		2.00			
16	Amer. Assoc. for Jewish Studies					
16	Audio-Visual Review		2.76	15.75		
16	Anti-Defamation League - bok	236.14				
16	New England Zionist Council - Speakers' fees & expenses	70.63				
16	Travel Expenses	250.00				
16	Speakers' fee	96.60				
16	Eastern expenses	171.80				
16	Speakers expense	75.60				

ITEM	DATE	MEETING, SPEAKERS FEES & EXPENSES	WRITTEN MATERIALS	RADIO & FILMS	SUBSCRIPTIONS
	May 15	Speakers expenses 62.50			
	15	Speakers expenses 57.00			
	15	Speakers expenses 24.10			
	15	Speakers expenses 29.86			
	15	Speakers expenses 35.34			
	15	Speakers expenses 12.00			
	16	The Bip - subscription	4.00		
	16	Foreign Policy Assn subscrip.	4.40		
	16	Bloch Pub. Co. - Book	4.75		
	16	Encyclopedia Britanica-Book	5.30		
	16	Editor & Publisher - subscrip	5.26		
	16	Christian Century - subscription	7.50		
	16	Central Conf American Rabbi.-	5.00		
	16	The American Press - subscription	5.00		
	16	Jewish Post & Opinion subscription	7.00		
	22	Council for M.E. Affairs Press-	15.00		
	23	The United Synagogue - booklet	.75		
	23	U.S. Committee for UN - booklet	.72		
	23	Professional Services & expenses 50.00			
	23	Fee 25.00			
	23	Inter-University Comm on Israel-allocation		333.33	
	27	Professional Services 250.00			
	26	Professional Serv & Expenses 100.00			
	27	Professional Services	250.00		
	27	Professional Services	350.00		
	29	Professional Services 50.00			
	29	Fee 125.00			
	29	Fee 300.00			
	29	Fee 150.00			
	29	Fee & travel expenses 300.50			
	29	Fee & travel expenses 110.00			
	29	Professional services 50.00			
June 6	Fee 200.00			
	13	Convention	200.00		2,000.00
	13	Fee 300.00			
	13	Fee & expenses 86.90			330.00
	13	Travel expenses 15.91			300.00
	20	Fee 50.00			222.19

APPENDIX

ITEM	DATE		MEETINGS, SPEAKERS, FEES & EXPENSES	WRITTEN MATERIALS	RADIO & FILMS	SUBVENTIONS	
18	May 16	Speakers expenses	62.50				
19	16	Speakers expenses	57.00				
20	16	Speakers expenses	24.16				
21	16	Speakers expenses	29.86				
22	16	Speakers expenses	95.34				
23	16	Speakers expenses	12.00				
24	16	The Sign - subscription		4.00			
25	16	Foreign Policy Assn. subscrip.		2.40			
26	16	Bloch Pub. Co. - Book		4.95			
27	16	Encyclopedia Britanica-Book		5.39			
28	16	Maier & Publisher - subscrip.		5.26			
29	16	Christian Century - subscription		7.50			
30	16	Central Conf. American Rabis."		9.00			
31	16	The American Press - subscription		5.00			
32	16	Jewish Post & Opinion subscription		7.00			
33	16	Council for N.A. Affairs Press."		15.00			
34	23	The United Synagogue - booklet		.75			
35	23	U.S. Committee for UN - booklets		.72			
36	23	Professional Services & expenses	50.00				
37	23	Fee	85.00				
38	23	Inter-University Comm on Israel-allocation			333.33		
39	23	Professional Services					310.00
40	28	Professional Serv. & Expenses					300.00
41	29	Professional Services	250.00				222.19
42	29	Professional Services	100.00				
43	29	Professional Services		250.00			
44	29	Professional Service		150.00			
45	29	Professional Services	50.00				
46	29	Fee	125.00				
47	29	Fee	300.00				
48	29	Fee & travel expenses	150.00				
49	29	Fee	309.92				
50	29	Professional services	110.00				
51	June 6	Fee	50.00				
52	12	Subvention				2,000.00	
53	13	Fee	200.00	200.00			
54	13	Fee	300.00				
55	13	Fee & expenses	86.90				
56	13	Travel expenses	15.91				
57	20	Fee	50.00				

AMERICAN ZIONIST COUNCIL
Department of Information and Public Relations
Disbursements for the
period of April 1, 1962 to June 30, 1962

ITEM	NAME
1	Frank J. Doft Foundation
2	Frances Sussna, Educator
5	Milton Krents, Consultant (Radio & TV)
6	Alisa Ber, Representative in Israel
7	Albert Ghosn, Consultant
8	Miriam Jackson, Consultant (Civic groups)
9	Rev. Karl Baehr, Director American Christian Assn. for Israel
10	Rabbi David Greenberg
11	Mortimer Kroll, Press and Publicity
12	Clement Mihanovitch, Professor St. Louis Univ. Missouri
13	Frank J. Doft Foundation
16	Ray Levin, Field Representative
23	John Stoessinger, Professor, Hunter College, New York
24	Nasrollah Fatemi, Professor, Fairleigh Dickinson Univ., N.J.
27	Jacques Torczyner, Member of Executive Committee
33	Shaul Ramati, Israel Consul
34	Clement Mihanovitch, Professor, St. Louis University, Missouri
35	Matityahu Dagan, Israeli Consul
36	Yaacov Nash, Israeli Consul
37	Zev Sufott, Israeli Consul
38	David Tesher, Israeli Consul
39	Eliezer Preminger, student, candidate PH.D.
40	Yakov Aviad, Israeli Consul
41	Arieh Eshel, Israeli Consul
42	Michael Pragai, Israeli Consul
43	Joseph B. Schechtman, Member of Executive Committee
56	Alisa Ber, Representative in Israel
57	Abraham Grobard, entertainer
58	Ella Steffens, social worker
60	Milton Krents, consultant (Radio & TV)
61	Alisa Ber, representative in Israel
62	Rev. Karl Baehr, Director American Christian Assn. for Israel
63	Miriam Jackson, Consultant (civic groups)
64	Mortimer Kroll, Press & Publicity
65	Rev. Karl Baehr, Director, American Christian Assn. for Israel
66	Rabbi David Greenberg
67	Sanford Griffith, Professor, New School for Social Research, N.Y.
68	Nasrollah Fatemi, Professor, Fairleigh Dickinson Univ., N.J.
69	Rabbi David Greenberg
70	Rabbi Herbert Weiner
71	Albert Ghosn, Consultant
72	Frances Sussna, Consultant
73	Frank J. Doft Foundation

-2-

NAME

74 Sanford Griffith, Professor, New School for Social Research
75 Rev. Karl Hollier Tomlin, Minister
76 Tamar Eshel, Member, Israel Delegation to the UN
77 Saul Panofsky, Field Representative
78 Frances Sussma, Educator
82 Tamar Eshel, Israel Delegate to the UN
83 Yeoshna Tadmar, Israeli Consul
84 Rev. James Sheldon, Exec. Secy, American Anti-Nazi League
85 Mordecai Shalev, Israeli Consul
86 Shaul Ramati, Israeli Consul
87 Sanford Griffith, Profession New School for Social Research
88 Milton Krents, Consultant (Radio & TV)
89 Alisa Ber, Representative in Israel
90 Rev. Karl Baehr, Director, American Christian Assoc. for Israel
91 Rabbi David Greenberg
92 Albert Ghosn, Consultant
93 Mortimer J. Kroll, Press & Publicity
94 Miriam Jackson, Consultant Civic Groups
95 Gabe Sanders, Professor, N.J. State Teachers College
108 Abraham Glassner, Educator

Yeagley Memo on AZC FARA File 5/10/1965

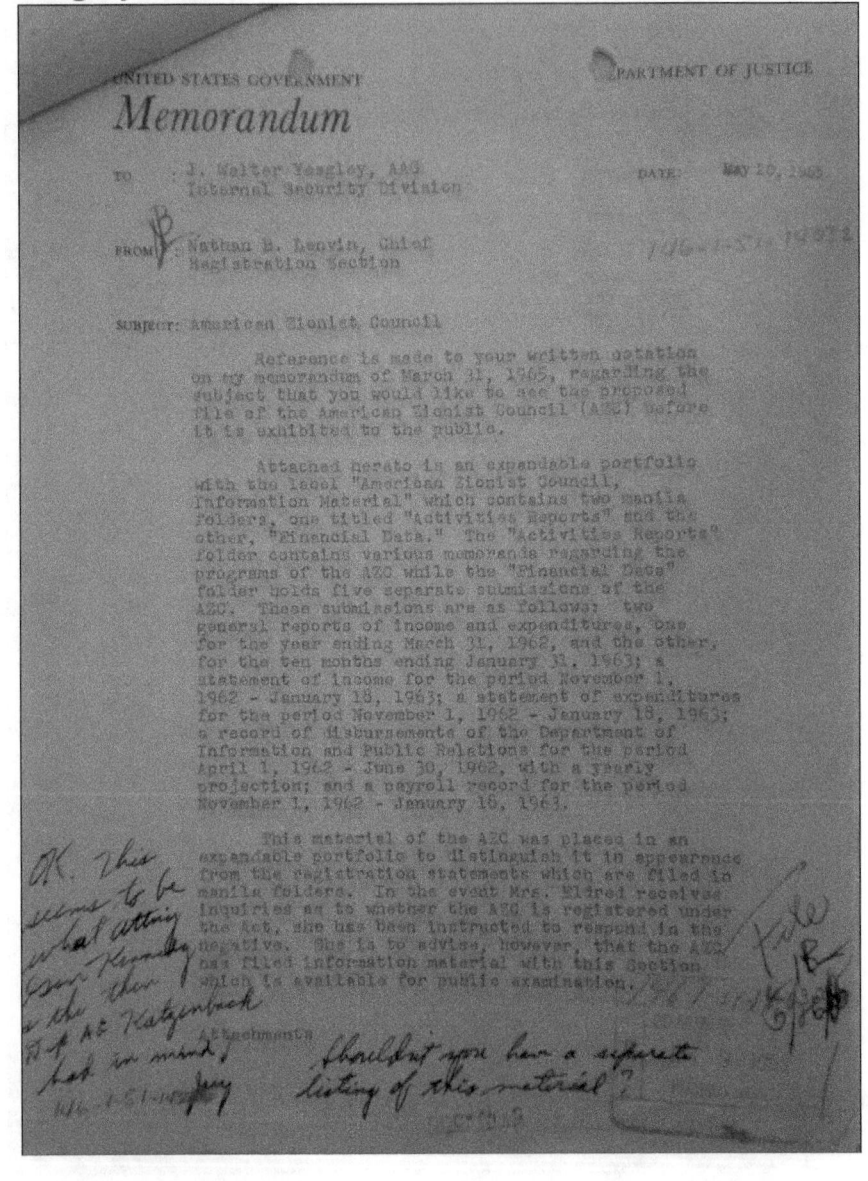

Analysis of Cartoons from the Near East Report

Cartoons from early editions of the *Near East Report* reveal deeply held positions of the newsletter's editor, Isaiah L. Kenen. Today many would be seen as invoking harmful stereotypes, though certainly not in all quarters of American society. Arabs were almost always depicted as backward, heavily armed, and engaged in violence or some type of duplicity. Institutions under constant fire in prose and portrayal include the news media, the U.S. Department of State, and the United Nations.

Many editions of the *Near East Report* also contained witty prose, deep insight, and cutting-edge analysis. However, the huge foreign subsidy Kenen received to start, produce, and distribute the *NER* in historical hindsight makes much of it appear to be exactly what it was: foreign government propaganda that should have borne a FARA declaration stamp.

Comments and critical analysis in the captions below each figure are made by the author.

Figure 9 Stereotypical armed, underdeveloped, and mistrustful Arabs. They are unable to cross into modernity or make peace with Israel, metaphorically depicted as the very same concept in this cartoon.

In the United States, some metaphors are so deeply rooted in bigotry that they simply cannot be made. Or at least that is an assertion made by the leader of one organization. In July of 2004, Abraham Foxman of the Anti-Defamation League (ADL) and Barbara Balser, the ADL's national chairman, issued a public letter about the illegitimacy of depicting Israel as any kind of "puppeteer" when discussing its influence on the U.S. Congress:

> We write to object to your characterization of the White House and Congress as "puppets" of the Israeli government. Reasonable people can and do disagree with American policy related to the Middle East, and specifically American support for Israel.
>
> However, there is a line between thoughtful, reasoned, constructive disagreements and offensive hyperbole. Indeed, one may disagree with America's Middle East approach, but to assert that U.S. policy in such a complex and volatile region is the product of wholesale manipulation by a foreign government fails to take into account important U.S. interests that are involved. Moreover, the image of the Jewish State as a "puppeteer," controlling the powerful U.S. Congress feeds into many age-old stereotypes which have no place in legitimate public discourse. [442]

Isaiah Kenen, however, delighted in portraying various Arab or Islamic figures in the role of sometimes violent puppeteers. This was an ongoing theme in early newsletter editions.

Figure 10 Syria's Hafez Assad portrayed as a regional puppeteer.

Figure 11 Shiite Islam puppeteer simultaneously killing off "sanity," "reason," and "civilized behavior."

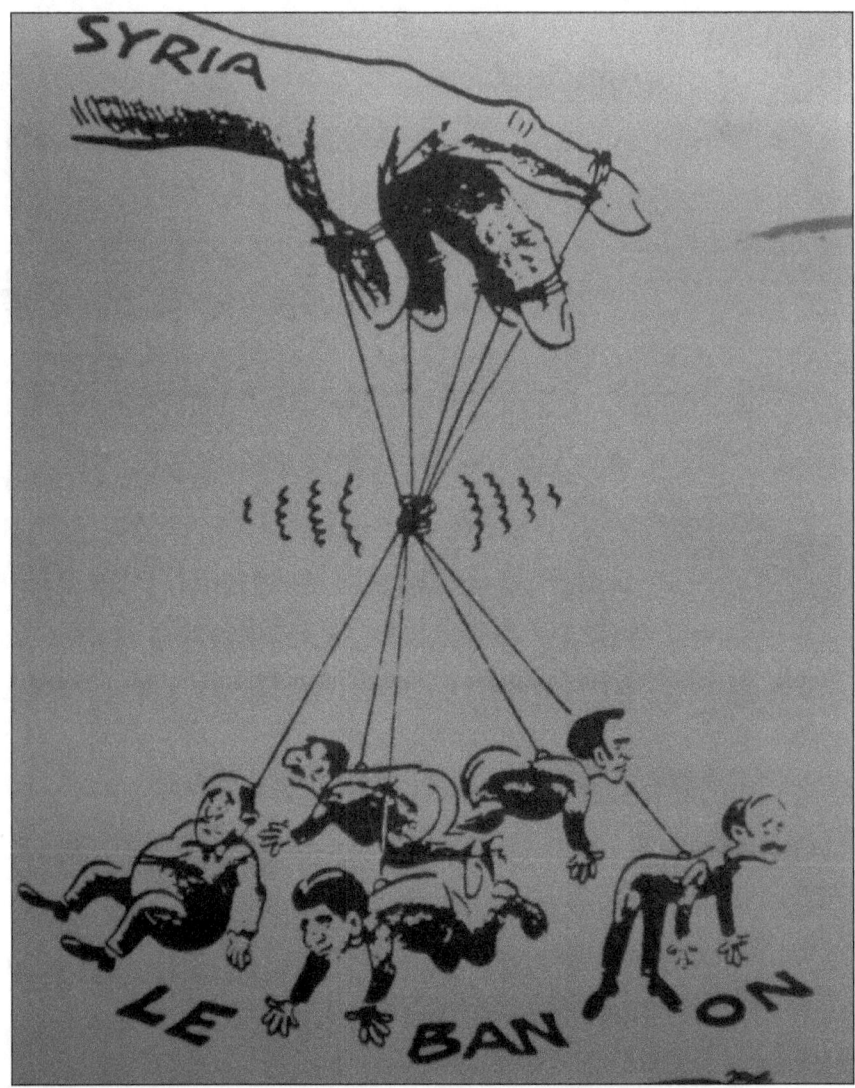

Figure 12 Syria once again as the puppeteer of Lebanon, directly controlling a wide range of politicians.

The *Near East Report* not only counted votes at the UN and in Congress, but also constantly worked to shape perceptions about the United Nations and the U.S. State Department in prose and cartoons.

Figure 13 In this Jewish Telegraphic Agency cartoon in the Near East Report, an elfish Israel is about to be jumped by the United Nations' dark-alley assortment of thugs, bomb throwers, and shady characters.

The U.S. State Department in particular was frequently portrayed by Kenen as naïve, misguided, and fundamentally ignorant of nearly all aspects of the Middle East. The following cartoon captures the quintessence of the buffoonish "Arabist" State Department bureaucrat Kenen depicted in numerous editions.

Figure 14 "Arabist" State Department official holds forth on the Middle East, but does not know the map is upside down.

The *Near East Report* also periodically lauded up-and-coming journalists such as Charles Krauthammer, profiled explaining how to combat "anti-Israel" bias in the mainstream media. The early editions also lampooned the media's supposed obsession with bad news from Israel.

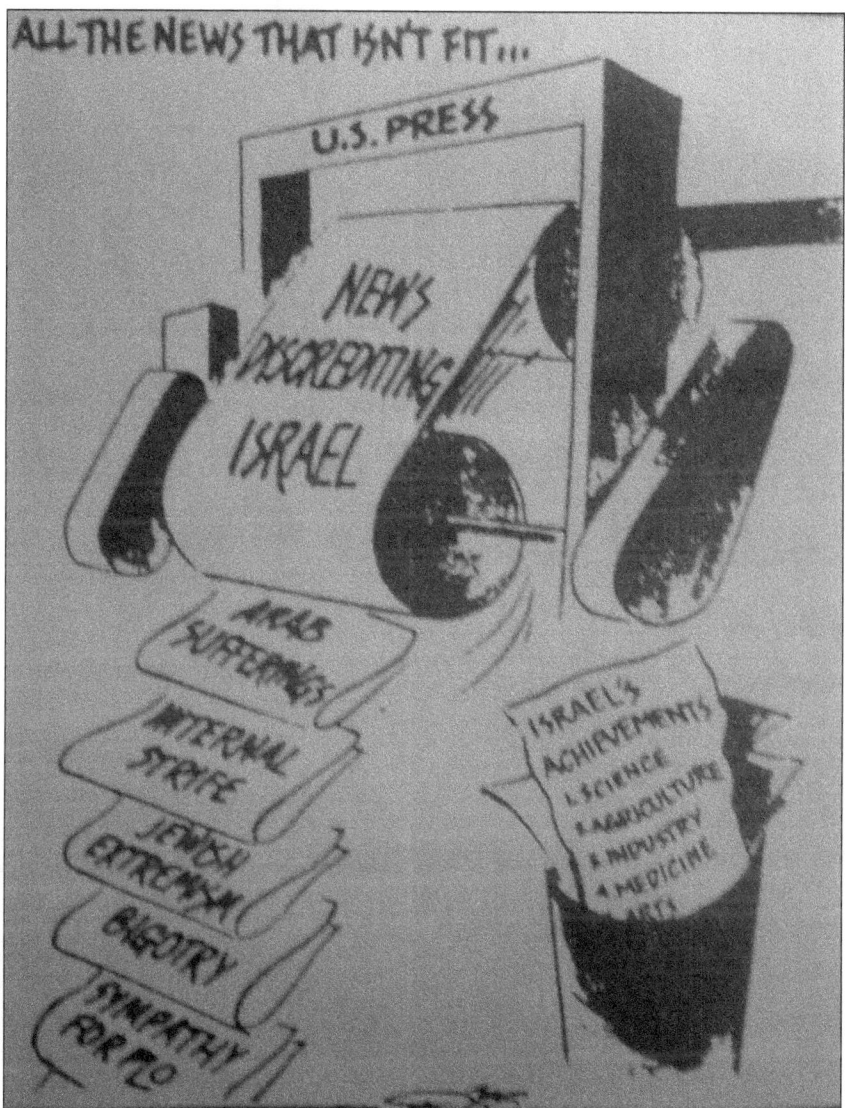

Figure 15 Satirizing the *New York Times* slogan in use since 1897, "All the news that's fit to print," the *NER* depicts print media as accentuating the negative.

Many of the cartoons appearing in the *Near East Report* were provided by the Jewish Telegraphic Agency, owned by the Jewish Agency Executive in Israel through a holding company.[443] Long after Kenen left day-to-day editorial duties, the *NER* continued to publish JTA cartoons. The following, which presents the racially charged " Arab Mind."

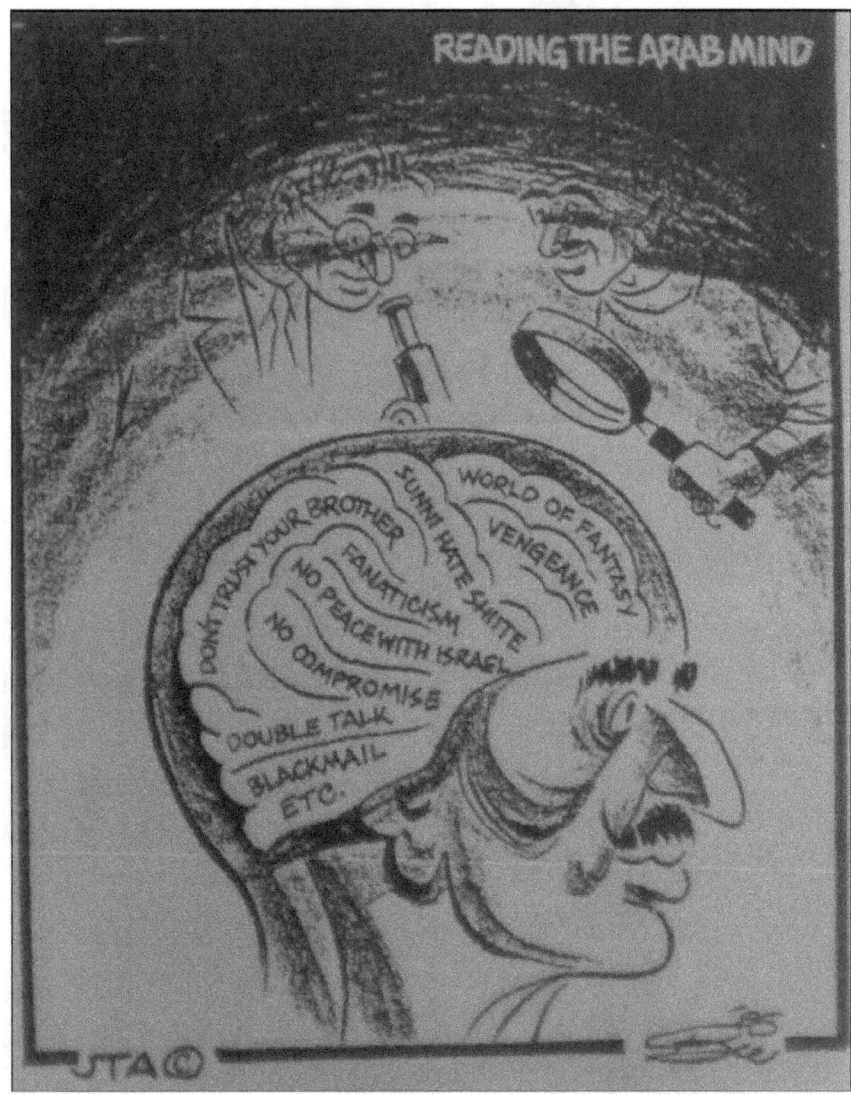

Figure 16 Jewish Telegraphic Agency cartoon in the *Near East Report* depicting the Arab psyche as the object of warranted Western clinical analysis of its embedded "fanaticism," "double talk," and "vengeance."

Other Incidents and Non-Enforcement

2014 The pressure group for economic and kinetic warfare on Iran, "United Against a Nuclear Iran" obtains classified U.S. national defense information it uses to target Greek Shipping magnate Victor Restis for alleged trade with Iran in violation of U.S. sanctions. When Restis sues UANI, the Department of Justice intervenes to shut down the case

2012 Veteran NASA employee sells classified information to Israel Aerospace Industries via his nonprofit charity. Rather than investigate and roll up IAI's spy ring, the FBI entraps only Nozette into offering secrets for sale to an FBI agent posing as a Mossad officer.

2009 Veteran Middle East diplomat Dennis Ross considered for U.S. State Department post. Serves at the Jewish People Policy Planning Institute (JPPPI) in Jerusalem, established by the Jewish Agency in 2002. Ross fails to register as a Jewish Agency foreign agent. Named by Secretary of State Hillary Clinton as Special Advisor for the Gulf and Southwest Asia.

2008 Israeli American media mogul and major AIPAC supporter Haim Saban is accused by four individual witnesses of attempting to bribe two superdelegates to support presidential candidate Hillary Clinton in exchange for a $1 million contribution to a nonprofit organization. Presumably Saban was attempting to obtain influence and political appointments for his subsidized group of Israel lobbyists, Dennis Ross, Martin Indyk, and Kenneth Pollack.

2008 Ben-Ami Kadish is charged with violating the 1917 Espionage Act and failing to register under FARA for alleged spying against the U.S. between 1979 and 1985. Although the statute of limitations had run out for the most active period of alleged spying, 2008 phone calls to his handler in Israel provide grounds for criminal indictments.

2005 Pentagon official Lawrence Franklin and AIPAC executives Keith Weissman and Steve Rosen are indicted for violating the 1917 Espionage Act. Franklin is given prison time, indefinitely suspended pending the outcome of the Rosen and Weissman trial. The case is dismissed by a judge stating they may not have been in a "state of mind" to commit espionage. Rep Jane Harman is taped conversing with an Israeli foreign agent promising to "waddle into" the case to end it.

2005 U.S.A Today and other news sources reveal that the World Zionist Organization, Jewish Agency, and affiliated nonprofits were found by an Israeli prosecutor to be breaking Israeli law through land confiscation and illegal colonization projects in the West Bank. In November, U.S. law enforcement officials send deputies to attend a Russell Senate Office briefing about the mechanics of nonprofit Israel lobby money laundering toward illegal colonization, and potential terrorist blowback, as well as the applicable U.S. criminal statutes. No action is taken.

2002 Israeli American Haim Saban donates $13 million for Brookings Institute to establish the "Saban Center for Middle East policy." Former AIPAC executive Martin Indyk becomes its director and beings publishing Op/Eds to give the impression of "centrist" support for the immanent U.S. invasion of Iraq.

2002 Sibel Edmonds alleges that while she was working as an FBI contract translator, she discovered that high officials linked to the U.S. Israel lobby were involved in smuggling nuclear secrets, money laundering, and bribery of public officials. At the request of FBI Director Robert Mueller, Attorney General John Ashcroft imposes a gag order on Sibel Edmonds, citing potential damage to sensitive diplomatic relations and national security.

1993-2016 Israel lobbyists pressure U.S. presidents Bill Clinton, George W. Bush, Barak Obama and Donald Trump to issue letters at the beginning of their terms promising never to pressure the Israeli government into signing the Treaty on the Non-Proliferation of Nuclear Weapons (NPT) or publicly discuss Israel's nuclear weapons program. All sign. The National Archives refuses to release any of the letters after being sued under FOIA.

1993 The Anti-Defamation League runs a covert operation in California to collect information and violate the privacy rights of anti-apartheid and Palestine solidarity activists. The ADL's operative forwards the information to Israel and apartheid-South Africa. In 1994 the FBI Los Angeles division closes down the investigation following AG Janet Reno's secret meeting on the matter with Israeli Minister of Justice David Libai.

1990 Former AIPAC director Michael Goland is indicted for 1988 campaign law violations that result in the AIPAC-favored candidate winning a California Senate seat. Goland is sentenced to 90 days in federal prison, but the rigged election results go unchallenged.

1989 A group of former U.S. government officials file an FEC complaint after it is revealed by the *Washington Post* in 1986 that AIPAC allegedly formed and coordinated political action committees in violation of federal campaign laws. The case rises to the Supreme Court, which refuses to address the merits of the case. The case is sent back to district court, where it remained unresolved.

1987 A report prepared for the Department of Defense titled Critical Technology Assessment in Israel and Nato Nations finds Israel has used Atoms for Peace funding from the U.S. and charitable funding from the U.S. arms of the Weizmann Institute for Scient and others to fund national laboratories producing nuclear weapons and researching hydrogen bomb development that mirror U.S. national laboratories. No action is taken.

1986 In 1986, AIPAC needed Alan Cranston to win the California senate race. So ex-AIPAC Director Michael Goland illegally funneled campaign cash to spoiler candidate Ed Vallen. The crooked ploy worked. Vallen drew enough votes from Cranston's opponent for Cranston to win. Although Goland was later convicted and given a slap on the wrist, Cranston shoveled billions in U.S. aid to Israel, none of which was affected by the criminal boost to his election.

1986 A lawsuit is brought by Americans and Palestinians residing on the West Bank challenging the IRS tax-exempt status of six United States–based Zionist nonprofit organizations, including the Jewish National Fund, the Jewish Agency–American Section (JA), the World Zionist Organization American Section (WZO), the United Israel Appeal (UIA), the United Jewish Appeal (UJA), and Americans for a Safe Israel.

Plaintiffs allege that these organizations were acting simply as blind "conduits" rather than legitimate U.S. charities and were channeling funds over which they had no ultimate control to Israel. The organizations were alleged to be confiscating lands of plaintiffs with the funds, in violation of plaintiff rights and in contravention of official U.S. policy. The plaintiffs also alleged that the organizations violated a Section 501 (c) (3) rule prohibiting tax-exempt organizations from "carrying on propaganda, or otherwise attempting to influence legislation," and participating in or intervening in (including the publishing or distributing of statements) "any political campaign on behalf of any candidate for public office." The six organizations allegedly violated this rule in their extensive and well-organized grassroots campaigning in support of Israel-lobby-preferred political candidates and their support of or opposition to legislation affecting Israel.

District Court of the District of Columbia presiding Judge Jackson refused to rule on merits, finding that plaintiffs lacked "standing" and had not shown sufficient injury.[444]

1986 AIPAC Deputy Political Director Elizabeth Schrayer illegally coordinates supposedly "independent" political action committees with misleading names (in fact set up by AIPAC) to contribute funds to support AIPAC-favored candidates. Decades of court actions, which rise to the level of the Supreme Court, resulted in no accountability for AIPAC. AIPAC continues to "score" each vote in Congress in its publications.

1984 An FBI investigation reveals that AIPAC obtained classified International Trade Organization documents that it then allegedly used to negotiate more favorable terms for Israel's free trade agreement with the U.S.. No indictments are issued.

1979-1973 California-based MILCO International Inc. ships 15 orders totaling 810 krytrons to the Israeli Ministry of Defense between 1979 and 1983. Israeli movie producer Arnon Milchan's Heli Trading Company brokers the transactions. A krytron is a gas-filled tube used as a high-speed switch. Export from the U.S. requires a U.S. State Department munitions license because krytrons can be used as triggers for nuclear weapons. The U.S. rejected several requests for krytron export licenses to Israel. MILCO obtained the krytrons from EG&G Inc. but listed them as "pentode" radio tubes before shipment to Israel. The ruse was finally uncovered by the FBI in 1983. Milchan is never prosecuted and also receives a 10 year via to remain in the U.S. after Israeli Prime Minister Benjamin Netanyahu, who was also part of the smuggling ring, pressures the U.S. Department of State in 2015-2016.

1978 Senate Foreign Relations Committee staff member and former AIPAC employee Stephen Bryan is overheard relaying classified information and discussing military aid coordination with Israeli government officials. After an 18-month FBI investigation, the Justice Department decides not to prosecute. Green goes on to establish the Jewish Institute for National Security Affairs, which lobbies the U.S. for military cooperation and arms sales to Israel.

1978 Paul Wolfowitz, while at the Arms Control and Disarmament Agency, allegedly passes classified information through AIPAC to Israel. No indictments are issued.

1970 On June 9, 1970, the Department of Justice compels the Jewish Agency–American Section to file its secret "Covenant" agreement with the Israeli government. No penalties for decades of deficient filings are assessed. The Jewish Agency then stops filing under FARA and the World Zionist Organization simultaneously registers a new American Section entity residing in the same New York City building, with leadership and functions identical to those of the Jewish Agency.   It claims the new entity is "non-government controlled."

1962-1965 The U.S. Department of Justice investigates and compels the American Zionist Council to register as a foreign agent. The Senate Foreign Relations Committee reveals financial records and internal reports documenting that the American Zionist Council acted as a conduit for Jewish Agency funds supporting unregistered lobbying, public relations, and other activities within the United States. An unprecedented accommodation is made for a "non-public" AZC disclosure held at the FARA section of the DOJ. AZC shifts activities to AIPAC.

1959-1970 A group of high officials of the Zionist Organization of America set up a privately owned nuclear fuel processing contractor for the U.S. Navy. NUMEC "loses" more highly enriched, U.S. government owned uranium than any other facility in U.S. history. Despite evidence of top Israeli spies entering the plant, and its president secretly smuggling canisters of weapons grade uranium to Israel, no charges are ever filed. The U.S. Army Corps of Engineers estimates the toxic cleanup of the smuggling site could cost half a billion dollars.

1953 A U.S. government agency rules that the American Zionist Council used tax-exempt funds for lobbying Congress. No legal action is taken.

1951 Isaiah Kenen is advised to file a new Foreign Agent Registration by the FARA section for public relations work on behalf of the Israeli government. Kenen never files and the Department of Justice takes no action.

1948 The Israel Office of Information's Foreign Agent registration filings are continually found to be "deficient" and the FBI alleges it is circulating propaganda that does not bear proper disclosure stamps. No action is taken.

1938-1960 The Zionist Organization of America is ordered seven times to register as an Israeli foreign agent, but never complies.

The Logan Act
953. Private correspondence with foreign governments

Any citizen of the United States, wherever he may be, who, without authority of the United States, directly or indirectly commences or carries on any correspondence or intercourse with any foreign government or any officer or agent thereof, with the intent to influence the measures or conduct of any foreign government or of any officer or agent thereof, in relation to any disputes or controversies with the United States, or to defeat the measures of the United States shall be fined under this title or imprisoned not more than three years, or both.

This section shall not abridge the right of a citizen to apply, himself or his agent, to any foreign government or the agents thereof for redress of any injury which he may have sustained from such government or any of its agents or subjects.

Delayed Disclosures 1933-2008

The following table provides a list of documents and events. The author asserts that they warranted immediate disclosure, which in turn would have resulted in more intelligent policymaking through democratic pressures. Instead, the releases of most were delayed on average four decades.

Document/Event	Disclosure	Impact
The 1933 Nazi-Zionist Transfer Agreement	This agreement was not widely discussed, understood, documented, or popularized until Edwin Black published his book *The Transfer Agreement* in 1984.	Deeper understanding of global Zionist lobbying and boycott movements. In this case, an in-depth account of an ill-fated decision that facilitated the economic growth of Germany under Hitler and immigration to Palestine. Comprehensive information release is delayed for 51 years.
Haganah Arms Theft and Smuggling from the United States	CIA reports from 1948 on airborne operations were finally released in 2001 after tell-all books such as Leonard Slater's *The Pledge* began appearing in 1970.	Relevant public information on how Truman's arms embargo and arms decommissioning laws had no effect on the flow of arms from the U.S. to Palestine is delayed 53 years.
Details of the Financial Backing for the 1948 "Whistlestop" Campaign	In 1973 the Truman Library tape-recorded a detailed interview with Abraham Feinberg about his role in financing the 1948 whistlestop campaign. The library publicly released a transcript in 1984.	Validating accounts from individuals directly involved in the most critical aspect of the 1948 presidential election are delayed for 36 years.
Draft Agency 1948 Position Papers to President Harry S Truman Analyzing U.S. Interests in the Middle East	In 1973, documents expressing both State and War Department recommendations are declassified.	Public release of specific national security rationales for non-recognition or alternative regional policies is delayed for 25 years.
Document/Event	Disclosure	Impact

APPENDIX

1948 Isaiah L. Kenen FARA Declaration	This formerly public information about AIPAC's founder and related DOJ files could only be obtained under FOIAs filed in 2007.	The first public audit of Kenen's FARA declarations against his own statements and lobbying activities is delayed for sixty years.
1953 Jewish Agency Covenant	This agreement between the Jewish Agency and the Israeli government covering political and financial prerogatives reveals the true nature of the Jewish Agency's quasi-governmental status and true foreign principal.	In 1963, the Fulbright hearings requested the relevant organizing documents of the Jewish Agency, but did not receive them. The Department of Justice issued a warning to the Jewish Agency–American Section, which filed its "Covenant" with FARA in 1969, revealing the true extent of Israeli government influence in the U.S. lobbying program sixteen years after implementation. The JA soon stopped filing as a foreign agent and restructured as the World Zionist Organization–American Section, claiming no government principal.
1967 Six-Day War	Johnson administration and U.S. State Department cables documenting urgent diplomatic maneuvers between the U.S. and Egypt before the Israelis launched a preemptive strike on June 5, 1967.	The U.S. State Department Office of Historian releases classified documents on the Six-Day War on January 12, 2004, thirty-seven years after the war. Documents detail how the U.S. wished to restrain an Israeli attack and found Israeli intelligence estimates justifying requests for U.S. weapons to be overblown, and how a high-level diplomatic visit by Egyptian envoys to wind down the confrontation was detected by Israel days before it launched its attack.

Document/Event	Disclosure	Impact
U.S. Department of Justice Internal Security Division File on the American Zionist Council	Complete working documents of the DOJ effort to compel AIPAC's predecessor organization, the American Zionist Council, to register as the agent of a foreign principal are released on June 10, 2008.	Until the release of the AZC file, there was no public record of law enforcement activity after the 1963 Fulbright foreign agents hearings revealed massive money laundering and Israel's covert public relations activity in the United States. The contents of the file reveal how an asymmetrical response via political pressures exerted on the FARA section and the environment created by the death of JFK led to a special "caveat" for the AZC. Americans can now understand that the DOJ's institutional reticence about upholding the law vis-à-vis the Israel lobby is based on the secret history of the subverted FARA registration attempt. This disclosure is made forty-three years after it was secretly implemented.

APPENDIX

Charter Memo of the Senate Foreign Relations Committee Investigation of Nondiplomatic Activities of Representatives of Foreign Governments, March 17, 1961

87th Congress, 2d Session — ~~CONFIDENTIAL~~ COMMITTEE PRINT

NONDIPLOMATIC ACTIVITIES OF REPRESENTATIVES OF FOREIGN GOVERNMENTS

A PRELIMINARY STUDY

PREPARED BY THE STAFF

JULY 1962

OF THE

COMMITTEE ON FOREIGN RELATIONS

UNITED STATES SENATE

March 17, 1961

CONFIDENTIAL

Senator:

Here are some thoughts which Pat, John, and I have developed on the subject of a Committee investigation of the nature and extent of efforts of foreign governments to influence the content and direction of United States foreign policy.

GENERAL:

In recent years there has been an increasing number of incidents involving attempts by foreign governments, or their agents, to influence the conduct of American foreign policy by techniques outside normal diplomatic channels. This is a subject of increasing concern to the Executive, to Congress, and to the American people generally. Activities of the China Lobby, the Spanish Lobby, the Dominican lobby, the Vietnamese lobby, and others, are frequently referred to in the press, but there is no very precise information on what they do or how they do it. Indigenous groups based on racial or national origins have been organized in the United States, and have often concentrated on influencing United States foreign policy in directions designed primarily to promote the interests of other states. Many foreign governments with diplomatic representation in Washington retain the services of public relations counsel or law firms, primarily to assist in bringing particular foreign policy points of view to the attention of the United States Government and people. Finally, there have been occasions when representatives of other governments have been privately accused of engaging in covert activities within the United States and elsewhere, for the purpose of influencing United States policy (the Lavon Affair).

The purpose of examining this subject is not to prove that all these activities are necessarily wrong. Rather, it is that the Committee has a responsibility to obtain for itself, for the Senate, and for the American people a full and accurate picture of activities of this kind. Perhaps legislative action will be suggested, perhaps not.

- 2 -

PROCEDURE:

By way of most preliminary planning, it is suggested that hearings (after preparation described below), might proceed in the following stages:

I. Public receipt of testimony from Department of Justice and Department of State.

The Attorney General might be called upon to give a brief history of the Foreign Agents Registration Act, describing how Justice got jurisdiction away from State. He should outline the present operation. Who registers; what information is supplied; prosecutions for failure to register, etc.

He should then discuss with the Committee specific examples of registration. Who represents China, Spain, Soviet Union, Dominican Republic, France, the United Kingdom, etc.

The Secretary of State might be called upon to describe influence through "normal diplomatic channels."

II. Public receipt of testimony from selected law and public relations firms. (Dewey, Acheson, Clark, etc.)

Perhaps these hearings should be preceded by a questionnaire, but in any event witnesses should be asked to discuss what they do and how much they get paid.

III. Executive (perhaps public) receipt of testimony on the Lavon Affair, and similar "gray area" activities.

IV. Public receipt of testimony of officers of such groups as the Committee of a Million, the Zionists, Captive Nations groups, the English Speaking Union, etc.

COMMENT:

Probably enough has been written to suggest that an investigation along these lines could be explosive in the extreme. At the same time, facts would probably be brought out that should be better known to the American people.

- 3 -

There would undoubtedly (even with care) be instances which would lead to foreign governmental protests, to violent attacks by special groups in the United States, and finally, there might be an overall public reaction in the direction of isolationism.

SUGGESTIONS:

That the Chairman instruct John Newhouse to devote full time to this project during the next six weeks to see what can be developed along the lines of this memorandum.

That the Chairman consider attaching to the staff (after discussion with Senators Sparkman and Hickenlooper) for a six-week period, Douglas Cater or Walter Pincus, both of whom have done work in this field.

That nothing be made public about this activity until such time as sufficient examples have been developed to justify the Chairman proposing to the Committee that several hearings are justified.

Finally, after you have read this memo, I suggest that Pat, John, and I discuss this with you at greater length.

CM:mej

Index

Abourezk, James 111
Adelson, Sheldon 189
All My Causes 12, 113, 213, 309
American Bank and Trust Company .34
American Civil Liberties Union
 (ACLU) 55
American Council for Judaism (ACJ)
 21, 23, 29, 96, 97, 98, 99, 101, 113,
 114, 118, 140, 148, 149, 159, 161,
 187
American Emergency Committee for
 Zionist Affairs (AECZA) .. 9, 10, 27,
 44
American Israel Public Affairs
 Committee (AIPAC) ... 1, 2, 3, 8, 11,
 30, 41, 73, 83, 84, 86, 88, 95, 109,
 111, 112, 120, 125, 126, 128, 129,
 156, 176, 177, 179, 189, 190, 191,
 192, 193, 194, 195, 196, 197, 199,
 200, 213, 217, 289, 290, 291, 292,
 296, 297, 309
American Jewish Conference 11, 20,
 28, 78, 115, 197, 212, 217
American Newspaper Guild 8, 212
American Zionist Council (AZC).2, 11,
 30, 54, 82, 84, 86, 87, 88, 90, 91,
 94, 95, 96, 98, 99, 107, 109, 112,
 113, 114, 116, 117, 118, 119, 120,
 121, 122, 123, 124, 125, 126, 127,
 128, 129, 132, 133, 136, 137, 140,
 141, 142, 143, 144, 146, 148, 154,
 160, 163, 164, 166, 168, 171, 173,
 174, 176, 185, 188, 190, 212, 216,
 292
Amtorg 15, 48
Anglo-American Committee 24, 25
anti-Semitism ... 5, 9, 12, 29, 45, 61, 62,
 63, 89, 98, 113
Arab Higher Committee 27
Arab League 31, 53, 183
Arabist 29, 285, 286

Arazi, Yehuda 65
Attlee, Clement 24, 26, 37
Attorney General 46, 48, 49, 51, 53, 55,
 56, 76, 83, 132, 133, 141, 142, 143,
 152, 158, 161, 162, 164, 166, 168,
 175, 191, 198, 221, 224, 225, 226,
 227, 228, 229, 230, 231, 232, 290
Balfour Declaration 5, 7, 11, 16, 17, 29,
 59
Bank Leumi 34, 149
Bank Secrecy Act 195
Bartlett, Charles L. 135
Basel program 12
Ben-Gurion, David ... 10, 31, 64, 79, 87,
 88, 103, 105, 107, 108, 109, 118,
 215
Berger, Rabbi Elmer. 93, 96, 97, 98, 99,
 114, 148, 185, 187, 199, 201
Bergson, Peter H. 18, 20, 21, 53, 58, 59,
 61, 62, 63
Betar 59, 60, 61, 62
Bevin, Ernest 36, 37
Binet, Max 107
Blitzer, Wolf 111
B'nai B'rith 193, 194
Bolshevik revolution 5, 6
Bookniga 48
Boukstein, Maurice M.... 112, 118, 119,
 124, 125, 128, 129, 130, 136, 137,
 138, 169, 173, 184, 186
Bowman, Irene A. ... 147, 148, 163, 165,
 168, 170, 171, 172, 173, 175, 176,
 177
Brandeis, Louis D. 10, 25, 189, 217
bylaws 71, 119, 219, 226
Carl Byoir & Associates 44
Carmon, Yosef 107
Carter, Billy 179, 181, 182, 183, 196
Carter, Jimmy 179, 181
cartoons 102, 108, 284, 287
Cassini, Igor 153, 196

caveat 4, 126, 162, 163, 297
Celler, Emanuel 24, 93, 94
Central Intelligence Agency (CIA) .. 39, 57, 58, 62, 64, 67, 69, 295
Chertoff, Mordecai 74
Clayton, William L 16
Cleveland News 7, 212
Cleveland Zionist District 8, 212
CNN 111
Coca-Cola 34, 158
Cold War 105, 134, 153
Committee for a Jewish Army .... *See* Jewish Army
Committee on Information and Public Relations ... 120, 145, 146, 163, 164, 165, 167, 168, 169, 172
Communist Party 7, 75
conduit(s) 117, 126, 138, 149, 161, 291, 292
Connolly, Matthew J. 24
Cosmopolitan 75
Council for the National Interest (CNI) 194
Covenant 185, 186, 187, 215, 259, 260, 261, 292, 296
Covington & Burlington 182
coyotes 58
Cuban missile crisis 132
Czechoslovakia 67, 69
Dafni, Reuven 75
Democratic Party .. 35, 89, 93, 104, 134, 135, 180
Dewey, Thomas 26, 33
DeWind, Adrian W. 145
Dimona nuclear weapons facility ... 154, 156, 159
Dominican Republic 52, 55, 57, 152, 153, 179, 182
Dreyfus Affair 12
Eban, Abba 70, 72, 78, 79, 159
Egypt 11, 18, 28, 30, 106, 108, 110, 296
Eisenhower, Dwight D. ... 83, 94, 95, 98, 112, 114, 134, 153
Elath, Eliahu 75
Eshkol, Levi 107, 108, 155
espionage 3, 53, 108, 179, 189, 190
Fahrnkopf, Nancy 145
false-flag 39, 67, 69, 106
Fatemi, Nasrollah 170
Federal Bureau of Investigation (FBI) 1, 41, 52, 53, 55, 64, 66, 76, 80, 126, 130, 147, 148, 174, 183, 190, 191, 198, 212, 290, 291, 292
Feinberg, Abraham J.33, 34, 35, 36, 37, 42, 85, 89, 134, 135, 158, 160, 189, 295
Feldman, Myer (Mike) 135, 160
First Amendment 55, 182
Foreign Agents Registration Act (FARA) ... 1, 2, 3, 43, 44, 45, 46, 47, 48, 49, 50, 51, 52, 53, 54, 55, 56, 57, 70, 71, 72, 73, 74, 76, 77, 79, 80, 81, 82, 83, 89, 90, 91, 92, 93, 94, 95, 96, 109, 116, 117, 119, 120, 126, 130, 132, 133, 136, 139, 140, 141, 142, 143, 144, 145, 146, 147, 148, 149, 150, 152, 153, 157, 160, 162, 163, 165, 167, 168, 171, 172, 173, 175, 176, 177, 178, 179, 180, 181, 182, 183, 184, 185, 186, 187, 190, 195, 196, 198, 199, 212, 214, 215, 233, 242, 247, 256, 257, 258, 264, 266, 278, 279, 289, 292, 296, 297
Forward, The 193, 194
Frank, John Joseph 55
Freedom of Information Act (FOIA) .. 2, 46, 71, 195
Fulbright, James W. ... 50, 80, 101, 102, 103, 109, 112, 113, 117, 118, 119, 123, 124, 125, 126, 127, 128, 129, 130, 131, 132, 133, 139, 141, 143, 146, 147, 148, 150, 152, 156, 169, 172, 178, 179, 181, 186, 201, 212, 296, 297
gestor 13, 14
Goland, Michael 191, 290
Goldschmidt, Ruth 64, 74
Göring, Hermann Wilhelm 61
Greenspun, Hank 66, 135
Grew, Joseph C. 22
Grossman, Rita 73
Haaretz 94
Haganah . 34, 35, 39, 57, 59, 62, 64, 65, 66, 67, 78, 79, 295
Hall, Thomas K. 138, 147
Hamlin, Isadore 112, 123, 126, 184, 185, 186, 188, 214
Hearst 63, 153
Hebrew University 61
Herzl, Theodor ... 11, 12, 14, 15, 16, 17, 29, 40, 60, 104, 214

INDEX

Hitler, Adolf 10, 18, 30, 31, 45, 60, 135, 295
Holocaust 37, 38, 118
Honest Leadership and Open Government Act of 2006 195
Ibn Saud 22, 53
Internal Security Division 95, 131, 132, 133, 139, 173, 174, 297
International Trade Organization (ITO) 41, 291
Inter-University Committee 121, 122
Iran ... 41, 113, 134, 170, 179, 180, 181, 194, 195, 212
Iran Air 181
Iraq 18, 43
Irgun. 18, 19, 20, 21, 25, 30, 31, 37, 38, 40, 53, 57, 58, 59, 61, 62, 79
Iron Wall 59
isolationists 9
Israel Office of Information (IOI) 2, 70, 71, 72, 73, 74, 76, 77, 80, 81, 82, 111, 181, 199, 212, 233, 246, 247, 255, 293
Jabotinsky, Vladimir 57, 58, 59, 60, 61, 62, 63, 107, 170
Jacobson, Edward 18, 29, 36
Javits, Marion 179, 180, 181, 196
Jenkins, Walter 160
Jerusalem Post 73, 107
Jewish Agency 2, 14, 20, 26, 27, 28, 29, 30, 34, 45, 47, 50, 56, 57, 64, 65, 73, 77, 78, 79, 80, 87, 90, 96, 106, 107, 108, 109, 111, 112, 113, 115, 116, 117, 118, 119, 123, 124, 125, 126, 129, 130, 131, 132, 133, 136, 137, 138, 139, 140, 141, 142, 143, 146, 148, 149, 160, 161, 162, 165, 167, 169, 170, 171, 173, 174, 176, 177, 184, 185, 186, 187, 188, 189, 190, 192, 193, 212, 214, 215, 216, 217, 259, 287, 289, 291, 292, 296
Jewish Army 18, 19, 20, 21, 40, 58, 61, 62
Jewish Company, The 13, 14
Jewish Front Tribute 59
Jewish relief .. 10, 12, 98, 114, 118, 138
Jewish Relief Commission 6
Jewish State, The 12
Jewish Telegraphic Agency (JTA) ... 50, 191, 287, 288
Johnson, Lyndon B. (LBJ) 17, 133, 134, 158, 168

Johnson, Paul 38
Jordan 57, 59, 60, 122, 170
Katzenbach, Nicholas 133, 141, 142, 143, 145, 147, 148, 149, 152, 158, 160, 161, 162, 163, 164, 165, 166, 167, 168, 170, 171, 173, 175, 272
Kay, Sam 35, 66
Kayser-Roth Corporation 34
Kenen Committee 120, 125
Kenen, Peter 9
Kennedy, Jacqueline 153
Kennedy, John F. (JFK) 17, 83, 103, 104, 132, 134, 135, 150, 152, 158
Kennedy, Robert F. (RFK) 17, 132, 143, 166, 175
Khomeini, Ayatollah 181
Kiep, Otto Karl 45
Kiev 6
King David Hotel 26, 62, 79
Knesset 184, 186
Kollek, Teddy 65
Korff, Rabii 38
Krauthammer, Charles 286
Kroll, Mortimer J. 169
La Follette, Robert M. 52
Lavon Affair 105, 106, 107, 108
Legislative Transparency and Accountability Act of 2006 195
Lenvin, Nathan B. 1, 81, 133, 136, 137, 138, 141, 145, 161, 166, 167, 171, 173, 174, 175, 182
Library of Congress (LOC) 54, 230
Libya 180, 181, 182
Likud 192
Lipsky, Louis 9, 11, 80, 84, 90, 96
machine guns 66
Mallison, William T. 148, 185, 187
Mapai 107, 108
Marshall, George C. 26, 33
Martial & Company 153
McDonald, James G. 34
McGoff, John 183
McNulty, Paul 191
Merriam, Gordon P. 33
Middle East i
Middle East Institute 121
Mildenstein, Baron Leopold von 60
milk-can bombs 62
Miller, Rabbi Irving 65, 88, 124, 137
Mitchell, James P. 137
money laundering 2, 109, 112, 192, 193, 194, 195, 198, 289, 290, 297

Monsky, Henry...................................11
Mossad...75
Moyers, Bill 160
Mufti of Jerusalem 30, 31, 40
Nasser, Gamal Abdul 106
Nation Magazine, The 9, 31, 40
National Archives and Records
    Administration (NARA) 54
National Jewish Post 139
National Military Organization (NMO)
   19
Nazi Germany 18, 44, 46
Near East Report 2, 3, 99, 100, 101,
    102, 103, 104, 105, 107, 108, 109,
    110, 111, 112, 113, 117, 125, 126,
    127, 128, 154, 156, 157, 169, 188,
    199, 212, 213, 279, 284, 286, 287,
    288
Near East Research ... 91, 111, 213, 309
negotiorum gestio...................14, 17, 40
Neutrality Act.....................................64
New Republic, The 9
New York Times ... 3, 21, 34, 40, 47, 89,
    90, 113, 140, 154, 169, 176, 309
New Yorker Magazine 169
Niles, David K....................................24
Non-Sectarian Anti-Nazi League 53
nuclear weapons....................................i
Nuremberg 11
offshore entities and transactions .2, 69,
    118, 119, 188, 189
Ohio Bar Association 8, 212
Olney, Warren....................................76
Operation Susannah 106, 107
opposition research........................9, 105
Organization of American States
    (OAS)..153
Ottoman emperor 12
Pahlevi, Ashref................................180
Palestine ... 1, 2, 5, 7, 10, 11, 12, 16, 17,
    18, 19, 20, 21, 22, 23, 24, 25, 26,
    27, 28, 29, 30, 31, 33, 34, 35, 37,
    39, 40, 47, 53, 57, 58, 59, 60, 61,
    62, 63, 64, 65, 66, 67, 68, 69, 73,
    78, 79, 80, 84, 86, 87, 90, 93, 94,
    97, 115, 118, 162, 212, 214, 215,
    216, 295
Palestinian refugees. 103, 104, 156, 185
Paul, Weiss, Rifkind, Wharton &
    Garrison LLP 137, 140, 141, 145
Pendergast, Thomas Joseph...............18
People Magazine..............................180

Plain Dealer..7
plank..............................104, 105, 217
Pledge, The..64
political action committees (PACs)..95,
    105, 290
Post Office....................................54, 55
Presidential Railroad Commission ..137
propaganda3, 22, 23, 44, 45, 46, 47, 48,
    50, 51, 53, 54, 55, 70, 71, 74, 76,
    83, 90, 91, 97, 100, 104, 106, 111,
    115, 116, 117, 121, 133, 136, 141,
    147, 149, 150, 152, 161, 171, 181,
    182, 183, 224, 225, 229, 230, 231,
    232, 279, 291
prosecutorial discretion 46, 56
Provisional Executive Committee for
    Zionist Affairs.............................10
puppets 111, 281
quasi ex contractu..............................13
Raji, Parviz C. 180
Reader's Digest..................................75
Redimix..18
Republican Party 85, 95, 104, 180
Rifkind, Simon H. ...137, 138, 141, 142,
    143, 147, 148, 149, 161, 164, 165
Roosevelt, Franklin Delano (FDR).8, 9,
    17, 20, 22, 24, 31, 45, 46, 51, 63, 85
Rosen, Steve..................191, 195, 289
Rosenwald, Lessing J. 23, 29, 94, 97,
    115, 117
Rothenberg, Nathanial S.146, 147, 161,
    162, 163, 164, 166, 167, 168, 170,
    171, 172, 176
Rubirosa, Porfirio............................153
Ruder & Finn 180, 181
Rumsfeld, Donald 144, 146
Russia.................... 5, 6, 38, 45, 48, 154
Saban, Haim....................................189
Sabin, Barry 194
Sason, Talia.................192, 193, 194
Saud, Ibn 22
Saudi Arabia................................22, 53
Savak..180, 181
Schalit, Elie.......................................65
Schechtman, Joseph P. 170
Schwimmer, Al 66, 67
Scribner, Fred...........................116, 125
Senate Foreign Relations Committee .1,
    56, 84, 112, 117, 125, 126, 130,
    131, 147, 152, 162, 172, 292
Shah of Iran..............................180, 181
Shamir, Yitzhak.................................19

Shapiro, Ezra 8
Sharett, Moshe 31, 75, 78, 79
Shiloah Reuven 75
short form 72, 77
Silver, Abba Hillel 28, 31, 80, 84, 85
Sirhan Sirhan 175
Six-Day War 110, 111, 181, 296
Slater, Leonard 64, 295
Sloan, Sam 65
Society of Jews, The 13
Somers, Andrew 20
Somoza, Anastasio 66
Sonneborn Institute 64
Sonneborn, Rudolf Goldschmidt 64
South Africa 34, 183
Soviet Union 29, 33, 45, 48
state secrets 197
Stern, Avraham 19
Stevenson, Adlai 134
Stoessinger, John 170
Syria 18, 146, 195, 282, 284
tax-deductible. 109, 111, 114, 117, 118, 189, 216
tax-exempt 54, 70, 82, 95, 96, 109, 114, 117, 120, 125, 128, 186, 189, 190, 193, 216, 217, 291, 292
The Pledge 295
Time Magazine 44, 45, 51
Tonkon, L. Edward 143, 144, 177
Toronto 5, 7, 212
Toronto Star 7
Transfer Agreement (Ha'avarah Agreement) 60, 61, 295
Transocean News 48
Trujillo, Rafael 55, 153
Truman, Harry S 16, 17, 18, 20, 21, 22, 23, 24, 25, 26, 27, 28, 29, 30, 31, 32, 33, 34, 35, 36, 37, 39, 40, 42, 51, 56, 58, 64, 81, 83, 85, 86, 89, 93, 134, 197, 295
U.S. Department of Defense 2, 42
U.S. Department of Justice. 1, 2, 11, 46, 47, 49, 51, 53, 55, 70, 71, 72, 74, 77, 78, 79, 80, 81, 82, 83, 89, 91, 95, 96, 99, 112, 113, 114, 116, 117, 120, 126, 130, 131, 132, 133, 136, 137, 140, 142, 143, 144, 145, 146, 148, 150, 151, 152, 157, 158, 162, 163, 166, 167, 168, 171, 172, 174, 175, 177, 181, 183, 185, 186, 187, 189, 194, 212, 230, 268, 271, 292, 296, 297

U.S. Department of State.. 2, 17, 21, 26, 30, 31, 32, 33, 34, 40, 46, 47, 48, 49, 52, 53, 55, 59, 63, 80, 83, 84, 85, 86, 93, 94, 98, 110, 134, 135, 150, 151, 152, 155, 182, 199, 284, 285, 286, 296
U.S. Information Service 106
U.S.A Today 192, 289
United Jewish Appeal (UJA) 21, 64, 110, 114, 115, 118, 133, 186, 188, 215, 216, 291
United Nations (UN) 22, 26, 27, 28, 30, 31, 34, 53, 70, 73, 78, 81, 90, 93, 159, 170, 212, 215, 279, 284
US Department of Justice 132, 309
Vanunu, Mordechai 156
Viereck, George Sylvester 45, 51, 52, 55
Vietnam 159
Wagner, Robert F. 25
Wall Street Journal, The. 143, 144, 146, 191
Wallace, George 175
War Assets Administration (WAA) .64, 65, 66
War Refugee Board (WRB) 63
Washington Post, The 117, 183, 191
Weisman, Leonard 65
Weissman, Keith 191, 289
Weizmann, Chaim 16, 34, 59, 60
Weldon, James L. 164
whistlestop 35, 295
White Paper 10, 17, 57, 61, 94
Wise, Stephen 80, 85, 217
World Zionist Congress 12, 39, 60, 194
World Zionist Organization (WZO) .12, 59, 60, 61, 62, 80, 87, 118, 184, 186, 187, 188, 190, 192, 193, 194, 199, 214, 215, 289, 291, 292, 296
WQXR 169
WWI 10, 16, 18, 59
WWII 8, 33, 37, 45, 51, 64, 66, 197
Yeagley, J. Walter .. 132, 133, 136, 137, 138, 139, 140, 141, 145, 146, 147, 148, 149, 160, 161, 162, 163, 164, 166, 167, 168, 171, 172, 173, 174, 175, 176, 272, 278
Zionist Organization of America (ZOA) . 11, 28, 80, 84, 88, 132, 170, 216

Sources

[1] "Learn About AIPAC," AIPAC website, accessed on May 7, 2008 www.aipac.org/about_AIPAC/26.asp
[2] Taylor, Henry, Great Bend Tribune, Wednesday, December 19, 1973
[3] Kenen, Isaiah L., All My Causes in an 80-Year Life Span, Washington, DC: Near East Research, 1985, p. 12
[4] Kenen, Isaiah L., All My Causes in an 80-Year Life Span, Washington, DC: Near East Research, 1985, p. vi
[5] Kenen, Isaiah L., All My Causes in an 80-Year Life Span, Washington, DC: Near East Research, 1985, p. vi
[6] Kenen, Isaiah L., All My Causes in an 80-Year Life Span, Washington, DC: Near East Research, 1985, p. 1
[7] Isaiah Kenen Obituary, New York Times, March 25, 1988
[8] Isaiah L. "Si" Kenen, FBI file released on August 8, 2011, under FOIA. https://www.israellobby.org/kenen/1160456-000Kenen_Isaiahxrs.pdf
[9] Kenen, Isaiah L., All My Causes In An 80-Year Life Span, Washington, DC: Near East Research, 1985, p. 18
[10] Kenen, Isaiah L., All My Causes In an 80-Year Life Span, Washington, DC: Near East Research, 1985, p. 19
[11] Isaiah Kenen Form FA-1 filing, US Department of Justice, September 1, 1948
[12] Kenen, Isaiah L. All My Causes in an 80-Year Life Span, Washington, DC: Near East Research, 1985, p. 30
[13] Goldberg, David Howard, Foreign Policy and Ethnic Interest Groups: American and Canadian Jews Lobby, Westport, CT, Greenwood Publishing Group, Inc. p. 16
[14] Kenen, Isaiah L., All My Causes in an 80-Year Life Span, Washington, DC: Near East Research, 1985, pp. 32-33
[15] Goldberg, David Howard, Foreign Policy and Ethnic Interest Groups: American and Canadian Jews Lobby, Westport, CT, Greenwood Publishing Group, Inc. page 16
[16] Kenen, Isaiah L., Israel's Defense Line: Her Friends and Foes in Washington, New York, New York, Prometheus Books, p. 11
[17] Kenen, Isaiah L., Israel's Defense Line: Her Friends and Foes in Washington, New York, New York, Prometheus Books, p. 37
[18] Isaiah Kenen Form FA-1 filing, US Department of Justice, September 1, 1948
[19] Goldberg, David Howard, Foreign Policy and Ethnic Interest Groups: American and Canadian Jews Lobby, Westport, CT, Greenwood Publishing Group, Inc. p. 16
[20] Kenen, Isaiah L., Israel's Defense Line: Her Friends and Foes in Washington, New York, New York, Prometheus Books, p. 8
[21] Mendelsson, David, "From the First Zionist Congress (1897) to the Twelfth (1921)," The Jewish Virtual Library, http://www.jewishvirtuallibrary.org/jsource/Zionism/firstcong.html
[22] Kenen, Isaiah L. All My Causes in an 80-Year Life Span, Washington, DC: Near East Research, 1985, p. 2
[23] Herzl, Theodor, The Jewish State, translation of the original 1896 version published in 1946, New York, New York, American Zionist Emergency Council

[24] Herzl, Theodor, The Jewish State, translation of the original 1896 version published in 1946, New York, New York, American Zionist Emergency Council
[25] Herzl, Theodor, The Jewish State, translation of the original 1896 version published in 1946, New York, New York, American Zionist Emergency Council
[26] Herzl, Theodor, The Jewish State, translation of the original 1896 version published in 1946, New York, New York, American Zionist Emergency Council
[27] "Zionist Aliyot (1882-2002)," The Jewish Agency website, http://www.jewishagency.org/
[28] Herzl, Theodor, The Jewish State, translation of the original 1896 version published in 1946, New York, New York, American Zionist Emergency Council
[29] "The Wonderful Wastebasket," Time Magazine, March 24, 1952
[30] Polkehn, Klaus, "The Secret Contacts: Zionism and Nazi Germany, 1933-1941," Journal of Palestine Studies, Vol. 5, No. 3/4 (Spring – Summer, 1976), pp. 54-82
[31] Letter from Congressman Andrew L. Somers to Harry S Truman, Harry S Truman Library & Museum, January 26, 1942
[32] Peck, Sarah E., "The Campaign for an American Response to the Nazi Holocaust, 1943-1945," Journal of Contemporary History, Vol. 15, No. 2 (April 1980), p. 375
[33] Letter from Senator Harry S Truman to Andrew L. Somers, Harry S Truman Library & Museum, January 28, 1942
[34] Kenen, Isaiah L., Israel's Defense Line: Her Friends and Foes in Washington, New York, New York, Prometheus Books, p. 17
[35] Peck, Sarah E., "The Campaign for an American Response to the Nazi Holocaust, 1943-1945," Journal of Contemporary History, Vol. 15, No. 2 (April 1980), pp. 367-400
[36] Letter from Senator Harry S Truman to Peter Bergson, Harry S Truman Library & Museum, May 7, 1943
[37] Truman, Harry S, Memoirs of Harry S Truman, vol. 2: "Years of Trial and Hope 1946-1952," New York, Doubleday & Co., p. 158
[38] Letter from Secretary of State Edward Stettinius to President Harry S Truman, Harry S Truman Library & Museum, April 18, 1945
[39] Letter from Undersecretary of State Joseph C. Grew to President Harry S Truman, Harry S Truman Library & Museum, May 1, 1945
[40] Letter from Undersecretary of State Joseph C. Grew to President Harry S Truman, Harry S Truman Library & Museum, May 28, 1945
[41] Lessing J. Rosenwald, memorandum on his meeting with Harry S Truman, Harry S Truman Library & Museum, December 4, 1945
[42] Kenen, Isaiah L., Israel's Defense Line: Her Friends and Foes in Washington, New York, New York, Prometheus Books, p. 16
[43] Letter from Congressman Emanuel Celler to Harry S Truman, Harry S Truman Library & Museum, March 20, 1946
[44] Letter from Senator Harry S Truman to Emanuel Celler, Harry S Truman Library & Museum, March 23, 1942
[45] Memo from David K. Niles to Matt Connelly, Harry S Truman Library & Museum, May 1, 1946
[46] Letter from Senator Robert Wagner to President Harry S Truman, Harry S Truman Library & Museum, June 21, 1942
[47] A.J. McFarland, Joint Chiefs of Staff, Harry S Truman Library & Museum, June 21, 1946

[48] Letter from Prime Minister Attlee to President Harry S Truman, Harry S Truman Library & Museum, July 25, 1946
[49] Kenen, Isaiah L., Israel's Defense Line: Her Friends and Foes in Washington, New York, New York, Prometheus Books, p. 36
[50] Kenen, Isaiah L., Israel's Defense Line: Her Friends and Foes in Washington, New York, New York, Prometheus Books, p. 37
[51] Kenen, Isaiah L., Israel's Defense Line: Her Friends and Foes in Washington, New York, New York, Prometheus Books, p. 37
[52] Kenen, Isaiah L., Israel's Defense Line: Her Friends and Foes in Washington, New York, New York, Prometheus Books, pp. 40-41
[53] "US Would Allow Zionists a UN Voice, Flushing Delegation Shifts Its View after Protests to Washington by Groups," New York Times, May 2, 1947
[54] Blewett, David, "Christian Support For Israel," Speech at the January 2003 National Christian Leadership Conference for Israel

Blewett notes that while the lobbying coalition had been around since 1932, it lacked cohesiveness and reason to exist after lobbying for Israel was successful: "Similar Christian organizations were developed in other countries, but the most energetic expression of political support for a Jewish homeland in Palestine came from Christians in the United States. Rev. Edward Russell founded the Pro-Palestine Federation (PPF) in 1930, composed primarily of pastors and a few priests. In 1932 the American Palestine Committee was founded with a membership that included a number of prominent public figures, statesmen and elected officials. Feeling the need for an overtly Christian organization, the Christian Council of Palestine (CCP) was founded in 1942 and soon grew to a membership of 3,000 clergymen, primarily from liberal churches. In order to maximize effectiveness, the two organizations merged in 1946 and became the American Christian Palestine Committee (ACPC), with a membership of over 15,000 Christians.

After the UN partition vote in 1947, the ACPC found itself just one among many similar organizations, Jewish and non-Jewish, that urged a quick implementation of the UN Special Committee on Palestine plan. The American Christian Palestine Committee continued for several more years to organize local programs and conferences, lobby national leaders and to publish a monthly magazine, *Land Reborn*, always focused on communicating the justice of the Zionist cause and strengthening sympathy in Christian communities for the Jewish State."

Concluding that its work was done, the ACPC disbanded.

[55] The Political Action Committee for Palestine was led by Republican Congressman Joseph Clark Baldwin, who represented New York's 17th congressional district from 1941 to 1947. Active in state politics, Baldwin had worked as a reporter for the *New York Tribune*. He served as administrative chairman for the short-lived group, and Baldwin's signature would often appear above ads placed in major US newspapers publicizing and defending the Zionist cause, although at times he claimed he was not personally responsible for particularly harsh declarations.

In 1946, the group pressed Truman to reject a British request for US troops to act as peacekeepers in Palestine. This PAC would present 100,000 petitions containing

2,000,000 signatures asking Congress to support partition on April 13, 1948. While the PAC generally called for an end to terror attacks by Irgun, it defended the group's kidnapping and flogging of four British soldiers on December 29, 1946, as just retribution. (See article "Aide of Baldwin Defends Flogging; Irgun Zvai Leumi Provoked, Says Official of Political Action Group for Palestine 1941–1947," New York Times, January 1, 1947)

[56] "US Would Allow Zionists a UN Voice, Flushing Delegation Shifts Its View after Protests to Washington by Groups," New York Times, May 2, 1947

[57] Isaiah L. Kenen Foreign Agent Registration, Exhibit A, US Department of Justice, September 1, 1948

[58] Kenen, Isaiah L. All My Causes in an 80-Year Life Span, Washington, DC: Near East Research, 1985, p. 67

[59] "UN Is Asked to Bar Jewish State by American Council for Judaism: Anti-Zionist Group Insists That Nationhood Would Harm Entire People—Assails Balfour Declaration on Palestine," New York Times, June 9, 1947

[60] Henry Morgenthau resigned when Harry S Truman became president. Morgenthau was the author of the 1944 Morgenthau Plan for postwar Germany. The plan called for Germany to be partitioned into separate states, stripped of its industrial capacity, and forcibly returned to an agrarian economy. The plan was used by German propaganda minister Joseph Goebbels in an attempt to motivate the Axis war effort, and partially adopted in a Truman occupation directive in 1945 to slow the reindustrialization of Germany. Morgenthau was later a leading participant in the Bretton Woods Conference, which led to the creation of the International Monetary Fund and the International Bank for Reconstruction and Development (the World Bank). See http://www.trumanlibrary.org/oralhist/connly3.htm.

[61] Truman, Harry S, Diary Entry, Harry S Truman Library & Museum, July 21, 1947

[62] Truman, Harry S, Diary Entry, Harry S Truman Library & Museum, July 21, 1947

[63] Kenen, Isaiah L., Israel's Defense Line: Her Friends and Foes in Washington, New York, New York, Prometheus Books, p. 38

[64] Niles, David, Memo to President Harry S Truman, Harry S Truman Library & Museum, May 12, 1947

[65] Niles, David, Memo to President Harry S Truman, Harry S Truman Library & Museum, May 12, 1947

[66] Kenen, Isaiah L., All My Causes in an 80-Year Life Span, Washington, DC: Near East Research, 1985, p. 39

[67] Kenen, Isaiah L., All My Causes in an 80-Year Life Span, Washington, DC: Near East Research, 1985, p. 39

[68] Foreign Relations of the United States, 1948. V. 5: The Near East, South Asia, and Africa, Part III. US Department of State, publication number 8840, 1976, p. 1222

[69] "Truman Appoints Mission to Israel, J.G. McDonald to Represent U.S.-Eliahu Epstein Will Act Here for New State," New York Times, June 23, 1948

[70] Obituary "Abraham Feinberg, 90, Philanthropist for Israel," New York Times, December 7, 1998

[71] Hersh, Seymour M., The Samson Option: Israel's Nuclear Option and American Foreign Policy, New York, Random House, 1991, p. 66

[72] Hersh, Seymour M., The Samson Option: Israel's Nuclear Option and American Foreign Policy, New York, Random House, 1991, p. 94

[73] Oral History Interview with Abraham Feinberg, Harry S Truman Library & Museum, Interview conducted in New York, NY on August 23, 1978, released in 1984

[74] Truman, Harry S, Memoirs of Harry S Truman, vol. 2: "Years of Trial and Hope 1946-1952," New York, Doubleday & Co., p. 153
[75] Oral History Interview with Abraham Feinberg, Harry S Truman Library & Museum, Interview conducted in New York, NY on August 23, 1978, released in 1984
[76] Oral History Interview with Abraham Feinberg, Harry S Truman Library & Museum, Interview conducted in New York, NY on August 23, 1978, released in 1984
[77] Oral History Interview with Abraham Feinberg, Harry S Truman Library & Museum, Interview conducted in New York, NY on August 23, 1978, released in 1984
[78] British Cabinet Minutes CP47/259, September 18, 1947, p. 4
[79] "Jewish groups plotted to kill Bevin," The Telegraph, May 22, 2003
[80] Johnson, Paul, A History of the Jews, New York, Harper and Row, 1987, p. 526
[81] "Two Planes Seized at Jersey Airport: Constellations at Millville Are Linked to Mysterious B-17 Detained in Halifax," New York Times, July 14, 1948
[82] "Zionist Groupings Are Active in U.S." New York Times, December 27, 1948
[83] Berger, Elmer, "Memoirs of an Anti-Zionist Jew," Journal of Palestine Studies, Vol. 5, No. ½ (Autumn 1975–Winter 1976), University of California Press on behalf of the Institute for Palestine Studies, p. 13
[84] US State Department investigates AIPAC Director Morris Amitay's acquisition of classified Hawk missile data, FOIA release January 2, 2012, online at https://www.israellobby.org/amitay/
[85] US Israel Free Trade Agreement Damage Assessment, Bilaterals.org, IRmep.org June 20, 2019, https://www.bilaterals.org/?us-israel-free-trade-agreement
[86] "Nazi Probe," Time Magazine, June 18, 1934
[87] "Hitler Kept List of Dead Plotters; Germans Disclose a Document Recording Executions After Blast July 20, 1944," New York Times, June 11, 1946
[88] "Dies Asks Curb on Foreign Groups," Associated Press, October 7, 1938
[89] "Test Set for Curb on Foreign Agents: First Trial Under Law Which Requires Registrations Will Open at Capital May 19. Soviet Activity Charged. Three Defendants Are Linked to the Distribution Here of Propaganda Literature," New York Times, May 4, 1941
[90] Foreign Agents Registration Act, cited in USC 1940 Edition Volume 2, Title 21, Section 352. See Appendices for complete text.
[91] "Influence Peddling Laws, History of the Lobbying Disclosure Act," Public Citizen, July 26, 2005, http://www.lobbyinginfo.org/laws/page.cfm?pageid=15
[92] "Influence Peddling Laws, History of the Lobbying Disclosure Act," Public Citizen, July 26, 2005, http://www.lobbyinginfo.org/laws/page.cfm?pageid=15
[93] "Warns All Agents of Foreign Groups: State Department Stresses Thursday Deadline for Registration Under Law," New York Times, October 2, 1938
[94] Kenen, Isaiah L., All My Causes in an 80-Year Life Span, Washington, DC: Near East Research, 1985, p. 12
[95] "15 More Registered as Foreign Agents: Total Filing Under the New Law Is Brought up to 317," New York Times, March 28, 1939
[96] "371 Registered as Propagandists: State Department Lists All Those Agents Working for Foreign Principals," New York Times, November 12, 1939
[97] "Propagandists Fined for Hiding Moscow Tie in Agents' Registry: Two Russians, Officers of Bookniga Admit Violation—Counsel Says Book-Selling Concern Will Be Dissolved," New York Times, December 28, 1939
[98] "Test Set for Curb on Foreign Agents," New York Times, May 4, 1941

[99] "News Agency on Trial: Nazi Transocean Accused of Violating Registration Act," New York Times, July 18, 1941
[100] "Amtorg Group Files Registration Data," New York Times, October 28, 1949
[101] Foreign Agents Registration Act, cited in USC 1946 Edition Volume 2, Title 22, Section 267B. The President initially made the transfer under the War Powers Act of 1941. See Appendices for full text.
[102] Foreign Agents Registration Act, cited in USC 1946 Edition Volume 2, Title 22, Section 267B. The President initially made the transfer under the War Powers Act of 1941. See Appendices for full text.
[103] Smith, Grant F., <u>Foreign Agents: The American Israel Public Affairs Committee from the 1963 Fulbright Hearings to the 2005 Espionage Scandal</u>, Washington, DC, Institute for Research: Middle Eastern Policy, pp. 57-59
[104] "Convict 2 as Japanese Agents," New York Times, June 2, 1942
[105] "F.B.I. Net Spread for Foes in Nation: Biddle Reviews Year's Task of Uncovering and Punishing Spies, Saboteurs, Traitors," New York Times, December 6, 1942
[106] "Allied Agents Must File Statements of Activity," New York Times, October 9, 1946
[107] "Votes Closer Check on Alien Agencies: House Exempts Allied Governments in New Registry Bill," New York Times, April 22, 1942
[108] "Nazi Probe," Time Magazine, June 18, 1934
[109] "Viereck Is Convicted by Federal Jury of Violating the Foreign Agents' Act," New York Times, July 17, 1943
[110] "Viereck. Convicted In War, Is Paroled," New York Times, June 27, 1947
[111] La Follette Jr, Robert M., Op/Ed, "Some Lobbies Are Good," New York Times, May 16, 1948
[112] "Saud Protests Search: King Calls Entry of Arab Office in U.S. 'A Hostile Act,'" New York Times, March 20, 1947
[113] "Arab Inquiry Demanded: Anti-Nazi League Thinks Acts of Agencies Violate U.S. Law," New York Times, November 27, 1947
[114] Peck, Sarah E., "The Campaign for an American Response to the Nazi Holocaust, 1943-1945," Journal of Contemporary History, Vol. 15, No. 2 (April 1980), pp. 367-400
[115] "58 Foreign Agents File: New Registrants in '53 Bring Total to 252, Brownwell Says," New York Times, May 24, 1952
[116] "US Would Raise Tax-Exempt Veil: Treasury Will Seek Law for Public Inspection of Bids by Nonprofit Groups," New York Times, November 10, 1955
[117] "Policy of Seizing Red Mail Studied: Senate Unit Is Investigating 10-Year Postal Practice After Many Protests," New York Times, May 22, 1960
[118] "U.S. to End Seizure of Soviet-Bloc Mail," New York Times, March 17, 1961
[119] "Frank's Sentence up to Two Years: Ex-FBI Man Was Illegal Agent for Trujillo in U.S.—Freed Pending Appeal," New York Times, December 20, 1957
[120] "Conviction Upset in Trujillo Case," New York Times, October 21, 1958
[121] "The Objectives and Activities of the Irgun Zvai Leumi," 10/13/1944, released by the US Central Intelligence Agency in 2003, CIA Freedom of Information Act electronic reading room
[122] "The Objectives and Activities of the Irgun Zvai Leumi," 10/13/1944, released by the US Central Intelligence Agency in 2003, CIA Freedom of Information Act electronic reading room

[123] "The Objectives and Activities of the Irgun Zvai Leumi," 10/13/1944, released by the US Central Intelligence Agency in 2003, CIA Freedom of Information Act electronic reading room
[124] Jabotinsky, Vladimir, "The Iron Wall (We and the Arabs)," (Berlin) Rassviet, November 4, 1923
[125] Hoffman, Joseph Paul, "The Price of Flight: German Jews, the Nazi regime and the finance of the Ha'avarah Agreement, 1933–1939," The George Washington University, 2002, Publication Number AAT 3045176
[126] Black, Edwin, The Transfer Agreement, New York, Carroll & Graf, 2001, p. xi
[127] Black, Edwin, The Transfer Agreement, New York, Macmillan Publishing Company, 1984, p. 70
[128] Brenner, Lenni, "Zionist-Revisionism: The Years of Fascism and Terror," Journal of Palestine Studies, Vol. 13, No. 1 (Autumn 1983), pp. 66-92
[129] Brenner, Lenni, "Zionist-Revisionism: The Years of Fascism and Terror," Journal of Palestine Studies, Vol. 13, No. 1 (Autumn 1983), pp. 66-92
[130] Peck, Sarah E., "The Campaign for an American Response to the Nazi Holocaust, 1943-1945," Journal of Contemporary History, Vol. 15, No. 2 (April 1980), pp. 367-400
[131] Peck, Sarah E., "The Campaign for an American Response to the Nazi Holocaust, 1943-1945," Journal of Contemporary History, Vol. 15, No. 2 (April 1980), pp. 367-400
[132] Obituary, "Rudolf Sonneborn American Zionism Leader, 87," Boston Globe, June 5, 1986
[133] Kollek, Teddy and Amos, "For Jerusalem, a Life," New York, Random House, p. 10
[134] Kollek, Teddy and Amos, "For Jerusalem, a Life," New York, Random House, pp. 68-69
[135] Obituary, "Mrs. N. A. Bernstein, Assisted Haganah," New York Times, December 28, 1965
[136] Calhoun, Ricky-Dale, "Arming David: The Haganah's Illegal Arms Procurement Network in the United States, 1945-1949," Journal of Palestine Studies, Vol. 36, No. 4 (Summer 2007)
[137] Calhoun, Ricky-Dale, "Arming David: The Haganah's Illegal Arms Procurement Network in the United States, 1945-1949," Journal of Palestine Studies, Vol. 36, No. 4 (Summer 2007)
[138] Obituary, "Hawaii Residents Aided Underdog Israel's Struggle," Honolulu Star Bulletin, October 15, 2006
[139] Calhoun, Ricky-Dale, "Arming David: The Haganah's Illegal Arms Procurement Network in the United States, 1945-1949," Journal of Palestine Studies, Vol. 36, No. 4 (Summer 2007)
[140] "Clandestine Air Transport Operations: Memorandum for the Secretary of Defense," Central Intelligence Agency, May 28, 1948, Declassified and released on September 27, 2001, CIA Freedom of Information Act electronic reading room
[141] "Clandestine Air Transport Operations: Memorandum for the Secretary of Defense," Central Intelligence Agency, May 28, 1948, Declassified and released on September 27, 2001, CIA Freedom of Information Act electronic reading room
[142] "Clandestine Air Transport Operations: Memorandum for the Secretary of Defense," Central Intelligence Agency, May 28, 1948, Declassified and released on September 27, 2001, CIA Freedom of Information Act electronic reading room

[143] Israel Office of Information Foreign Agent Registration, <u>US Department of Justice</u>, October 6, 1948
[144] Israeli Embassy chooses FARA reporting dates for Israel Office of Information, <u>US Department of Justice</u>, November 1, 1948
[145] Foreign Agents Registration Section Deficiency Notice to the Israel Office of Information, <u>US Department of Justice</u>, June 17, 1948
[146] Foreign Agents Registration Section Deficiency Notice to the Israel Office of Information, <u>US Department of Justice</u>, June 17, 1948
[147] Isaiah L. Kenen Foreign Agent Registration, Exhibit A, <u>US Department of Justice</u>, September 1, 1948
[148] Israel Office of Information Budget, Foreign Agent Registration Act report Appendix A, <u>US Department of Justice</u>, October 30, 1950
[149] Israel Office of Information FARA Declaration—3 offices—I.L. Kenen, <u>US Department of Justice</u>, October 30, 1950, June 30, 1950
[150] "Jerusalem Issue Danger Stressed," <u>Los Angeles Times</u>, December 7, 1949
[151] Kenen, Isaiah L., <u>All My Causes in an 80-Year Life Span</u>, Washington, DC: Near East Research, 1985, p. 48
[152] Israel Office of Information FARA Declaration—Activities, <u>US Department of Justice</u>, October 30, 1950, January 1-June 30, 1951
[153] Israel Office of Information FARA Declaration—Personnel, <u>US Department of Justice</u>, January 1-June 30, 1951. Chertoff would later file as a registered foreign agent for the World Zionist Organization from May of 1974 until December of 1990, according to the FARA online database: http://www.usdoj.gov/criminal/fara/links/search.html
[154] Taken from a certified letter from Assistant Attorney General, Internal Security Division G. Walter Yeagley to the American Zionist Council, November 21, 1962; released under Freedom of Information Act on June 10, 2008
[155] Isaiah L. "Si" Kenen, FBI file released on August 8, 2011, under FOIA. https://www.israellobby.org/kenen/1160456-000Kenen_Isaiahxrs.pdf
[156] Isaiah L. "Si" Kenen, FBI file released on August 8, 2011, under FOIA. https://www.israellobby.org/kenen/1160456-000Kenen_Isaiahxrs.pdf
[157] Isaiah L. "Si" Kenen, FBI file released on August 8, 2011, under FOIA. https://www.israellobby.org/kenen/1160456-000Kenen_Isaiahxrs.pdf
[158] Isaiah L. "Si" Kenen, FBI file released on August 8, 2011, under FOIA. https://www.israellobby.org/kenen/1160456-000Kenen_Isaiahxrs.pdf
[159] Israel Office of Information Violation Investigation, <u>US Department of Justice</u>, April 21, 1953
[160] Israel Office of Information Foreign Agent Registration, <u>US Department of Justice</u>, October 6, 1948
[161] Isaiah Kenen form FA-1 filing, <u>US Department of Justice</u>, September 1, 1948
[162] Kenen, Isaiah L., <u>Israel's Defense Line: Her Friends and Foes in Washington</u>, New York, New York, Prometheus Books, p. 122
[163] Kenen, Isaiah L., <u>All My Causes in an 80-Year Life Span</u>, Washington, DC: Near East Research, 1985, p. 49
[164] Kenen, Isaiah L., <u>All My Causes in an 80-Year Life Span</u>, Washington, DC: Near East Research, 1985, p. 34
[165] Kenen, Isaiah L., <u>All My Causes in an 80-Year Life Span</u>, Washington, DC: Near East Research, 1985, p. 34

[166] Kenen, Isaiah L., Israel's Defense Line: Her Friends and Foes in Washington, New York, New York, Prometheus Books, p. 69
[167] "US Zionist Leaders Will Go to Palestine," New York Times, July 1, 1946
[168] Nathan Lenvin FARA Section Memo About Isaiah Kenen Visit, US Department of Justice, January 17, 1951
[169] Kenen, Isaiah L., Israel's Defense Line: Her Friends and Foes in Washington, New York, New York, Prometheus Books, p. 68
[170] Kenen, Isaiah L., Israel's Defense Line: Her Friends and Foes in Washington, New York, New York, Prometheus Books, p. 69
[171] Isaiah Kenen Termination Letter to the Department of Justice, US Department of Justice, February 13, 1951
[172] "Shake-up Nears in Zionist Council," New York Times, December 26, 1944
[173] "Shake-up Nears in Zionist Council," New York Times, December 26, 1944
[174] Oral History Interview with Abraham Feinberg, Harry S Truman Library & Museum, Interview conducted in New York, NY on August 23, 1978, released in 1984
[175] Kenen, Isaiah L., All My Causes in an 80-Year Life Span, Washington, DC: Near East Research, 1985, pp. 66-67
[176] Kenen, Isaiah L., Israel's Defense Line: Her Friends and Foes in Washington, New York, New York, Prometheus Books, p. 7
[177] Kenen, Isaiah L., All My Causes in an 80-Year Life Span, Washington, DC: Near East Research, 1985, pp. 52-53
[178] "Zionists Propose a New US Set-up," New York Times, November 24, 1952
[179] "Miller New Head of Zionist Council," New York Times, February 27, 1954
[180] Kenen, Isaiah L., Israel's Defense Line: Her Friends and Foes in Washington, New York, New York, Prometheus Books, p. 66
[181] "Miller New Head of Zionist Council," New York Times, February 27, 1954
[182] Stork, Joe and Rose, Sharon, "Zionism and American Jewry," Journal of Palestine Studies, Vol. 3, No. 3 (Spring 1974), pp. 39-57
[183] Obituary, "Abraham Feinberg, 90, Philanthropist for Israel," New York Times, December 7, 1998
[184] "I.L. Kenen in Zionist Unit Post," New York Times, February 29, 1952
[185] Letter to FARA Section Chief from Isaiah Kenen, US Department of Justice, March 14, 1952
[186] Letter to Isaiah Kenen from FARA Section Chief, US Department of Justice, March 26, 1952
[187] Kenen, Isaiah L., Israel's Defense Line: Her Friends and Foes in Washington, New York, New York, Prometheus Books, p. 106
[188] Kenen, Isaiah L., All My Causes in an 80-Year Life Span, Washington, DC: Near East Research, 1985, p. 54
[189] Kenen, Isaiah L., All My Causes in an 80-Year Life Span, Washington, DC: Near East Research, 1985, pp. 54-55
[190] "Dr. Bunche Attacked: Celler Says He Takes Orders from State Department," New York Times, October 22, 1948
[191] "The Nation: A Gray Law Illuminates Billy Carters Foreign Deals," New York Times, July 20, 1980
[192] Berger, Elmer, "Memoirs of an Anti-Zionist Jew," Journal of Palestine Studies, Vol. 5, No. ½ (Autumn 1975–Winter 1976), University of California Press on behalf of the Institute for Palestine Studies, pp. 3-55

[193] Kenen, Isaiah L., Israel's Defense Line: Her Friends and Foes in Washington, New York, New York, Prometheus Books, p. 106

[194] Kenen, Isaiah L., Israel's Defense Line: Her Friends and Foes in Washington, New York, New York, Prometheus Books, p. 106

[195] Mittleman, Alan, Licht, Robert A., and Sarna, Jonathan D., Jewish Polity and American Civil Society, Lanham, Maryland, Rowman and Littlefield, 2002, p. 113

[196] Kenen, Isaiah L., Israel's Defense Line: Her Friends and Foes in Washington, New York, New York, Prometheus Books, p. 106

[197] Kenen, Isaiah L., Israel's Defense Line: Her Friends and Foes in Washington, New York, New York, Prometheus Books, p. 107

[198] "Lipsky Quits Post in Zionist Council," New York Times, November 22, 1950.

[199] "Rabbi Criticizes U.S. Jewish Units," New York Times, January 23, 1959

[200] "Rabbi Criticizes U.S. Jewish Units," New York Times, January 23, 1959

[201] "Council for Judaism Objects to Implication That All American Jews Back Zionist Aims," New York Times, October 1, 1945

[202] "Council for Judaism Objects to Implication That All American Jews Back Zionist Aims," New York Times, October 1, 1945

[203] "Zionists Concepts Called Dangerous," New York Times, May 11, 1953

[204] "Zionists Concepts Called Dangerous," New York Times, May 11, 1953

[205] "Zionists Concepts Called Dangerous," New York Times, May 11, 1953

[206] Near East Report, Washington, DC, 1959 issues

[207] Near East Report, Washington, DC, Vol. 4, No. 4, July 15, 1960

[208] Near East Report, Washington, DC, Vol. 4, No. 1, June 2, 1960

[209] Near East Report, Washington, DC, Vol. 4, No. 1, June 2, 1960

[210] Near East Report, Washington, DC, Vol. 6, No. 10, May 8, 1962

[211] Near East Report, Washington, DC, Vol. 4, No. 3, July 1, 1960

[212] Near East Report, Washington, DC, Vol. 4, No. 3, July 1, 1960

[213] Near East Report, Washington, DC, Vol. 4, No. 4, July 15, 1960

[214] Near East Report, Washington, DC, Vol. 4, No. 4, July 15, 1960

[215] Near East Report, Washington, DC, Vol. 4, No. 17, February 1, 1961

[216] "Egyptian-Jewish spy ring gets belated salute," Jerusalem Post, March 31, 2005

[217] Shalom, Zakai, Ben-Gurion's Political Struggles, 1963-1967: A Lion in Winter, New York, Routledge, 2006, pp. 31-32

[218] Shalom, Zakai, Ben-Gurion's Political Struggles, 1963-1967: A Lion in Winter, New York, Routledge, 2006, pp. 31-32

[219] Near East Report, Washington, DC, Vol. 4, No. 15, November 2, 1961

[220] Senate Foreign Relations Committee Investigation into the Activities of Agents of Foreign Principals in the United States, 88th Congress, 1st session, Washington, US Government Printing Office, May 23, 1963, p. 1211

[221] Kenen, Isaiah L., Israel's Defense Line: Her Friends and Foes in Washington, New York, New York, Prometheus Books, p. 107

[222] Kenen, Isaiah L., Israel's Defense Line: Her Friends and Foes in Washington, New York, New York, Prometheus Books, p. 107

[223] Faris, Fuad, "Zionism and American Jews," Middle East Research and Information Project, Merip Reports, No. 29 (June 1974), pp. 3-13 + 26

[224] Smith, Charles, University of Arizona Near Eastern Studies Professor Speech, "The 1967 War Revisited: New Sources and Their Implications," U.S. State Department, 1/12/2004, video at rtsp://cspanrm.fplive.net/cspan/archive/iraq/iraq011204_statedept.rm

[225] Kenen, Isaiah L., Israel's Defense Line: Her Friends and Foes in Washington, New York, New York, Prometheus Books, p. 302

[226] Abourezk, James, Email to the Author, July 7, 2008

[227] Kenen, Isaiah L., All My Causes in an 80-Year Life Span, Washington, DC: Near East Research, 1985, p. 102

[228] Kenen, Isaiah L., All My Causes in an 80-Year Life Span, Washington, DC: Near East Research, 1985, p. 103

[229] "US Studies Status of Zionist Council," New York Times, March 13, 1963

[230] "US Studies Status of Zionist Council," New York Times, March 13, 1963

[231] Faris, Fuad, "Zionism and American Jews," Middle East Research and Information Project, Merip Reports, No. 29 (June 1974), pp. 3-13 + 26

[232] Berger, Elmer, "Memoirs of an Anti-Zionist Jew," Journal of Palestine Studies, Vol. 5, No. ½ (Autumn 1975–Winter 1976), University of California Press on behalf of the Institute for Palestine Studies, pp. 3-55

[233] Kenen, Isaiah L., Israel's Defense Line: Her Friends and Foes in Washington, New York, New York, Prometheus Books, p. 10

[234] "Zionists to Form Territorial Units," New York Times, January 1, 1954

[235] "Zionists Accused of Fund Control," New York Times, May 14, 1960

[236] "Zionists Accused of Fund Control," New York Times, May 14, 1960

[237] "Zionists Accused of Fund Control," New York Times, May 14, 1960

[238] "Zionists Accused of Fund Control," New York Times, May 14, 1960

[239] "Fulbright Scores Agency of Israel, Its Use of US Zionist Body Is Said to Skirt Statute," New York Times, August 2, 1963

[240] Senate Foreign Relations Committee Investigation into the Activities of Agents of Foreign Principals in the United States, 88th Congress, 1st session, Washington, US Government Printing Office, May 23, 1963, pp. 1307-1312

[241] Senate Foreign Relations Committee Investigation into the Activities of Agents of Foreign Principals in the United States, 88th Congress, 1st session, Washington, US Government Printing Office, May 23, 1963, pp. 1347-1348

[242] Senate Foreign Relations Committee Investigation into the Activities of Agents of Foreign Principals in the United States, 88th Congress, 1st session, Washington, US Government Printing Office, May 23, 1963, p. 1343

[243] Senate Foreign Relations Committee Investigation into the Activities of Agents of Foreign Principals in the United States, 88th Congress, 1st session, Washington, US Government Printing Office ,May 23, 1963, p. 1344

[244] Senate Foreign Relations Committee Investigation into the Activities of Agents of Foreign Principals in the United States, May 23, 1963, p. 1344

[245] Senate Foreign Relations Committee Investigation into the Activities of Agents of Foreign Principals in the United States, 88th Congress, 1st session, Washington, US Government Printing Office, May 23, 1963, p. 1344

[246] Senate Foreign Relations Committee Investigation into the Activities of Agents of Foreign Principals in the United States, 88th Congress, 1st session, Washington, US Government Printing Office, May 23, 1963, p. 1346

[247] Senate Foreign Relations Committee Investigation into the Activities of Agents of Foreign Principals in the United States, 88th Congress, 1st session, Washington, US Government Printing Office, May 23, 1963, p. 1347

[248] Senate Foreign Relations Committee Investigation into the Activities of Agents of Foreign Principals in the United States, 88th Congress, 1st session, Washington, US Government Printing Office, May 23, 1963, p. 1347

[249] Senate Foreign Relations Committee Investigation into the Activities of Agents of Foreign Principals in the United States, 88th Congress, 1st session, Washington, US Government Printing Office, May 23, 1963, p.1347

[250] Senate Foreign Relations Committee Investigation into the Activities of Agents of Foreign Principals in the United States, 88th Congress, 1st session, Washington, US Government Printing Office, May 23, 1963, p. 1344

[251] Senate Foreign Relations Committee Investigation into the Activities of Agents of Foreign Principals in the United States, 88th Congress, 1st session, Washington, US Government Printing Office, May 23, 1963, p. 1345

[252] Senate Foreign Relations Committee Investigation into the Activities of Agents of Foreign Principals in the United States, 88th Congress, 1st session, Washington, US Government Printing Office, May 23, 1963, p. 1345

[253] In 1940, Robert Soblen and his brother Jack were sent to America via Canada by Soviet Secret Police Chief Lavrenty Beria. During World War II, Robert Soblen provided the Soviets with secret documents from the Office of Strategic Services and data from the Sandia nuclear weapons development center at Albuquerque, New Mexico. In December 1960, the FBI arrested him on a charge of wartime espionage, which could have carried a death sentence, but they did not consider him to be a flight risk. Soblen fled to Israel in June 1962, touching off a national debate in Israel over whether it should extradite criminals for prosecution unless they could be returned to serve time in Israel.

[254] Senate Foreign Relations Committee Investigation into the Activities of Agents of Foreign Principals in the United States, 88th Congress, 1st session, Washington, US Government Printing Office, May 23, 1963, p. 1345

[255] Senate Foreign Relations Committee Investigation into the Activities of Agents of Foreign Principals in the United States, 88th Congress, 1st session, Washington, US Government Printing Office, May 23, 1963, p. 1355

[256] Senate Foreign Relations Committee Investigation into the Activities of Agents of Foreign Principals in the United States, 88th Congress, 1st session, Washington, US Government Printing Office, May 23, 1963, p. 1346

[257] Senate Foreign Relations Committee Investigation into the Activities of Agents of Foreign Principals in the United States, 88th Congress, 1st session, Washington, US Government Printing Office, May 23, 1963, p. 1346

[258] Senate Foreign Relations Committee Investigation into the Activities of Agents of Foreign Principals in the United States, May 23, 1963, pp. 1348-1350

[259] Senate Foreign Relations Committee Investigation into the Activities of Agents of Foreign Principals in the United States, 88th Congress, 1st session, Washington, US Government Printing Office, May 23, 1963, pp. 1326-1328

[260] Senate Foreign Relations Committee Investigation into the Activities of Agents of Foreign Principals in the United States, 88th Congress, 1st session, Washington, US Government Printing Office, August 1, 1963, pp. 1735-1741

[261] Senate Foreign Relations Committee Investigation into the Activities of Agents of Foreign Principals in the United States, 88th Congress, 1st session, Washington, US Government Printing Office, August 1, 1963, p. 1719

[262] Senate Foreign Relations Committee Investigation into the Activities of Agents of Foreign Principals in the United States, Washington, US Government Printing Office, August 1, 1963, pages 1704-1709

[263] Obituary, "J. Walter Yeagley, 81, Former Justice Official," New York Times, May 1, 1990. The obituary emphasizes Yeagley's role heading a division that "investigated organizations and individuals suspected of Communist affiliations" but makes no specific mention of broader foreign agent registration efforts.

[264] Memo from Assistant Attorney General, Internal Security Division G. Walter Yeagley to Attorney General Robert F. Kennedy, October 31, 1962; Released under Freedom of Information Act on June 10, 2008

[265] Edwin Guthman, Inventory of Personal Papers, John F. Kennedy Presidential Library, http://www.jfklibrary.org/Historical+Resources/Archives/Archives+and+Manuscripts/fa_guthman.htm

[266] Memo from Edwin Guthman Director of Public Information to Robert F. Kennedy, Attorney General, copied to Nicholas Katzenbach November 14, 1962; Released under Freedom of Information Act on June 10, 2008

[267] Oral History Interview with Abraham Feinberg, Harry S Truman Library & Museum, Interview conducted in New York, NY on August 23, 1978, released in 1984

[268] Hersh, Seymour M., The Samson Option: Israel's Nuclear Option and American Foreign Policy, New York, Random House, 1991, pp. 96-97

[269] "Greenspun Wins '50 Case Pardon: Nevada Editor Convicted in Israel Arms Case" New York Times, October 28, 1961

[270] Hersh, Seymour M., The Samson Option: Israel's Nuclear Option and American Foreign Policy, New York, Random House, 1991, pp. 98-100; 108-109

[271] Certified Letter from Assistant Attorney General, Internal Security Division G. Walter Yeagley to the American Zionist Council, November 21, 1962; Released under Freedom of Information Act on June 10, 2008

[272] Memo from Nathan B. Lenvin, Chief Registration Section to Files, page 1, November 6, 1962; Released under Freedom of Information Act on June 10, 2008

[273] Memo from Nathan B. Lenvin, Chief Registration Section to Files, page 2, November 6, 1962; Released under Freedom of Information Act on June 10, 2008 J. Walter Yeagley handwrote, "I would expect this" and initialed the document in the left margin, referencing the text "would be a non-pressing by A.G. of any request for registration on the basis of bona fide representations that the Jewish Agency no longer would contribute funds to the American Zionist Council."

[274] Letter from Rabbi Irving Miller, Chairman of the American Zionist Council to Nathan B. Lenvin, Chief Registration Section, December 6, 1962; Released under Freedom of Information Act on June 10, 2008

[275] Records of Temporary Committees, Commissions and Boards, Presidential Railroad Commission, The National Archives and Records Administration, http://www.archives.gov/research/guide-fed-records/groups/220.html#220.9.15

[276] Appleton Post-Crescent, March 5, 1962

[277] Memo from Thomas K. Hall, Executive Assistant, Internal Security Division to Files, page 1, January 24, 1962; Released under Freedom of Information Act on June 10, 2008

[278] Memo from Nathan B. Lenvin, Chief Registration Section to Files, page 1, February 8, 1963; Released under Freedom of Information Act on June 10, 2008

[279] Memo from Thomas K. Hall, Executive Assistant, Internal Security Division to Files, page 1, January 24, 1962; Released under Freedom of Information Act on June 10, 2008

[280] Memo from Thomas K. Hall, Executive Assistant, Internal Security Division to Files, page 2, January 24, 1962; Released under Freedom of Information Act on June 10, 2008

[281] Memo from Thomas K. Hall, Executive Assistant, Internal Security Division to Files, page 2, January 24, 1962; Released under Freedom of Information Act on June 10, 2008

[282] AZC Gives Up $ to Avoid Foreign Agent Registration, National Jewish Press, 1/25/1963

[283] American Council for Judaism, Bulletin, February 19, 1963

[284] Memo from Justin O'Shea to Thomas K. Hall, Executive Assistant, Internal Security Division to Files, p. 1, March 7, 1963; Released under Freedom of Information Act on June 10, 2008

[285] Paul, Weiss, Rifkind, Wharton & Garrison Letter to Nathan B. Lenvin, Chief Registration Section, March 21, 1963

[286] Paul, Weiss, Rifkind, Wharton & Garrison Letter to Nathan B. Lenvin, Chief Registration Section, March 21, 1963

[287] Memo from Walter Yeagley to Thomas K. Hall, Executive Assistant, Internal Security Division, p. 1, April 5, 1963; Released under Freedom of Information Act on June 10, 2008

[288] Memo from Nathan B. Lenvin, Chief Registration Section to Files, pp. 1-3, May 2, 1963, reviewed by Katzenbach on 5/20/1963; Released under Freedom of Information Act on June 10, 2008

[289] Memo from Nathan B. Lenvin, Chief Registration Section to Files, pp. 1-3, May 2, 1963, reviewed by Katzenbach on 5/20/1963; Released under Freedom of Information Act on June 10, 2008

[290] "Federal Lawyers", Wall Street Journal, June 28, 1963

[291] Telegram from L. Edward Tonkon, Tonkon Millinery Company to Robert F. Kennedy, Copied to the Honorable John Tower, Ralph Yarborough, J. William Fulbright, Bruce Alger

[292] Letters entered into Internal Security Section central files about the American Zionist Council.

[293] Letter from Congressman Donald Rumsfeld to Robert F. Kennedy, July 15, 1963

[294] Memo from Irene Bowman, Registration Section to Files, p. 1, July 2, 1963; Released under Freedom of Information Act on June 10, 2008

[295] Memo from Nancy Fahrnkopf, Registration Section to Nathan Lenvin, pp. 1-3, July 17, 1963; Released under Freedom of Information Act on June 10, 2008

[296] Memo from Irene Bowman, Registration Section to Files, p. 1, July 2, 1963; Released under Freedom of Information Act on June 10, 2008

[297] Memo from J. Walter Yeagley, Assistant Attorney General, Internal Security Division to Files, p. 1, July 17, 1963; Released under Freedom of Information Act on June 10, 2008

[298] Letter from J. Walter Yeagley, Assistant Attorney General, Internal Security Division to Donald Rumsfeld, July 22, 1963; Released under Freedom of Information Act on June 10, 2008

[299] Theresa L. Green, Registration Section to Nathan Lenvin, July 26, 1963; Released under Freedom of Information Act on June 10, 2008

[300] Memo from Deputy Attorney General Nicholas Katzenbach to J. Walter Yeagley, Assistant Attorney General, July 30, 1963; Released under Freedom of Information Act on June 10, 2008

[301] Memo from Thomas K. Hall, Executive Assistant, Internal Security Division to Nathan Lenvin, p. 1, August 15, 1963; Released under Freedom of Information Act on June 10, 2008

[302] Memo from Nathan B. Lenvin, Chief Registration Section to J. Walter Yeagley, August 20, 1963, Reviewed by Katzenbach on 5/20/1963; Released under Freedom of Information Act on June 10, 2008

[303] Letter from J. Walter Yeagley, Assistant Attorney General, Internal Security Division to FBI Director J. Edgar Hoover, August 23, 1963; Released under Freedom of Information Act on June 10, 2008

[304] Memo from Irene Bowman, Registration Section to Files, pp. 1-3, October 14, 1963; Released under Freedom of Information Act on June 10, 2008

[305] Memo from J. Walter Yeagley, Assistant Attorney General, Internal Security Division to Files, pp. 1-3, October 17, 1963; Released under Freedom of Information Act on June 10, 2008

[306] Memo from J. Walter Yeagley, Assistant Attorney General, Internal Security Division to Files, pp. 1-3, October 17, 1963; Released under Freedom of Information Act on June 10, 2008

[307] "Senate Study Finds Laxity in Checking Foreign Lobbyists," New York Times, July 22, 1962

[308] "Senate Study Finds Laxity in Checking Foreign Lobbyists," New York Times, July 22, 1962

[309] "Senate Study Finds Laxity in Checking Foreign Lobbyists," New York Times, July 22, 1962

[310] "Senate Study Finds Laxity in Checking Foreign Lobbyists," New York Times, July 22, 1962

[311] "Senators Told of Lobby Check: More Effectual Law Proposed; New Legal Procedure American Agents Hired," New York Times, February 7, 1963

[312] "Senators Told of Lobby Check; More Effectual Law Proposed," New York Times, February 7, 1963

[313] Obituary, "Igor Cassini, Hearst Columnist, Dies at 86," New York Times, January 9, 2002

[314] "Igor Cassini Gets $10,000 Fine for Failing to Register as Agent," New York Times, January 11, 1964

[315] "Igor Cassini, Hearst Columnist, Dies at 86," New York Times, January 9, 2002

[316] Near East Report, Vol. 4, No. 15, November 2, 1961

[317] Near East Report, Vol. 4, No. 15, November 2, 1961

[318] Near East Report, Vol. 4, No. 15, November 2, 1961

[319] Secret Letter from John F. Kennedy, President of the United States, to Levi Eshkol, July 5, 1963. Obtained from the Israel State Archive and the published at George Washington University's National Security Archive website: http://www.gwu.edu/~nsarchiv/israel/documents/exchange/

[320] Hersh, Seymour M. The Samson Option: Israel's Nuclear Option and American Foreign Policy, New York, Random House, 1991, p. 181

[321] Hersh, Seymour M., The Samson Option: Israel's Nuclear Option and American Foreign Policy, New York, Random House, 1991, p. 210
[322] Hersh, Seymour M., The Samson Option: Israel's Nuclear Option and American Foreign Policy, New York, Random House, 1991, p. 271
[323] "Jimmy Carter says Israel had 150 nuclear weapons," Times of London, May 26, 2008
[324] Near East Report, Vol. 7, No. 24, November 19, 1963
[325] Hersh, Seymour M., The Samson Option: Israel's Nuclear Option and American Foreign Policy, New York, Random House, 1991, p. 192
[326] Hersh, Seymour M., The Samson Option: Israel's Nuclear Option and American Foreign Policy New York, Random House, 1991, p. 191
[327] Hersh, Seymour M., The Samson Option: Israel's Nuclear Option and American Foreign Policy, New York, Random House, 1991, p. 191
[328] "President's View on Jews Is Sought," New York Times, September 21, 1966
[329] Hersh, Seymour M., The Samson Option: Israel's Nuclear Option and American Foreign Policy, New York, Random House, 1991, p. 193
[330] Rifkind, Simon H., Letter to Nicholas Katzenbach, Deputy Attorney General, December 11, 1963
[331] Memo from J. Walter Yeagley, Assistant Attorney General, Internal Security Division to Nicholas Katzenbach, December 13, 1963; Released under Freedom of Information Act on June 10, 2008
[332] Routing Slip from J. Walter Yeagley, Assistant Attorney General, Internal Security Division to Nathan Lenvin, January 1, 1964; Released under Freedom of Information Act on June 10, 2008
[333] Letter from Deputy Attorney General, Nicholas Katzenbach to Simon F. Rifkind, January 10, 1964; Released under Freedom of Information Act on June 10, 2008
[334] Memo from Nathan B. Lenvin, Chief Registration Section to Files, pp. 1-3, February 3, 1963; Released under Freedom of Information Act on June 10, 2008
[335] "Jewish National Organizations" American Jewish Yearbook, p. 687, Directories and Lists, American Jewish Committee Archives http://www.ajcarchives.org/AJC_DATA/Files/1937_1938_6_DirectoriesLists.pdf
[336] Handwritten Memo from Irene Bowman, Internal Security Division to Walter Yeagley and Edwin Guthman. This handwritten memo lists the date as 1/3/1964 but is date-stamped February 24, 1964. Since it refers to the January 31, 1964, meeting between Rifkind, Lenvin, and Rothenberg written up on February 3, the date digit of the handwritten date is no doubt a "2" rather than a "1." Edwin Guthman's typed memo to Yeagley transmitting Bowman's concerns verbatim is dated February 10, 1964. Released under Freedom of Information Act on June 10, 2008
[337] Memo Response from Walter Yeagley to Irene Bowman, Edwin Guthman, Nathan Lenvin, p. 1, February 10, 1963; Released under Freedom of Information Act on June 10, 2008
[338] Letter from Assistant Attorney General, Internal Security Division G. Walter Yeagley, Signed by Nathan Lenvin, to Nathaniel S. Rothenberg, February 10, 1964; Released under Freedom of Information Act on June 10, 2008
[339] Letter from Nathanial S. Rothenberg, Counselor at Law, to Nathan B. Lenvin, March 16, 1964
[340] Routing Slip from J. Walter Yeagley, Assistant Attorney General, Internal Security Division to Thomas Weldon, March 16, 1964; Released under Freedom of Information Act on June 10, 2008

[341] Confidential Cover Memo from J. Walter Yeagley, Assistant Attorney General, Internal Security to Nicholas Katzenbach; Released under Freedom of Information Act on June 10, 2008
[342] Letter from Deputy Attorney General, Nicholas Katzenbach to Nathaniel S. Rothenberg, October 7, 1964; Released under Freedom of Information Act on June 10, 2008
[343] Memo from Irene Bowman, Registration Section to Files, pp. 1-2, October 20, 1964; Released under Freedom of Information Act on June 10, 2008
[344] Memo from Irene Bowman, Registration Section to Files, pp. 1-2, October 20, 1964; Released under Freedom of Information Act on June 10, 2008
[345] Memo from Irene Bowman, Registration Section to Files, pp. 1-2, October 20, 1964; Released under Freedom of Information Act on June 10, 2008
[346] Memo from Nathan B. Lenvin, Chief Registration Section to Files, October 30, 1964; Released under Freedom of Information Act on June 10, 2008
[347] Memo from Nathan B. Lenvin, Chief Registration Section to Files, October 30, 1964; Released under Freedom of Information Act on June 10, 2008
[348] Memo from Nathan B. Lenvin, Chief Registration Section to Files, October 30, 1964; Released under Freedom of Information Act on June 10, 2008
[349] Memo from Nathan B. Lenvin, Chief Registration Section to Files, October 30, 1964; Released under Freedom of Information Act on June 10, 2008
[350] Memo from Nathan B. Lenvin, Chief Registration Section to Files, October 30, 1964; Released under Freedom of Information Act on June 10, 2008
[351] Letter from Nathanial S. Rothenberg, Counselor at Law, to Nathan B. Lenvin, November 4, 1964
[352] Letter from J. Walter Yeagley, Assistant Attorney General, Internal Security Division to Nathaniel S. Rothenberg, November 18, 1964; Released under Freedom of Information Act on June 10, 2008
[353] Letter from Nathanial S. Rothenberg, Counselor at Law, to Nathan B. Lenvin, November 23, 1964
[354] Memo from Irene Bowman, Registration Section to Nathan B. Lenvin, Chief, Registration Section, January 19, 1965; Released under Freedom of Information Act on June 10, 2008
[355] "Katzenbach Is Appointed Attorney General, Katzenbach Gets Top Post," New York Times, January 29, 1965
[356] Memo from Nathan B. Lenvin, Chief Registration Section to Irene Bowman and Files, February 23, 1965; Released under Freedom of Information Act on June 10, 2008
[357] Cover Letter from Harry A. Steinberg, Executive Director of the American Zionist Organization to Nathan B. Lenvin, March 2, 1965
[358] Senate Foreign Relations Committee Investigation into the Activities of Agents of Foreign Principals in the United States, Washington, US Government Printing Office, August 1, 1963, p. 1735
[359] American Zionist Council Department of Information & Public Relations, Disbursements for the Period of April 1, 1962 to June 30, 1962. Coded disbursements: p. 1, name index, p. 1.
[360] Senate Foreign Relations Committee Investigation into the Activities of Agents of Foreign Principals in the United States, Washington, US Government Printing Office, August 1, 1963, pp. 1735-1741

[361] Obituary, "Fatemi, Shayesteh S.," New York Times, December 20, 2004
[362] American Zionist Council Department of Information & Public Relations, Disbursements for the Period of April 1, 1962 to June 30, 1962. Coded disbursements: p. 2, name index: p. 1
[363] Routing Slip from Nathan B. Lenvin to Irene Bowman, March 4, 1965; Released under Freedom of Information Act on June 10, 2008
[364] Memo from Irene Bowman, Registration Section to Nathan B. Lenvin, March 23, 1965; Released under Freedom of Information Act on June 10, 2008
[365] Memo from Irene Bowman, Registration Section to Files, March 24, 1965; Released under Freedom of Information Act on June 10, 2008
[366] Memo from Nathan Lenvin to J. Walter Yeagley, March 31, 1965; Released under Freedom of Information Act on June 10, 2008
[367] Senate Foreign Relations Committee Investigation into the Activities of Agents of Foreign Principals in the United States, Washington, US Government Printing Office, August 1, 1963, pp. 1735-1741
[368] Thomas K. Hall Routing Slip to J. Walter Yeagley, March 31, 1965; Released under Freedom of Information Act on June 10, 2008
[369] Memo from Nathan Lenvin to Ulda Eldred, April 8, 1965; Released under Freedom of Information Act on June 10, 2008
[370] Memo from J. Walter Yeagley, Assistant Attorney General, Internal Security Division to Director, Federal Bureau of Investigation, May 14, 1965; Released under Freedom of Information Act on June 10, 2008
[371] Memo from J. Walter Yeagley, Assistant Attorney General, Internal Security Division to Nathan Lenvin, May 17, 1965; Released under Freedom of Information Act on June 10, 2008
[372] Memo from Nathan Lenvin to J. Walter Yeagley, May 20, 1965; Released under Freedom of Information Act on June 10, 2008
[373] Obituary, "J. Walter Yeagley, 81, Former Justice Official," New York Times, May 1, 1990
[374] Letter from Michael W. Lenvin to the Author, July 3, 2008
[375] Obituary, "Geraldine Lensh Lenvin Dies; Taught English in N. Virginia," Washington Post, June 15, 1998
[376] "Rethinking Israel's David-and-Goliath past: Little-noticed details in declassified U.S. documents indicate that Israel's Six-Day War may not have been a war of necessity," Salon, June 4, 2007
[377] "9 Zionist Groups Agree on Program", New York Times, May 17, 1965
[378] "2062 Foreign Agents Registration Act Enforcement," US Department of Justice, October 1997
[379] "Foreign Lobbies Face Gift Curbs: Fulbright Proposes Ban on Campaign Contributions," New York Times, April 27, 1963
[380] Effectiveness of the Foreign Agents Registration Act of 1938 as Amended, and its Administration by the Department of Justice, Comptroller General of the United States, Document Number 701879, March 13, 1974, http://archive.gao.gov/f0302/095964.pdf
[381] Crawford, Clare, "On Being the Senator's Partner," People Magazine, June 3, 1974
[382] "Marion Javits Quits Role as a Consultant for Iran," New York Times, January 28, 1976

[383] Israel Information Services, June 30, 1970 Supplemental Statement, Foreign Agents Registration Section, US Department of Justice, received August 20, 1970
[384] "Documents Show Shah Sought US Lobby," New York Times, May 30, 1979
[385] "U.S. Is Suing a Washington Law Firm for Files as a Representative of Guinea," New York Times, July 31, 1975
[386] "A Gray Law Illuminates Billy Carter's Foreign Deals," New York Times, July 20, 1980
[387] Memo from Irene Bowman, Registration Section to Files, pp. 1-3, October 14, 1963; Released under Freedom of Information Act on June 10, 2008
[388] "Billy Carter Settles Charges by US and Registers as an Agent of Libya," New York Times, July 15, 1980
[389] "Jury Studying Ties of a US Publisher," New York Times, September 8, 1979
[390] Obituary, "John McGoff, 73, Entrepreneur And Conservative Fund-Raiser," New York Times, February 4, 1998
[391] Exhibit A, Jewish Agency–American Section FARA Declaration, Registrant 208, US Department of Justice, May 27, 1968
[392] Exhibit A, Jewish Agency–American Section FARA Declaration, Registrant 208, US Department of Justice, May 27, 1968
[393] Berger, Elmer, "Memoirs of an Anti-Zionist Jew," Journal of Palestine Studies, Vol. 5, No. ½ (Autumn 1975–Winter 1976), University of California Press on behalf of the Institute for Palestine Studies, pp. 3-55
[394] Nelson, Nancy Jo, "The Zionist Organizational Structure," Journal of Palestine Studies, Autumn 1980
[395] Request for Review of Public File, Registration Section Internal Security Division, Requested by William T. Mallison on September 3, 1969, Sent to Central Files on October 17, 1969; Released under Freedom of Information Act on June 10, 2008
[396] Covenant between the Government of Israel and the Zionist Executive, called also the Executive of the Jewish Agency, US Department of Justice, July 26, 1954. See Appendices for full text.
[397] Supplemental Statement, Jewish Agency–American Section FARA declaration, US Department of Justice, March 1969
[398] Nelson, Nancy Jo, "The Zionist Organizational Structure," Journal of Palestine Studies, Autumn 1980
[399] "Zionism, Freedom of Information, and the Law, American," Arab Affairs, Washington, March 31, 1988
[400] "Resolutions of the Twenty-Eighth Zionist Congress, 1972," Journal of Palestine Studies, Vol. 1, No. 3 (Spring 1972), pp. 175-202
[401] "Resolutions of the Twenty-Eighth Zionist Congress, 1972," Journal of Palestine Studies, Vol. 1, No. 3 (Spring 1972), pp. 175-202
[402] Mittleman, Alan, Licht, Robert A., and Sarna, Jonathan D., Jewish Polity and American Civil Society, Lanham, Maryland, Rowman and Littlefield, 2002, p. 122
[403] Smith, Grant F., Foreign Agents: The American Israel Public Affairs Committee from the 1963 Fulbright Hearings to the 2005 Espionage Scandal, Washington, DC, Institute for Research: Middle Eastern Policy, p. 69
[404] US Israel Free Trade Agreement Damage Assessment, Bilaterals.org, IRmep.org June 20, 2019 https://www.bilaterals.org/?us-israel-free-trade-agreement

[405] Smith, Grant F., Foreign Agents: The American Israel Public Affairs Committee from the 1963 Fulbright Hearings to the 2005 Espionage Scandal, Washington, DC, Institute for Research: Middle Eastern Policy, p. 78

[406] Smith, Grant F., Foreign Agents: The American Israel Public Affairs Committee from the 1963 Fulbright Hearings to the 2005 Espionage Scandal, Washington, DC, Institute for Research: Middle Eastern Policy, p. 97

[407] Ellis, Judge T.S., US vs. Steven J. Rosen and Keith Weissman, Memorandum Opinion, Court Order Denying Motion to Dismiss, Case 1:05-cr-00225-TSE, PACER, August 9, 2006

[408] Pearlstine, Norman, Op/Ed, "A Test for Mr. Mukasey: The attorney general should drop the chilling 'espionage' prosecution against two pro-Israel lobbyists," Wall Street Journal, November 12, 2007, http://opinionjournal.com/editorial/feature.html?id=110010853

[409] "Rosen lawyer wants Jews to 'rise up,'" Jewish Telegraphic Agency, May 14, 2008

[410] "No one knows full cost of Israel's settlement ambitions," USA Today, August 14, 2005

[411] Popper, Nathaniel, "Jewish Officials Profess Shock Over Report on Zionist Body," The Forward, March 18, 2005

[412] Smith, Grant F., Speech at the Russell Senate Office Building, "US Charitable Contributions, Illegal Settlements, and Suicide Terrorism," 11/21/2005, http://www.irmep.org/11212005.htm

[413] Department of Justice returned mail to Author indicating employee Justin Dempsey was "transferred to Anti-Trust". Court dockets reveal his later active pursuit of anti-trust litigation.

[414] Amanda Michanczyk, Acting Disclosure Officer, Department of Treasury Financial Crimes Enforcement Network Letter to Author, December 10, 2007. "This letter is in response to your Freedom of Information Act (FOIA) request to the Department of Treasury dated September 27, 2007, in which you requested documents about Treasury Department investigations triggered by public revelations that U.S. charitable funds flows are used to illegally confiscate Palestinian lands and commit crimes overseas. Additionally, you requested information about Treasury Department programs designed to combat U.S. charitable money laundering to the West Bank, and certain meeting minutes of key Treasury Department officials, specifically Mr. Levey and Mr. Szubin....FinCEN..could find no records responsive to your request...The statutory provision that specifically exempts records collected under the Bank Secrecy Act from disclosure under FOIA can be found in Section 5319 of Title 31 of the United States Code."

[415] Massing, Michael, The Nation, June 10, 2002

[416] Jerusalem Post, August 27, 2004

[417] Lobbying Report, American Israel Public Affairs Committee, 8/10/2006, filed under the Lobbying Disclosure Act of 1995.

[418] Lobbying Report, American Israel Public Affairs Committee, 8/10/2006, filed under the Lobbying Disclosure Act of 1995.

[419] Lobbying Report, American Israel Public Affairs Committee, 2/14/2007, filed under the Lobbying Disclosure Act of 1995.

[420] Kenen, Isaiah L., Israel's Defense Line: Her Friends and Foes in Washington, New York, New York, Prometheus Books, p. 46

[421] Rice, Condoleezza, "Remarks at Opening Dinner of the 102nd Annual Meeting of the American Jewish Committee," Capital Hilton; US Department of State, Washington, DC, April 28, 2008, http://www.state.gov/secretary/rm/2008/04/104220.htm

[422] Berger, Elmer, "Memoirs of an Anti-Zionist Jew," Journal of Palestine Studies, Vol. 5, No. ½ (Autumn 1975–Winter 1976), University of California Press on behalf of the Institute for Palestine Studies, pp. 3-55

[423] "Economics and the rule of law—Order in the jungle," The Economist, May 13, 2008

[424] Charter Memo of the Senate Foreign Relations Committee Investigation of Nondiplomatic Activities of Representatives of Foreign Governments, March 17, 1961 https://www.israellobby.org/forrel

[425] Singer, Paul Jay, "The Disturbing Legacy of 'Operation Susannah' and the Lavon Affair, The Jewish Press, March 30, 2022 https://www.jewishpress.com/sections/features/features-on-jewish-world/the-disturbing-legacy-of-operation-susannah-and-the-lavon-affair/2022/03/30/

[426] Senate Foreign Relations Committee Investigation into the Activities of Agents of Foreign Principals in the United States, 88th Congress, 1st session, Washington, US Government Printing Office, May 23, 1963, pp. 1403-1422

[427] Senate Foreign Relations Committee Investigation into the Activities of Agents of Foreign Principals in the United States, 88th Congress, 1st session, Washington, US Government Printing Office, May 23, 1963, pp. 1242

[428] Isaiah L. Kenen Foreign Agent Registration, Exhibit A, US Department of Justice, September 1, 1948

[429] Obituary, New York Times, March 25, 1988

[430] Kenen, Isaiah L., Israel's Defense Line: Her Friends and Foes in Washington, New York, New York, Prometheus Books, p. 5

[431] Obituary, New York Times, March 25, 1988

[432] Kenen, Isaiah L., Israel's Defense Line: Her Friends and Foes in Washington, New York, New York, Prometheus Books, p. 14

[433] New York Times, June 7, 1948

[434] Kenen, Isaiah L., Israel's Defense Line: Her Friends and Foes in Washington, New York, New York, Prometheus Books, p. 109

[435] "Jewish Agency for Israel (JAFI)," The Jewish Virtual Library, http://www.jewishvirtuallibrary.org/jsource/Orgs/jafi.html

[436] "Zionism, Freedom of Information, and the Law, American," Arab Affairs, Washington, March 31, 1988

[437] Brandeis, Louis Dembitz, Urofsky, Melvin I., and Levy, David W., Letters of Louis D. Brandeis vol. 4, New York, SUNY Press, p. 193

[438] Bierbrier, Doreen, "The American Zionist Emergency Council: An Analysis of a Pressure Group," American Jewish History, London, England, Taylor & Francis, p. 82

[439] Bierbrier, Doreen, "The American Zionist Emergency Council: An Analysis of a Pressure Group," American Jewish History, London, England, Taylor & Francis, p. 93

[440] Peck, Sarah E., "The Campaign for an American Response to the Nazi Holocaust, 1943-1945," Journal of Contemporary History, Vol. 15, No. 2 (April 1980), p. 383

[441] Senate Foreign Relations Committee Investigation into the Activities of Agents of Foreign Principals in the United States, 88th Congress, 1st session, Washington, <u>US Government Printing Office,</u> May 23, 1963, pp. 1339-1340

[442] "ADL Objects To Ralph Nader's Characterization of U.S. Government As 'Puppet' to Israel," Anti-Defamation League, New York, New York, July 2, 2004, http://www.adl.org/PresRele/IslME_62/4527_62.htm

[443] Smith, Grant F., <u>Foreign Agents: The American Israel Public Affairs Committee from the 1963 Fulbright Hearings to the 2005 Espionage Scandal,</u> Washington, DC, Institute for Research: Middle Eastern Policy, pp. 57-59

[444] Kareem Khalaf et al. v. Donald Regan et al, CA. No. 83-2963 (D.D.C.), Memorandum and Order, January 7, 1985

www.ingramcontent.com/pod-product-compliance
Lightning Source LLC
Chambersburg PA
CBHW070959160426
43193CB00012B/1841